Calligrammes

Calligrammes

Poems of Peace and War (1913-1916)

Guillaume Apollinaire

Translated by ANNE HYDE GREET
With an Introduction by S. I. LOCKERBIE
and Commentary by ANNE HYDE GREET
and S. I. LOCKERBIE

University of California Press Berkeley • Los Angeles • London

University of California Press
Berkeley and Los Angeles, California

University of California Press, Ltd.
London, England

Library of Congress Cataloging in Publication Data

Apollinaire, Guillaume, 1880-1918.
Calligrammes.

Bibliography: p. 509
L. European War, 1914-1918—Poetry. I. Greet, Anne Hyde. II. Title.
PQ2601. P6C313 1980 841'912 73-149946
ISBN 0-520-01968-7

Book Design: Linda M. Robertson

Printed in the United States of America

A la mémoire
du plus ancien de mes camarades
RENÉ DALIZE
mort au Champ d'Honneur
le 7 mai 1917.

Table des Matières
Contents

Sketches by Apollinaire in the margins of the galleys for *Calligrammes*

"Le Musicien de Saint-Merry"
  Soldier's head
  House and musician

"Un Fantôme de Nuées"
  Acrobat
  Horse and its shadow
  Tree and château

"Tour"
  Tower and Ferris wheel

"L'Inscription Anglaise"
  Sailboat

"Dans l'Abri-Caverne"
  Cat

"L'Avenir"
  Harbor

"La Victoire"
  Fish

Photographer: Bernard Décaudin, Paris

Acknowledgments

A transatlantic correspondence was the beginning of a long collaboration, mainly carried out in letters. The eventual coming-to-terms of two Apollinaireans with quite different notions about a poet they both love is expressed on every page of this book.

Among those who have helped us to understand verbal and physical complexities of the era, special thanks go to Madame Claude Tournadre and Professor André Chervel who generously shared their knowledge of military slang, to Pierre Marcel Adéma who patiently and humorously provided an unexpected answer to every question, and, last but not least, to Professor Michel Décaudin, always a resource in time of trouble, who spent a memorable afternoon in an Apollinairean café with mirrored walls, drawing *hexaèdres barbelés, douilles d'obus,* and the *2e canonnier conducteur* seated behind an elegant steed and pulling a cannon that pointed backward.

The French text used in this edition is that of the original edition published in 1918 by the Mercure de France. We have followed the practice of later editions, notably the Pléiade edition, in correcting obvious misprints in the original text (a full list will be found on p. 1078 of the Pléiade edition). Like the Pléiade, however, we have refrained from correcting handwritten calligrams, thus leaving unaltered the omission of a letter in "La Mandoline l'Œillet et le Bambou" and the misprint *Xexaèdres* instead of *Hexaèdres* in "Loin du Pigeonnier."

The justification for using the Mercure de France text is that Apollinaire personally supervised its printing. Yet subsequent editions—with the notable exception of the edition by Michel Décaudin, published by the Club du Meilleur Livre in 1955—have taken considerable liberties with the typographical layout of the poems, and with the order in which they were originally printed. In both respects the present edition seeks to present the text as Apollinaire intended it to appear.

We are able to use the first edition of *Calligrammes,* thanks to Special Collections, University of California, Santa Barbara, and to its curator, Christian Brun. Our thanks are owing also to François Chapon, curator of the Bibliothèque Littéraire Jacques Doucet in Paris, who allowed the photographing of unedited material, and to the photographer Bernard Décaudin.

Special thanks go to Robert Y. Zachary of the University of California Press for his inspiration and his warm support.

Last but not least, we thank two remarkable women, Sandy McDonald, typist, and Grace Stimson, editor, who, each in her own way, helped us to bring order out of chaos, in preparing the manuscript.

Introduction

THE MODERNISM OF CALLIGRAMMES

Calligrammes is, with *Alcools*, the second major volume of poetry on which rests Guillaume Apollinaire's reputation as one of the great modern poets in French literature. Linking the two volumes are deep and persistent continuities, rooted in Apollinaire's vision of the world and the fundamental nature of his lyric gift. There is also a marked proximity in time, for the first poems of *Calligrammes* were written in December 1912 and early 1913, immediately after the completion of *Alcools* in November 1912. Yet these affinities do not prevent most readers being struck—and rightly so—by considerable differences in tone, style, and theme between the two volumes. *Calligrammes*, particularly the first section entitled "Ondes," reveals a novelty of accent and composition which clearly rests on aesthetic assumptions different from those underlying the main poems of *Alcools*, assumptions that can conveniently be drawn together under the concept of modernism.

Although a modern note is frequently struck in *Alcools*, and increasingly so as we move from the earlier to the later poems, Apollinaire's conception of poetry in that volume is one that essentially derives from Symbolism. It is an introspective poetry in which the poet is concerned with the troubled depths of the psyche, the transitoriness of experience, and the quest for identity and permanence. The shadowy and obsessive nature of the poet's states of mind is reflected in elliptical, elusive, and sometimes hermetic expression. Like the great Symbolist poets, Apollinaire finds deep aesthetic satisfaction in the beauties of obscurity and allusiveness of utterance. Even the supremely musical short poems on which his fame as a popular lyric poet rests—"Le Pont Mirabeau" and others—acquire their melodic ease through a process of distillation and condensation which makes them more appealing than immediately intelligible.

The force with which an urgent form of consciousness is increasingly deployed in this poetry, tempering the melancholy, widening the imaginative span, and revitalizing the language, is Apollinaire's major creative achievement in *Alcools.* But, with some exceptions, it is an achievement that does not seek to renew the poet's vision of the world. This is so even in "Zone," the opening poem but the last to be written, which in its early lines makes the first forceful statement of the new enthusiasm for the modern world which was to burst out in *Calligrammes.* The initial optimism, however, is not sustained. The final mood that is established is one of anguish and suffering, and the poem ends with the poet assuming what is his most characteristic role throughout the volume, that of the lonely wanderer in the hostile and ominous environment of the modern city.

In *Calligrammes,* on the other hand, the mood reflects much greater confidence and enthusiasm for life. In the first part of "Liens" and "Les Fenêtres" the poet is no longer posited as a lonely wanderer in a harsh cityscape but as a "new man" whose vision radiates across frontiers and continents and unites the modern world in a network of concordances. The shadowy, claustrophobic atmosphere of earlier poems now gives way to urgent, syncopated rhythms and to the play of sensuous color and light. The final lines of "Les Fenêtres,"

> *La fenêtre s'ouvre comme une orange*
> *Le beau fruit de la lumière*
>
> [The window opens like an orange
> The lovely fruit of light]

symbolize a new openness to experience in the poet and a sense of communion with the world, even in its farther-flung reaches.

It is not only in Apollinaire that this remarkable change in outlook is encountered. The whole prewar generation of artists in Paris was caught up in a similar wave of extrovert enthusiasm. It was a change of mood that stemmed ultimately from the rapid technological advances of the early years of the twentieth century and the general widening of horizons brought about by such inventions as the motorcar, the airplane, radiography, cinematography, and radio communications. Suddenly modern man seemed to be living in a totally different context from the older, slower world of the nineteenth century. His ability to manipulate his environment, and his capacity for experience, had been infinitely increased. Now he seemed the triumphant master of his own destiny.

It is not surprising that this new sensibility should produce a new tempo in the arts and a general desire for artistic change. All the prewar movements, from the Futurists to the most ephemeral and obscure, declared that the artistic forms of the past were no longer adequate to express the new spirit and had to be radically renewed. Apollinaire stands out as the most masterly innovator in an avant-garde hectically devoted to experiment, not because his ideas were the most original, but because he had the creative genius to transform aesthetic concepts that were in general circulation into powerful and appealing poetry.

Central among these aesthetic ideas was the notion that the modern work of art must adequately reflect the global nature of contemporary consciousness. In the conditions of modern life man has achieved totality of awareness: through worldwide communications he is as aware of what is happening in New York as in Paris; through newspapers, radio, and the cinema his imagination is stimulated by a constantly changing stream of information and ideas; in the streets and cafés his senses are assailed by a kaleidoscopic multiplicity of sights, sounds, and sensations. To be able to mirror such a multiple form of consciousness the work of art had to abandon linear and discursive structures, in which events are arranged successively, in favor of what Apollinaire called *simultaneity:* a type of structure that would give the impression of a full and instant awareness within one moment of space-time.

Essentially this conception led Apollinaire to a radical dislocation of poetic structure. To create an impression of multiple and simultaneous consciousness, perceptions and ideas are abruptly juxtaposed in the poems in an arrangement that, at first reading, seems to be one of considerable disorder. Many poems of *Alcools* had already been characterized by elliptical syntax and collocations of disparate images, but the novelty in *Calligrammes* is that the discontinuities are much more radical, forcing the reader into a greater effort of synthesis to discover the underlying unity. It was this effort of synthesis that, for Apollinaire, produced the "simultanist" vision, insofar as it short-circuits the normal discursive process of reading and requires the reader to reassemble the apparently random fragments in a new order that is independent of the flow of time and is experienced in one global act of consciousness.

Undeniably Apollinaire was encouraged in his thinking by the similar fragmentation of structure he observed in Cubist painting, particularly in the work of Picasso, which he also considered to stem from the simultaneous depiction of the same object from several viewpoints. What he admired above all in Picasso was the sheer imaginative boldness with which the painter had broken with all previous conceptions in Western painting. He describes Picasso in *Les Peintres Cubistes* as a heroic figure who had dared to disrupt the established order of the universe and to rearrange it as he thought fit:

> *La grande révolution des arts qu'il a accomplie presque seul, c'est que le monde est sa nouvelle représentation. . . . C'est un nouveau-né qui met de l'ordre dans l'univers pour son usage personnel, et aussi afin de faciliter ses relations avec ses semblables. Ce dénombrement a la grandeur de l'épopée.*[1]
>
> [The great revolution in the arts which he almost alone has accomplished is that the world is now in his image. . . . He is a newborn babe who rearranges the universe for his personal convenience and to facilitate understanding with his fellowmen. His cataloguing has an epic grandeur.]

The important thing here is that the elaborating of a new structure is identified with personal creativity of the highest order. The process of reordering the world according to the artist's own vision testifies not only to his global, all-embracing consciousness but also to his unique powers as an inventor. The distinguishing feature of the modern artist is that he produces a new art object, profoundly original in conception and form and freed from servile imitation of nature, which becomes the projection of his own creative personality onto the world.

The different emphases in Apollinaire's own experiments in poetic form which emerge implicitly from his account of Picasso can be traced, in greater or lesser degree, in most of the poems of "Ondes," the section of *Calligrammes* which contains his prewar innovative work, but are particularly evident in the two poems that Apollinaire himself dubbed "conversation poems": "Les Fenêtres" and "Lundi Rue Christine." The descriptive label refers to the fact that frequent use is made of snippets of spoken language, assembled from what seem to be unrelated and disconnected conversations being held in some public place. The intention seems to be to face the reader

1. *PC*, p. 67.

with a mass of unintegrated details, not unlike the profusion of planes that, at first sight, obscure the overall design and organization of a cubist painting. The difference between the poems is that when a synthesis begins to emerge from the jigsaw, it is achieved in a high key in "Les Fenêtres" and in a lower and subtler key in "Lundi Rue Christine." In "Les Fenêtres" the mixing into the jumble of conversation of sensuous evocations of light and color, and flashing impressions of a worldwide scene, quickly suggests that there is a powerful controlling consciousness at the heart of the poem, unifying it through the force of its own aspiration. In this poem, therefore, simultanist form is directly expressive of the creator's personality and power of vision. In "Lundi Rue Christine," on the other hand, the poet is virtually absent, or is reduced to the role of an eavesdropper, and the reader has to build up the picture of a café scene from quizzical hints that arise in the disorderly buzz of conversation. Here the emphasis falls on the autonomy of the work of art that has been created: it stands out as an arbitrary but fascinating construction whose existence is justified by its status as a deliberately fabricated object. The distinction, however, is not absolute. In both poems, and in its many other uses in the poems of "Ondes," the terse, fragmented structure operates on two levels at once, suggesting both the multiple consciousness of the poet at the center of the modern world and the formal intricacy of an innovatory approach to poetic form.

A similar judgment can be made of the use of language in the conversation poems. The question of language is as central to modernism as the notion of simultaneity. One of Apollinaire's principal convictions was that a poetry that seeks to express the quintessence of the modern world must also use the direct and forceful speech of contemporary life. Already in "Zone" there is the statement that the stylistic models for the modern poet should be those that he can find in the public uses of language all around him:

Tu lis les prospectus les catalogues les affiches
qui chantent tout haut
Voilà la poésie ce matin et pour la prose il y a
les journaux

[You read handbills catalogues advertisements that
sing out loud and clear
There is where poetry is this morning and for prose
there are the newspapers]

And in many other contexts the poet who had once argued for the necessary obscurity of poetry now condemns the convoluted nature of Symbolist verse and declares his faith in an art that has broad popular appeal.[2]

The use of fragments of ordinary speech in the conversation poems is a striking example of the extension of poetic language to include popular usage. Phrases that have none of the characteristics of conventional poetic diction are shown to acquire meaning and expressiveness when manipulated in a certain way. This amounts to the destruction of any notion of hierarchy in language and to the removal of artificial barriers between the kinds of speech that can be used by poets. In this sense Apollinaire can be said to have stripped the remaining ornaments of rhetoric from the language of poetry. But here also there are implications that are formal and internal. It is because he is defeated in his attempt to find an immediate discursive meaning linking the various fragments that the reader is thrown back onto the text and interrogates the linguistic network more closely, discovering unexpected resonances and connections in apparently banal phrases. The poem thus becomes a self-reflexive object, in which it is the internal echoes and the relationships of the snippets of language among themselves which provide the aesthetic pleasure, as much as any externally directed act of communication.

The interaction of style and structure throughout the modernist poems makes it clear that they are creatively original and independent of the painters. However much Apollinaire may have been stimulated by the example of Picasso, and for a shorter period by that of Robert Delaunay,[3] he could draw no more than general inspiration from them. It is only through particular combinations of words and images that the poems achieve their success, and in this respect they are as innovatory at the level of poetic style as they are at the level of structure.

The range of Apollinaire's modernism can be gauged from the fact that it is expressed not only in the simultanist experiments, but also in poems that, in technique and conception, are at the opposite extreme. Where the experimental pieces abandon linear and discursive structures and turn their back on narration and description, two major poems of "Ondes"—"Un Fantôme de Nuées" and "Le Musicien de Saint-Merry"—adopt a linear form and discursive narration as their fundamental modes of expression. Moreover, in these poems and others ("Sur les Prophéties" and many later pieces) coherence and continuity are restored to language. The language remains the casual speech of everyday life, but, as against the elliptical juxtapositions of

2. Cf. *TS*, p. 55, where Apollinaire describes late Symbolist verse as being directed at "les snobs férus de mysticité" [snobs enamored of obscurity]. Again, in *LM*, p. 53, he wishes a socially diverse audience for his own poetry.

3. See note on "Les Fenêtres."

the conversation poems, the registers of the spoken language are used in a fluent, relaxed way, producing an impression of spontaneity and naturalness of utterance.

Narration, description, unforced naturalness of style—these conventions imply a respect for empirical reality and an acceptance of its intrinsic value. Rather than manipulate the real world in order to impose his highly structured vision upon it, the poet, in this approach, sees it as a continuum and tries to preserve its homogeneity. This is, to an extent, a rehabilitation of mimesis as a literary mode, a confidence in the power of literature to render the essence of unadorned reality through attentive observation. It testifies to the pull of the real world on Apollinaire's imagination, counterbalancing the powerful attraction of artistic innovation, and demonstrates the strength of his ambition to make his poetry a truly popular art, accessible to an undifferentiated public. Few French poets in the twentieth century have gone so far in capturing what Zola called the everyday "sense of the real," or written poems so immediately readable and appealing as "Un Fantôme de Nuées" and "Le Musicien de Saint-Merry."

In this approach the personal vision of the poet is not absent but is allowed to grow out of the common area of experience that the poem renders. Apollinaire's delight in the ordinary world stemmed not only from its colorful diversity but also from its multilayered ambiguity, which he saw as the task of the poet to explore and exploit. It was at this time that he began to formulate the concept of surprise as a key element in a modernist aesthetic and to suggest, in "Sur les Prophéties," that magical and superstitious interpretations of reality have their own validity. It is symptomatic that he was also drawn to the works of such eminently surprising and enigmatic painters as Chirico and Chagall, whose disconcerting canvases undoubtedly stimulated his interest in the dimension of the irrational. (There does seem to be some influence of Chagall behind Apollinaire's first attempts in "A Travers l'Europe" to use the kind of apparently unmotivated imagery that points in the direction of surrealism.) These strands in his view of reality come together in the concept of *surnaturalisme*,[4] which may be described as a blend of realism and fantasy in the poet's approach to the world, allowing him to move easily between both poles and to suggest, as in "Sur les Prophéties," that the marvelous is an integral part of our everyday experience. The

4. The term was applied to Apollinaire's poetry in a note in his own review, *Les Soirées de Paris* (May 1914). He also used the term "Orphism" which he coined in 1913 to describe the painting of Delaunay. Cf. *OC*, III, 939: "Orphisme ou surnaturalisme, c'est à dire un art qui n'est pas le naturalisme photographique uniquement et qui cependant soit la nature . . . cette nature intérieure aux merveilles insoupçonnées, impondérables, impitoyables et joyeuses" [Orphism or surnaturalism, that is, an art that is not merely photographic naturalism and yet is

successful application of this aesthetic is to be seen in "Un Fantôme de Nuées" and "Le Musicien de Saint-Merry." The first is remarkable in bringing about an untroubled epiphany with minimal departures from a casual narrative tone. The second is no less so in encompassing the whole range of Apollinaire's conflicting emotions within the framework of a narrative fable, set in the heart of modern Paris. The past and the present, fatalistic obsession with the loss of love and delight in the multiplicity of the modern world, are all brought together, in perfect balance, in what is indeed a new form of twentieth-century *merveilleux:* a sense of the real suffused with personal vision.

It is not only in "Le Musicien de Saint-Merry" but throughout "Ondes" that a state of inner anxiety, reminiscent of the mood of *Alcools,* makes itself felt. For all the novelty of accent and outlook of *Calligrammes,* Apollinaire's sensibility remains one haunted by uncertainty and doubt. This is what distinguishes his modernism from the more aggressive and strident version of his contemporaries. Where they were condemning subjectivity as outmoded and self-indulgent, he declares only partial loyalty to the bright new world of extrovert energy and admits to an enduring attachment to the poetry of personal emotion and elegiac sadness. Far from seeking to minimize his inner contradictions, he articulates them clearly in the prefatory poem "Liens," raising self-division to the rank of the major theme around which the whole modernist section of the volume is constructed. His instinctive gravitation toward images of sadness and pain, and the melodious incantatory phrases in which they naturally seek expression, are not to be explained solely in terms of the unhappiness that followed his separation from Marie Laurencin in 1913—although echoes of the suffering that produced the late lyric masterpieces of *Alcools* are certainly among the most plangent notes of *Calligrammes.* Beyond that, there is a more general anxiety in the face of experience which seeks refuge in the comfort of the past and fears, rather than welcomes, confrontation with the new. This explains why, on occasion, even the modern world, and the future itself, can lose their dynamic associations for the poet and become equivocal and ominous. In "Arbre" it is a barren and comfortless world that is about to be born. The new beings who will usher it in bear the mark of divinity in the mystic number three, but nevertheless hark back to the *acteurs inhumains*

---

nature . . . that inner nature of unsuspected, imponderable, unrelenting, and joyous marvels]. It was he who gave currency to the word "surrealism," which he applied to his own play *Les Mamelles de Tirésias* and to the ballet *Parade,* but for him it was a synonym of orphism and surnaturalism, rather than what the surrealist movement later made of it.

claires bêtes nouvelles of "Le Brasier" [inhuman actors bright new beasts], symbolizing a soulless new race, insensitive to the old world of emotion and memory.

Every dynamic theme in "Ondes," therefore, has its antithesis which reverses the mood and the associations. Despite the apparent assertion of "Liens," this represents not so much a conflict within the poet—although for vividness of expression images of conflict are often used—as a creative tension between two states of sensibility that are felt to be indivisible parts of the self. Melancholy and confidence are each so instinctive in Apollinaire that only when they have been resolved and brought into balance can he feel that he has fully expressed the wholeness of his personality. His lyricism derives all its power and rich ambiguities precisely from this resolution of inner contradictions into a complex but profoundly unified state of sensibility.

It was no doubt to ensure that the depth of personal experience which characterizes Apollinaire's modernism was adequately represented that he included "Les Collines" in "Ondes," out of chronological order. Not written until 1917, after the poet had gone through the maturing turmoil of war, this poem presents, more powerfully than any other in the section, the commitment to modernism as a testing spiritual adventure. The picture it gives of the modern poet as an innovator and a prophet radically enlarges that notion as it was expressed in "Sur les Prophéties." Rather than the gift of everyday observation within the power of any man, prophecy now becomes the prerogative of the poet as a seer who acquires his privileged insights into the mysteries of the universe through struggle, trial, and suffering. The poet again takes on the persona of the martyr-hero of *Alcools*, mourning the loss of youth, wracked by the exceptional experiences he undergoes, but gaining as his prize a multiplication of his powers and an oneiric understanding of life and death. In its exalted tone, denseness of allusion, and complexity of expression, "Les Collines" thus achieves the higher resolution of all Apollinaire's complexities and colors the whole context of "Ondes." Inevitably the reader is induced to see the poet's modernism, even in its more apparently fanciful experiments, as a poetic undertaking of the highest seriousness of purpose.

THE CALLIGRAMMES

The calligrams may have seemed fanciful experiments to many contemporary and later commentators, but they were not so in Apollinaire's eyes. By giving to the whole volume the title he invented for these exercises in what he called "visual lyricism"—even though only a small minority of poems are composed in that style—he made plain the importance he attached to them. His famous lecture in 1917, "L'Esprit Nouveau et les Poètes" [The New Spirit and the Poets], leaves no doubt that he saw visual or spatial poetry as an important new development, and had he lived he would probably have pursued it much further.

In conception the calligram derives directly from the techniques of fragmentation and recombination employed in the conversation poems. It stems from the conviction that the simultaneous nature of consciousness can be even more powerfully rendered by abandoning not only discursive expression but also the traditional linear layout of the poem as well. In a phrase that has had a famous history, a friendly critic described this typographical revolution as inevitable "because it is necessary that our intelligence become accustomed to understanding synthetico-ideographically instead of analytico-discursively."[5] That is to say that in a spatial layout, where the poem is displayed in a multiplicity of patterns on the page rather than being arranged in one linear sequence, the reader is forced to grasp the complex interrelationship of the whole in a global perception which is (apparently) more instantaneous than his recombination of the fragmented structure of the conversation poem and leads to a more powerful illumination. The fact that some of his understanding comes to him through a visual, as well as a verbal, communication of ideas further reinforces the direct sensory awareness that is characteristic of a modern consciousness.

While Apollinaire was certainly encouraged in his thinking about this concept by a desire to emulate his painter friends, as is demonstrated by his original intention to publish the poems separately under the title "Et Moi Aussi Je Suis Peintre" [I, too, am a painter], the calligram remains indisputably a form of poetry that, in its combination of spatial and linguistic factors, points toward the concrete poetry movement of recent years. Yet, intriguingly, his implementation of his bold plan has served to obscure the originality of his thought and has led to some misunderstanding of the poems. The confusion arises from what seems like a dramatic change of heart between the publication of the first calligram, "Lettre-Océan," and those that followed.

In an article about "Lettre-Océan" published in Apollinaire's own review, *Les Soirées de Paris,* G. Arbouin[6] welcomed the poem as a revolutionary innovation but expressed the important reservation that the new technique

5. The phrase is from the article by G. Arbouin on "Lettre-Océan" published in *Les Soirées de Paris* in July-August 1914, the same number in which the "new-style" calligrams appeared. Most commentators have assumed erroneously that Arbouin was a pseudonym of Apollinaire's.

6. See note 5.

could destroy the rhythmic basis of poetry, on which the communication of emotion depended, and thus create an arcane art reserved for the initiated. One must assume that these views reflected Apollinaire's own uncertainties about the proper mode of application of spatial poetry and his own constant desire to combine innovation with broad popular appeal. He must, therefore, have been susceptible to Arbouin's argument that the calligram would perforce evolve toward a pictorial shape directly related to its subject matter. Inwardly he must have felt that to give the spatial poem a pictorial shape was to restore it to a more immediately intelligible form and one that was more compatible with the rhythmic expression of feeling.

That is indeed what happened. After "Lettre-Océan," in which a global view of the modern world is imprinted on the page in an exploded structure of radiating lines and pulverized language, the calligrams that immediately follow it are composed of coherent phrases fashioned into extremely simple and instantly recognizable shapes. Any intention of expressing a simultaneous consciousness seems to have disappeared, so that some readers have fallen into the trap of thinking that the shape is simply a tautological repetition of what the referential or discursive meaning of the words already clearly conveys.

But to do so is to misunderstand the different nature of the reading operations involved in even the simplest association of word and picture. Tautology is impossible between a linguistic statement and the instant impression conveyed by a shape. Inevitably, and in poetic use deliberately, the words refine and add connotations and overtones that extend and complicate the initial response. The eye and the mind of the reader describe a circle that leads from recognition of the object to the exploration of the poet's reflections on it, and back again to the picture overlaid with a new significance. This significance must be considerable when, as in most of Apollinaire's poems, the language is richly lyrical. Whether in compact or languorous form—in "Paysage" or in "Il Pleut"—the calligrams encapsulate much of his most incantatory writing. It is, in fact, the nature of their lyricism, more than their mode of operation, which distinguishes the pictorial calligrams from "Lettre-Océan." Rather than expressing the poet's delight in the pulsating modern world, they are concerned with the realm of private feeling; however, the process by which an instantaneous graphic perception is enriched by the accumulated associations of extended reading is common to both. In a nonfigurative poem like "Lettre-Océan," the eye can take a larger number of paths through the shape, and the mind may have to hold together a larger number of different associations, but the delayed-reaction effect, before the experience is complete, is the same. Provided that one understands that "simultaneity" is really the eventual end result of a process of reading rather than the instant perception that Apollinaire sometimes implied, it can be seen that "Lettre-Océan" and the pictorial poems share one kind of simultaneity that distinguishes them from noncalligrammatic poems like the conversation pieces: the fusing together of two different modes of apprehension of the same idea or feeling, one mode working through visual association and the other through verbal.

Such a manner of operation gives particular satisfaction when the picture itself carries immediately as much impact as the words. If in some of the calligrams the picture is emblematic and acquires its richness of significance from the words in an initially one-way process, as is possibly true of the watch, the house, or the crown, other shapes instantly impress themselves on the eye with their own suggestive power before being enriched by the words. The vivid outline of the lovers in "Paysage," the oval of the mirror, the graceful lines of the fountain, the falling rain, the shell, the smoking cigar, the harmonious balance of forms in "La Mandoline l'OEillet et le Bambou"—all these and others demonstrate that Apollinaire immensely increased the capacity of figured verse to assume a wide variety of flexible and striking forms. Since antiquity pictorial poetry had confined itself to a relatively small number of elementary shapes, which were solidly filled with unbroken lines of type. Departing from this static tradition, Apollinaire's calligrams use single lines of type to trace bold or delicate outlines on the printed page with all the spontaneity of handwriting, producing a much wider range of plastic images. The fluid nature of his composition has always posed problems for printers, but by the same token, when the calligrams are successfully realized in type, they have a freshness of effect that gives them immediate expressiveness and explains why they have been so often reproduced and imitated, even by advertisers.

In a significant number of examples the inherent expressiveness of the graphic form adds a dimension of meaning to the poem which is inseparable from its appearance on the printed page and cannot emerge from the words alone. The shape of the lovers in "Paysage" can be interpreted pictorially in different ways, with considerable consequences for the overall meaning of the poem, and, whatever the interpretation, the shape says something that the words do not. The same is true in many other poems. Nor are the visual implications necessarily restricted to those associated with the object that is pictured. In calligrammatic compositions, no less than in visual art generally, graphic form itself can be directly expressive. It is instructive, from this point of view, to compare the three different typographical representations of rain in Apollinaire's work (see notes on "Il Pleut" and "Du Coton dans les Oreilles") where the different nature of type, line, and spacing on each occasion produces three quite different statements. It can even happen that certain graphic forms—notably the sinuous line—are so imprinted with associations that they contradict the verbal statement that the poem is making and create a much more complex mood than is immediately apparent (see note on first page of "Du Coton").

It is observable that Apollinaire becomes increasingly sensitive to the possibilities of spatial expression. While the earlier poems, with the exception of "Lettre-Océan," are pictorial, later sections of the volume show his interest in less figurative uses of the medium. In the section "Case d'Armons" there are examples of handwritten script and bold layout which make their effect in purely plastic terms. In the calligrams proper, in the same section, abstract graphic values can be seen to assume equal importance with the representational. Even a simple emblematic likeness of a gun in "S P" has formal qualities that transcend the shape, whereas in "Loin du Pigeonnier" and "Visée" the graphic form is sophisticated and suggestive on several levels. Again, if a figurative intention is present in the later works, such as "Aussi Bien Que les Cigales" and "Éventail des Saveurs," these poems also make an impact as a pleasing pattern of lines and as an exercise in the formal grouping of shapes on the page. A freer approach to layout is to be found even in conventionally printed poems, as in the marginal additions or offset lines of "Saillant," "Échelon," and "Oracles." These have less an explicit significance than the general function of calling attention to the poem as a deliberate composition in both structural and plastic terms, and thus of raising the reader's consciousness of the spatial dimension.

Within these freer designs, language is used in a freer way also, sometimes in marked contrast with the coherent, well-formed phrases of most of the picture poems. Apollinaire realized that one of the most potent features of the calligram is the heightening effect it has on the words from which it is made, and that it thus lent itself to his constant endeavors to restore high expressiveness to language. One of the ways in which the form serves this purpose is to act as a vehicle for the dense allusive utterances that he had favored since his Symbolist beginnings. The one-line poem "Chantre," which he added at the last moment to the proofs of *Alcools*, is a formulation of this kind, and it could be read as the first tentative calligram. Poems such as "Visée" and "Éventail des Saveurs," however, not only multiply the power of "Chantre" tenfold, by accumulating a succession of such "autonomous" lines, but confer visual as well as auditory eloquence on the statements by the beauty of their graphic composition. More boldly, the expressions that are encapsulated in other calligrams are in a much lower poetic register. These can be prosaic, repetitive slogans ("Aussi Bien Que les Cigales"), fragmentary phrases ("Loin du Pigeonnier"), or simple declarative sentences and exclamations ("1915," "Carte Postale à Jean Royère"), but here also the intention is clearly to elevate the statement through its isolation in a striking graphic structure and thus give it the self-sufficiency of a complete poetic thought.

However few in number, therefore, the calligrams are a significant poetic achievement. Nothing could be more mistaken than to think of their shape, whether pictorial or more abstract, as incidental or merely decorative. On the contrary, their graphic form interacts with the verbal text to create a new form of poetry in which Apollinaire has had many successors. They also play their part, like the conversation poems before them, in extending the range of poetic expression and increasing the number of uses of language in which we can find aesthetic satisfaction.

THE WAR POEMS

The war poetry, although the product of circumstance, is far from circumstantial in the pejorative sense. The vast poetic output (only part of which found its way into *Calligrammes*) of the fifteen months between December 1914, when Apollinaire enlisted in the artillery, and March 1916, when he was wounded in the head, testifies to the stimulating effect of events on his imagination. The drama of a creative personality faced with a phenomenon on an unprecedented scale unfolds through the five sections of the volume which chronicle his changing reactions to the different aspects of war.

Throughout its evolution the commanding feature of Apollinaire's attitude is his desire to respond to these events as a new dimension of experience. The general social climate at the outbreak of hostilities—which was, curiously, one of eager anticipation—together with the more specific optimism and energy of his own modernist outlook led him to welcome the coming conflict as the opening of a new era of infinite promise. It takes only a reading of "La Petite Auto," the poem that is virtually the overture for everything that follows, to see that his vision of the war was an epic one. The almost apocalyptic images that swell the tone of this poem represent the simultanist vision of the 1913-1914 period carried to a new pitch of intensity. Embracing within himself the dimensions of earth, sky, and ocean as well as the armies spreading across the face of Europe, the poet feels that coming events can only multiply his powers further. The pattern that can be traced throughout the succeeding work is that of Apollinaire's attempt to maintain this larger vision in face of the realities of war. Aragon's belief that "ce serait un crime de montrer les beaux côtés de la guerre . . . même si elle en avait"[7] [it would be a crime to show the attractive face of war . . . even if it had one] is the very antithesis of what Apollinaire was trying to achieve.

7. From an article in which Aragon is highly critical of Apollinaire's attempt to find beauty in war: "Beautés de la guerre et leurs reflets dans la littérature" [Beauties of war and their reflection in literature], *Europe* (December 1935), 474-480.

The division of the effects of war into horrors and beauties is one that he sought to transcend in order to grasp it as a total experience that could multiply his imaginative powers and his capacity for living.

The synthesis was perhaps easiest to achieve in the period covered by "Étendards" and "Case d'Armons." Novelty enhanced the enthusiasm with which Apollinaire entered upon his training as a soldier and underwent his first engagements in artillery combat at the front. He was proud that, as an intellectual and a poet, he could prove the equal of the other recruits (mostly much younger than himself) in becoming a man of action, and he derived immense satisfaction from mastering the pragmatic skills of soldiering. The sense of being part of a vast collective effort, and the experience of comradeship, brought the kind of fulfillment that was sought in more imaginative terms in the prewar period. Echoing the proud statement of a liberated personality in "Le Musicien de Saint-Merry"—"J'ai enfin le droit de saluer des êtres que je ne connais pas"—the enlisted poet can say with equal force but more literal truth, "Me voici libre et fier parmi mes compagnons." That is not to say that Apollinaire felt none of the alienating effects of his situation. The loneliness and the apprehension that could afflict him are strongly expressed in "La Colombe Poignardée et le Jet d'Eau," while the reinforcement of the basic polarities of his nature, under pressure of the war situation, is densely formulated in one line of "Visée": "Guerre paisible ascèse solitude métaphysique." But at this early stage inner doubts are conquered by an effort of the will and the imagination. The sense of purpose felt in his life spills over into his creative activity. As in the prewar period, his self-confidence is expressed equally in vigorous simplicity of expression and lively formal innovations, represented on the one hand by the easy discursive verse of "2^e^ Canonnier Conducteur," "A Nîmes," and "Veille," and on the other by the typographical experiments and bold plastic values of many poems of "Case d'Armons."

The recurring image in "Case d'Armons" which crystallizes the freedom of spirit of the early months at the front is that of *le bois* or *la forêt*, suggesting a private enclave, a time out of war, which the poet has created for himself. It is a fact that Apollinaire's battery was stationed during this period (April-June 1915) in a small wood at some distance from the front line. His letters are full of delighted accounts of its plant and animal life and the hours of leisure he enjoyed within it, in relative safety, writing and making rings out of shell cases. But the poems—"Échelon" especially, with the white wound of the trenches seen beyond the wood and Death dangling at the perimeter—heighten this real-life situation by a process of fabulation in which the wood takes on the associations of a privileged, almost magic, sanctuary. A sense of security, therefore, spreads throughout the poems, exorcising danger. An artillery bombardment becomes an exciting and enchanting event: "La forêt merveilleuse où je vis donne un bal." Death-dealing shells are transformed into swift and beautiful birds of prey, pastoral harbingers of love, or tightrope dancers full of the grace of spring. Because he is sheltered by the wood, the soldier of "Les Saisons" can see his life as an ordered succession of happy moments, the time of war being indistinguishable from the time of peace. This is not escapism, or obliviousness of death and danger, whose presence is acknowledged in the background and occasionally filters into the poems. It is rather that the ominous associations of war are sublimated in a release of energy, prompted by a situation with an unusual appeal to the poet's imagination and stimulating him to a unique appreciation of life, given greater force by its context.

At this and all subsequent stages love is, of course, one of the major ways in which Apollinaire tried to sustain his vision. The significant group of poems here are those written for Madeleine Pagès. The dying loves for Marie Laurencin and Louise de Coligny[8] add to the singular richness of love themes in the volume, generating elegiac poems in that vein of condensed and evocative lyricism of which he was a consummate master. The sequence of quatrains in "Lueurs des Tirs" which he wrote for Marie conceal ambivalent depths of meaning beneath a limpid surface with a skill that he rarely surpassed. What is special about the poems to Madeleine, however, is the way in which they are deliberately made to fulfill a vital need for spiritual replenishment and creative stimulation. Particularly in the autumn and winter of 1915, when the first euphoria of war had subsided and his battery had moved forward into front-line combat in one of the major battle zones of the war, Madeleine is made the focal point of his determination to be equal to events as a poet no less than as a man. In a real sense, as "Dans

8. The liaison between Apollinaire and the painter Marie Laurencin, begun in 1907, went through a period of strain in 1912-1913 and was finally broken by Marie's marriage in June 1914, although he continued to send her love poems after that. His passionate erotic liaison with Louise de Coligny-Châtillon (Lou) began in Nice in September 1915, before his enlistment in the army. She inspired most of the love poems in "Étendards" and "Case d'Armons," but after Apollinaire left Nîmes for the front there was a rapid cooling off on her side—hence the growing note of melancholy in the poems in these sections. He met Madeleine Pagès in January 1915 while returning from leave to his barracks in Nîmes, but he did not begin to exchange letters with her until April-May. There followed a rapid courtship by letter, culminating in a proposal in August, and a visit to her home in Algeria in January 1916. During this time he continued to correspond with Lou as well as Madeleine, but the majority of his love poems from May 1915 are inspired by Madeleine, although sometimes they were also sent to Lou! He broke off his engagement with Madeleine in late 1916, after being wounded at the front. The last love poem of *Calligrammes*, "La Jolie Rousse," was inspired by Jacqueline Kolb, whom he married in May 1918, some months before his death.

l'Abri-Caverne" lucidly recognizes, his love is as much a creation of his imagination as actual feeling for another person. Although such poems as "Simultanéités," "Chevaux de Frise," "Désir," and "Un Oiseau Chante" often have the enraptured tone and ecstatic imagery of highly self-conscious love poetry, literary *préciosité* does not arise, because the aim is clearly to invest a grim reality with human significance. The metaphoric connections that are woven so persistently between the battlefield and the distant object of the poet's dreams draw together two widely different realities and, by enlarging the poet's awareness of both, allow him to transcend his immediate situation.

Remarkably, the escalating eroticism of the poems is made to fulfill a similar function. The whole violence of war is colored by the poet's sexual longing and becomes the expression, not of a destructive aim, but of a fierce celebration of passion. Ultimately the erotic drive extends beyond the poet himself and is projected in many poems as a fundamental life-force which is larger than hate and unites the combating nations in "le terrible amour des peuples" [the terrible love of the (warring) peoples] ("Le Chant d'Amour"). This is not a Freudian hypothesis about the link between sex and aggression, but rather an attitude of quasi-religious awe at the convulsion which shakes humanity. It is an attempt to humanize and make sense of violence by seeing it as an expression of a vital urge which ultimately transcends its death-dealing function.

The dangers of celebrating violence at so high-flown a level are only too obvious, and Apollinaire has more than once been accused—but shortsightedly—of turning a horrific situation into a private egotistical "fête" and thus of revealing serious emotional inadequacy. Undoubtedly the greatest challenge to his powers as a poet was that of finding a convincing form and style in which to convey his epic vision of the war, without insensitivity to the real horror and suffering that were involved. The solution is found in a constant striving to elevate events to a mythic dimension, beyond the notions of death and destruction. In some instances ("La Petite Auto," "Merveille de la Guerre") it is the poet's own self that is mythologized so that he takes on a larger identity, capable of seeing beyond the cataclysm to the transfigured future that will be born from it. In other poems ("Chant de l'Horizon en Champagne," "Le Vigneron Champenois") there is a suggestion that events are seen from the viewpoint of larger-than-life deities and thus take on, in their broader vision, a significance that escapes the merely human eye. A wider imaginative perspective is also created by uses of the simultanist technique of the modernist period (("Il y a"), by the involvement of extrahuman, as well as human, forces ("Chant de l'Honneur"), and by the visionary qualities of much of the imagery (the long night of labor of "Désir," for example). By these means there is a successful heightening of the traumatic events of war, which does not imply blindness to death and suffering but rather an optimistic conviction that humanity can survive the holocaust and emerge magnified by the experience.

There is ample evidence in the poems from the last months of Apollinaire's service that he was aware of the real horrors of war. The poems written after his transfer to the infantry at the end of November 1915 are increasingly grave. In the artillery the dugout had been, like the wood, a symbol of security, but now that it is a front-line infantry dugout it is given, in the hallucinatory images of "Océan de Terre," new associations of dread and fear. "L'Avenir" and "Exercice," in their sobriety of form and statement, are overshadowed by an awareness of death; they speak of the need for a stoic retreat within the self as the only safeguard against the dehumanizing effect of war. Yet, even in this period of great gravity, Apollinaire is still impelled to prove himself equal as a poet to the scale of the conflict in which he is enmeshed. "Du Coton dans les Oreilles," one of the last poems written at the front, is also one of his major compositions in its successful attempt to match, in the span and controlled confusion of its parts, the cacophony and frenzy of war. It is at once a definitive expression of the anarchy of war and yet, in the way the wild sweep of events is artistically channeled, a demonstration of the poet's control over disorder.

It is, therefore, by the overall breadth of his vision and the quality of his artistic achievement that Apollinaire is to be judged as a war poet, and not—as has too often been done—by the single criterion of the degree of pathos that he achieves in selected poems. War for him was a total and complex experience whose contradictions can be reconciled only within a heightened poetic vision. His achievement is that his war poetry as a whole successfully embodies that vision.

THE NEW SPIRIT

The final creative period of Apollinaire's life is the short span of two years between the autumn of 1916, following his (partial) recovery from a head wound received in March 1916, to his death in November 1918. The dominating aesthetic ideas of this period are a more mature and more pronounced form of his prewar modernism. They are most fully elaborated in his famous lecture "L'Esprit Nouveau et les Poètes" in November 1917, whose central theme is the need for constant experiment and innovation if poetry is to maintain its place in the modern world. The miracles achieved by contemporary science and technology are so staggering, according to Apollinaire, that poetry risks being left behind in the ability to express the creative spirit of man. To rival the achievements of the scientists, poets have to rid themselves of outmoded forms and conventions and seek to renew their art by every means possible. The new spirit in poetry will be distinguished by its power of absolute invention and its capacity to surprise and astonish. As in the prewar period, but in a much stronger sense, prophecy and surprise are proclaimed to be the two cardinal virtues of a modern poetics. Through prophecy the artist will constantly be able to look into the unknown and anticipate the mysteries of the future; through surprise the new will constantly be created and recreated.

This radical commitment to innovation is qualified by the statement that a modernist aesthetic should nevertheless seek to retain the finest elements of the past. If the new spirit inherits from Romanticism its restless quest for novelty, it must draw from classicism certain traditional qualities. Limits are set to innovation, dictated by common sense and an awareness of the need for discipline and order: by these standards some of the more hectic of recent experiments are suggested to be puerile. These concessions to tradition, however, strengthen rather than weaken a paean of praise which performs the considerable rhetorical feat of bestowing on the avant-garde spirit both a cloak of heroic glamour and a mantle of authority.

The ideas of "L'Esprit Nouveau" form the very stuff of the last great poems of *Calligrammes*—"La Victoire," "La Jolie Rousse," and, of course, "Les Collines," which truly belongs to this period—but are developed there with a significant difference of tone and mood. Whereas the lecture was enthusiastic and confident, anxiety and uncertainty again invade the poems. "La Victoire" may seem to be calling for an uninhibited assault on traditional poetic language which is consistent with the lecture and Apollinaire's previous practice, but the constant faltering of the tone points to underlying inhibitions and self-doubt. More strikingly still, where the alliance between the old and the new seems easy and unproblematic in the lecture, there is a sharper polarization in "La Jolie Rousse" which speaks of a "long quarrel" between tradition and invention, which the poet will have to struggle to surmount, knowing that there will be many compromises and failures on the way.

It is sometimes said that this note of self-doubt is attributable to personal difficulties and changing circumstances in the last two years of Apollinaire's life. His head wound had left him debilitated and frequently depressed; as "Tristesse d'une Étoile" seems to hint, he may even have feared permanent impairment of his poetic powers. He also suddenly found himself elevated to the status of a recognized master for a whole new generation of poets, but he was uneasily aware that some of his disciples were prepared to be more radically iconoclastic than himself (hence some veiled criticisms in the lecture). There is no doubt some substance in these explanations, but, looking deeper, the most profound reason for the tone of the poems is less a failure of purpose than a positive choice of conflict and tension as a preferred creative state of mind. As in the 1913-1914 period, Apollinaire is intuitively aware of the inspiration he can find in doubt and uncertainty, and he values the dramatic heightening of mood that results from a clash between optimism and anxiety. He needs, even more strongly than in "Liens" and the prewar work, to bring all his conflicting emotions to bear on a theme that is of central importance to him and to make a definitive statement that embraces all aspects of his creative personality.

This theme is the heroic anguish of the poet as the explorer of the future. Whereas in "Liens" the conflict was experienced in the private area of Apollinaire's own sensibility and attitude to the world, the emphasis in "La Victoire," "Les Collines," and "La Jolie Rousse" is thrown entirely onto the poet's public persona as an artist undertaking an arduous responsibility on behalf of humanity. It is this sense of a mission, requiring all the vision and courage of a man who had lived through the tumult of war and suffered personally, which provides the resolution between anguish and optimism and makes the final poems, particularly "Les Collines" and "La Jolie Rousse," the definitive statement of Apollinaire's credo. The moving quality of "La Jolie Rousse" comes partly from our knowledge that it was virtually Apollinaire's last word before his untimely death. But, even without this extraneous knowledge, it stands as a remarkably complete summation of his achievement and genius as they now appear before history. He can rightly claim to be the one poet above all others who unites the virtues of a long poetic tradition and those of a new phase of bold experiment and change. In the depth of his vision and his consummate mastery of poetic language he is in complete continuity with the great poetry of the past. In his determination to make poetry assume an adventurous and pioneering role in creating a new sensibility for a new and rapidly changing world, he is a man of the future. It is fitting that his poetic testament should be so lucid and poignant a recognition of his unique position.

University of Stirling
August 1978

S. I. Lockerbie

Ondes
Waves

Liens

Cordes faites de cris

Sons de cloches à travers l'Europe
Siècles pendus

Rails qui ligotez les nations
Nous ne sommes que deux ou trois hommes
Libres de tous liens
Donnons-nous la main

Violente pluie qui peigne les fumées
Cordes
Cordes tissées
Câbles sous-marins
Tours de Babel changées en ponts
Araignées-Pontifes
Tous les amoureux qu'un seul lien a liés

Chains

Cords made of cries

Sounds of bells across Europe
Hanging centuries

Rails binding the nations
We are only two or three men
Free of all chains
Let's join hands

Violent rain combing the smoke
Cords
Woven cords
Submarine cables
Towers of Babel changed to bridges
Spider-Pontiffs
All the lovers a single chain has joined together

D'autres liens plus ténus
Blancs rayons de lumière
Cordes et Concorde

J'écris seulement pour vous exalter
O sens ô sens chéris
Ennemis du souvenir
Ennemis du désir

Ennemis du regret
Ennemis des larmes
Ennemis de tout ce que j'aime encore

Other more tenuous chains
White rays of light
Cords and Concord

I write only to exalt you
Oh senses oh cherished senses
Enemies of memory
Enemies of desire

Enemies of regret
Enemies of tears
Enemies of all I still love

Les Fenêtres

Du rouge au vert tout le jaune se meurt
Quand chantent les aras dans les forêts natales
Abatis de pihis
Il y a un poème à faire sur l'oiseau qui n'a qu'une aile
Nous l'enverrons en message téléphonique
Traumatisme géant
Il fait couler les yeux
Voilà une jolie jeune fille parmi les jeunes Turinaises
Le pauvre jeune homme se mouchait dans sa cravate blanche
Tu soulèveras le rideau
Et maintenant voilà que s'ouvre la fenêtre
Araignées quand les mains tissaient la lumière
Beauté pâleur insondables violets
Nous tenterons en vain de prendre du repos
On commencera à minuit
Quand on a le temps on a la liberté
Bignorneaux Lotte multiples Soleils et l'Oursin du couchant
Une vieille paire de chaussures jaunes devant la fenêtre

Windows

From red to green all the yellow dies
When parakeets sing in their native forests
Giblets of pihis
There's a poem to be done on the bird with only one wing
We'll send it by telephone
Giant traumatism
It makes your eyes run
Do you see that pretty girl among the young women of Turin
The poor young man blew his nose with his white tie
You'll raise the curtain
And now see the window opening
Spiders when hands wove the light
Beauty paleness fathomless violets
Vainly we'll try to take some rest
We'll begin at midnight
When you have time you have liberty
Winkles Codfish multiple Suns and the Sea Urchin of sunset
An old pair of yellow boots in front of the window

Tours
Les Tours ce sont les rues
Puits
Puits ce sont les places
Puits
Arbres creux qui abritent les Câpresses vagabondes
Les Chabins chantent des airs à mourir
Aux Chabines marronnes
Et l'oie oua-oua trompette au nord
Où les chasseurs de ratons
Raclent les pelleteries
Étincelant diamant
Vancouver
Où le train blanc de neige et de feux nocturnes fuit l'hiver
O Paris
Du rouge au vert tout le jaune se meurt
Paris Vancouver Hyères Maintenon New-York et les Antilles
La fenêtre s'ouvre comme une orange
Le beau fruit de la lumière

Towers
Towers are the streets
Well
Wells are the squares
Wells
Hollow trees sheltering vagabond mulattoes
The Chabins sing melancholy songs
To brown Chabines
And the wa-wa wild goose honks to the north
Where raccoon hunters
Scrape the fur skins
Glittering diamond
Vancouver
Where the train white with snow and lights flashing through the dark runs away from winter
Oh Paris
From red to green all the yellow dies
Paris Vancouver Hyères Maintenon New York and the Antilles
The window opens like an orange
The lovely fruit of light

Paysage

V
OI
LA
CI MAISON
Où NAISSENT
LES È
TOI LES
ET LES DIVINITÉS

CET
ARBRISSEAU
QUI SE PRÉPARE
A FRUCTIFIER
TE
RES
SEM
BLE

UN CIGARE a
l
l
u
m
é
q
u
i
f
u
m
e

C
O
U
C
H
É
S

a

E
L
B
M
E
S
N
E

MANTS
VOUS
VOUS
SÉ
PA MES
RE MEM
R BRES
E
Z

Landscape

H
ERE THE ?
IS MANSION
WHERE ARE BORN
THE S
TA RS
AND THE DIVINITIES

THIS
LITTLE TREE
BEGINNING
TO BEAR FRUIT
RE
SEM
BLES
YOU

A LIGHTED cigar that smokes

L
Y
I
N
G

R
E
H
T
E
G
O
T

l
OVERS
YOU
WILL
SE
PA MY
RA MEM
T BERS
E

Les Collines

Au-dessus de Paris un jour
Combattaient deux grands avions
L'un était rouge et l'autre noir
Tandis qu'au zénith flamboyait
L'éternel avion solaire

L'un était toute ma jeunesse
Et l'autre c'était l'avenir
Ils se combattaient avec rage
Ainsi fit contre Lucifer
L'Archange aux ailes radieuses

Ainsi le calcul au problème
Ainsi la nuit contre le jour
Ainsi attaque ce que j'aime
Mon amour ainsi l'ouragan
Déracine l'arbre qui crie

The Hills

High over Paris one day
Two enormous airplanes fought
One was red and one was black
Meanwhile in the zenith flamed
The eternal solar plane

One was all my youth
And the other was the future
They raged against each other
So struggled with Lucifer
The radiant-winged Archangel

Thus calculation reckons with the problem
Night strives against the day
Thus what I love
My love assails A hurricane
Uproots the shrieking tree

Mais vois quelle douceur partout
Paris comme une jeune fille
S'éveille langoureusement
Secoue sa longue chevelure
Et chante sa belle chanson

Où donc est tombée ma jeunesse
Tu vois que flambe l'avenir
Sache que je parle aujourd'hui
Pour annoncer au monde entier
Qu'enfin est né l'art de prédire

Certains hommes sont des collines
Qui s'élèvent d'entre les hommes
Et voient au loin tout l'avenir
Mieux que s'il était le présent
Plus net que s'il était passé

Ornement des temps et des routes
Passe et dure sans t'arrêter
Laissons sibiler les serpents
En vain contre le vent du sud
Les Psylles et l'onde ont péri

Ordre des temps si les machines
Se prenaient enfin à penser
Sur les plages de pierreries
Des vagues d'or se briseraient
L'écume serait mère encore

Moins haut que l'homme vont les aigles
C'est lui qui fait la joie des mers
Comme il dissipe dans les airs
L'ombre et les spleens vertigineux
Par où l'esprit rejoint le songe

Voici le temps de la magie
Il s'en revient attendez-vous

But look what sweetness everywhere
Paris like a young girl
Awakens languidly
Shakes out her long hair
And sings her lovely song

What has happened to my youth
See the future is ablaze
Bear in mind I speak today
Announcing to the entire world
The art of prophecy at last is born

Some men are hills
Rising higher than other men
The distant future they descry
Better than if it were at hand
More clearly than if it had passed by

Adornment of roads and seasons
Pass on endure and never end
Let's leave the serpents to hiss
Vainly against a south wind
The Psylli and their wave have perished

Order of our days
If machines began at last to think
Against beaches of precious stones
Waves of gold would break
Sea-foam would once more be mother

Lower than man the eagles fly
It's man who makes the seas exult
As he dissipates in the air
The shadow and the dizzy spleens
By which the spirit communicates with dreams

This is the time of magic
It's coming back You may expect

A des milliards de prodiges
Qui n'ont fait naître aucune fable
Nul les ayant imaginés

Profondeurs de la conscience
On vous explorera demain
Et qui sait quels êtres vivants
Seront tirés de ces abîmes
Avec des univers entiers

Voici s'élever des prophètes
Comme au loin des collines bleues
Ils sauront des choses précises
Comme croient savoir les savants
Et nous transporteront partout

La grande force est le désir
Et viens que je te baise au front
O légère comme une flamme
Dont tu as toute la souffrance
Toute l'ardeur et tout l'éclat

L'âge en vient on étudiera
Tout ce que c'est que de souffrir
Ce ne sera pas du courage
Ni même du renoncement
Ni tout ce que nous pouvons faire

On cherchera dans l'homme même
Beaucoup plus qu'on n'y a cherché
On scrutera sa volonté
Et quelle force naîtra d'elle
Sans machine et sans instrument

Les secourables mânes errent
Se compénétrant parmi nous
Depuis les temps qui nous rejoignent
Rien n'y finit rien n'y commence
Regarde la bague à ton doigt

Billions of prodigies
They have fathered no fable
For no one has yet imagined them

Depths of consciousness
We'll fathom you tomorrow
And who knows what living beings
Will be drawn from those abysses
Along with entire universes

Now prophets loom
Like distant hills of blue
Precise things will they know
Like what scientists claim to know
And they'll transport us everywhere

The supreme force is desire
Come let me kiss you on the brow
You who are nimble as a flame
Yours is all its pain
All its ardor and all the glitter

An age is coming when we'll examine
What it is to suffer pain
It's not a matter of taking heart
Or even of renunciation
Or of anything that we can do

We'll seek in man himself
Far more than we sought before
We'll test the human will
And the vigor born of it
Without machine or instrument

Helpful spirits wander
And mingle among men
In these times that overtake us
Here nothing ends nothing begins
Look at the ring on your finger

Temps des déserts des carrefours
Temps des places et des collines
Je viens ici faire des tours
Où joue son rôle un talisman
Mort et plus subtil que la vie

Je me suis enfin détaché
De toutes choses naturelles
Je peux mourir mais non pécher
Et ce qu'on n'a jamais touché
Je l'ai touché je l'ai palpé

Et j'ai scruté tout ce que nul
Ne peut en rien imaginer
Et j'ai soupesé maintes fois
Même la vie impondérable
Je peux mourir en souriant

Bien souvent j'ai plané si haut
Si haut qu'adieu toutes les choses
Les étrangetés les fantômes
Et je ne veux plus admirer
Ce garçon qui mime l'effroi

Jeunesse adieu jasmin du temps
J'ai respiré ton frais parfum
A Rome sur les chars fleuris
Chargés de masques de guirlandes
Et des grelots du carnaval

Adieu jeunesse blanc Noël
Quand la vie n'était qu'une étoile
Dont je contemplais le reflet
Dans la mer Méditerranée
Plus nacrée que les météores

Duvetée comme un nid d'archanges
Ou la guirlande des nuages

Time of deserts of crossroads
Time of city squares and hills
I've come here to perform some tricks
In which a talisman plays its part
Dead and yet subtler than life

I have at last detached myself
From all natural things
I can die but may not sin
And what no one has ever touched
I have touched I have felt

And I've explored what no man
Can imagine in any way
Often I've weighed
Even life the imponderable
I can die with a smile

Often I have soared so high
So high that farewell everything
Phantoms and wonders
No longer shall I admire
That boy who mimics fear

Youth farewell jasmine of time
I've inhaled your fresh perfume
On flowered wagons in Rome
Bearing masks and garlands
And bells of carnivals

Farewell youth white Noel
When life was a single star
I gazed at its reflection
In the Mediterranean
More pearly than a meteor

And downy as an archangel's nest
Or a wreath of cloud

Et plus lustrée que les halos
Émanations et splendeurs
Unique douceur harmonies

Je m'arrête pour regarder
Sur la pelouse incandescente
Un serpent erre c'est moi-même
Qui suis la flûte dont je joue
Et le fouet qui châtie les autres

Il vient un temps pour la souffrance
Il vient un temps pour la bonté
Jeunesse adieu voici le temps
Où l'on connaîtra l'avenir
Sans mourir de sa connaissance

C'est le temps de la grâce ardente
La volonté seule agira
Sept ans d'incroyables épreuves
L'homme se divinisera
Plus pur plus vif et plus savant

Il découvrira d'autres mondes
L'esprit languit comme les fleurs
Dont naissent les fruits savoureux
Que nous regarderons mûrir
Sur la colline ensoleillée

Je dis ce qu'est au vrai la vie
Seul je pouvais chanter ainsi
Mes chants tombent comme des graines
Taisez-vous tous vous qui chantez
Ne mêlez pas l'ivraie au blé

Un vaisseau s'en vint dans le port
Un grand navire pavoisé
Mais nous n'y trouvâmes personne
Qu'une femme belle et vermeille
Elle y gisait assassinée

More glowing than halos
Emanations and splendors
Unique sweetness harmonies

I pause to see
On the incandescent lawn
A serpent wander it is I
Who am the flute I play
And the whip to chastise men

A time will come for suffering
A time will come for kindness
Farewell youth In that time
We'll know the future
And not die of our knowledge

It will be a time of ardent grace
When only human will can act
Seven years of incredible trials
Man will become a god
Purer more alive and knowing

And he'll discover other worlds
The spirit shrivels like a flower
From it sweet fruits will spring
We'll watch them ripening
On the sunlit slope

I tell you what life really is
Only I could sing this way
My songs are scattering like seeds
Hush all you others who sing
Don't mix your darnel with my grain

A vessel glided into the haven
A huge ship decked with flags
But in it we found no one
Only a lovely crimson woman
Who lay there slain

Une autre fois je mendiais
L'on ne me donna qu'une flamme
Dont je fus brûlé jusqu'aux lèvres
Et je ne pus dire merci
Torche que rien ne peut éteindre

Où donc es-tu ô mon ami
Qui rentrais si bien en toi-même
Qu'un abîme seul est resté
Où je me suis jeté moi-même
Jusqu'aux profondeurs incolores

Et j'entends revenir mes pas
Le long des sentiers que personne
N'a parcourus j'entends mes pas
A toute heure ils passent là-bas
Lents ou pressés ils vont ou viennent

Hiver toi qui te fais la barbe
Il neige et je suis malheureux
J'ai traversé le ciel splendide
Où la vie est une musique
Le sol est trop blanc pour mes yeux

Habituez-vous comme moi
A ces prodiges que j'annonce
A la bonté qui va régner
A la souffrance que j'endure
Et vous connaîtrez l'avenir

C'est de souffrance et de bonté
Que sera faite la beauté
Plus parfaite que n'était celle
Qui venait des proportions
Il neige et je brûle et je tremble

Maintenant je suis à ma table
J'écris ce que j'ai ressenti

I was begging another time
But was given only a flame
That burnt me to the lips
No word of thanks could I say
Torch nothing can extinguish

Where are you then my friend
Withdrawn within yourself so far
That only an abyss remains
Where I have flung myself
Into the colorless depths

I hear my footsteps coming back
Along the track where no one
Has been I hear my steps
At any hour they pass by
Slow or hurried they come and go

Winter while you shave your chin
It's snowing and I suffer
I've traversed the glowing sky
Where life is a melody
The earth is too white for my eyes

Accustom yourself as I have done
To these prodigies I announce
To the kindness that will rule
To the suffering I endure
And you will know what is to come

Of suffering and kindness
Beauty will be composed
More perfect than the beauty
That arose from symmetry
It snows I burn and I tremble

Now seated at my table
I write what I have felt

Et ce que j'ai chanté là-haut
Un arbre élancé que balance
Le vent dont les cheveux s'envolent

Un chapeau haut de forme est sur
Une table chargée de fruits
Les gants sont morts près d'une pomme
Une dame se tord le cou
Auprès d'un monsieur qui s'avale

Le bal tournoie au fond du temps
J'ai tué le beau chef d'orchestre
Et je pèle pour mes amis
L'orange dont la saveur est
Un merveilleux feu d'artifice

Tous sont morts le maître d'hôtel
Leur verse un champagne irréel
Qui mousse comme un escargot
Ou comme un cerveau de poète
Tandis que chantait une rose

L'esclave tient une épée nue
Semblable aux sources et aux fleuves
Et chaque fois qu'elle s'abaisse
Un univers est éventré
Dont il sort des mondes nouveaux

Le chauffeur se tient au volant
Et chaque fois que sur la route
Il corne en passant le tournant
Il paraît à perte de vue
Un univers encore vierge

Et le tiers nombre c'est la dame
Elle monte dans l'ascenseur
Elle monte monte toujours
Et la lumière se déploie
Et ces clartés la transfigurent

And what I sang up there
A slender tree swayed by the wind
With streaming hair

A top hat rests upon
A table bearing fruit
Near an apple the gloves lie dead
A lady wrings her neck
Beside a man who gulps himself

The dance whirls in the depths of time
I've killed the handsome bandleader
And now I peel for my friends
The orange whose flavor is
A marvelous fireworks display

They are all dead the maitre d'hôtel
Pours them an unreal champagne
It foams up like a snail
Or like a poet's brain
And all the while a rose was singing

The slave grasps a naked sword
Like fountains and like rivers
And every time he lowers it
A universe is disemboweled
From which new worlds arise

The chauffeur grips the steering wheel
And every time along the road
He sounds his horn around a curve
There appears on the horizon
A universe still virgin

And the third number is the lady
Going up in the elevator
She keeps on going going up
And the light keeps spreading out
And those clarities transform her

Mais ce sont de petits secrets
Il en est d'autres plus profonds
Qui se dévoileront bientôt
Et feront de vous cent morceaux
A la pensée toujours unique

Mais pleure pleure et repleurons
Et soit que la lune soit pleine
Ou soit qu'elle n'ait qu'un croissant
Ah! pleure pleure et repleurons
Nous avons tant ri au soleil

Des bras d'or supportent la vie
Pénétrez le secret doré
Tout n'est qu'une flamme rapide
Que fleurit la rose adorable
Et d'où monte un parfum exquis

But these are petty secrets
There are other deeper ones
That soon will be unveiled
And divide you into a hundred pieces
Still having one common thought

But weep weep and again weep
And may the moon wax full
Or may she wane to a crescent
Ah! weep weep and again weep
We have laughed so long in the sunlight

Golden arms sustain life
Find out the gilded secret
That all is only a rapid flame
Adorned by the adorable rose
And shedding a delicate perfume

Arbre

A Frédéric Boutet

Tu chantes avec les autres tandis que les phonographes galopent
Où sont les aveugles où s'en sont-ils allés
La seule feuille que j'aie cueillie s'est changée en plusieurs mirages
Ne m'abandonnez pas parmi cette foule de femmes au marché
Ispahan s'est fait un ciel de carreaux émaillés de bleu
Et je remonte avec vous une route aux environs de Lyon

Je n'ai pas oublié le son de la clochette d'un marchand de coco d'autrefois
J'entends déjà le son aigre de cette voix à venir
Du camarade qui se promènera avec toi en Europe
Tout en restant en Amérique

Un enfant
Un veau dépouillé pendu à l'étal
Un enfant
Et cette banlieue de sable autour d'une pauvre ville au fond de l'est
Un douanier se tenait là comme un ange
A la porte d'un misérable paradis
Et ce voyageur épileptique écumait dans la salle d'attente des premières

Tree

For Frédéric Boutet

You sing with the others while phonographs gallop
Where are the blind where have they gone
The only leaf I've picked has become several mirages
Don't desert me in this crowd of women at the market
There is a sky at Ispahan of enameled blue tiles
And I go with you along a road near Lyons

I haven't forgotten the long-ago sound of a licorice vendor's bell
Already I hear the shrill sound of that future voice
Of the friend who will walk with you in Europe
While he remains in America

A child
A skinned calf hanging at the butcher's stall
A child
And that suburb of sand around a beggarly town in the depths of the east
A customs officer stood there like an angel
At the door of a shabby paradise
And the epileptic traveler foamed in the first-class waiting room

Engoulevent Blaireau
Et la Taupe-Ariane
Nous avions loué deux coupés dans le transsibérien
Tour à tour nous dormions le voyageur en bijouterie et moi
Mais celui qui veillait ne cachait point un revolver armé

Tu t'es promené à Leipzig avec une femme mince déguisée en homme
Intelligence car voilà ce que c'est qu'une femme intelligente
Et il ne faudrait pas oublier les légendes
Dame-Abonde dans un tramway la nuit au fond d'un quartier désert
Je voyais une chasse tandis que je montais
Et l'ascenseur s'arrêtait à chaque étage

Entre les pierres
Entre les vêtements multicolores de la vitrine
Entre les charbons ardents du marchand de marrons
Entre deux vaisseaux norvégiens amarrés à Rouen
Il y a ton image

Elle pousse entre les bouleaux de la Finlande

Ce beau nègre en acier

La plus grande tristesse
C'est quand tu reçus une carte postale de La Corogne

Le vent vient du couchant
Le métal des caroubiers
Tout est plus triste qu'autrefois
Tous les dieux terrestres vieillissent
L'univers se plaint par ta voix
Et des êtres nouveaux surgissent
Trois par trois

Whippoorwill Badger
And the Mole-Ariadne
We had rented two compartments in the Trans-Siberian
In turn we slept the jewel salesman and I
But the one who kept watch made no effort to conceal his loaded revolver

You walked in Leipzig with a thin woman disguised as a man
Intelligence for that's what an intelligent woman is
And it's best to keep the legends in mind
Lady-Plentiful in a tramway at night in the depths of a deserted
neighborhood
I saw a hunt while I was going up
And the elevator stopped at every floor

Between the stones
Between the multicolored clothes in the window
Between the glowing coals of the chestnut seller
Between two Norwegian ships anchored at Rouen
I see your image

It springs up between birches in Finland

The beautiful steel negro

The greatest sadness
Was when you received a postcard from La Corogne

The wind blows from the sunset
The metal of carob trees
Everything is sadder than it used to be
All earth's gods are growing old
The universe complains with your voice
And new beings are rising
Three by three

Lundi Rue Christine

La mère de la concierge et la concierge laisseront tout passer
Si tu es un homme tu m'accompagneras ce soir
Il suffirait qu'un type maintînt la porte cochère
Pendant que l'autre monterait

Trois becs de gaz allumés
La patronne est poitrinaire
Quand tu auras fini nous jouerons une partie de jacquet
Un chef d'orchestre qui a mal à la gorge
Quand tu viendras à Tunis je te ferai fumer du kief

Ça a l'air de rimer

Des piles de soucoupes des fleurs un calendrier
Pim pam pim
Je dois fiche près de 300 francs à ma probloque
Je préférerais me couper le parfaitement que de les lui donner

Monday in Christine Street

The concierge's mother and the concierge will let everyone through
If you're a man you'll come with me tonight
All we need is one guy to watch the main entrance
While the other goes upstairs

Three gas burners lit
The proprietress is consumptive
When you've finished we'll play a game of backgammon
An orchestra leader who has a sore throat
When you come through Tunis we'll smoke some hashish

That almost rhymes

Piles of saucers flowers a calendar
Bing bang bong
I owe damn almost 300 francs to my landlady
I'd rather cut off you know what than give them to her

Je partirai à 20 h. 27
Six glaces s'y dévisagent toujours
Je crois que nous allons nous embrouiller encore davantage
Cher monsieur
Vous êtes un mec à la mie de pain
Cette dame a le nez comme un ver solitaire
Louise a oublié sa fourrure
Moi je n'ai pas de fourrure et je n'ai pas froid
Le Danois fume sa cigarette en consultant l'horaire
Le chat noir traverse la brasserie

Ces crêpes étaient exquises
La fontaine coule
Robe noire comme ses ongles
C'est complètement impossible
Voici monsieur
La bague en malachite
Le sol est semé de sciure
Alors c'est vrai
La serveuse rousse a été enlevée par un libraire

Un journaliste que je connais d'ailleurs très vaguement

Écoute Jacques c'est très sérieux ce que je vais te dire

Compagnie de navigation mixte

Il me dit monsieur voulez-vous voir ce que je peux faire d'eaux-fortes et de tableaux
Je n'ai qu'une petite bonne

Après déjeuner café du Luxembourg
Une fois là il me présente un gros bonhomme
Qui me dit
Écoutez c'est charmant
A Smyrne à Naples en Tunisie
Mais nom de Dieu où est-ce
La dernière fois que j'ai été en Chine

I'm leaving at 8:27 P.M.
Six mirrors keep staring at one another
I think we're going to get into an even worse mess
Dear sir
You are a crummy fellow
That dame has a nose like a tapeworm
Louise forgot her fur piece
Well I don't have a fur piece and I'm not cold
The Dane is smoking his cigarette while he consults the schedule
The black cat crosses the restaurant

Those pancakes were divine
The water's running
Dress black as her nails
It's absolutely impossible
Here sir
The malachite ring
The ground is covered with sawdust
Then it's true
The redheaded waitress eloped with a bookseller

A journalist whom I really hardly know

Look Jacques it's extremely serious what I'm going to tell you

Shipping company combine

He says to me sir would you care to see what I can do in etchings and
pictures
All I have is a little maid

After lunch at the Café du Luxembourg
When we get there he introduces me to a big fellow
Who says to me
Look that's charming
In Smyrna in Naples in Tunisia
Bus in God's name where is it
The last time I was in China

C'est il y a huit ou neuf ans
L'Honneur tient souvent à l'heure que marque la pendule
La quinte major

That was eight or nine years ago
Honor often depends on the time of day
The winning hand

Lettre-Océan

je traverse la ville nez en avant et je la coupe en 2

J'étais au bord du Rhin quand tu partis pour le Mexique
Ta voix me parvient malgré l'énorme distance
Gens de mauvaise mine sur le quai à la Vera Cruz

Juan Aldama

Les voyageurs de *l'Espagne* devant faire
le voyage de Coatzacoalcos pour s'embarquer
je t'envoie cette carte aujourd'hui au lieu

Correos
Mexico
4 centavos

YPIRANGA

REPUBLICA MEXICANA
TARJETA POSTAL

11 45
29 - 5
14
Rue des Batignolles

de profiter du courrier de Vera Cruz qui n'est pas sûr
Tout est calme ici et nous sommes dans l'attente
des événements.

U. S. Postage
2 cents 2

Vive la Ré pu bli que

Zut pour M. Zun

Ar ré tez co cher

Hou le croquant

Vi ve le Roy

Des clefs j'en ai vu mille et mille

Sur la rive gauche devant le pont d'Iéna

Evviva il Papa

A bas la ca lot te

Jac ques c'é tait dé li cieux

La Tu ni sie tu fondes, un jour nal

non si vous avez une mous tache

ta gueule mon vieux pad

T

S

F

BONJOUR ANOMO ANORA TU, NE CONNAITRAS JAMAIS BIEN

LES

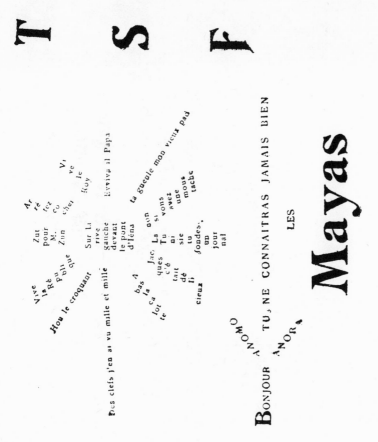

Mayas

Ocean-Letter

nose in the air
I cross the city
and i cut it in 2

I was on the banks of the Rhine when you left for Mexico
Your voice reaches me in spite of the huge distance
Seedy-looking people on the pier at Vera Cruz

Since the travelers on the *Espagne* are supposed
Juan Aldama — to go to Coatzacoalcos in order to embark
I send you this card today instead

Correos
Mexico
4 centavos

YPIRANGA

REPUBLICA MEXICANA
TARJETA POSTAL

11 45
29 – 5
14
Rue des Batignolles

of profiting by the Vera Cruz mails which aren't dependable
Everything is quiet here and we are awaiting events.

U. S. Postage
2 cents 2

Long live the Re pub lic

Nuts to Mr. Zun

Sto p driv er

Long li ve the King

Boo the peasant

On the left bank in front of Iéna bridge

I have seen thousands of keys

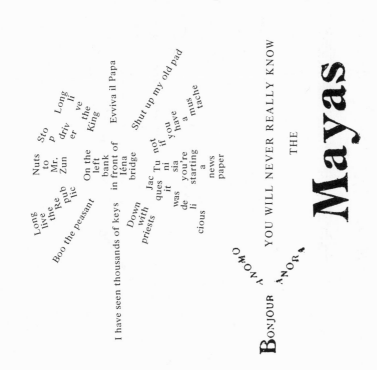

Evviva il Papa

Down with priests

Jac ques it was de li cious

Tu ni sia you're starting a news paper

not if you have a mus tache

Shut up my old pad

T

S

F

BONJOUR ANOMO ANORA

YOU WILL NEVER REALLY KNOW

THE

Mayas

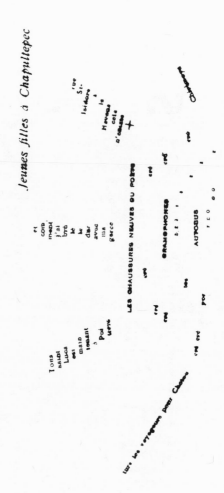

Te souviens-tu du tremblement de terre entre 1885 et 1890
on coucha plus d'un mois sous la tente

BONJOUR MON FRÈRE ALBERT à Mexico

Jeunes filles à Chapultepec

Tous
saint
Luca
est
main
tenant
à
Poi
tiers

et
com
ment
j'ai
brû
lé
le
dar
avec
ma
gorge

rue
St-
Isidore
à
la
Havane
cela
n'existe

LES CHAUSSURES NEUVES DU POETE

cré cré cré cré

GRAMOPHONES

cré cré

tire les voyageurs pour Chapultepec

cré cré cré

AUTOBUS

cré

Chapultepec

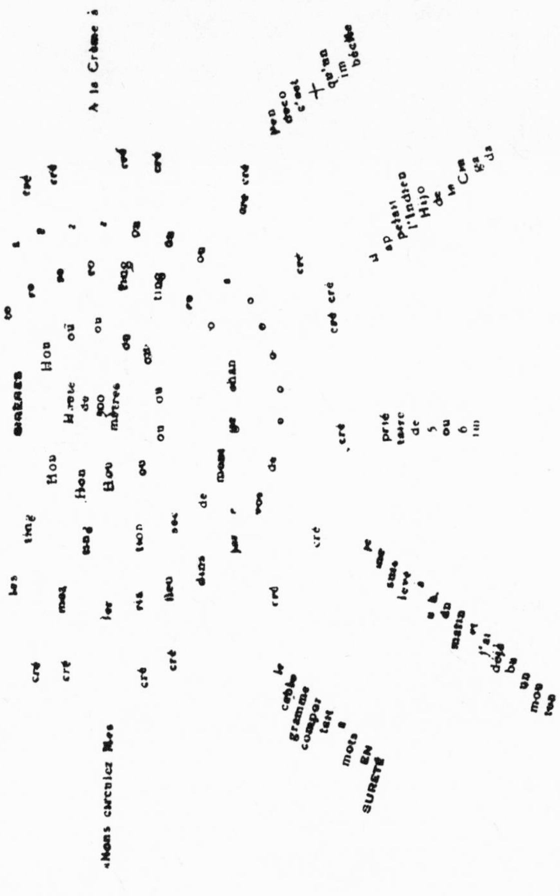

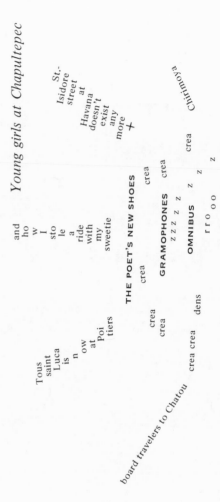

Do you remember the earthquake between 1885 and 1890
people slept in tents for more than a month

HELLO MY BROTHER ALBERT in Mexico

Young girls at Chapultepec

and
ho
w
I
sto
le
a
ride
with
my
sweetie

Tous
saint
Luca
is
n
ow
at
Poi
tiers

St.-
Isidore
street
at
Havana
doesn't
exist
any
more
+

THE POET'S NEW SHOES

crea
crea
crea
crea
crea

GRAMOPHONES
z z z z z

board travelers to Chatou

crea crea

dens

OMNIBUS

r r o o o

z
z
z

crea

Chirimoya

gar SIRENS to crea
z
crea ting Boo ro z crea
crea ing Boo ro
ting Boo 300 oo z
Move on please ladies and flower meters oo ro z With Cream in
Boo high
crea your ne oo oo ting ou crea
crea of li oo oo oo ting ou crea
tes the ro ou
of end the o o
ga the o crea crea
crea shut o o o o
crea crea
crea crea crea

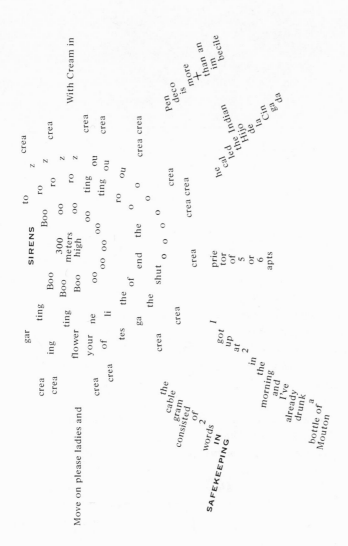

the
cable
gram
consisted
of
2
words
IN
SAFEKEEPING

I
got
up
at
2
in
the
morning
and
I've
already
drunk
a
bottle of
Mouton

prie
tor
of
5
or
6
apts

he
cal
led
the Indian
Hijo
de
la
Cin
ga
da

Pen
deco
is
more
+
than an
im
becile

Sur les Prophéties

J'ai connu quelques prophétesses
Madame Salmajour avait appris en Océanie à tirer les cartes
C'est là-bas qu'elle avait eu encore l'occasion de participer
A une scène savoureuse d'anthropophagie
Elle n'en parlait pas à tout le monde
En ce qui concerne l'avenir elle ne se trompait jamais

Une cartomancienne céretane Marguerite je ne sais plus quoi
Est également habile
Mais Madame Deroy est la mieux inspirée
La plus précise
Tout ce qu'elle m'a dit du passé était vrai et tout ce qu'elle
M'a annoncé s'est vérifié dans le temps qu'elle indiquait
J'ai connu un sciomancien mais je n'ai pas voulu qu'il interrogeât mon ombre
Je connais un sourcier c'est le peintre norvégien Diriks

On Prophecies

I've known a few prophetesses
Madame Salmajour learned in Oceania to tell fortunes by cards
It was there too she had occasion to participate
In a tasty scene of anthropophagy
She didn't mention it to everyone
Concerning the future she was never wrong

A Ceretanian cartomanceress Marguerite something or other
                Is just as clever
But Madame Delroy is the most inspired
                The most precise
Everything she's told me about the past was true and everything she
Predicted has come true in the time she said
I know a sciomantic but I didn't want him to interview my shadow
I know a water diviner he's the Norwegian painter Diriks

Miroir brisé sel renversé ou pain qui tombe
Puissent ces dieux sans figure m'épargner toujours
Au demeurant je ne crois pas mais je regarde et j'écoute et notez
Que je lis assez bien dans la main
Car je ne crois pas mais je regarde et quand c'est possible j'écoute

Tout le monde est prophète mon cher André Billy
Mail il y a si longtemps qu'on fait croire aux gens
Qu'ils n'ont aucun avenir qu'ils sont ignorants à jamais
Et idiots de naissance
Qu'on en a pris son parti et que nul n'a même l'idée
De se demander s'il connaît l'avenir ou non
Il n'y a pas d'esprit religieux dans tout cela
Ni dans les superstitions ni dans les prophéties
Ni dans tout ce que l'on nomme occultisme
Il y a avant tout une façon d'observer la nature
Et d'interpréter la nature
Qui est très légitime

Broken mirror spilt salt or scattered bread
May those faceless gods spare me always
All the same I don't believe but I look and listen and please note
I read hands rather well
For I don't believe but I look and when it's possible I listen

Everybody is a prophet my dear André Billy
But for so long people have been made to believe
They have no future and are ignorant forever
                    And born idiots
That they've become resigned and it never even occurs to anyone
To wonder if he knows the future or not
There's nothing religious in any of these matters
In the superstitions or in the prophecies
Or in anything that people call the occult
There is above all a way of observing nature
And of interpreting nature
Which is completely legitimate

Le Musicien de Saint-Merry

J'ai enfin le droit de saluer des êtres que je ne connais pas
Ils passent devant moi et s'accumulent au loin
Tandis que tout ce que j'en vois m'est inconnu
Et leur espoir n'est pas moins fort que le mien

Je ne chante pas ce monde ni les autres astres
Je chante toutes les possibilités de moi-même hors de ce monde et des astres
Je chante la joie d'errer et le plaisir d'en mourir

Le 21 du mois de mai 1913
Passeur des morts et les mordonnantes mériennes
Des millions de mouches éventaient une splendeur
Quand un homme sans yeux sans nez et sans oreilles
Quittant le Sébasto entra dans la rue Aubry-le-Boucher
Jeane l'homme était brun et ce couleur de fraise sur les joues
Homme Ah! Ariane
Il jouait de la flûte et la musique dirigeait ses pas
Il s'arrêta au coin de la rue Saint-Martin

The Musician of Saint-Merry

At last I have the right to hail unknown beings
They pass by me and gather in the distance
While all that I see of them is strange to me
And their hope is no frailer than mine

I sing neither of this world nor of the other stars
I sing of my own possibilities beyond this world and the stars
I sing the joy of wandering and the pleasure of the wanderer's death

The 21st of May 1913
Ferryman of the dead and of buzzing Saint-Merryites
Thousands of flies were fanning a splendor
When a man with no eyes or nose or ears
Turned out of Sebasto and started down Aubry-le-Boucher Street
He was a young man and dark his cheeks were strawberry pink
Man Oh! Ariadne
He played a flute and the music guided his steps
He paused at the corner of Saint-Martin Street

Jouant l'air que je chante et que j'ai inventé
Les femmes qui passaient s'arrêtaient près de lui
Il en venait de toutes parts
Lorsque tout à coup les cloches de Saint-Merry se mirent à sonner
Le musicien cessa de jouer et but à la fontaine
Qui se trouve au coin de la rue Simon-Le-Franc
Puis Saint-Merry se tut
L'inconnu reprit son air de flûte
Et revenant sur ses pas marcha jusqu'à la rue de la Verrerie
Où il entra suivi par la troupe des femmes
Qui sortaient des maisons
Qui venaient par les rues traversières les yeux fous
Les mains tendues vers le mélodieux ravisseur
Il s'en allait indifférent jouant son air
Il s'en allait terriblement

Puis ailleurs
A quelle heure un train partira-t-il pour Paris

A ce moment
Les pigeons des Moluques fientaient des noix muscades
En même temps
Mission catholique de Bôma qu'as-tu fait du sculpteur

Ailleurs
Elle traverse un pont qui relie Bonn à Beuel et disparaît à travers Pützchen

Au même instant
Une jeune fille amoureuse du maire

Dans un autre quartier
Rivalise donc poète avec les étiquettes des parfumeurs

En somme ô rieurs vous n'avez pas tiré grand-chose des hommes
Et à peine avez-vous extrait un peu de graisse de leur misère
Mais nous qui mourons de vivre loin l'un de l'autre
Tendons nos bras et sur ces rails roule un long train de marchandises

Tu pleurais assise près de moi au fond d'un fiacre

Playing the tune I'm singing and have invented
Women passing by gathered near him
They came from every direction
When suddenly the bells of Saint-Merry began to ring
The musician stopped playing and drank at the fountain
At the corner of Simon-Le-Franc Street
Then Saint-Merry was still
The stranger began to play his flute once more
And retracing his steps walked as far as La Verrerie Street
He started down it followed by the troupe of women
Who left the houses
And came by the cross streets with maddened eyes
Their hands stretched toward the melodious ravisher
He continued indifferently on his way playing his tune
He continued on his way terribly

And somewhere else
What time will a train leave for Paris

At that moment
Spice Island pigeons made nutmeg droppings
At the same time
Catholic mission of Boma what have you done with the sculptor

Somewhere else
She crosses a bridge joining Bonn to Beuel and disappears across Pützchen

At the same moment
A young girl in love with the mayor

In another neighborhood
Emulate poet the labels of perfumers

In sum oh laughers you haven't gotten a great deal from men
And scarcely have you obtained a little grease from their misery
But we who die because we live far from each other
Stretch out our arms and on those rails rolls a long train of merchandise

You wept sitting beside me in the depths of a taxi

Et maintenant
Tu me ressembles tu me ressembles malheureusement

Nous nous ressemblons comme dans l'architecture du siècle dernier
Ces hautes cheminées pareilles à des tours

Nous allons plus haut maintenant et ne touchons plus le sol

Et tandis que le monde vivait et variait
Le cortège des femmes long comme un jour sans pain
Suivait dans la rue de la Verrerie l'heureux musicien

Cortèges ô cortèges
C'est quand jadis le roi s'en allait à Vincennes
Quand les ambassadeurs arrivaient à Paris
Quand le maigre Suger se hâtait vers la Seine
Quand l'émeute mourait autour de Saint-Merry

Cortèges ô cortèges
Les femmes débordaient tant leur nombre était grand
Dans toutes les rues avoisinantes
Et se hâtaient raides comme balle
Afin de suivre le musicien
Ah! Ariane et toi Pâquette et toi Amine
Et toi Mia et toi Simone et toi Mavise
Et toi Colette et toi la belle Geneviève
Elles ont passé tremblantes et vaines
Et leurs pas légers et prestes se mouvaient selon la cadence
De la musique pastorale qui guidait
Leurs oreilles avides

L'inconnu s'arrêta un moment devant une maison à vendre
Maison abandonnée
Aux vitres brisées
C'est un logis du seizième siècle
La cour sert de remise à des voitures de livraisons
C'est là qu'entra le musicien
Sa musique qui s'éloignait devint langoureuse
Les femmes le suivirent dans la maison abandonnée

And now
You resemble me unhappily you resemble me

We resemble each other as do in nineteenth-century architecture
Those high chimneys like towers

We go higher now and no longer touch the earth

And while the world lived and changed
The procession of women as long as a day without bread
Followed along La Verrerie Street the lucky musician

Processions oh processions
As when long ago the king went to Vincennes
When ambassadors arrived in Paris
When skinny Suger rushed to the Seine
When the riot died around Saint-Merry

Processions oh processions
The women overflowed there were so many
Into all the neighboring streets
Hurrying like a flung ball
Following after the musician
Ah! Ariadne and you Paquette and you Amine
And you Mia and you Simone and you Mavise
And you Colette and you lovely Genevieve
They passed by trembling and vain
And their light eager steps moved in cadence
With the pastoral music that guided
Their avid ears

The stranger stopped for a moment in front of a house for sale
Deserted house
With broken windows
It's a sixteenth-century dwelling
The courtyard's used as a garage for delivery trucks
The musician went in
His music as it receded grew languorous
The women followed him into the deserted house

Et toutes y entrèrent confondues en bande
Toutes toutes y entrèrent sans regarder derrière elles
Sans regretter ce qu'elles ont laissé
Ce qu'elles ont abandonné
Sans regretter le jour la vie et la mémoire
Il ne resta bientôt plus personne dans la rue de la Verrerie
Sinon moi-même et un prêtre de Saint-Merry
Nous entrâmes dans la vieille maison

Mais nous n'y trouvâmes personne

Voici le soir
A Saint-Merry c'est l'Angélus qui sonne
Cortèges ô cortèges
C'est quand jadis le roi revenait de Vincennes
Il vint une troupe de casquettiers
Il vint des marchands de bananes
Il vint des soldats de la garde républicaine
O nuit
Troupeau de regards langoureux des femmes
O nuit
Toi ma douleur et mon attente vaine
J'entends mourir le son d'une flûte lointaine

All of them entered together in a group
All all entered without a backward glance
Without regretting what they had left
Or abandoned
Without regretting the day their life or their memory
Soon no one was left in La Verrerie Street
Except myself and a Saint-Merry priest
We entered the old house

But we didn't find anyone there

Now it's evening
At Saint-Merry the Angelus is ringing
Processions oh processions
As when long ago the king came back from Vincennes
There came a troupe of hatters
There came banana sellers
There came soldiers of the republican guard
Oh night
Flock of languorous feminine looks
Oh night
You my sorrow and my futile waiting
I hear the dying sound of a distant flute

La Cravate et la Montre

LA CRAVATE
DOU
LOU
REUSE
QUE TU
PORTES
ET QUI T'
ORNE O CI
VILISÉ
OTE- TU VEUX
LA BIEN
SI RESPI
RER

COMME L'ON
S'AMUSE
BI
EN

la
beau
té
de
la
vie
pas
se
la
dou
leur
de
mou
rir

Mon
cœur

les
yeux

l'enfant

Agla

la main

Tircis

semaine

l'infini
redressé
par un fou
de philosophe

les Muses
aux portes de
ton corps

le bel
inconnu

et le
vers
dantesque
luisant et
cadavérique

les
heures

Il
est
—
5
en
fin

Et
tout
se
ra
fi
ni

The Tie and the Watch

THE TIE
SO
SOR
ROWFUL
THAT YOU
WEAR
AND THAT
ADORNS YOU
OH CIVILIZED
ONE TAKE
IT IF YOU
OFF WISH
TO BREATHE

WHAT A GOOD
TIME WE'RE
HAV
ING

the
hours

the
beau
ty
of
life
sur
pass
es

My
heart

and the
Dantean
verse
shining and
corpselike

the handsome
stranger

the
eyes

It's
—
5
at
last

And
all
will
en
d

the Muses
at the doors of
your body

the child

the
sor
row
of
dy
ing

Agla

the infinite
righted
by a mad
philosopher

week

the hand

Tircis

Un Fantôme de Nuées

Comme c'était la veille du quatorze juillet
Vers les quatre heures de l'après-midi
Je descendis dans la rue pour aller voir les saltimbanques

Ces gens qui font des tours en plein air
Commencent à être rares à Paris
Dans ma jeunesse on en voyait beaucoup plus qu'aujourd'hui
Ils s'en sont allés presque tous en province

Je pris le boulevard Saint-Germain
Et sur une petite place située entre Saint-Germain-des-Prés et la statue de Danton
Je rencontrai les saltimbanques

La foule les entourait muette et résignée à attendre
Je me fis une place dans ce cercle afin de tout voir
Poids formidables
Villes de Belgique soulevées à bras tendu par un ouvrier russe de Longwy

Phantom of Clouds

Since it was the day before July fourteenth
Around four in the afternoon
I went down to the street to see the jugglers

Those people who give open-air performances
Are beginning to be rare in Paris
In my youth you saw many more of them
They've nearly all gone to the provinces

I took the Boulevard Saint-Germain
And in a little square between Saint-Germain-des-Prés and Danton's statue
I found the jugglers

The crowd surrounding them was silent and resigned to waiting
I found a place in the circle where I could see everything
Tremendous weights
Belgian cities raised at arm's length by a Russian worker from Longwy

Haltères noirs et creux qui ont pour tige un fleuve figé
Doigts roulant une cigarette amère et délicieuse comme la vie

De nombreux tapis sales couvraient le sol
Tapis qui ont des plis qu'on ne défera pas
Tapis qui sont presque entièrement couleur de la poussière
Et où quelques taches jaunes ou vertes ont persisté
Comme un air de musique qui vous poursuit

Vois-tu le personnage maigre et sauvage
La cendre de ses pères lui sortait en barbe grisonnante
Il portait ainsi toute son hérédité au visage
Il semblait rêver à l'avenir
En tournant machinalement un orgue de Barbarie
Dont la lente voix se lamentait merveilleusement
Les glouglous les couacs et les sourds gémissements

Les saltimbanques ne bougeaient pas
Le plus vieux avait un maillot couleur de ce rose violâtre qu'ont aux joues certaines jeunes filles fraîches mais près de la mort

Ce rose-là se niche surtout dans les plis qui entourent souvent leur bouche
Ou près des narines
C'est un rose plein de traîtrise

Cet homme portait-il ainsi sur le dos
La teinte ignoble de ses poumons

Les bras les bras partout montaient la garde

Le second saltimbanque
N'était vêtu que de son ombre
Je le regardai longtemps
Son visage m'échappe entièrement
C'est un homme sans tête

Un autre enfin avait l'air d'un voyou
D'un apache bon et crapule à la fois

Hollow black dumbbells whose stem is a frozen stream
Fingers rolling a cigarette as bittersweet as life

A number of dirty rugs covered the ground
Rugs with wrinkles that won't come out
Rugs that are almost entirely dust-colored
And with some yellow or green stains persistent
Like a tune that pursues you

Do you see the man who's savage and lean
His father's ashes sprouted in his graying beard
And he bore his whole heredity in his face
He seemed to be dreaming about the future
Turning his barrel organ all the while
Its lingering voice lamented in marvelous
Glug-glugs squawks and muffled groans

The jugglers didn't move
The oldest wore a sweater the rose-violet color you see in the fresh cheeks
 of young girls who are dying

That rose nestles above all in the creases surrounding their mouths
Or near their nostrils
It's a rose full of treachery

Thus he bore on his back
The lowly hue of his lungs

Arms arms everywhere mounted guard

The second juggler
Wore only his shadow
I watched him for a long time
His features escape me entirely
He's a headless man

Then there was another who resembled a tough thug
With a kind heart and a dirty mind

Avec son pantalon bouffant et les accroche-chaussettes
N'aurait-il pas eu l'apparence d'un maquereau à sa toilette

La musique se tut et ce furent des pourparlers avec le public
Qui sou à sou jeta sur le tapis la somme de deux francs cinquante
Au lieu des trois francs que le vieux avait fixés comme prix des tours

Mais quand il fut clair que personne ne donnerait plus rien
On se décida à commencer la séance
De dessous l'orgue sortit un tout petit saltimbanque habillé de rose pulmonaire
Avec de la fourrure aux poignets et aux chevilles
Il poussait des cris brefs
Et saluait en écartant gentiment les avant-bras
Mains ouvertes

Une jambe en arrière prête à la génuflexion
Il salua ainsi aux quatre points cardinaux
Et quand il marcha sur une boule
Son corps mince devint une musique si délicate que nul parmi les spectateurs n'y fut insensible
Un petit esprit sans aucune humanité
Pensa chacun
Et cette musique des formes
Détruisit celle de l'orgue mécanique
Que moulait l'homme au visage couvert d'ancêtres

Le petit saltimbanque fit la roue
Avec tant d'harmonie
Que l'orgue cessa de jouer
Et que l'organiste se cacha le visage dans les mains
Aux doigts semblables aux descendants de son destin
Fœtus minuscules qui lui sortaient de la barbe
Nouveaux cris de Peau-Rouge
Musique angélique des arbres
Disparition de l'enfant

Les saltimbamques soulevèrent les gros haltères à bout de bras
Ils jonglèrent avec les poids

With his baggy trousers and garters to hold up his socks
Didn't he look dressed up like a pimp

The music stopped and there were negotiations with the public
Who sou by sou threw down on the rug the sum of two and a half francs
Instead of the three francs the old man had set as the price of the show

But when it was clear no one was going to give any more
They decided to begin the performance
From beneath the organ appeared a tiny juggler dressed in pulmonary pink
With fur at his wrists and ankles
He gave little cries
And saluted by gracefully lifting his forearms
And spreading wide his fingers

One leg back ready to kneel
He saluted the four points of the compass
And when he balanced on a sphere
His thin body became such delicate music that none of the onlookers could resist it
A small inhuman sprite
Each of them thought
And that music of shapes
Destroyed the music of the mechanical organ
That the man with the ancestor-covered face was grinding out

The tiny juggler turned cartwheels
With such harmony
That the organ stopped playing
And the organist hid his face in his hands
His fingers resembled descendants of his destiny
Miniscule fetuses appearing in his beard
New cries like Redskins
Angelic music of the trees
Vanishing of the child

The jugglers raised the huge dumbbells at arm's length
They juggled with weights

Mais chaque spectateur cherchait en soi l'enfant miraculeux
Siècle ô siècle des nuages

But every spectator searched in himself for the miraculous child
Century oh century of clouds

Cœur Couronne et Miroir

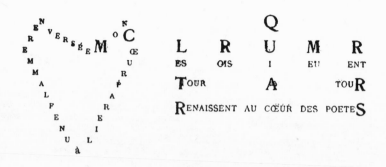

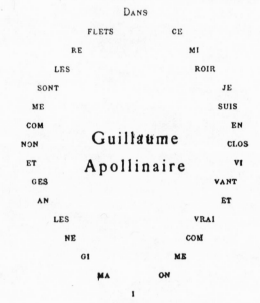

MON CŒUR PAREIL À UNE FLAMME RENVERSÉE

LES ROIS QUI MEURENT TOUR À TOUR RENAISSENT AU CŒUR DES POETES

DANS CE MIROIR JE SUIS ENCLOS VIVANT ET VRAI COMME ON IMAGINE LES ANGES ET NON COMME SONT LES REFLETS

Guillaume Apollinaire

Heart Crown and Mirror

L
F A
M
D E M^Y H T K H D IE
E E
T HE INGS O A
R
E R O^NE B^Y ON E
V T
N A^RE REBORN IN POETS' HEARTS
I L
N I
A K
E

W

IN
TIONS THIS
FLEC MIR
RE ROR
LIKE I
ALL AM
AT EN
NOT Guillaume CLOSED
AND LI
GELS Apollinaire VING
AN AND
THE REAL
NE JUST
GI AS
MA YOU
I

Tour

A R. D.

Au Nord au Sud
Zénith Nadir
Et les grands cris de l'Est
L'Océan se gonfle à l'Ouest
La Tour à la Roue
S'adresse

Turning Tower

To R. D.

To the North to the South
Zenith Nadir
And the great cries of the East
The Ocean swells to the West
The Tower to the Ferris Wheel
Appeals

Voyage

ADIEU AMOUR NUAGE QUI
FUIS REFAIS LE VOYAGE DE DANTE
ET N'A PAS CHU PLUIE FÉCON

OU VA DONC CE TRAIN QUI MEURT
DANS LES VALS ET LES BEAUX BOIS

DOUCE

LA

NUIT

ETOILES

D

PLEINE

NE

JE

TÉLÉGRAPHE

OISEAU QUI LAISSE TOMBER SES AILES PARTOUT

?
E
L
A
P

AU LOIN
FRAIS DU
TENDRE ÉTÉ SI P

L U N A I R E ET

C' EST TON SA
VI GE

QUE

V O I S PLU
S

Trip

FAREWELL LOVE CLOUD THAT
FLEES MAKE AGAIN DANTE'S JOURNEY
AND HASN'T FALLEN FERTILE RAIN

WHERE DOES THIS TRAIN GO THAT DIES
INTO THE VALLEYS AND BEAUTIFUL FRESH

W
S E
ET
T
H
G
I
N
T
H
E
S
of T
A
U
R
F
L
L
S
N
O
I

TELEGRAPH
B I R D
THAT F A L L
L E T S
HIS WINGS EVERYWHERE

?
E
L
A
FAR AWAY
WOODS OF **TENDER SUMMER SO P**

M O

O N AND
I
S
H

I S YOUR
A
F C
E
THAT

L
O
N SE
G E
E
R

A Travers l'Europe

A M. Ch.

Rotsoge
Ton visage écarlate ton biplan transformable en hydroplan
Ta maison ronde où il nage un hareng saur
Il me faut la clef des paupières
Heureusement que nous avons vu M. Panado
Et nous sommes tranquilles de ce côté-là
Qu'est-ce que tu vois mon vieux M. D...
90 ou 324 un homme en l'air un veau qui regarde à travers le ventre de sa mère

J'ai cherché longtemps sur les routes
Tant d'yeux sont clos au bord des routes
Le vent fait pleurer les saussaies
Ouvre ouvre ouvre ouvre ouvre
Regarde mais regarde donc
Le vieux se lave les pieds dans la cuvette
Una volta ho inteso dire Chè vuoi
Je me mis à pleurer en me souvenant de vos enfances

Across Europe

To M. Ch.

Rotsoge
Your scarlet face your biplane transformable to hydroplane
Your round house where a sour herring swims
I lack the key of eyelids
Luckily we saw Mr. Panado
And we're not worried in that respect
What do you see my old M. D...
90 or 324 a man in the air a calf looking through his mother's stomach

I looked a long while along the roads
So many eyes are shut at the edge of the roads
The wind makes the willows weep
Open open open open open
Look but look
The old man is washing his feet in the basin
Una volta ho inteso dire Chè vuoi
I began to weep remembering your childhood

Et toi tu me montres un violet épouvantable

Ce petit tableau où il y a une voiture m'a rappelé le jour
Un jour fait de morceaux mauves jaunes bleus verts et rouges
Où je m'en allais à la campagne avec une charmante cheminée tenant sa chienne en laisse
Il n'y en a plus tu n'as plus ton petit mirliton
La cheminée fume loin de moi des cigarettes russes
La chienne aboie contre les lilas
La veilleuse est consumée
Sur la robe ont chu des pétales
Deux anneaux d'or près des sandales
Au soleil se sont allumés
Mais tes cheveux sont le trolley
A travers l'Europe vêtue de petits feux multicolores

And you you show me a dreadful violet hue

That little painting of a car reminds me of the day
A day made of pieces of mauve yellow blue green and red
When I went to the country with a charming chimney who had her dog on a leash
There's nothing left you no longer have your little bauble
The chimney smokes Russian cigarettes far away from me
The dog barks at the lilacs
The night-light has burnt out
On the dress petals have fallen
Two gold rings near some sandals
In the sunlight have ignited
But your hair is the trolley
Across Europe clad in tiny multicolored lights

Il Pleut

Il pleut des voix de femmes comme si elles étaient mortes même dans le souvenir

cest vous aussi quil pleut merveilleuses rencontres de ma vie ô gouttelettes

et ces nuages cabrés se prennent à hennir tout un univers de villes auriculaires

écoute sil pleut tandis que le regret et le dédain pleurent une ancienne musique

écoute tomber les liens qui te retiennent en haut et en bas

It's Raining

its raining womens voices as if they were dead even in memory
its raining you too marvelous encounters of my life oh droplets
and those clouds rear and begin to whinny a universe of auricular cities
listen to it rain while regret and disdain weep an ancient music
listen to the fetters falling that bind you high and low

Étendards
Banners

La Petite Auto

Le 31 de mois d'Août 1914
Je partis de Deauville un peu avant minuit
Dans la petite auto de Rouveyre

Avec son chauffeur nous étions trois

Nous dîmes adieu à toute une époque
Des géants furieux se dressaient sur l'Europe
Les aigles quittaient leur aire attendant le soleil
Les poissons voraces montaient des abîmes
Les peuples accouraient pour se connaître à fond
Les morts tremblaient de peur dans leurs sombres demeures

Les chiens aboyaient vers là-bas où étaient les frontières
Je m'en allais portant en moi toutes ces armées qui se battaient
Je les sentais monter en moi et s'étaler les contrées où elles serpentaient
Avec les forêts les villages heureux de la Belgique
Francorchamps avec l'Eau Rouge et les pouhons

The Little Car

August 31, 1914
A little before midnight I left Deauville
In Rouveyre's little car

Counting the chauffeur we were three

We said farewell to a whole era
Furious giants were rising over Europe
Eagles flew from their eyrie to wait for the sun
Voracious fish ascended from abysses
Nations hurled together so they might learn to know one another
The dead trembled fearfully in their dark dwellings

Dogs barked yonder where the frontiers were
I went off carrying within me all those armies that were fighting
I felt them rise within me and where they meandered the landscape
  spread out
With forests happy villages in Belgium

Région par où se font toujours les invasions
Artères ferroviaires où ceux qui s'en allaient mourir
Saluaient encore une fois la vie colorée
Océans profonds où remuaient les monstres
Dans les vieilles carcasses naufragées
Hauteurs inimaginables où l'homme combat
Plus haut que l'aigle ne plane
L'homme y combat contre l'homme
Et descend tout à coup comme une étoile filante

Je sentais en moi des êtres neufs pleins de dextérité
Bâtir et aussi agencer un univers nouveau
Un marchand d'une opulence inouïe et d'une taille prodigieuse
Disposait un étalage extraordinaire
Et des bergers gigantesques menaient
De grands troupeaux muets qui broutaient les paroles
Et contre lesquels aboyaient tous les chiens sur la route

Francorchamps where the Red Water is and the springs
Region where invasions always start
Railway arteries where those going off to die
Hailed once more brightly colored life
Deep oceans where monsters were moving
In old shipwrecked carcasses
Unimaginable heights where man fights
Higher than the eagle glides
Man fights there against man
And suddenly falls like a shooting star

I felt within me skillful new beings
Build and even arrange a new universe
A merchant with unheard-of wealth and whose size was prodigious
Arranged an extraordinary showcase
And giant shepherds led
Great silent flocks that nibbled words
They were barked at by all the dogs on the road

Je n'oublierai jamais ce voyage nocturne où nul de nous ne dit un mot

O départ sombre où mouraient nos 3 phares
O nuit tendre d'avant la guerre
O villages où se hâtaient
MARECHAUX-FERRANTS RAPPELES
ENTRE MINUIT ET UNE HEURE DU MATIN

vers LISIEUX la très bleue
ou bien
vers Versailles d'or

et 3 fois nous nous arrêtâmes pour changer un pneu qui avait éclaté

I shall never forget that nocturnal journey where none of us said a word

O
dark
de-
parture
where our 3
headlights died

O
tender
night
before
the war

O
vil
lages where h a s t e n e d t h e

FARRIERS SUMMONED

BETWEEN MIDNIGHT AND ONE IN THE MORNING

to
w a r d s
L I S I E U X
s o b l u
e

or else

v
e r s
a i l l e
s the gol
den

and 3 times we stopped to change a flat tire

Et quand après avoir passé l'après-midi
Par Fontainebleau
Nous arrivâmes à Paris
Au moment où l'on affichait la mobilisation
Nous comprîmes mon camarade et moi
Que la petite auto nous avait conduits dans une époque
Nouvelle
Et bien qu'étant déjà tous deux des hommes mûrs
Nous venions cependant de naître

And when after spending the afternoon
Near Fontainebleau
We arrived in Paris
Just as they were posting the draft
We realized my friend and I
That the little car had driven us into a New era
And although we were both already mature men
We had just been born

La Mandoline l'Œillet et le Bambou

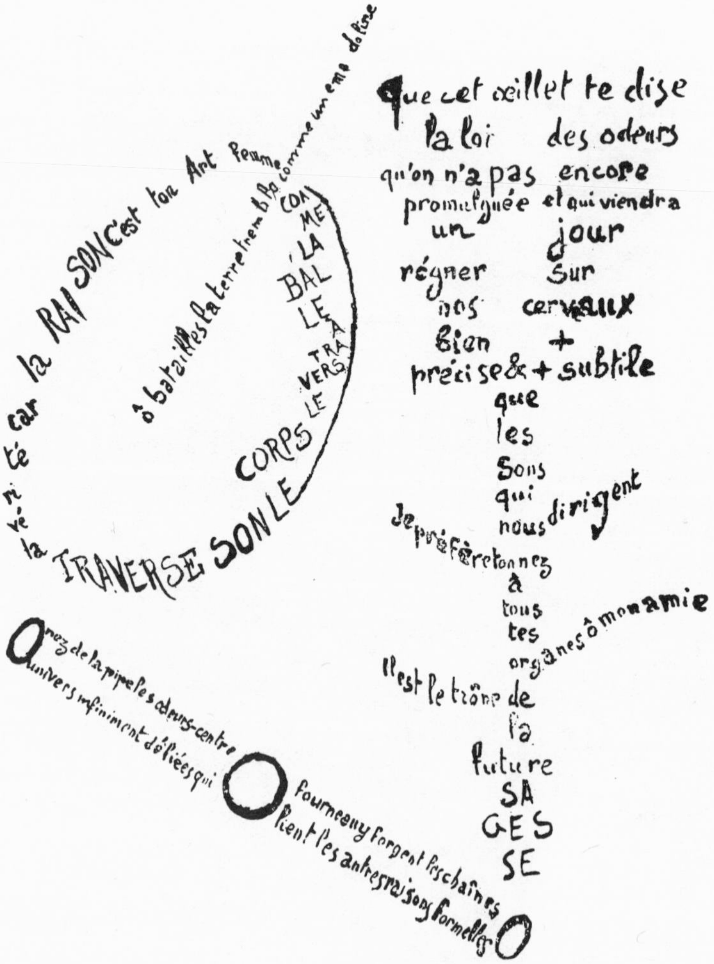

Mandolin Carnation and Bamboo

Let this carnation tell you
the law of odors
that has not yet been
promulgated and will
some day
rule over
our brains
far more +
precisely & + subtly
than
the
sounds
which
direct us
I prefer your nose
to
your
other organs oh my dear
It is the throne
of
the
future
WI
SDO
M

the truth for REASON is your Art woman
oh battles earth trembles like a mandolin
AS
THE
BUL
LET
PIERCES
THE
BODY
the PIERCES SOUND

O nose of the pipe the pivotal odors
O universe they're infinitely long and supple
O furnace are forging there the chains
linking the other formal reasons O

Fumées

Et tandis que la guerre
Ensanglante la terre
Je hausse les odeurs
Près des couleurs-saveurs

Et je fu
m
e
du
ta
bac
de
*Zo*NE

Des fleurs à ras du sol regardent par bouffées
Les boucles des odeurs par tes mains décoiffées
Mais je connais aussi les grottes parfumées
Où gravite l'azur unique des fumées

Smoke

And while war
Bloodies the earth
I hoist odors
Near the taste-colors

And I sm
ok
e
tob
ac
co from
the
ZoNE

Flowers barely touching the ground glimpse in whiffs
The ringlets of odors tousled by your hands
But I know too the perfumed grottoes
Where smoke's unrivaled azure spirals

Où plus doux que la nuit et plus pur que le jour
Tu t'étends comme un dieu fatigué par l'amour
Tu fascines les flammes
Elles rampent à tes pieds
Ces nonchalantes femmes
Tes feuilles de papier

Where softer than night and purer than day
You sprawl like a god wearied by love
                    You bewitch the flames
                    They crawl at your feet
                    Those nonchalant women
                    Your leaves of paper

A Nîmes

A Émile Léonard

Je me suis engagé sous le plus beau des cieux
Dans Nice la Marine au nom victorieux

Perdu parmi 900 conducteurs anonymes
Je suis un charretier du neuf charroi de Nîmes

L'Amour dit Reste ici Mais là-bas les obus
Épousent ardemment et sans cesse les buts

J'attends que le printemps commande que s'en aille
Vers le nord glorieux l'intrépide bleusaille

Les 3 servants assis dodelinent leurs fronts
Où brillent leurs yeux clairs comme mes éperons

Un bel après-midi de garde à l'écurie
J'entends sonner les trompettes d'artillerie

At Nimes

For Émile Léonard

I enlisted under a beautiful sky
In seaside Nice named for victory

Lost among 900 anonymous drivers
I'm a carter in Nimes's ninth transport division

Love said Linger But far off the bombshells
Ardently continue to espouse their goals

I am waiting till springtime orders forth
The intrepid greenhorns to the glorious north

The 3 gunners sit and cradle their brows
Their eyes glitter as bright as my spurs

A fine afternoon on guard at the stable
I hear the artillery trumpets blow

J'admire la gaieté de ce détachement
Qui va rejoindre au front notre beau régiment

Le territorial se mange une salade
A l'anchois en parlant de sa femme malade

4 pointeurs fixaient les bulles des niveaux
Qui remuaient ainsi que les yeux des chevaux

Le bon chanteur Girault nous chante après 9 heures
Un grand air d'opéra toi l'écoutant tu pleures

Je flatte de la main le petit canon gris
Gris comme l'eau de Seine et je songe à Paris

Mais ce pâle blessé m'a dit à la cantine
Des obus dans la nuit la splendeur argentine

Je mâche lentement ma portion de boeuf
Je me promène seul le soir de 5 à 9

Je selle mon cheval nous battons la campagne
Je te salue au loin belle rose ô tour Magne

I admire the gaiety of this detachment
We'll rejoin at the front our fine regiment

The territorial munching a salad leaf
And anchovies talks of his sick wife

4 checkers steadied the clinometer levels
That like horses' eyes bobbed and trembled

The good singer Girault sings opera airs
At night As you listen you shed tears

I stroke with my hand the little gray cannon
Gray like Seine water and I dream of Paris

But at the canteen a pale wounded soldier
Told of the bombshells' silver splendor

Slowly I eat my portion of beef and alone
I take an evening walk from 5 to 9

I saddle my horse we scour the meadows
I hail you from afar Great Tower oh lovely rose

La Colombe Poignardée et le Jet d'Eau

Douces figures poignardées Chères lèvres fleuries
MIA MAREYE
YETTE LORIE
ANNIE et toi MARIE
où êtes-
vous ô
jeunes filles
MAIS
pres d'un
jet d'eau qui
pleure et qui prie
cette colombe s'extasie

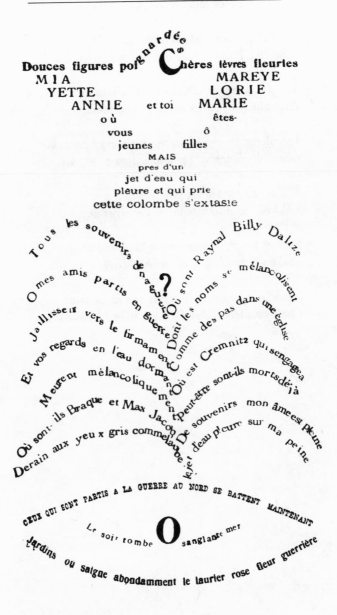

Tous les souvenirs de naguère
O mes amis partis en guerre
Jaillissent vers le firmament
Et vos regards en l'eau dormant
Meurent mélancoliquement
Où sont-ils Braque et Max Jacob
Derain aux yeux gris comme l'aube
Où sont Raynal Billy Dalize
Dont les noms se mélancolisent
Comme des pas dans une église
Où est Cremnitz qui sengagea
Peut-être sont-ils morts déjà
De souvenirs mon âme est pleine
Le jet d'eau pleure sur ma peine

CEUX QUI SONT PARTIS A LA GUERRE AU NORD SE BATTENT MAINTENANT
Le soir tombe O sanglante mer
Jardins ou saigne abondamment le laurier rose fleur guerrière

The Bleeding-Heart Dove and the Fountain

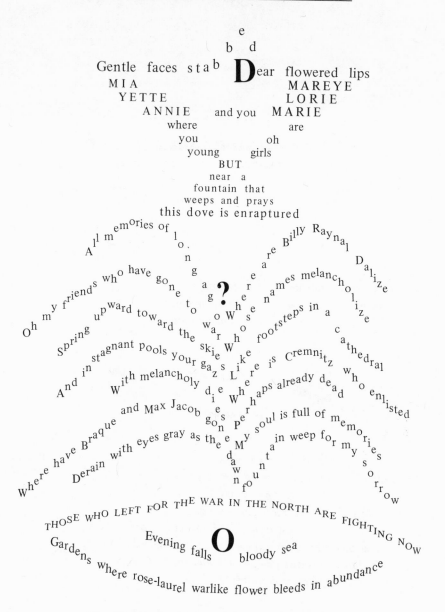

Gentle faces stabbed Dear flowered lips
MIA MAREYE
YETTE LORIE
ANNIE and you MARIE
where are
you oh
young girls
BUT
near a
fountain that
weeps and prays
this dove is enraptured

All memories of long ago
Oh my friends who have gone to war
Spring upward toward the skies
And in stagnant pools your gazes
With melancholy die
Where have Braque and Max Jacob gone
Derain with eyes gray as the dawn
Where are Billy Raynal Dalize
Whose names melancholize
Like footsteps in a cathedral
Where is Cremnitz who enlisted
Perhaps already dead
My soul is full of memories
The fountain weeps for my sorrow

THOSE WHO LEFT FOR THE WAR IN THE NORTH ARE FIGHTING NOW
Evening falls O bloody sea
Gardens where rose-laurel warlike flower bleeds in abundance

2e Canonnier Conducteur

Me voici libre et fier parmi mes compagnons
Le Réveil a sonné et dans le petit jour je salue
La fameuse Nancéenne que je n'ai pas connue

AS-
TU CON
NU LA QUI
PU TAIN A FOUTU LA VXXXXX A TOUTE L'ARTILLERIE
DE N
ANCY L'ARTILLERIE ne
s'est
pas
aperçu qu'elle avait
mal
au
. .

Les 3 servants bras dessus bras dessous se sont endormis sur l'avant-train
Et conducteur par mont par val sur le porteur
Au pas au trot ou au galop je conduis le canon
Le bras de l'officier est mon étoile polaire
Il pleut mon manteau est trempé et je m'essuie parfois la figure
Avec la serviette-torchon qui est dans la sacoche du sous-verge
Voici des fantassins aux pas pesants aux pieds boueux
La pluie les pique de ses aiguilles le sac les suit

2d Gunnery Driver

Here I am free and proud among my companions
Reveille has sounded and in the morning twilight I salute
The famous woman of Nancy whom I never knew

DID
YOU KN
OW THE
WH ORE WHO GAVE THE POX TO THE WHOLE ARTILLERY
OF N
ANCY THE ARTILLERY shared a sick
its had
blunt not knowing she

The 3 gunners arm in arm have fallen asleep on the front seat
And driving up hill and down dale on the carrier
At a walk at a trot at a gallop I haul the cannon
The officer's arm is my polar star
It's raining my coat is drenched and sometimes I dry my face
With the rag from the saddlebag on the off horse
Here come some foot soldiers with a heavy tramp with muddy feet
The rain stings them with needles their kit bag pursues them

SA
CRÉ NOM
DE DIEU
Q U E L L E
AL LU
RE NOM
DE DIEU
QUEL LE
L
A L U R E
N
U
I
T
C
E
P E N D
ANT
que la
D C
E E
S N
D

SOU V E
NIRS D E
P A R I S
AVANT LA
GUERRE ILS
SERONT BIEN
PLUS DOUX
APRÈS LA
VICTOIRE

S
A
LUT
M'
O N
D E
DONT
JE SUIS
LA LAN
GUE É
LOQUEN
TE QUESA
BOUCHE
O PARIS
TIRE ET TIRERA
TOU JOURS
AUX A L
LEM ANDS

GOOD

GOD AL

MIGH TY

W H A T A

SP EED

GOD AL

MIGH TY

WHAT A

E
P E D
S

N
I
G
H
the T is
I L L
N THE MEAN A I
TIME F N
G

MEM O R
IES O F
P A R I S
BEFORE THE
WAR THEY
WILL BE MUCH
SWEETER
A F T E R
VICTORY

H
A
I L
W O
R LD
WHOSE
ELOQUE
NT TON
GUE I A
M THAT ITS
M O U T H
OH PARIS
STICKS OUT AND
ALWAYS W I L L
A T THE
GER MANS

Fantassins
Marchantes mottes de terre
Vous êtes la puissance
Du sol qui vous a faits
Et c'est le sol qui va
Lorsque vous avancez
Un officier passe au galop
Comme un ange bleu dans la pluie grise
Un blessé chemine en fumant une pipe
Le lièvre détale et voici un ruisseau que j'aime
Et cette jeune femme nous salue charretiers
La Victoire se tient après nos jugulaires
Et calcule pour nos canons les mesures angulaires
Nos salves nos rafales sont ses cris de joie
Ses fleurs sont nos obus aux gerbes merveilleuses
Sa pensée se recueille aux tranchées glorieuses

J'ENTENDS CHA N
L
E TER l'oiseau
B E
EL OISEAU RAPAC

Foot soldiers
Lumps of earth marching
You are the strength
Of the soil that made you
And the soil moves
When you advance
An officer goes galloping by
Like a blue angel in the gray rain
A casualty plods on smoking his pipe
The hare scampers away and here is a stream I love
And that young woman is waving to us drivers
Victory clings to our chin straps
And calculates for our cannons the width of the angles
Our salvos and bursts of gunfire are her cries of joy
Her flowers are the bombshells and their marvelous sheaves
Her thought broods over the glorious trenches

I HEAR THE B
T
I
H
RD singing
E
EY
BEAUTIFUL BIRD OF PR

Veille

Mon cher André Rouveyre
Troudla la Champignon Tabatière
On ne sait quand on partira
Ni quand on reviendra

Au Mercure de France
Mars revient tout couleur d'espérance
J'ai envoyé mon papier
Sur papier quadrillé

J'entends les pas des grands chevaux d'artillerie allant au trot sur la grand-route où moi je veille
Un grand manteau gris de crayon comme le ciel m'enveloppe jusqu'à l'oreille

Quel
Ciel
Triste
Piste

Night Watch

My dear André Rouveyre
Tra-la the Mushroom Snuff and Tobacco
We don't know when we're leaving
Or when we're coming back

At the Mercure de France
March arrives pink with expectation
I've sent in my paper
On graph paper

I hear the tread of the big artillery horses trotting along the highroad where
  I keep watch
A huge mantle chalky gray like the sky covers me from head to toe
My
Sky
Sad
Road
Where

Où
Va le
Pâle
Sou-
rire
De la lune qui me regarde écrire

Sails the
Pale
Smile
Of the moon that watches me write

Ombre

Vous voilà de nouveau près de moi
Souvenirs de mes compagnons morts à la guerre
L'olive du temps
Souvenirs qui n'en faites plus qu'un
Comme cent fourrures ne font qu'un manteau
Comme ces milliers de blessures ne font qu'un article de journal
Apparence impalpable et sombre qui avez pris
La forme changeante de mon ombre
Un Indien à l'affût pendant l'éternité
Ombre vous rampez près de moi
Mais vous ne m'entendez plus
Vous ne connaîtrez plus les poèmes divins que je chante
Tandis que moi je vous entends je vous vois encore
Destinées
Ombre multiple que le soleil vous garde
Vous qui m'aimez assez pour ne jamais me quitter
Et qui dansez au soleil sans faire de poussière

Shadow

Here you are near me once more
Memories of my comrades dead in battle
Olive of time
Memories composing now a single memory
As a hundred furs make only one coat
As those thousands of wounds make only one newspaper article
Impalpable dark appearance you have assumed
The changing form of my shadow
An Indian hiding in wait throughout eternity
Shadow you creep near me
But you no longer hear me
You will no longer know the divine poems I sing
But I hear you I see you still
Destinies
Multiple shadow may the sun watch over you
You who love me so much you will never leave me
You who dance in the sun without stirring the dust

Ombre encre du soleil
Écriture de ma lumière
Caisson de regrets
Un dieu qui s'humilie

Shadow solar ink
Handwriting of my light
Caisson of regrets
A god humbling himself

C'est Lou Qu'on la Nommait

Il est des loups de toute sorte
Je connais le plus inhumain
Mon cœur que le diable l'emporte
Et qu'il le dépose à sa porte
N'est plus qu'un jouet dans sa main

Les loups jadis étaient fidèles
Comme sont les petits toutous
Et les soldats amants des belles
Galamment en souvenir d'elles
Ainsi que les loups étaient doux

Mais aujourd'hui les temps sont pires
Les loups sont tigres devenus
Et les Soldats et les Empires
Les Césars devenus Vampires
Sont aussi cruels que Vénus

They Called Her Lou

There are wolves of every kind
I know the most inhuman
May the devil take my heart
And leave it at her door
It's only a toy in her hand

Wolves long ago were loyal
As little puppies are
And soldiers who adore the fair
Gallantly in their memory
Like the wolves were gentle

But times today are worse
Now wolves have become tigers
And Soldiers and Empires
Caesars turned to Vampires
Have become cruel as Venus

J'en ai pris mon parti Rouveyre
Et monté sur mon grand cheval
Je vais bientôt partir en guerre
Sans pitié chaste et l'œil sévère
Comme ces guerriers qu'Épinal

Vendait Images populaires
Que Georgin gravait dans le bois
Où sont-ils ces beaux militaires
Soldats passés Où sont les guerres
Où sont les guerres d'autrefois

I've resigned myself to this Rouveyre
And mounted on my huge charger
Soon I shall be off to war
Pitiless chaste with gaze severe
Like those warriors Epinal

Used to sell Folk heroes Georgin would
Engrave on wood
Where are those handsome army men
And soldiers gone Where are the wars
Where are the wars of long ago

Case d'Armons
Flutchel

La 1re édition à 25 exemplaires de «Case d'Armons» a été polygraphiée sur papier quadrillé, à l'encre violette, au moyen de gélatine, à la batterie de tir (45e batterie, 38e Régiment d'artillerie de campagne) devant l'ennemi, et le tirage a été achevé le 17 juin 1915.

The 1st edition of 25 copies of "Case d'Armons" was polygraphed on graph paper, in violet ink, by means of gelatin, at the battery of heavy guns (45th battery, 38th Regiment of field artillery) facing the enemy, and the printing was completed June 17, 1915.

Loin du Pigeonnier

Et vous savez pourquoi

Pour quoi la chère cou leu vre se love de la mer jusqu'à l'espoir a tten dri ssant de l'Est

Malourène 75 Canteraine

Xexa
èdres
bar
belés
mais un secret
collines bleues
en sentinelle

dans la
Forêt
où
nous chantons

O gerbes
des
3o5
en déroute

Far From the Dovecote

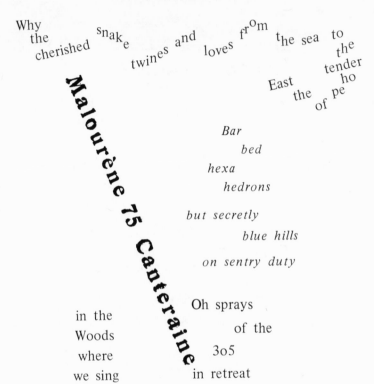

And you know why

Why the cherished snake twines and loves from the sea to the tender ho pe of the East

Malourène 75 Canteraine

Bar
bed
hexa
hedrons

but secretly
blue hills

on sentry duty

in the
Woods
where
we sing

Oh sprays
of the
3o5
in retreat

Reconnaissance

A Mademoiselle P...

Un seul bouleau crépusculaire
Pâlit au seuil de l'horizon
Où fuit la mesure angulaire
Du coeur à l'âme et la raison

Le galop bleu des souvenances
Traverse les lilas des yeux

Et les canons des indolences
Tirent mes songes vers
les
cieux

Reconnaissance

For Mademoiselle P...

A single twilit birch tree
Pales on the horizon's sill
Where flees the measured angle
Of heart to soul and reason

A blue gallop of memories
Traverses the lilac of eyes

And the cannons of indolence
Fire my dreams toward
                                        the
                                              skies

SP

Au maréchal des logis
René Berthier

Qu'est-ce qu'on y met
Dans la case d'armons
Espèce de poilu de mon cœur

Pan pan pan
Perruque perruque
Pan pan pan
Perruque à canon

Pour lutter contre les vapeurs
les lunettes pour protéger les yeux
au moyen d'un masque nocivité gaz
un tissu trempé mouchoir des nez

dans
la so
lution
de bi
carbo
nate de
sodium

Les masques seront sim
plement mouillés des lar
mes de rire de rire

SP

To the maréchal des logis
René Berthier

What do we put
In the flutchel
My heart's doughboy

Bang bang bang
Peruke peruke
Bang bang bang
Cannon peruke

To fight against fumes
glasses that shield the eyes
by means of a gas mask
a wet cloth or handkerchief

dipped in
a so
lution
of bi
carbo
nate of
soda

The masks will simply
be wet with tears
of laughter of laughter

Visée

A Madame René Berthier

Chevaux couleur cerise limite des Zélandes
Des mitrailleuses d'or coassent les légendes
Je t'aime liberté qui veilles dans les hypogées
Harpe aux cordes d'argent ô pluie ô ma musique
L'invisible ennemi plaie d'argent au soleil
Et l'avenir secret que la fusée élucide
Entends nager le Mot, poisson subtil
Les villes ' tour à tour deviennent des clefs
Le masque bleu comme met Dieu son ciel
Guerre paisible ascése solitude métaphysique
Enfant aux mains . coupées parmi les roses oriflammes

Aim

For Madame René Berthier

Cherry-color horses boundary of Zeeland
Machine guns of gold are croaking legends
I love you liberty keeping watch in the catacombs
Harp with silver strings oh rain oh my music
The invisible enemy a silver wound in the sunlight
And the secret future a flare illuminates
Listen to the Word swim subtle fish
The cities one by one become keys
My blue mask as God puts on his sky
War peaceful ascesis metaphysical solitude
Child with severed hands among roses oriflamme

1915

Soldats
de Faïence
et d'Esca-
rboucl
e
ô amour

1915

Soldiers
of porcelain
AND GAR-
NET
Ō LOVE

Carte Postale

à Jean Royère

CORRESPONDANCE

Nous sommes bien
mais l'auto-bazar qu'on
dit merveilleux
ne vient pas jusqu'ici.

LUL

on les
aura

faire suivre
transparente route
France

ESPONDANCE
LA RÉPUBLIQUE
NCHISÉ

Postcard

to Jean Royère

CORRESPONDENCE

We're doing fine
but the grocery car which they
say is marvelous
doesn't come this far

LUL

We'll get
them yet

please forward
transparent
route
France

Saillant

A André Level

Rapidité attentive à peine un peu d'incertitude
Mais un dragon à pied sans armes
Parmi le vent quand survient la

	S	torpille aérienne	
	A	Le balai de verdure	**Grain**
Salut	L	T'en souviens-tu	**de**
Le Rapace	U	Il est ici dans les pierres	**blé**
	T	Du beau royaume dévasté	

Mais la couleuvre me regarde dressée comme une épée

Vive comme un cheval pif
Un trou d'obus propre comme une salle de bain
Berger suivi de son troupeau mordoré
Mais où est un coeur et le svastica

Salient

For André Level

Wary haste just a little uncertainty
But a dragoon on foot weaponless
In the wind when arrives the

aerial torpedo

Hail
Bird of Prey

H
A
I
L

Broom of greenery
Do you remember
It is here among the stones
Of the beautiful ruined kingdom

Grain
of
wheat

But the snake poised like a sword watches me

As lively as a horse bang
A shell crater as clean as a bathroom
    Shepherd followed by his bronze flock
        But where is a heart and the swastika

Aÿ Ancien nom du renom
Le crapaud chantait les saphirs nocturnes

Lou VIVE
Lou Verzy LE
CAPISTON

Et le long du canal des filles s'en allaient

Aÿ Ancient name of renown
A toad sang nocturnal sapphires

Lou   LONG LIVE
                   THE
Lou Verzy   CAPTAIN

And along the canal girls were walking

Guerre

Rameau central de combat
Contact par l'écoute
On tire dans la direction «des bruits entendus»
Les jeunes de la classe 1915
Et ces fils de fer électrisés
Ne pleurez donc pas sur les horreurs de la guerre
Avant elle nous n'avions que la surface
De la terre et des mers
Après elle nous aurons les abîmes
Le sous-sol et l'espace aviatique
Maîtres du timon
Après après
Nous prendrons toutes les joies
Des vainqueurs qui se délassent
Femmes Jeux Usines Commerce
Industrie Agriculture Métal
Feu Cristal Vitesse
Voix Regard Tact à part

War

Central combat sector
    Contact by sound
We're firing toward "noises that were heard"
The young men of the class of 1915
And those electrified wires
Then don't weep for the horrors of war
Before the war we had only the surface
Of the earth and the seas
After it we'll have the depths
Subterranean and aerial space
Masters of the helm
After after
We'll assume all the joys
Of conquerors in repose
Women Games Factories Trade
Industry Agriculture Metal
Fire Crystal Speed
Voice Gaze Touch separately

Et ensemble dans le tact venu de loin
De plus loin encore
De l'Au-delà de cette terre

And together in the touch of things from far away
From farther still
From the Beyond of this earth

Mutation

Une femme qui pleurait
Eh! Oh! Ha!
Des soldats qui passaient
Eh! Oh! Ha!
Un éclusier qui pêchait
Eh! Oh! Ha!
Les tranchées qui blanchissaient
Eh! Oh! Ha!
Des obus qui pétaient
Eh! Oh! Ha!
Des allumettes qui ne prenaient pas
Et tout
A tant changé
En moi
Tout
Sauf mon Amour
Eh! Oh! Ha!

Mutation

A woman weeping
    Eh! Oh! Ah!
Soldiers passing
    Eh! Oh! ah!
A lockkeeper fishing
    Eh! Oh! Ah!
Trenches whitening
    Eh! Oh! Ah!
Shells popping
    Eh! Oh! Ah!
Matches that wouldn't strike
    And everything
        Has changed so much
            In me
    Everything
        Except my Love
            Eh! Oh! Ah!

Oracles

Je porte votre bague
Elle est très finement ciselée
Le sifflet me fait plus plaisir
Qu'un palais égyptien
Le sifflet des tranchées
Tu sais
Tout au plus si je n'arrête pas
Les métros et les taxis avec
O Guerre
Multiplication de l'amour

Petit
Sifflet
à 2 trous

Avec un fil
on prend
la mesure
du doigt

Oracles

  I wear your ring
It is delicately engraved
The whistle thrills me more
  Than an Egyptian palace
The whistle of the trenches
    You know
I could almost stop
Subways and taxis with it
    Oh War
    Multiplication of love

Little
  Whistle
with 2 holes

With a thread
you take
the finger's
measure

14 Juin 1915

On ne peut rien dire
Rien de ce qui se passe
Mais on change de Secteur
Ah! voyageur égaré
Pas de lettres
Mais l'espoir
Mais un journal
Le glaive antique de la Marseillaise de Rude
S'est changé en constellation
Il combat pour nous au ciel
Mais cela signifie surtout
Qu'il faut être de ce temps
Pas de glaive antique
Pas de Glaive
Mais l'Espoir

June 14, 1915

We can't say anything
Anything of what's happening
But we're changing Sector
Ah! lost traveler
No letters
But hope
And a newspaper
The ancient sword of Rude's Marseillaise
Has changed to a constellation
It's fighting for us in the sky
And that means mostly
That you've got to be modern
No ancient sword
No Sword
But Hope

De la Batterie de Tir

Au maréchal des logis F. Bodard

Nous sommes ton collier France
Venus des Atlantides ou bien des Négrities
Des Eldorados ou bien des Cimméries
Rivière d'hommes forts et d'obus dont l'orient chatoie
Diamants qui éclosent la nuit
O Roses ô France
Nous nous pâmons de volupté
A ton cou penché vers l'Est
Nous sommes l'Arc-en-terre
Signe plus pur que l'Arc-en-Ciel
Signe de nos origines profondes
Étincelles
O nous les très belles couleurs

Battery of Heavy Guns

For the maréchal des logis F. Bodard

We are your necklace France
Arrived from Atlantis or the Negros Islands
From Eldorados or from Cimmerias
Rivière of strong men and bombshells whose orient glimmers
Diamonds blossoming at night
            Oh Roses oh France
We swoon with desire
At your neck leaning toward the East
We are earth's rainbow
Purer sign than heaven's rainbow
  Sign of our profound origins
            Sparks
Oh we who are the most beautiful colors

Échelon

Grenouilles et rainettes
Crapauds et crapoussins
Ascèse sous les peupliers et les frênes
La reine des près va fleurir
Une petite hutte dans la forêt
Là-bas plus blanche est la blessure

Le Ciel

Coquelicots
Flacon au col d'or
On a pendu la mort
A la lisière du bois
On a pendu la mort
Et ses beaux seins dorés
Se montrent tour à tour

On tire contre avions
Verdun

L'orvet
Le sac à malice
La trousse à boutons

Echelon

Frogs and tree frogs
Toads and toadies
Ascesis under poplars and ash trees
The queen of the meadows will flower
A small hut in the forest
Over there the wound grows paler

Sky

They are firing at planes
Verdun

Red poppies
Bottle with a gold neck
They have hung death
At the edge of the woods
They have hung death
And her beautiful gilded breasts
Glint in turn

The slow worm
Bag of tricks
Ditty bag

O rose toujours vive
O France
Embaume les espoirs d'une armée qui halète

Le Loriot chante

N'est-ce pas rigolo

Enfin une plume d'épervier

Oh rose forever alive
    Oh France
Perfume the hopes of a breathless army

The oriole sings

        Isn't it a riot

At last a hawk's feather

Vers le Sud

Zénith
Tous ces regrets
Ces jardins sans limite
Où le crapaud module un tendre cri d'azur
La biche du silence éperdu passe vite
Un rossignol meurtri par l'amour chante sur
Le rosier de ton corps dont j'ai cueilli les roses
Nos cœurs pendent ensemble au même grenadier
Et les fleurs de grenade en nos regards écloses
En tombant tour à tour ont jonché le sentier

Southward

Zenith
All those regrets
Those endless gardens
Where the toad modulates a tender cry of azure
The doe of bewildered silence moves quickly past
A nightingale wounded by love sings upon
The roses of your body whose roses I have gathered
Our hearts hang together from the same pomegranate tree
And the pomegranate flowers hatched in our gaze
Falling one by one have strewn the pathway

Les Soupirs du Servant de Dakar

C'est dans la cagnat en rondins voilés d'osier
Auprès des canons gris tournés vers le nord
Que je songe au village africain
Où l'on dansait où l'on chantait où l'on faisait l'amour
Et de longs discours
Nobles et joyeux

Je revois mon père qui se battit
Contre les Achantis
Au service des Anglais
Je revois ma soeur au rire en folie
Aux seins durs comme des obus
Et je revois
Ma mère la sorcière qui seule du village
Méprisait le sel
Piler le millet dans un mortier
Je me souviens du si délicat si inquiétant
Fétiche dans l'arbre

The Sighs of the Gunner from Dakar

In the log dugout hidden by osiers
Near gray cannons turned toward the north
I dream of the African village
Where we danced where we sang and made love
And made long speeches
Noble and joyful

I see again my father who fought
The Ashantis
In the service of the English
I see again my sister with the crazy laugh
With breasts hard as bombshells
And I see again
My mother the witch who alone in the village
Scorned salt
Crushing millet in a mortar
I remember the fetish so delicate so disturbing
In the tree

Et du double fétiche de la fécondité
Plus tard une tête coupée
Au bord d'un marécage
O pâleur de mon ennemi
C'était une tête d'argent
Et dans le marais
C'était la lune qui luisait
C'était donc une tête d'argent
Là-haut c'était la lune qui dansait
C'était donc une tête d'argent
Et moi dans l'antre j'étais invisible
C'était donc une tête de nègre dans la nuit profonde
Similitudes Pâleurs
Et ma soeur
Suivit plus tard un tirailleur
Mort à Arras

Si je voulais savoir mon âge
Il faudrait le demander à l'évêque
Si doux si doux avec ma mère
De beurre de beurre avec ma soeur
C'était dans une petite cabane
Moins sauvage que notre cagnat de canonniers-servants
J'ai connu l'affût au bord des marécages
Où la girafe boit les jambes écartées
J'ai connu l'horreur de l'ennemi qui dévaste
Le Village
Viole les femmes
Emmène les filles
Et les garçons dont la croupe dure sursaute
J'ai porté l'administrateur des semaines
De village en village
En chantonnant
Et je fus domestique à Paris
Je ne sais pas mon âge
Mais au recrutement
On m'a donné vingt ans
Je suis soldat français on m'a blanchi du coup
Secteur 59 je ne peux pas dire où

And the double fetish of fecundity
Later a severed head
Beside a swamp
Oh paleness of my enemy
It was a silver head
And in the marsh
The moon was shining
It was it was a silver head
The moon above was dancing
It was it was a silver head
And I in the cave was invisible
It was it was a Negro head in the dead of night
Resemblances Pallors
And later my sister
Went off with a rifleman
Who was killed at Arras

If I wanted to know my age
I'd have to ask the bishop
So gentle so gentle to my mother
So like butter like butter with my sister
It was in a little hut
Neater than our gunners' dugout
I've known the hiding place at the swamp's edge
Where the giraffe drinks with legs spread apart
I've known the horror of the enemy that plunder
The Village
Rape the women
Lead away the girls
And the boys whose hard rumps quiver
I've guided the administrator for weeks
From village to village
Singing
And I was a servant in Paris
I don't know my age
But at the recruiting
They wrote down twenty years old
I'm a French soldier and so they turned me white
Sector 59 I can't say where

Pourquoi donc être blanc est-ce mieux qu'être noir
Pourquoi ne pas danser et discourir
Manger et puis dormir
Et nous tirons sur les ravitaillements boches
Ou sur les fils de fer devant les bobosses
Sous la tempête métallique
Je me souviens d'un lac affreux
Et de couples enchaînés par un atroce amour
Une nuit folle
Une nuit de sorcellerie
Comme cette nuit-ci
Où tant d'affreux regards
Éclatent dans le ciel splendide

But why is it better to be white than black
Why not dance and make speeches
Eat and then sleep
And we shoot at the Boche supplies
Or at the iron wires in front of the doughboys
Under the metallic storm
I remember a hideous lake
And couples chained by an atrocious love
A crazy night
A night of sorcery
Like tonight
Where so many horrible eyes
Explode in the brilliant sky

Toujours

A Madame Faure-Favier

Toujours
Nous irons plus loin sans avancer jamais

Et de planète en planète
De nébuleuse en nébuleuse
Le don Juan des mille et trois comètes
Même sans bouger de la terre
Cherche les forces neuves
Et prend au sérieux les fantômes

Et tant d'univers s'oublient
Quels sont les grands oublieurs
Qui donc saura nous faire oublier telle ou telle partie du monde
Où est le Christophe Colomb à qui l'on devra l'oubli d'un continent

Perdre
Mais perdre vraiment

Always

For Madame Faure-Favier

Always
We'll go further without ever advancing

And from planet to planet
From nebula to nebula
The Don Juan of a thousand and three comets
Even without leaving the earth
Looks for new forces
And take ghosts seriously

And so many universes are forgotten
Then who are the great forgetters
And who will be able to make us forget this or that part of the world
Who is the Christopher Columbus to whom we will owe the forgetting of a continent

To lose

Pour laisser place à la trouvaille
Perdre
La vie pour trouver la Victoire

But to lose truly
To make way for the windfall
                    To lose
Life in order to Triumph

Fête

A André Rouveyre

Feu d'artifice en acier
Qu'il est charmant cet éclairage
  Artifice d'artificier
Mêler quelque grâce au courage

Deux fusants
Rose éclatement
Comme deux seins que l'on dégrafe
Tendent leurs bouts insolemment
IL SUT AIMER
        quelle épitaphe

Un poète dans la forêt
Regarde avec indifférence
  Son revolver au cran d'arrêt
Des roses mourir d'espérance

Festival

For André Rouveyre

Fireworks in steel
How delightful is this lighting
  An artificer's artifice
Mingling grace with valor

Two flares
Rose explosion
Like two breasts unbound
Raising their nipples insolently
HE KNEW HOW TO LOVE
          what an epitaph

A poet in the forest
Gazes languidly
  His revolver on its safety catch
At roses dying of hope

Il songe aux roses de Saadi
Et soudain sa tête se penche
Car une rose lui redit
La molle courbe d'une hanche

L'air est plein d'un terrible alcool
Filtré des étoiles mi-closes
Les obus caressent le mol
Parfum nocturne où tu reposes
Mortification des roses

He dreams of roses of Saadi
And suddenly his head bows
For a rose reminds him of
The soft curve of a hip

The air is full of a frightful alcohol
Filtered from half-closed stars
Bombshells caress the soft
Nocturnal perfume where you repose
    Mortification of roses

Madeleine

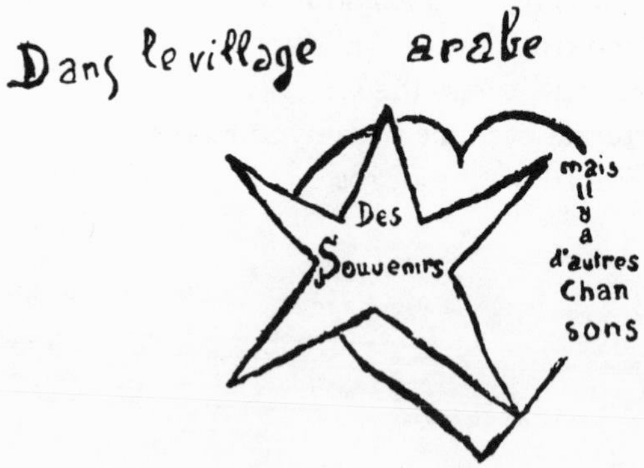
Dans le village arabe
Des
Souvenirs
mais
il
y
a
d'autres
Chan
sons

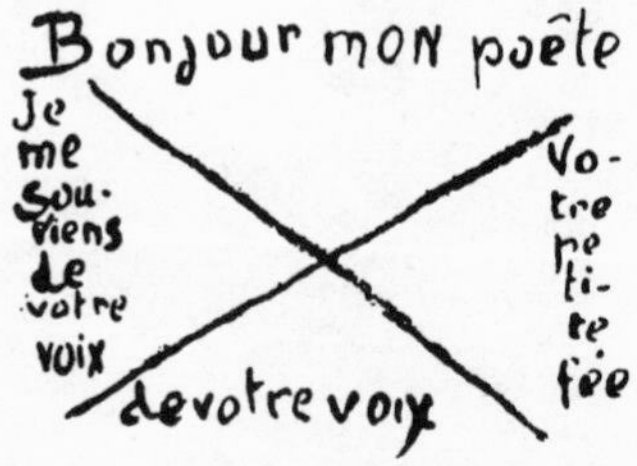
Bonjour mon poète
Je
me
sou-
viens
de
votre
voix
Vo-
tre
pe
ti-
te
fée
de votre voix

Photographie
tant attendue

Far
tiz
rose

Madeleine

In the Arab village

Hello my poet

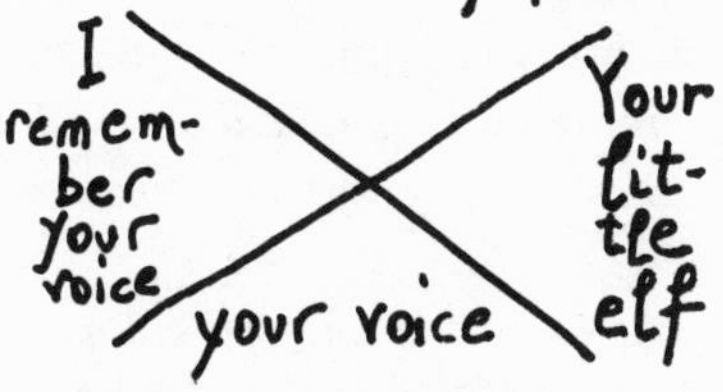

Long awaited snapshot

Les Saisons

C'était un temps béni nous étions sur les plages
Va-t'en de bon matin pieds nus et sans chapeau
Et vite comme va la langue d'un crapaud
L'amour blessait au coeur les fous comme les sages

As-tu connu Guy au galop
Du temps qu'il était militaire
As-tu connu Guy au galop
Du temps qu'il était artiflot
A la guerre

C'était un temps béni Le temps du vaguemestre
On est bien plus serré que dans les autobus
Et des astres passaient que singeaient les obus
Quand dans la nuit survint la batterie équestre

As-tu connu Guy au galop
Du temps qu'il était militaire

The Seasons

Those were happy days we strolled along the beach
Go early in the morning hatless and barefoot
And as swiftly as a toad's tongue darts
Love wounded crazy hearts as well as wise

Did you know Galloping Guy
In the days when he was a soldier
Did you know Galloping Guy
When he was an artilleryman
During the war

Those were happy days Days when letters came
We're far more crowded than in a bus
And stars passed by and the bombshells mocked them
When at night the cavalry guns drove up

Did you know Galloping Guy
In the days when he was a soldier

As-tu connu Guy au galop
Du temps qu'il était artiflot
A la guerre

C'était un temps béni Jours vagues et nuits vagues
Les marmites donnaient aux rondins des cagnats
Quelque aluminium où tu t'ingénias
A limer jusqu'au soir d'invraisemblables bagues

As-tu connu Guy au galop
Du temps qu'il était militaire
As-tu connu Guy au galop
Du temps qu'il était artiflot
A la guerre

C'était un temps béni La guerre continue
Les Servants ont limé la bague au long des mois
Le Conducteur écoute abrité dans les bois
La chanson que répète une étoile inconnue

As-tu connu Guy au galop
Du temps qu'il était militaire
As-tu connu Guy au galop
Du temps qu'il était artiflot
A la guerre

Did you know Galloping Guy
When he was an artilleryman
During the war

Those were happy days Vague days vague nights
The big shells furnished the log dugouts
With aluminum fragments so you spent your time
Polishing till evening incredible rings

Did you know Galloping Guy
In the days when he was a soldier
Did you know Galloping Guy
When he was an artilleryman
During the war

Those were happy days The war continues
The Gunners have polished their rings now for months
Sheltered in the woods the Driver listens
To the song rehearsed by an unknown star

Did you know Galloping Guy
In the days when he was a soldier
Did you know Galloping Guy
When he was an artilleryman
During the war

Venu de Dieuze

Claire-Ville-Neuve-En-Cristal-Eternel
fortes'allontanando
Funambule des lianes du printemps Tu assassines les arbres qui sont ver. g. v. c. La poule d'eau caquète et plonge à ton approche
Cantato
Ah! mon Dieu m'quiot' fille
L'homme qu'j'ai
C'est enn' mouqu' dans d' l'huile
Tout à fouait
Couple des marais Les turquoises
Hennissements partout
Amour sacré amour de la Patrie
Le général
Il était Antisthène et c'était Fabius

On Arrival from Dieuze

Shining-New-City-in-Eternal-Crystal

rope-dancer shell
in the vines
of springtime
you kill
the trees that are
your G.V.C. The moor
hen clucks and dives
at your approach

Cantato { Oh God! my little girl
That man of mine
What a fly in the ointment
Absolutely }

Swamp butterflies sky-blue mushrooms
Whinnies everywhere
Sacred love patriotic love
The general
He was Antisthenes and Fabius as well

La Nuit d'Avril 1915

A L. de C.-C.

Le ciel est étoilé par les obus des Boches
La forêt merveilleuse où je vis donne un bal
La mitrailleuse joue un air à triples-croches
Mais avez-vous le mot
Eh! oui le mot fatal
Aux créneaux Aux créneaux Laissez là les pioches

Comme un astre éperdu qui cherche ses saisons
Cœur obus éclaté tu sifflais ta romance
Et tes mille soleils ont vidé les caissons
Que les dieux de mes yeux remplissent en silence

Nous vous aimons ô vie et nous vous agaçons

Les obus miaulaient un amour à mourir
Un amour qui se meurt est plus doux que les autres
Ton souffle nage au fleuve où le sang va tarir
Les obus miaulaient

April Night 1915

For L. de C.-C.

The sky is starred by the Boche's shells
The marvelous forest where I live is giving a ball
The machine gun plays a tune in three-fourths time
But have you the word
                    Eh! yes the fatal word
To the loopholes To the loopholes Leave the picks there

Like a lost star searching for its seasons
Heart exploded shell you whistled your love song
And your thousand suns have emptied the caissons
That the gods of my eyes fill silently

We love you oh life and we get on your nerves

The shells whined a killing love
A dying love is sweeter than others
Your breath swims the river where blood will run dry
Shells were whining

Entends chanter les nôtres
Pourpre amour salué par ceux qui vont périr

Le printemps tout mouillé la veilleuse l'attaque

Il pleut mon âme il pleut mais il pleut des yeux morts

Ulysse que de jours pour rentrer dans Ithaque

Couche-toi sur la paille et songe un beau remords
Qui pur effet de l'art soit aphrodisiaque

Mais
orgues
aux fétus de la paille où tu dors
L'hymne de l'avenir est paradisiaque

Hear our shells sing
Their deep-purple love hailed by our men going to die

The wet springtime the night light the attack

It's raining my soul it's raining but it's raining dead eyes

Ulysses how many days to get back to Ithaca

Lie down in the straw and dream a fine remorse
Which as a pure effect of art is aphrodisiac

But
organ music
in the strawstack where you slumber
The hymn of the future is paradisiac

Lueurs des Tirs
Flash of Gunfire

La Grâce Exilée

Va-t'en va-t'en mon arc-en-ciel
Allez-vous-en couleurs charmantes
Cet exil t'est essentiel
Infante aux écharpes changeantes

Et l'arc-en-ciel est exilé
Puisqu'on exile qui l'irise
Mais un drapeau s'est envolé
Prendre ta place au vent de bise

Exiled Grace

Go my rainbow go
Go charming colors
You need this exile
Infanta in iridescent shawls

And the rainbow is exiled
For the exiler is the colorist
But a flag has flown away
To take your place in the north wind

La Boucle Retrouvée

Il retrouve dans sa mémoire
La boucle de cheveux châtains
T'en souvient-il à n'y point croire
De nos deux étranges destins

Du boulevard de la Chapelle
Du joli Montmartre et d'Auteuil
Je me souviens murmure-t-elle
Du jour où j'ai franchi ton seuil

Il y tomba comme un automne
La boucle de mon souvenir
Et notre destin qui t'étonne
Se joint au jour qui va finir

The Lock of Hair Found

He finds once more in his memory
The lock of chestnut-colored hair
Do you remember beyond belief
Our two strange destinies

The boulevard of La Chapelle
Charming Montmartre and Auteuil
These I remember she murmured and
The day I crossed your threshold

Then dropped like an autumn there
The lock of hair I remember
And our fate that stuns you
Joins with the day about to end

Refus de la Colombe

Mensonge de l'Annonciade
La Noël fut la Passion
Et qu'elle était charmante et sade
Cette renonciation

Si la colombe poignardée
Saigne encore de ses refus
J'en plume les ailes l'idée
Et le poème que tu fus

Refusal of the Dove

Lie of the Annuncione
Christmas became the Passion
How charming and agreeable
Was that renunciation

If the bleeding-heart dove
Still bleeds from its refusals
I pluck its feathers the idea
And the poem you once were

Les Feux du Bivouac

Les feux mouvants du bivouac
Éclairent des formes de rêve
Et le songe dans l'entrelacs
Des branches lentement s'élève

Voici les dédains du regret
Tout écorché comme une fraise
Le souvenir et le secret
Dont il ne reste que la braise

Campfires

The moving bivouac fires
Illuminate forms of dream
And the dream through interlacing
Branches slowly rises

Here are disdains born of regret
Raw as a strawberry
Here are memory and the secret
That have turned to embers

Les Grenadines Repentantes

En est-il donc deux dans Grenade
Qui pleurent sur ton seul péché
Ici l'on jette la grenade
Qui se change en un œuf coché

Puisqu'il en naît des coqs Infante
Entends-les chanter leurs dédains
Et que la grenade est touchante
Dans nos effroyables jardins

The Repentant Grenadines

Then are there two in Granada
Who weep for your single sin
Here they toss grenades
That change to marked eggs

Since cocks rise from them Infanta
Hear them sing out their disdain
How touching is the grenadine
In our frightful gardens

Tourbillon de Mouches

Un cavalier va dans la plaine
La jeune fille pense à lui
Et cette flotte à Mytilène
Le fil de fer est là qui luit

Comme ils cueillaient la rose ardente
Leurs yeux tout à coup ont fleuri
Mais quel soleil la bouche errante
A qui la bouche avait souri

Swirl of Flies

A cavalier rides over the plain
The young girl thinks of him
And that flotilla at Mytilene
Where the iron wire is gleaming

As they gathered the ardent rose
Their eyes did flower suddenly
But what a sun is the wandering mouth
At whom another mouth has smiled

L'Adieu du Cavalier

Ah Dieu! que la guerre est jolie
Avec ses chants ses longs loisirs
Cette bague je l'ai polie
Le vent se mêle à vos soupirs

Adieu! voici le boute-selle
Il disparut dans un tournant
Et mourut là-bas tandis qu'elle
Riait au destin surprenant

The Cavalier's Farewell

Oh God! what a lovely war
With its hymns its long leisure hours
I have polished and polished this ring
The wind with your sighs is mingling

Farewell! the trumpet call is sounding
He disappeared down the winding road
And died far off while she
Laughed at fate's surprises

Le Palais du Tonnerre

Par l'issue ouverte sur le boyau dans la craie
En regardant la paroi adverse qui semble en nougat
On voit à gauche et à droite fuir l'humide couloir désert
Où meurt étendue une pelle à la face effrayante à deux yeux réglementaires qui servent à l'attacher sous les caissons
Un rat y recule en hâte tandis que j'avance en hâte
Et le boyau s'en va couronné de craie semé de branches
Comme un fantôme creux qui met du vide où il passe blanchâtre
Et là-haut le toit est bleu et couvre bien le regard fermé par quelques lignes droites
Mais en deçà de l'issue c'est le palais bien nouveau et qui paraît ancien
Le plafond est fait de traverses de chemin de fer
Entre lesquelles il y a des morceaux de craie et des touffes d'aiguilles de sapin
Et de temps en temps des débris de craie tombent comme des morceaux de vieillesse
A côté de l'issue que ferme un tissu lâche d'une espèce qui sert généralement aux emballages

Thunder's Palace

By the door opening onto the chalky trench
Where the wall across from you looks like nougat
You can see to the left and right the empty wet tunnel fleeing
A shovel dies flung aside with its terrifying face and its two regulation eyes
that hook it under the caissons
A rat hastily withdraws as I hurry forward
And the trench goes on its way crowned with chalk sown with branches
Like a hollow phantom spreading emptiness where it passes palely
And overhead the roof is blue and caps the gaze blocked by a few straight
lines
But this side of the door is the brand-new palace looking old
Its ceiling is made of railroad ties
Between them are lumps of chalk and pine-needle tufts
And from time to time chalk fragments fall like lumps of old age
Beside the door covered by a loose cloth of a sort usually used in packing
We have a hole for a chimney and what burns there is a flame like a human
soul

Il y a un trou qui tient lieu d'âtre et ce qui y brûle est un feu semblable à l'âme
Tant il tourbillonne et tant il est inséparable de ce qu'il dévore et fugitif
Les fils de fer se tendent partout servant de sommier supportant des planches
Ils forment aussi des crochets et l'on y suspend mille choses
Comme on fait à la mémoire
Des musettes bleues des casques bleus des cravates bleues des vareuses bleues
Morceaux du ciel tissus des souvenirs les plus purs
Et il flotte parfois en l'air de vagues nuages de craie

Sur la planche brillent des fusées détonateurs joyaux dorés à tête émaillée
Noirs blancs rouges
Funambules qui attendent leur tour de passer sur les trajectoires
Et font un ornement mince et élégant à cette demeure souterraine
Ornée de six lits placés en fer à cheval
Six lits couverts de riches manteaux bleus

Sur le palais il y a un haut tumulus de craie
Et des plaques de tôle ondulée
Fleuve figé de ce domaine idéal
Mais privé d'eau car ici il ne roule que le feu jailli de la mélinite
Le parc aux fleurs de fulminate jaillit des trous penchés
Tas de cloches aux doux sons des douilles rutilantes
Sapins élégants et petits comme en un paysage japonais
Le palais s'éclaire parfois d'une bougie à la flamme aussi petite qu'une souris
O palais minuscule comme si on te regardait par le gros bout d'une lunette
Petit palais où tout s'assourdit
Petit palais où tout est neuf rien rien d'ancien
Et où tout est précieux où tout le monde est vêtu comme un roi
Une selle est dans un coin à cheval sur une caisse
Un journal du jour traîne par terre
Et cependant tout paraît vieux dans cette neuve demeure
Si bien qu'on comprend que l'amour de l'antique
Le goût de l'anticaille
Soit venu aux hommes dès le temps des cavernes
Tout y était si précieux et si neuf
Tout y est si précieux et si neuf

It swirls and is so inseparable from what it devours and so fugitive
Iron wires stretch everywhere they make a net that supports the planks
They also form hooks and you can hang a thousand objects on them
As one hangs things on memory
Blue haversacks blue helmets blue ties blue jackets
Lumps of sky a patchwork of the purest memories
And at times floating in the air are vague clouds of chalk

On the plank floor gleam flares detonators gilt jewels with enameled heads
Black white red
Acrobats waiting for their turn to fly over the trajectories
They make elegant thin ornaments for this underground residence
Adorned with six beds arranged like a horseshoe
Six beds covered with rich blue coats

Above the palace there's a tall barrow of chalk
And sheets of corrugated iron
Congealed river of an ideal domain
But without water because here there flows only fire struck from melinite
The park with flowers of fulminate gushes from sloping cannon holes
Pile of bells whose faint sounds are the ruddy shells
Elegant small pine trees as in a Japanese landscape
The palace is lit up at times by a candle with a mouse-size flame
Oh tiny palace as if someone were watching you from the wrong end of a
telescope
Small palace where everything becomes muffled
Small palace where everything is new and nothing nothing is old
And where everything is precious where everyone is dressed like a king
A saddle straddles a crate in the corner
A daily paper lies scattered over the floor
And still everything seems old in this new house
So you can understand men had a love for antiquity
A taste for antiquating
Even when they lived in caves
Everything there was so precious and new
Everything here is so precious and new
That something older or something already used seems
More precious still
Than what is at hand

Qu'une chose plus ancienne ou qui a déjà servi y apparaît
Plus précieuse
Que ce qu'on a sous la main
Dans ce palais souterrain creusé dans la craie si blanche et si neuve
Et deux marches neuves
Elles n'ont pas deux semaines
Sont si vieilles et si usées dans ce palais qui semble antique sans imiter l'antique
Qu'on voit que ce qu'il y a de plus simple de plus neuf est ce qui est
Le plus près de ce que l'on appelle la beauté antique
Et ce qui est surchargé d'ornements
A besoin de vieillir pour avoir la beauté qu'on appelle antique
Et qui est la noblesse la force l'ardeur l'âme l'usure
De ce qui est neuf et qui sert
Surtout si cela est simple simple
Aussi simple que le petit palais du tonnerre

In this underground palace hollowed out from such fresh white chalk
And two new steps
        They aren't two weeks old
Are so old and so beat up in this palace that seems ancient without imitating
  antiquity
You can see that what's simplest and newest is
Nearest to what's called antique beauty
And what's overladen with ornaments
Needs to age before it can acquire the beauty labeled antique
Which is nobility strength ardor soul and the attrition
Of what is new and which is useful
Above all if it is simple simple
As simple as thunder's small palace

Photographie

Ton sourire m'attire comme
Pourrait m'attirer une fleur
Photographie tu es le champignon brun
De la forêt
Qu'est sa beauté
Les blancs y sont
Un clair de lune
Dans un jardin pacifique
Plein d'eaux vives et de jardiniers endiablés
Photographie tu es la fumée de l'ardeur
Qu'est sa beauté
Et il y a en toi
Photographie
Des tons alanguis
On y entend
Une mélopée
Photographie tu es l'ombre
Du Soleil
Qu'est sa beauté

Snapshot

Your smile charms me the way
A flower charms me
Snapshot you are the brown mushroom
Of the forest
That is her beauty
There shades of white
Are moonlight
In a quiet garden
Full of running water and reckless gardeners
Snapshot you are the smoke of that ardor
That is her beauty
And in you
Snapshot
There are languishing colors
Among them I can hear
A single voice singing sadly
Snapshot you are the shadow
Of the Sun
That is her beauty

L'Inscription Anglaise

C'est quelque chose de si ténu de si lointain
Que d'y penser on arrive à le trop matérialiser
Forme limitée par la mer bleue
Par la rumeur d'un train en marche
Par l'odeur des eucalyptus des mimosas
Et des pins maritimes

Mais le contact et la saveur

Et cette petite voyageuse alerte inclina brusquement la tête sur le quai de la gare à Marseille
Et s'en alla
Sans savoir
Que son souvenir planerait
Sur un petit bois de la Champagne où un soldat s'efforce
Devant le feu d'un bivouac d'évoquer cette apparition
A travers la fumée d'écorce de bouleau
Qui sent l'encens minéen
Tandis que les volutes bleuâtres qui montent

The English Inscription

It's something so intangible so faraway
That just dwelling on it can bring it too close to earth
Shape limited by the blue sea
The sound of a train moving
The smell of eucalyptus of mimosas
And seaside pines

But touch and taste

And the brisk little traveler nodded her head brusquely on the platform of the railway station at Marseilles
And departed
Not knowing
That her memory would hover
Over a small wood in Champagne where a soldier
Beside a campfire tries to evoke that apparition
Through the smoke of birch bark
Smelling like Minyan incense
While bluish circles rising

D'un cigare écrivent le plus tendre des noms
Mais les nœuds de couleuvres en se dénouant
Écrivent aussi le nom émouvant
Dont chaque lettre se love en belle anglaise

Et le soldat n'ose point achever
Le jeu de mots bilingue que ne manque point de susciter
Cette calligraphie sylvestre et vernale

From a cigar write the fondest of names
But the knots of snakes uncoiling
Also write the thrilling name
Whose every letter twines in fine English

And the soldier doesn't dare finish
The bilingual pun that is evoked
By this springtime handwriting in the woods

Dans l'Abri-Caverne

Je me jette vers toi et il me semble aussi que tu te jettes vers moi
Une force part de nous qui est un feu solide qui nous soude
Et puis il y a aussi une contradiction qui fait que nous ne pouvons nous apercevoir
En face de moi la paroi de craie s'effrite
Il y a des cassures
De longues traces d'outils traces lisses et qui semblent être faites dans de la stéarine
Des coins de cassures sont arrachés par le passage des types de ma pièce
Moi j'ai ce soir une âme qui s'est creusée qui est vide
On dirait qu'on y tombe sans cesse et sans trouver de fond
Et qu'il n'y a rien pour se raccrocher
Ce qui y tombe et qui y vit c'est une sorte d'êtres laids qui me font mal et qui viennent de je ne sais où
Oui je crois qu'ils viennent de la vie d'une sorte de vie qui est dans l'avenir dans l'avenir brut qu'on n'a pu encore cultiver ou élever ou humaniser
Dans ce grand vide de mon âme il manque un soleil il manque ce qui éclaire
C'est aujourd'hui c'est ce soir et non toujours

In the Dugout

I project myself toward you and I think that you too project yourself toward me
A force issues from us it's a solid fire welding us together
And yet paradoxically we can't see each other
Facing me the chalk wall crumbles
Filled with fractures
Long traces of tools sleek traces that appear to be made of stearin
Edges of fractures are torn by the fellows in my room passing by
As for me tonight I have a soul that's hollow and empty
You could say in my soul someone keeps falling and finding no bottom
And there's nothing to grab onto
What keeps falling and living inside me is a crowd of ugly beings that hurt me I don't know where they come from
But I think they come from life from a kind of life still in the future a raw future not yet refined or exalted or humanized
In the huge emptiness of my soul there isn't any soul there's nothing that gives light
It's today it's tonight but it's not for always

Heureusement que ce n'est que ce soir
Les autres jours je me rattache à toi
Les autres jours je me console de la solitude et de toutes les horreurs
En imaginant ta beauté
Pour l'élever au-dessus de l'univers extasié
Puis je pense que je l'imagine en vain
Je ne la connais par aucun sens
Ni même par les mots
Et mon goût de la beauté est-il donc aussi vain
Existes-tu mon amour
Ou n'est-tu qu'une entité que j'ai créée sans le vouloir
Pour peupler la solitude
Es-tu une de ces déesses comme celles que les Grecs avaient douées pour moins s'ennuyer
Je t'adore ô ma déesse exquise même si tu n'es que dans mon imagination

Luckily it's just for tonight
Most days I cling to you
Most days I console myself for loneliness and all kinds of horrors
By imagining your beauty
And raising it above the ecstatic universe
Then I start wondering if I imagine it in vain
For I can't know your beauty by my senses
Or even by words
Then is my fondness for beauty also in vain
Do you really exist my love
Or are you only a being I created involuntarily
So that I might people my loneliness
Are you a goddess like those the Greeks instated so as to feel less weary
I worship you my delicate goddess even if you are only the creature of my thought

Fusée

La boucle des cheveux noirs de ta nuque est mon trésor
Ma pensée te rejoint et la tienne la croise
Tes seins sont les seuls obus que j'aime
Ton souvenir est la lanterne de repérage qui nous sert à pointer la nuit

En voyant la large croupe de mon cheval j'ai pensé à tes hanches

Voici les fantassins qui s'en vont à l'arrière en lisant un journal

Le chien du brancardier revient avec une pipe dans sa gueule

Un chat-huant ailes fauves yeux ternes gueule de petit chat et pattes de chat

Une souris verte file parmi la mousse

Le riz a brûlé dans la marmite de campement
Ça signifie qu'il faut prendre garde à bien des choses

Flare

The curl of black hair from the nape of your neck is my treasure
My thought finds you out and your thought meets mine
Your breasts are the only bombshells I love
Your memory is the searchlight focusing the night for us

Seeing the wide rump of my horse I thought of your haunches

There go the foot soldiers on their way to the rear reading a newspaper

The stretcher-bearer's dog comes back with a pipe in his mouth

A tawny owl yellow wings dull eyes beak of a little cat and cat paws

A green mouse darts off through the moss

The rice has scorched in the camp cooking pot
The meaning of that is you have to be careful about a lot of things

Le mégaphone crie
Allongez le tir

Allongez le tir amour de vos batteries

Balance des batteries lourdes cymbales
Qu'agitent les chérubins fous d'amour
En l'honneur du Dieu des Armées

Un arbre dépouillé sur une butte

Le bruit des tracteurs qui grimpent dans la vallée

O vieux monde du XIXe siècle plein de hautes cheminées si belles et si pures

Virilités du siècle où nous sommes
O canons

Douilles éclatantes des obus de 75
Carillonnez pieusement

The megaphone cries
Lengthen the range

Lengthen the range love of your guns

Indecision of guns heavy cymbals
Waved by cherubim crazy with love
In honor of the God of Armies

A bare tree on a knoll

The noise of tractors climbing a valley

Oh aged nineteenth-century world full of tall chimneys so handsome and pure

Virilities of our century
Oh cannons

Bursting powder charges of shells from 75's
Ring out your bells piously

Désir

Mon désir est la région qui est devant moi
Derrière les lignes boches
Mon désir est aussi derrière moi
Après la zone des armées

Mon désir c'est la butte du Mesnil
Mon désir est là sur quoi je tire
De mon désir qui est au-delà de la zone des armées
Je n'en parle pas aujourd'hui mais j'y pense

Butte du Mesnil je t'imagine en vain
Des fils de fer des mitrailleuses des ennemis trop sûrs d'eux
Trop enfoncés sous terre déjà enterrés

Ca ta clac des coups qui meurent en s'éloignant

En y veillant tard dans la nuit
Le Decauville qui toussote

Desire

My desire is the region that lies before me
Behind the Boche lines
My desire is also behind me
Beyond the armies' zone

My desire is the butte of Mesnil
My desire is far off where I'm firing
Of my desire that lies beyond the armies' zone
I shall not speak today but I think of it

Butte of Mesnil vainly I evoke you
Iron wire machine guns brazen enemies
Sunken too far underground already buried

Ca tac clac of gunfire that dwindles and dies

Watching there late at night
A Decauville railway coughing

La tôle ondulée sous la pluie
Et sous la pluie ma bourguignotte

Entends la terre véhémente
Vois les lueurs avant d'entendre les coups

Et tel obus siffler de la démence
Ou le tac tac tac monotone et bref plein de dégoût

Je désire
Te serrer dans ma main Main de Massiges
Si décharnée sur la carte

Le boyau Gœthe où j'ai tiré
J'ai tiré même sur le boyau Nietzsche
Décidément je ne respecte aucune gloire

Nuit violente et violette et sombre et pleine d'or par moments
Nuit des hommes seulement
Nuit du 24 septembre
Demain l'assaut
Nuit violente ô nuit dont l'épouvantable cri profond devenait plus intense de minute en minute
Nuit qui criait comme une femme qui accouche
Nuit des hommes seulement

Corrugated iron waving in the rain
And in the rain my helmet

Listen to the vehement earth
You see the flashes before you hear the gunfire

And a shell whistling demented
Or the monotonous brief tac tac full of disgust

I long
To grasp you in my hand Main de Massiges
So fleshless on the map

Goethe's trench I have fired at
I have even fired at the guts of Nietzsche
Decidedly I respect no glory

Night that is violet and violent and dark and momentarily full of gold
Night of men only
Night of September 24
Tomorrow the attack
Violent night oh night whose frightful deep cry became more intense every
  minute
Night crying like a woman in labor
Night of men only

Chant de l'Horizon en Champagne

A M. Joseph Granié

Voici le tétin rose de l'euphorbe verruquée
Voici le nez des soldats invisibles
Moi l'horizon invisible je chante
Que les civils et les femmes écoutent ces chansons
Et voici d'abord la cantilène du brancardier blessé

Le sol est blanc la nuit l'azure
Saigne la crucifixion
Tandis que saigne la blessure
Du soldat de Promission

Un chien jappait l'obus miaule
La lueur muette a jailli
A savoir si la guerre est drôle
Les masques n'ont pas tressailli

Mais quel fou rire sous le masque
Blancheur éternelle d'ici

Song of the Horizon in Champagne

For M. Joseph Granié

Here is the rose-colored nipple of warty spurge
Here are the noses of invisible soldiers
And I the invisible horizon I sing
Let civilians let the women listen to my songs
And first here is the lament of the wounded stretcher-bearer

The soil is white night paints it azure
The crucifixion bleeds
The soldier of the Promised Land
Bears a bloody wound

A dog was yelping bombshells whine
There came a silent blaze of light
We've yet to see if war's a scream
The gas masks didn't quiver

Behind the mask what crazy laughter
Eternal whiteness of here and now

Où la colombe porte un casque
Et l'acier s'envole aussi

Je suis seul sur le champ de bataille
Je suis la tranchée blanche le bois vert et roux
L'obus miaule
Je te tuerai
Animez-vous fantassins à passepoil jaune
Grands artilleurs roux comme des taupes
Bleu-de-roi comme les golfes méditerranéens
Veloutés de toutes les nuances du velours
Ou mauves encore ou bleu-horizon comme les autres
Ou déteints
Venez le pot en tête
Debout fusée éclairante
Danse grenadier en agitant tes pommes de pin
Alidades des triangles de visée pointez-vous sur les lueurs
Creusez des trous enfants de 20 ans creusez des trous
Sculptez les profondeurs
Envolez-vous essaims des avions blonds ainsi que les avettes
Moi l'horizon je fais le roue comme un grand Paon
Écoutez renaître les oracles qui avaient cessé
Le grand Pan est ressuscité
Champagne viril qui émoustille la Champagne
Hommes faits jeunes gens
Caméléon des autos-canons
Et vous classe 16
Craquements des arrivées ou bien floraison blanche dans les cieux
J'étais content pourtant ça brûlait la paupière
Les officiers captifs voulaient cacher leurs noms
Œil du Breton blessé couché sur la civière
Et qui criait aux morts aux sapins aux canons
Priez pour moi Bon Dieu je suis le pauvre Pierre

Boyaux et rumeur du canon
Sur cette mer aux blanches vagues
Fou stoïque comme Zénon
Pilote du cœur tu zigzagues

Where the dove wears a helmet
And steel is flying also

I am all alone on the battlefield
I am the white trench the green and red forest
The bombshell whines
I'm going to kill you
Start moving foot soldiers wearing yellow braid
Tall artillerymen red-haired like moles
Royal blue like Mediterranean bays
Downy with all the hues of velvet
Or else purple or horizon-blue like the others
Or faded
Come on get your helmets
Up brilliant flare
Dance grenadier waving your pinecones
Alidades measure the angles and aim toward the gunfire
Dig holes you twenty-year-olds dig holes
Carve out the depths
Fly off swarms of blond airplanes like bees
And I the horizon I spread my tail like a huge Peacock
Listen the oracles are renewed that were silent
Great Pan is reborn
Manly champagne that rouses Champagne
Grown men and boys
Chameleon of motorized cannon
And you class of 1916
The crunch of shells landing or white blossoming in the sky
I was serene and yet all this made one's eyelids burn
Officer prisoners wanted to conceal their names
The look in the eyes of the wounded Breton lying on the litter
Who cried out to the dead to the pine trees and the cannons
I'm poor Peter Good God pray for me

Trench-guts and cannon boom
Over the sea and its white foam
Like Zeno stoical and mad
Heart's pilot you follow a crooked road

Petites forêts de sapins
La nichée attend la becquée
Pointe-t-il des nez de lapins
Comme l'euphorbe verruquée

Ainsi que l'euphorbe d'ici
Le soleil à peine boutonne
Je l'adore comme un Parsi
Ce tout petit soleil d'automne

Un fantassin presque un enfant
Bleu comme le jour qui s'écoule
Beau comme mon cœur triomphant
Disait en mettant sa cagoule

Tandis que nous n'y sommes pas
Que de filles deviennent belles
Voici l'hiver et pas à pas
Leur beauté s'éloignera d'elles

O Lueurs soudaines des tirs
Cette beauté que j'imagine
Faute d'avoir des souvenirs
Tire de vous son origine

Car elle n'est rien que l'ardeur
De la bataille violente
Et de la terrible lueur
Il s'est fait une muse ardente

Il regarde longtemps l'horizon
Couteaux tonneaux d'eaux
Des lanternes allumées se sont croisées
Moi l'horizon je combattrai pour la victoire

Je suis l'invisible qui ne peut disparaître
Je suis comme l'onde
Allons ouvrez les écluses que je me précipite et renverse tout

Pine trees in a little wood
The nest awaits the cropful of food
Do rabbits' noses emerge
Like warty spurge

Like spurge that grows near here
The sun barely begins to bud
And like a Parsee I adore
This tiny autumnal sun

An infantryman still a child
Blue like the day flowing past
Handsome like my triumphant heart
Said as he donned his gas mask

While we're no longer there
How many girls begin to blossom
Now winter comes and step by step
Their beauty will withdraw from them

Oh sudden blazing of the guns
The beauty I imagine
Since I've no memories
Takes from you its origin

For it's nothing but the zeal
Of the violent battle
And from that frightful blaze
He fashioned himself an ardent muse

For a long while he watched the horizon
Knives casks of water
Bright lanterns have intersected
And I the horizon I'll fight for victory

I am the invisible one who cannot vanish
I am like a wave
Come on open the floodgates so I can rush in and capsize everything

Océan de Terre

A G. de Chirico

J'ai bâti une maison au milieu de l'Océan
Ses fenêtres sont les fleuves qui s'écoulent de mes yeux
Des poulpes grouillent partout où se tiennent les murailles
Entendez battre leur triple cœur et leur bec cogner aux vitres
Maison humide
Maison ardente
Saison rapide
Saison qui chante
Les avions pondent des œufs
Attention on va jeter l'ancre
Attention à l'encre que l'on jette
Il serait bon que vous vinssiez du ciel
Le chèvrefeuille du ciel grimpe
Les poulpes terrestres palpitent
Et puis nous sommes tant et tant à être nos propres fossoyeurs
Pâles poulpes des vagues crayeuses ô poulpes aux becs pâles
Autour de la maison il y a cet océan que tu connais
Et qui ne se repose jamais

Ocean of Earth

For G. de Chirico

I have built a house in the middle of the Ocean
Its windows are the rivers flowing from my eyes
Octopuses swarm all over the walls
Listen to their triple heartbeat and their beak knock at the windows
        Humid house
        Blazing house
        Swift season
        Singing season
    Airplanes are laying eggs
    Watch out they're going to sink the anchor
    Watch out for this ink they're throwing
Oh will you not descend from the sky
The honeysuckle of the sky is climbing
The earthly octopuses quiver
And so many of us dig our own graves
Pale octopuses of chalky waves oh octopuses with pale beaks
Around the house lies the ocean you know so well
The ocean that is never still

Obus Couleur de Lune
Moon-Colored Shells

Merveille de la Guerre

Que c'est beau ces fusées qui illuminent la nuit
Elles montent sur leur propre cime et se penchent pour regarder
Ce sont des dames qui dansent avec leurs regards pour yeux bras et cœurs

J'ai reconnu ton sourire et ta vivacité

C'est aussi l'apothéose quotidienne de toutes mes Bérénices dont les chevelures sont devenues des comètes
Ces danseuses surdorées appartiennent à tous les temps et à toutes les races
Elles accouchent brusquement d'enfants qui n'ont que le temps de mourir

Comme c'est beau toutes ces fusées
Mais ce serait bien plus beau s'il y en avait plus encore
S'il y en avait des millions qui auraient un sens complet et relatif comme les lettres d'un livre
Pourtant c'est aussi beau que si la vie même sortait des mourants

Mais ce serait plus beau encore s'il y en avait plus encore
Cependant je les regarde comme une beauté qui s'offre et s'évanouit aussitôt

Wonder of War

How lovely these flares are that light up the dark
They climb their own peak and lean down to look
They are dancing ladies whose glances become eyes arms and hearts

I recognize your smile and your vivacity

It's also the daily apotheosis of all my Berenices whose hair has turned to
comets' tails
These dancing girls twice gilded belong to all times and all races
Swiftly they give birth to children who have just time enough to die

How lovely all these flares are
But it would be finer if there were still more of them
If there were millions with a full and relative meaning like letters in a book
However it's as lovely as if life itself issued from those who are dying

But it would be finer still if there were still more of them
And yet I see them as a beauty who offers herself and immediately swoons
away

Il me semble assister à un grand festin éclairé a giorno
C'est un banquet que s'offre la terre
Elle a faim et ouvre de longues bouches pâles
La terre a faim et voici son festin de Balthasar cannibale

Qui aurait dit qu'on pût être à ce point anthropophage
Et qu'il fallût tant de feu pour rôtir le corps humain
C'est pourquoi l'air a un petit goût empyreumatique qui n'est ma foi pas désagréable
Mais le festin serait plus beau encore si le ciel y mangeait avec la terre
Il n'avale que les âmes
Ce qui est une façon de ne pas se nourrir
Et se contente de jongler avec des feux versicolores

Mais j'ai coulé dans la douceur de cette guerre avec toute ma compagnie au long des longs boyaux
Quelques cris de flamme annoncent sans cesse ma présence
J'ai creusé le lit où je coule en me ramifiant en mille petits fleuves qui vont partout
Je suis dans la tranchée de première ligne et cependant je suis partout ou plutôt je commence à être partout
C'est moi qui commence cette chose des siècles à venir
Ce sera plus long à réaliser que non la fable d'Icare volant

Je lègue à l'avenir l'histoire de Guillaume Apollinaire
Qui fut à la guerre et sut être partout
Dans les villes heureuses de l'arrière
Dans tout le reste de l'univers
Dans ceux qui meurent en piétinant dans le barbelé
Dans les femmes dans les canons dans les chevaux
Au zénith au nadir aux 4 points cardinaux
Et dans l'unique ardeur de cette veillée d'armes

Et ce serait sans doute bien plus beau
Si je pouvais supposer que toutes ces choses dans lesquelles je suis partout
Pouvaient m'occuper aussi
Mais dans ce sens il n'y a rien de fait
Car si je suis partout à cette heure il n'y a cependant que moi qui suis en moi

I seem to be at a great feast lighted *a giorno*
A banquet that earth offers herself
Hungrily she opens her long pale mouths
Earth is hungry and here is the feast of this cannibal Balthazar

Who would have said one could be so anthropophagous
Or that so much fire was needed to roast human flesh
That's why the air has a slight empyreumatic taste which by God is not unpleasant
But the feast would be finer still if the sky too dined with the earth
But it swallows only souls
Which is a way of not nourishing oneself at all
And it's content to juggle with multicolored lights

But I have flowed into the sweetness of this war with my whole company along the long trenches
A few cries of flame keep announcing my presence
I have hollowed out the bed where I flow and branch into a thousand small streams going everywhere
I am in the front-line trenches and still I am everywhere or rather I am beginning to be everywhere
For it is I who begin this affair of the centuries to come
It will be longer to realize than the myth of soaring Icarus

I bequeath to the future the story of Guillaume Apollinaire
Who was in the war and knew how to be everywhere
In the lucky towns behind the front lines
In all the rest of the universe
In those who died tangled in the barbed wire
In women in cannons in horses
At the zenith at the nadir at the four cardinal points
And in the unique ardor of this eve of battle

And of course it would be finer
If I could imagine that all these things in which I dwell
Invaded me too
But in this sense there's nothing doing
For if I am everywhere at this hour there is only myself who is in me

Exercice

Vers un village de l'arrière
S'en allaient quatre bombardiers
Ils étaient couverts de poussière
Depuis la tête jusqu'aux pieds

Ils regardaient la vaste plaine
En parlant entre eux du passé
Et ne se retournaient qu'à peine
Quand un obus avait toussé

Tous quatre de la classe seize
Parlaient d'antan non d'avenir
Ainsi se prolongeait l'ascèse
Qui les exerçait à mourir

Exercise

Towards a village in the rear
Marched four bombardiers
And they were covered with dirt
From head to foot

They stared at the vast plain
As they talked about the past
And they barely looked around
When a shell made a coughing sound

All four of class sixteen
Spoke of the past not future time
Thus the ascesis dragged on
That practiced them in dying

A l'Italie

A Ardengo Soffici

L'amour a remué ma vie comme on remue la terre dans la zone des armées
J'atteignais l'âge mûr quand la guerre arriva
Et dans ce jour d'août 1915 le plus chaud de l'année
Bien abrité dans l'hypogée que j'ai creusé moi-même
C'est à toi que je songe Italie mère de mes pensées

Et déjà quand von Kluck marchait sur Paris avant la Marne
J'évoquais le sac de Rome par les Allemands
Le sac de Rome qu'ont décrit
Un Bonaparte le vicaire espagnol Delicado et l'Arétin
Je me disais
Est-il possible que la nation
Qui est la mère de la civilisation
Regarde sans la défendre les efforts qu'on fait pour la détruire

Puis les temps sont venus les tombes se sont ouvertes
Les fantômes des Esclaves toujours frémissants
Se sont dressés en criant SUS AUX TUDESQUES

To Italy

For Ardengo Soffici

Love has upturned my life as the earth is upturned in the army zone
I was nearing my prime when the war began
And on this hottest day of August in the year 1915
Well screened in the hypogeum I dug myself
It's you I dream of Italy mother of my thought

Already when von Kluck marched on Paris before the Marne
I evoked Rome's plundering by the Germans
The sack of Rome described by
A Bonaparte the Spanish vicar Delicado and Aretino
I said to myself
Can a nation
Known as the mother of civilization
Witness attempts to destroy her child without defending it

Then the times rolled round and the tombs yawned
The phantoms of Slaves still trembling
Rose up and cried UP AND AT THE GERMANS

Nous l'armée invisible aux cris éblouissants
Plus doux que n'est le miel et plus simples qu'un peu de terre
Nous te tournons bénignement le dos Italie
Mais ne t'en fais pas nous t'aimons bien
Italie mère qui es aussi notre fille

Nous sommes là tranquillement et sans tristesse
Et si malgré les masques les sacs de sable les rondins nous tombions
Nous savons qu'un autre prendrait notre place
Et que les Armées ne périront jamais

Les mois ne sont pas longs ni les jours ni les nuits
C'est la guerre qui est longue

Italie
Toi notre mère et notre fille quelque chose comme une sœur
J'ai comme toi pour me réconforter
Le quart de pinard
Qui met tant de différence entre nous et les Boches
J'ai aussi comme toi l'envol des compagnies de perdreaux des 75
Comme toi je n'ai pas cet orgueil sans joie des Boches et je sais rigoler
Je ne suis pas sentimental à l'excès comme le sont ces gens sans mesure que leurs actions dépassent sans qu'ils sachent s'amuser
Notre civilisation a plus de finesse que les choses qu'ils emploient
Elle est au-delà de la vie confortable
Et de ce qui est l'extérieur dans l'art et l'industrie
Les fleurs sont nos enfants et non les leurs
Même la fleur de lys qui meurt au Vatican

La plaine est infinie et les tranchées sont blanches
Les avions bourdonnent ainsi que des abeilles
Sur les roses momentanées des éclatements
Et les nuits sont parées de guirlandes d'éblouissements
De bulles de globules aux couleurs insoupçonnées

Nous jouissons de tout même de nos souffrances
Notre humeur est charmante l'ardeur vient quand il faut
Nous sommes narquois car nous savons faire la part des choses

We the invisible army with our blazing cries
Sweeter than honey and simpler than a little earth
We gently turn our backs on you Italy
But don't be disturbed we're still your friends
Italy our mother and our daughter too

We're still here quite calm and without distress
And if in spite of the gas masks the sandbags and logs we should fall
We know someone else would take our place
For the Armies will never perish

The months aren't long neither are the days or nights
It's war that's long

Italy
You our mother and our daughter almost a sister
Like you I have a quart of vino
To cheer me up
And this is what makes us so different from the Huns
Like you I have the flight of flocks of partridges of the 75's
Like you I have nothing in common with the Huns' joyless pride and I know how to laugh
For I'm not overly sentimental like those immoderate people with their excessive actions and their inability to amuse themselves
Our civilization is subtler than the objects they use
It's beyond the comforts of life
Beyond what's external in art or industry
Flowers are our children and not theirs
Even the lily flower dying at the Vatican

The plain is endless the trenches are white
Airplanes buzz like bees
Over the momentary pinks of an explosion
And nights are adorned with garlands of glitter
With globular bubbles in unsuspected colors

We delight in everything even in pain
Our mood is bewitching and eagerness comes when it's needed

Et il n'y a pas plus de folie chez celui qui jette les grenades que chez celui qui plume les patates
Tu aimes un peu plus que nous les gestes et les mots sonores
Tu as à ta disposition les sortilèges étrusques le sens de la majesté héroïque et le courageux honneur individuel
Nous avons le sourire nous devinons ce qu'on ne nous dit pas nous sommes démerdards et même ceux qui se dégonflent sauraient à l'occasion faire preuve de l'esprit de sacrifice qu'on appelle la bravoure
Et nous fumons du gros avec volupeté

C'est la nuit je suis dans mon blockhaus éclairé par l'électricité en bâton
Je pense à toi pays des 2 volcans
Je salue le souvenir des sirènes et des scylles mortes au moment de Messine
Je salue le Colleoni équestre de Venise
Je salue la chemise rouge
Je t'envoie mes amitiés Italie et m'apprête à applaudir aux hauts faits de ta bleusaille
Non parce que j'imagine qu'il y aura jamais plus de bonheur ou de malheur en ce monde
Mais parce que comme toi j'aime à penser seul et que les Boches m'en empêcheraient
Mais parce que le goût naturel de la perfection que nous avons l'un et l'autre si on les laissait faire serait vite remplacé par je ne sais quelles commodités dont je n'ai que faire
Et surtout parce que comme toi je sais je veux choisir et qu'eux voudraient nous forcer à ne plus choisir
Une même destinée nous lie en cette occase

Ce n'est pas pour l'ensemble que je le dis
Mais pour chacun de toi Italie

Ne te borne point à prendre les terres irrédentes
Mets ton destin dans la balance où est la nôtre

Les réflecteurs dardent leurs lueurs comme des yeux d'escargots
Et les obus en tombant sont des chiens qui jettent de la terre avec leurs pattes après avoir fait leurs besoins

We like to banter for we know how to take things in our stride
And the man who tosses grenades is no crazier than the one who peels potatoes
You love more than we do gestures and sonorous words
You have at your disposal Etruscan enchantments a sense of fearless dignity and individual honor
We go in for smiles we guess what people don't tell us we're resourceful and even punks may show on occasion the spirit of sacrifice that's called bravura
And we smoke rough tobacco with relish

It's night I'm in my blockhouse wired for candles
I'm thinking of you land of 2 volcanoes
I hail the memory of sirens and of dead scyllas at the time of Messina
I hail the Colleoni horseman of Venice
I hail the red shirt
I send you my greetings Italy and I'm ready to applaud the noble deeds of your recruits
Not because I imagine there'll ever be more or less happiness or grief in this world
But because like you I prefer to think alone and the Huns would prevent me
And because if we left things to them the natural taste for perfection which you and I share would be swiftly replaced by God knows what unusable commodities
And above all because like you I know I want to choose and they would keep us from ever choosing again
Our fate's the same on this occasion

It's not as a generality that I say this
But for each one of you Italy

Don't confine yourself to taking the unredeemed lands
Place your destiny in the same scales as ours

Reflectors dart flashing gleams like snails' eyes
And falling bombshells are dogs scattering dirt with their paws after they have relieved themselves

Notre armée invisible est une belle nuit constellée
Et chacun de nos hommes est un astre merveilleux

O nuit ô nuit éblouissante
Les morts sont avec nos soldats
Les morts sont debout dans les tranchées
Ou se glissent souterrainement vers les Bien-Aimées
O Lille Saint-Quentin Laon Maubeuge Vouziers
Nous jetons nos villes comme des grenades
Nos fleuves sont brandis comme des sabres
Nos montagnes chargent comme cavalerie

Nous reprendrons les villes les fleuves et les collines
De la frontière helvétique aux frontières bataves
Entre toi et nous Italie
Il y a des patelins pleins de femmes
Et près de toi m'attend celle que j'adore
O Frères d'Italie

Ondes nuages délétères
Métalliques débris qui vous rouillez partout
O frères d'Italie vos plumes sur la tête
Italie
Entends crier Louvain vois Reims tordre ses bras
Et ce soldat blessé toujours debout Arras

Et maintenant chantons ceux qui sont morts
Ceux qui vivent
Les officiers les soldats
Les flingots Rosalie le canon la fusée l'hélice la pelle les chevaux
Chantons les bagues pâles les casques
Chantons ceux qui sont morts
Chantons la terre qui bâille d'ennui
Chantons et rigolons
Durant des années
Italie
Entends braire l'âne boche
Faisons la guerre à coups de fouets

Our invisible army is a lovely constellated night
And each of our men is a marvelous star

Oh night oh glittering night
The dead are with our soldiers
The dead stand in the trenches
Or glide underground toward the Best-Beloved
Oh Lille Saint-Quentin Laon Maubeuge Vouziers
We hurl our cities like grenades
Our rivers are brandished like swords
Our mountains charge like horsemen

We will take back the cities rivers and hills
From Switzerland to the Batavian border
Between you and us Italy
There are small towns full of women
And near you waits the one I love
Oh Italian brothers

Noxious waves and clouds
Metallic debris growing rusty everywhere
Oh Italian brothers with your feathered crests
Italy
Listen to Louvain cry see Rheims twist her arms
And Arras that wounded soldier still standing

And now let's sing of those who are dead
And those still alive
Officers soldiers
Rosalie the rifle cannon rockets propellers shovels horses
Sing pale rings and helmets
Sing you who are dead
Sing earth yawning with boredom
Sing and laugh
Down the years
Italy
Hear the Hun ass bray
Let's fight with whiplashes

Faits avec les rayons du soleil
Italie
Chantons et rigolons
Durant des années

Made of sunbeams
Italy
Let's sing and laugh
Down the years

La Traversée

Du joli bateau de Port-Vendres
Tes yeux étaient les matelots
Et comme les flots étaient tendres
Dans les parages de Palos

Que de sous-marins dans mon âme
Naviguent et vont l'attendant
Le superbe navire où clame
Le chœur de ton regard ardent

The Crossing

Of that charming boat from Porto Venere
Your eyes were the mariners
And how tender was each wave
In the latitudes of Spain

So many submarines in my soul
Cruise onward waiting for
The proud ship where clamors
The chorus of your piercing gaze

Il y a

Il y a un vaisseau qui a emporté ma bien-aimée
Il y a dans le ciel six saucisses et la nuit venant on dirait des asticots dont naîtraient les étoiles
Il y a un sous-marin ennemi qui en voulait à mon amour
Il y a mille petits sapins brisés par les éclats d'obus autour de moi
Il y a un fantassin qui passe aveuglé par les gaz asphyxiants
Il y a que nous avons tout haché dans les boyaux de Nietzsche de Gœthe et de Cologne
Il y a que je languis après une lettre qui tarde
Il y a dans mon porte-cartes plusieurs photos de mon amour
Il y a les prisonniers qui passent la mine inquiète
Il y a une batterie dont les servants s'agitent autour des pièces
Il y a le vaguemestre qui arrive au trot par le chemin de l'Arbre isolé
Il y a dit-on un espion qui rôde par ici invisible comme l'horizon dont il s'est indignement revêtu et avec quoi il se confond
Il y a dressé comme un lys le buste de mon amour
Il y a un capitaine qui attend avec anxiété les communications de la T. S. F. sur l'Atlantique

There Is There Are

There's a ship that has sailed away with my love
There are six sausages in the sky and night coming on you'd say maggots
  that will hatch into stars
There's an enemy submarine with designs on my love
There are a thousand little pines shattered by the bursting shells around me
There's a foot soldier passing by who is blinded by the asphyxiating gas
There's everything we have slashed to pieces in the gutlike trenches of
  Nietzsche Goethe and Cologne
There's my longing for a letter that doesn't come
There are snapshots in my wallet of my love
There are the prisoners going by with troubled looks
There's a battery whose gun crew is busy with the guns
There's the post orderly who arrives trotting along the trail of the lonesome
  pine
There's a spy they say who prowls by here invisible like the horizon which
  he is shamelessly wearing and which he blends with
There is erect like a lily the portrait of my love

Il y a à minuit des soldats qui scient des planches pour les cercueils
Il y a des femmes qui demandent du maïs à grands cris devant un Christ sanglant à Mexico
Il y a le Gulf Stream qui est si tiède et si bienfaisant
Il y a un cimetière plein de croix à 5 kilomètres
Il y a des croix partout de-ci de-là
Il y a des figues de Barbarie sur ces cactus en Algérie
Il y a les longues mains souples de mon amour
Il y a un encrier que j'avais fait dans une fusée de 15 centimètres et qu'on n'a pas laissé partir
Il y a ma selle exposée à la pluie
Il y a les fleuves qui ne remontent pas leurs cours
Il y a l'amour qui m'entraîne avec douceur
Il y avait un prisonnier boche qui portait sa mitrailleuse sur son dos
Il y a des hommes dans le monde qui n'ont jamais été à la guerre
Il y a des Hindous qui regardent avec étonnement les campagnes occidentales
Ils pensent avec mélancolie à ceux dont ils se demandent s'ils les reverront
Car on a poussé très loin durant cette guerre l'art de l'invisibilité

There's a captain waiting anxiously for messages from the TSF about the
Atlantic
There are soldiers at midnight sawing planks for coffins
There are women asking for corn with great cries before a bleeding Christ in
Mexico City
There's the Gulf Stream so lukewarm and so beneficial
There's a cemetery full of crosses 5 kilometers away
There are crosses everywhere on this side or that
There are Barbary figs on the cactus in Algeria
There are my love's long supple hands
There's an inkwell I made in a 15-centimeter rocket they didn't send off
There's my saddle out in the rain
There are the rivers that won't flow uphill again
There's love that gently allures me
There was a Boche prisoner carrying his machine gun on his back
There are men in the world who have never been to war
There are Hindus watching in astonishment the Western landscapes
They think sadly of their friends and wonder if they'll see them again
For we have pushed very far in this war the art of invisibility

L'Espionne

Pâle espionne de l'Amour
Ma mémoire à peine fidèle
N'eut pour observer cette belle
Forteresse qu'une heure un jour

Tu te déguises
A ta guise
Mémoire espionne du cœur
Tu ne retrouves plus l'exquise
Ruse et le cœur seul est vainqueur

Mais la vois-tu cette mémoire
Les yeux bandés prête à mourir
Elle affirme qu'on peut l'en croire
Mon cœur vaincra sans coup férir

The Spy

Love's pale spy
My memory barely faithful
Had only an hour one day
To chart that lovely citadel

You disguise yourself
                    As you please
Memory my heart's spy
That artful stratagem you'll recover
Never and the heart alone is winner

But do you see my memory
As blindfolded she prepares to die
Still insisting that she knows
My heart will win without a blow

Le Chant d'Amour

Voici de quoi est fait le chant symphonique de l'amour
Il y a le chant de l'amour de jadis
Le bruit des baisers éperdus des amants illustres
Les cris d'amour des mortelles violées par les dieux
Les virilités des héros fabuleux érigées comme des pièces contre avions
Le hurlement précieux de Jason
Le chant mortel du cygne
Et l'hymne victorieux que les premiers rayons du soleil ont fait chanter à Memnon l'immobile
Il y a le cri des Sabines au moment de l'enlèvement
Il y a aussi les cris d'amour des félins dans les jongles
La rumeur sourde des sèves montant dans les plantes tropicales
Le tonnerre des artilleries qui accomplissent le terrible amour des peuples
Les vagues de la mer où naît la vie et la beauté

Il y a là le chant de tout l'amour du monde

Love's Hymn

This is what love's symphonic hymn is composed of
There's the tune of ancient loves
The sound of mad kisses of famous lovers
The love cries of mortal women raped by the gods
The virilities of fabulous heroes erect like guns against planes
The precious moan of Jason
The mortal song of the swan
And the victorious song that the first rays of the sun have made motionless
Memnon sing
There's the cry of Sabine women when they were seized
There's also the cry of felines in the jungles
The dull noise of sap rising in tropical plants
The thunder of artilleries accomplishing the terrible love of nations
The waves of sea where life and beauty are born

Here is the hymn of all the love in the world

Aussi Bien que les Cigales

gens du midi   ne savez pas   M
gens du mi   creuser que   ais
di vous n'   vous ne sa   vous
avez donc   vez pas vous   savez
pas regar   éclairer ni   encore
dé les ciga   voir Que vous   boire com   le jour
les que vous   manque-t-il   me les ci   de gloire
donc pour   gales ô   se
voir aus   gens du mi   *c*   ra
si bien   di gens du   *reusez*   ce
que les   soleil gens qui   *voyez bu*   lui
ciga   devriez savoir   *vez pissez*   où
les   creuser et voir   *comme*   vous
aussi bien pour le   *les ciga*   sau
moins aussi bien   *les*   rez
que les cigales   creu
Eh quoi! vous savez   *gens du Midi il faut*   ser
boire et ne savez   *creuser voir boire*   pour
plus pisser utile   *pisser aussi bien que*   bien
ment comme les   *les cigales*   sor
cigales   LA JOIE   *pour chan*   tir
ADORABLE   *ter com*   au
DE LA PAIX   *me elles*   so
SOLAIRE   leil

As Well as the Cicadas

southern folks You don't know B
southern fo how to dig and so ut
lks then yo you don't you
u haven't know how to brighten still
looked at the up or know
cicadas and so see What's missing how to drink the day
that would like the ci of glory
help you see cadas oh will
just as southern fo *d* be
well lks sunshine *ig* the
as the folks folks who *look dr* one
cica ought to know *ink piss* when
das how to dig how to look *like* you
at least as *the cica* will
well as well *das* know
as the cicadas how to
Eh what! you know *southern folks you* dig
how to drink and don't know *have to dig look drink* so
how to piss useful *piss just as well as* as
ly like the *the cicadas* to
cicadas THE ADORABLE *so you can* reach
JOY OF *sing like* the
SOLAR *them* sun
PEACE

Simultanéités

Les canons tonnent dans la nuit
On dirait des vagues tempête
Des cœurs où pointe un grand ennui
Ennui qui toujours se répète

Il regarde venir là-bas
Les prisonniers L'heure est si douce
Dans ce grand bruit ouaté très bas
Très bas qui grandit sans secousse

Il tient son casque dans ses mains
Pour saluer la souvenance
Des lys des roses des jasmins
Éclos dans les jardins de France

Et sous la cagoule masqué
Il pense à des cheveux si sombres

Simultaneities

Cannon are thundering through the gloom
You might say waves or a storm
Or hearts where weariness grows
Weariness continually renewed

He watches prisoners passing by
The hour is so subdued
With that huge noise muffled low
So low yet loudening steadily

He holds his helmet in his hands
And salutes the memory
Of lilies of roses and of jasmine
Flowering in French gardens

And behind his gas mask he
Dreams of such dark hair

Mais qui donc l'attend sur le quai
O vaste mer aux mauves ombres

Belles noix du vivant noyer
La grand folie en vain vous gaule
Brunette écoute gazouiller
La mésange sur ton épaule

Notre amour est une lueur
Qu'un projecteur du cœur dirige
Vers l'ardeur égale du cœur
Qui sur le haut Phare s'érige

O phare-fleur mes souvenirs
Les cheveux noirs de Madeleine
Les atroces lueurs des tirs
Ajoutent leur clarté soudaine
A tes beaux yeux ô Madeleine

But who then waits for him on the pier
Oh vast sea of lilac shadows

Lovely nuts from the living tree
Folly vainly beats you down
Listen brown-haired girl to the twitter
Of the titmouse on your shoulder

Our passion is a blaze
Flung by the heart's searchlight
Toward another heart's twin fire
On top of the lofty Beacon

Oh beacon-blossom my memories
Madeleine's black hair
The atrocious blaze of gunfire
Adds its sudden clarity
To your lovely eyes my Madeleine

Du Coton dans les Oreilles

Tant d'explosifs sur le point **VIF !**

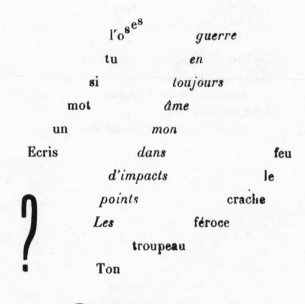

l'oses *guerre*

tu *en*

si *toujours*

mot *âme*

un *mon*

Ecris *dans* feu

d'impacts le

? *points* crache

Les féroce

troupeau

Ton

OMÉGAPHONE

Cotton in your Ears

So many explosives just about to be
ALIVE!

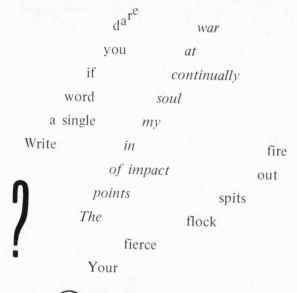

dare war
you at
if continually
word soul
a single my
Write in fire
of impact out
? points spits
The flock
fierce
Your

OMEGAPHONE

Ceux qui revenaient de la mort
En attendaient une pareille
Et tout ce qui venait du nord
Allait obscurcir le soleil

Mais que voulez-vous
c'est son sort
Allô la truie

C'est quand sonnera le réveil

ALLÔ LA TRUIE

La sentinelle au long regard

La sentinelle au long regard

Et la cagnat s'appelait

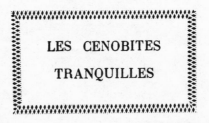

LES CENOBITES
TRANQUILLES

La sentinelle au long regard la sentinelle au large regard
Allô la truie

Tant et tant de coquelicots
D'où tant de sang a-t-il coulé
Qu'est-ce qu'il se met dans le coco
Bon sang de bois il s'est saoulé
Et sans pinard et sans tacot
Avec de l'eau
Allô la truie

Those who came back from death
Expected it the next time
And what came from the north
Almost obscured the sun

But what would you have
It's his fate
Come in the sow

That's when reveille will sound

COME IN THE SOW

The sentinel with the long gaze

The sentinel with the long gaze

And the dugout was called

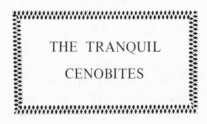

THE TRANQUIL
CENOBITES

The sentinel with the long gaze the sentinel with the lingering gaze
Come in the sow

So so many scarlet poppies
Where did all that blood come from
He's not half chugalugging
God bless the skunk he's rotten drunk
With no vino and no brandy
Just with water
Come in the sow

Le silence des phonographes
Mitrailleuses des cinémas
Tout l'échelon là-bas piaffe
Fleurs de feu des lueurs-frimas
Puisque le canon avait soif
Allô la truie
Et les trajectoires cabrées
Trébuchements de soleils-nains
Sur tant de chansons déchirées

Il a l'Étoile du Benin
Mais du singe en boîtes carrées
Crois-tu qu'il y aura la guerre
Allô la truie
Ah! s'il vous plaît
Ami l'Anglais
Ah! qu'il est laid
Ton frère ton frère ton frère de lait

Et je mangeais du pain de Gênes
En respirant leurs gaz lacrymogènes
Mets du coton dans tes oreilles
D'siré

Puis ce fut cette fleur sans nom
A peine un souffle un souvenir
Quand s'en allèrent les canons
Au tour des roues heure à courir
La baleine a d'autres fanons
Éclatements qui nous fanons

Mais mets du coton dans tes oreilles
Évidemment les fanions
Des signaleurs
Allô la truie

Ici la musique militaire joue
Quelque chose

The hush of phonographs
Machine guns from the movies
The entire echelon is pacing up and down
Fire flowers of flashing sleet
Since the cannon was thirsty
        Come in the sow
And the trajectories bucked
And dwarf suns trembled
Over so many mangled songs

He has the Star of Benin
But bully beef in square tins
Do you think there'll be a war
        Come in the sow
    Ah! if you please
    Friend Englishman
    What a fester
Your brother your brother your foster brother

    I was nibbling almond cakes
While inhaling their tear gas
    Put cotton in your ears
                    M'love

Then there rose that nameless flower
Scarcely a breath a memory
When the cannon went their way
At the wheels' turn an hour to run
The whale has other whalebones
Explosions we who fade

But put cotton in your ears
Obviously the flags
    Of signalmen
            Come in the sow

Here the military band plays
                Something

Et chacun se souvient d'une joue
Rose
Parce que même les airs entraînants
Ont quelque chose de déchirant quand on les entend à la guerre

Écoute s'il pleut écoute s'il pleut

*puis
é
cou
tez
tom
ber
la
pluie
si
ten
dre
et
si
dou
ce*

*sol
dats
a
veu
gles
per
dus
par
mi
les
che
vaux
de
fri
se
sous
la
lu
ne
li
qui
de*

*des
Flan
dres
à
l'
a
go
nie
sous
la
pluie
fi
ne
la
pluie
si
ten
dre
et
si
dou
ce*

*con
fon
dez-
vous
a
vec
l'
ho
ri
zon
beaux
ê
tres
in
vi
si
bles
sous
la
pluie
fi
ne*

*la
pluie
si
ten
dre
la
pluie
si
dou
ce*

*Les longs boyaux où tu chemines
Adieu les cagnats d'artilleurs
Tu retrouveras
La tranchée en première ligne
Les éléphants des pare-éclats
Une girouette maligne
Et les regards des guetteurs las
Qui veillent le silence insigne
Ne vois-tu rien venir*

And each one remembers a pink
Cheek
Because even martial airs
Have something heartrending when you hear them at the war

Listen to it raining listen to it rain

then
lis
ten
to
the
rain
fall
ing
so
ten
der
ly
and
gent
ly

bl
ind
sol
diers
lo
st
a
mong
the
che
vaux
de
fri
se
un
der
the
li
qui
d
mo
on

of
Flan
ders
in
a
go
ny
un
der
the
thi
n
rain
the
rain
so
ten
der
and
so
gent
le

min
gle
with
the
ho
ri
zon
beau
ti
ful
in
vi
si
ble
be
ings
un
der
the
thi
n
rain

the
rain
so
ten
der
the
rain
so
gent
le

The long trenches where you trudge
Farewell dugouts of artillerymen
Once more you'll find
The front-line trench
The heaped-up elephant parapets
A mischievous weathercock
And weary look-out men
Brooding over the strange silence
Don't you see anything coming

au
Pé
ris
co
pe

La balle qui froisse le silence
Les projectiles d'artillerie qui glissent
Comme un fleuve aérien
Ne mettez plus de coton dans les oreilles
Ça n'en vaut plus la peine
Mais appelez donc Napoléon sur la tour
Allô

Le petit geste du fantassin qui se gratte au cou où les totos le démangent
La vague
Dans les caves
Dans les caves

in
the
Pe
ris
co
pe

Bullet ruffling the silence
Artillery projectiles sliding past
        Like an aerial river
Put no more cotton in your ears
        It's no longer worthwhile
But call Napoleon on the tower
                Contact

The slight gesture of the foot soldier scratching his neck where the lice bite
The wave
        To the cellars
   To the cellars

La Tête Étoilée
The Starry Head

Le Départ

Et leurs visages étaient pâles
Et leurs sanglots s'étaient brisés

Comme la neige aux purs pétales
Ou bien tes mains sur mes baisers
Tombaient les feuilles automnales

The Departure

And their faces grew pale
And their sobs were broken

Like snow on pure petals
Or your hands on my kisses
Fell the autumn leaves

Le Vigneron Champenois

Le régiment arrive
Le village est presque endormi dans la lumière parfumée
Un prêtre a le casque en tête
La bouteille champenoise est-elle ou non une artillerie
Les ceps de vigne comme l'hermine sur un écu
Bonjour soldats
Je les ai vus passer et repasser en courant
Bonjour soldats bouteilles champenoises où le sang fermente
Vous resterez quelques jours et puis remonterez en ligne
Échelonnés ainsi que sont les ceps de vigne
J'envoie mes bouteilles partout comme les obus d'une charmante artillerie

La nuit est blonde ô vin blond
Un vigneron chantait courbé dans sa vigne
Un vigneron sans bouche au fond de l'horizon
Un vigneron qui était lui-même la bouteille vivante
Un vigneron qui sait ce qu'est la guerre
Un vigneron champenois qui est un artilleur

The Vine Grower of Champagne

The soldiers are coming
The village is almost asleep in the perfumed light
A priest wears a helmet
A bottle of champagne is artillery yes or no
Vine stocks like ermine on a coat of arms
Hello soldiers
I saw them running to and fro
Hello soldiers you bottles of champagne in which the blood ferments
You'll linger a few days and then return to your lines
Arranged in echelon like the vine plants
I hurl my bottles everywhere like charming artillery shells

The night is a blonde oh blond wine
A vine grower sang bowed over his vineyard
A mouthless vine grower in the depths of the horizon
A vine grower who was himself the living bottle
A vine grower who knows what war is
A vine grower of Champagne who is also an artilleryman

C'est maintenant le soir et l'on joue à la mouche
Puis les soldats s'en iront là-haut
Où l'Artillerie débouche ses bouteilles crémantes
Allons Adieu messieurs tâchez de revenir
Mais nul ne sait ce qui peut advenir

Now it's evening they're playing blackjack
Then the soldiers will depart for the front
Where the Artillery uncorks its frothy bottles
Let's be off Good-bye friends try to come back
But no one can tell the outcome

Carte Postale

Je t'écris de dessous la tente
Tandis que meurt ce jour d'été
Où floraison éblouissante
Dans le ciel à peine bleuté
Une canonnade éclatante
Se fane avant d'avoir été

Postcard

I write to you in my tent
While this summer day is dying
Now in the faintly azured sky
A gaudy flower
Of bursting gunfire
Fades before it happens

Éventail des Saveurs

Attols singuliers .
de brownings quel
goût
de viv
re Ah!

Des lacs versicolores
Dans les glaciers solaires

1 tout
petit
oiseau
qui n'a pas
de queue et
qui s'envole
quand on
lui en met
u ' ne

Mes tapis de la saveur moussons des sons obscurs
et ta bouche au souffle
azur

ouïs ouïs le cri les pas le pho
NOGRAPHE ouïs ouïs L'ALOÈS
éclater et le petit mirliton

Fan of Flavors

Fantastic atolls
of revolvers what
a taste
for liv
ing Ah!

Multicolored lakes
in solar glaciers

1 very
small
bird
that hasn't any
tail and
that flies off
when you
give him
o ne

My carpets of taste let's foam obscure sounds
and your mouth with its breath
of azure

hark hark the cry footsteps pho
NOGRAPH hark hark THE ALOE
bursts open and the tiny flute

Souvenirs

Deux lacs nègres
Entre une forêt
Et une chemise qui sèche

Bouche ouverte sur un harmonium
C'était une voix faite d'yeux
Tandis qu'il traîne de petites gens

Une toute petite vieille au nez pointu
J'admire la bouillotte d'émail bleu
Mais le rat pénètre dans le cadavre et y demeure

Un monsieur en bras de chemise
Se rase près de la fenêtre
En chantant un petit air qu'il ne sait pas très bien
Ça fait tout un opéra

Toi qui te tournes vers le roi
Est-ce que Dieu voudrait mourir encore

Memories

Two negro lakes
    Between a forest
        And a shirt drying

Mouth open above a harmonium
It was a voice composed of eyes
While the poor people lingered

A tiny old woman with a pointed nose
I admire the enameled blue foot warmer
But the rat penetrates the cadaver and stays there

A man in his shirt-sleeves
Is shaving near the window
And singing a little song he doesn't know very well
That kind of thing makes a whole opera

You who turn toward the king
Does God want to die all over again

L'Avenir

Soulevons la paille
Regardons la neige
Écrivons des lettres
Attendons des ordres

Fumons la pipe
En songeant à l'amour
Les gabions sont là
Regardons la rose

La fontaine n'a pas tari
Pas plus que l'or de la paille ne s'est terni
Regardons l'abeille
Et ne songeons pas à l'avenir

Regardons nos mains
Qui sont la neige
La rose et l'abeille
Ainsi que l'avenir

The Future

Let's lift up the straw
And look at the snow
And write some letters
Let's wait for orders

We'll smoke our pipes
And dream of love
The gabions are there
Let's gaze at the rose

The fountain hasn't dried up
Any more than the straw's gold has dulled
Let's look at the bee
But we'll not dream of the future

Let's stare at our hands
For they are the snow
The rose and the bee
As well as the future

Un Oiseau Chante

Un oiseau chante ne sais où
C'est je crois ton âme qui veille
Parmi tous les soldats d'un sou
Et l'oiseau charme mon oreille

Écoute il chante tendrement
Je ne sais pas sur quelle branche
Et partout il va me charmant
Nuit et jour semaine et dimanche

Mais que dire de cet oiseau
Que dire des métamorphoses
De l'âme en chant dans l'arbrisseau
Du cœur en ciel du ciel en roses

L'oiseau des soldats c'est l'amour
Et mon amour c'est une fille

A Bird Is Singing

A bird is singing I can't tell where
He is I think your soul that waits
Among all the twopenny soldiers
And the singing bird enchants my ear

Listen to him sing tenderly
I can't tell on what branch he sits
And everywhere he bewitches me
Day and night the whole week long

But what can I tell you about the bird
Or about the metamorphosis
Of the soul to a song in the shrubbery
Of the heart to sky or of sky to roses

The bird of all soldiers is love
And my love is a girl

La rose est moins parfaite et pour
Moi seul l'oiseau bleu s'égosille

Oiseau bleu comme le cœur bleu
De mon amour au cœur céleste
Ton chant si doux répète-le
A la mitrailleuse funeste

Qui claque à l'horizon et puis
Sont-ce les astres que l'on sème
Ainsi vont les jours et les nuits
Amour bleu comme est le cœur même

A rose is less perfect than she is
And to me alone does the bluebird call

Bird as blue as the blue heart
Of my love whose heart is heavenly
Warble that sweet song once more
To the deadly burst of machine-gun fire

Chattering on the horizon Say
Are those the stars someone is sowing
This is how days and nights flow by
Love as blue as the heart itself

Chevaux de Frise

Pendant le blanc et nocturne novembre
Alors que les arbres déchiquetés par l'artillerie
Vieillissaient encore sous la neige
Et semblaient à peine des chevaux de frise
Entourés de vagues de fils de fer
Mon cœur renaissait comme un arbre au printemps
Un arbre fruitier sur lequel s'épanouissent
Les fleurs de l'amour

Pendant le blanc et nocturne novembre
Tandis que chantaient épouvantablement les obus
Et que les fleurs mortes de la terre exhalaient
Leurs mortelles odeurs
Moi je décrivais tous les jours mon amour à Madeleine
La neige met de pâles fleurs sur les arbres
Et toisonne d'hermine les chevaux de frise
Que l'on voit partout
Abandonnés et sinistres

Chevaux-de-Frise

On those white November nights
When trees slashed by artillery
Were aging still under the snow
And seemed faintly like chevaux-de-frise
Drowned in waves of barbed wire
My heart revived like a tree in springtime
A fruit tree where love's flowers
Open

On those gray November nights and days
When bombshells sang horribly
And earth's dead flowers breathed forth
Their deadly odors
I described my love each day to Madeleine
Snow sticks pale flowers to the trees
It fleeces with ermine the chevaux-de-frise
You see them everywhere
Abandoned and sinister

Chevaux muets
Non chevaux barbes mais barbelés
Et je les anime tout soudain
En troupeau de jolis chevaux pies
Qui vont vers toi comme de blanches vagues
Sur la Méditerranée
Et t'apportent mon amour
Roselys ô panthère ô colombes étoile bleue
O Madeleine
Je t'aime avec délices
Si je songe à tes yeux je songe aux sources fraîches
Si je pense à ta bouche les roses m'apparaissent
Si je songe à tes seins le Paraclet descend
O double colombe de ta poitrine
Et vient délier ma langue de poète
Pour te redire
Je t'aime
Ton visage est un bouquet de fleurs
Aujourd'hui je te vois non Panthère
Mais Toutefleur
Et je te respire ô ma Toutefleur
Tous les lys montent en toi comme des cantiques d'amour et d'allégresse
Et ces chants qui s'envolent vers toi
M'emportent à ton côté
Dans ton bel Orient où les lys
Se changent en palmiers qui de leurs belles mains
Me font signe de venir
La fusée s'épanouit fleur nocturne
Quand il fait noir
Et elle retombe comme une pluie de larmes amoureuses
De larmes heureuses que la joie fait couler
Et je t'aime comme tu m'aimes
Madeleine

Mute horses
Not Barbary horses but barbed
And I change them suddenly
Into a herd of pretty piebald horses
They run toward you like white waves
On the Mediterranean
And bear my love to you
Roselily oh panther oh doves blue star
Oh Madeleine
I love you with delight
If I think of your eyes I think of cool springs
If I think of your mouth I see roses
If I dream of your breasts the Paraclete descends
Oh twofold dove of your breast
And comes to loosen my poet's tongue
To tell you again
I love you
Your face is a bouquet of flowers
Today I see you not as Panther
But Allflower
And I breathe you my Allflower
All your lilies rise in you like canticles of love and joy
And those songs winging toward you
Bear me to your side
Into your fair Orient where lilies
Change to palm trees with their lovely hands
They signal to me draw near
The rocket opens nocturnal flower
When it's dark
And scatters like a rain of amorous tears
Happy tears flowing for joy
And I love you as you love me
Madeleine

Chant de l'Honneur

LE POÈTE

Je me souviens ce soir de ce drame indien
Le Chariot d'Enfant un voleur y survient
Qui pense avant de faire un trou dans la muraille
Quelle forme il convient de donner à l'entaille
Afin que la beauté ne perde pas ses droits
Même au moment d'un crime
Et nous aurions je crois
A l'instant de périr nous poètes nous hommes
Un souci de même ordre à la guerre où nous sommes

Mais ici comme ailleurs je le sais la beauté
N'est la plupart du temps que la simplicité
Et combien j'en ai vu qui morts dans la tranchée
Étaient restés debout et la tête penchée
S'appuyant simplement contre le parapet

Honor's Hymn

THE POET

I remember tonight that Indian drama
The Boy's Chariot a thief arrives
Who considers before he cuts a hole in the wall
What shape to give to the notch
So that beauty will never lose her rights
Even at a moment of crime
                And I think we should show
At the instant of dying we poets we men
The same kind of concern in this war we are in

But in this I know as in all things beauty
Is mainly no more than simplicity
So many I have seen dead in the trenches
Who remained standing their heads bowed
Leaning simply against the parapet

J'en vis quatre une fois qu'un même obus frappait
Ils restèrent longtemps ainsi morts et très crânes
Avec l'aspect penché de quatre tours pisanes

Depuis dix jours au fond d'un couloir trop étroit
Dans les éboulements et la boue et le froid
Parmi la chair qui souffre et dans la pourriture
Anxieux nous gardons la route de Tahure

J'ai plus que les trois cœurs des poulpes pour souffrir
Vos cœurs sont tous en moi je sens chacque blessure
O mes soldats souffrants ô blessés à mourir

Cette nuit est si belle où la balle roucoule
Tout un fleuve d'obus sur nos têtes s'écoule
Parfois une fusée illumine la nuit
C'est une fleur qui s'ouvre et puis s'évanouit
La terre se lamente et comme une marée
Monte le flot chantant dans mon abri de craie
Séjour de l'insomnie incertaine maison
De l'Alerte la Mort et la Démangeaison

LA TRANCHÉE

O jeunes gens je m'offre à vous comme une épouse
Mon amour est puissant j'aime jusqu'à la mort
Tapie au fond du sol je vous guette jalouse
Et mon corps n'est en tout qu'un long baiser qui mord

LES BALLES

De nos ruches d'acier sortons à tire-d'aile
Abeilles le butin qui sanglant emmielle
Les doux rayons d'un jour qui toujours renouvelle
Provient de ce jardin exquis l'humanité
Aux fleurs d'intelligence à parfum de beauté

I once saw four hit by a single shell
Dead they still stood full of guts
With the leaning look of four Pisan towers

For ten days at the end of a skintight passage
In landslides and mud and cold
Among agonized or rotting flesh
Uneasily we guard the road to Tahure

I have more than an octopus's triple heart to suffer with
I contain your hearts within me I feel each wound
Oh suffering soldiers oh my soldiers wounded to death

This night is so beautiful where the bullet coos
A huge river of shells flows over our heads
At times a flare illuminates the night
It's a flower that opens and then disappears
The earth laments and like the tides
A singing wave rises to my chalk shelter
Abode of insomnia uncertain house
Of Alarms of Death and of Itchings

THE TRENCH

Young men I offer myself to you like a bride
My love is strong for I love until death
Squatting on the ground I watch you with envy
And my entire body is only one long biting kiss

THE BULLETS

From our steel hives let's fly swiftly
Bees the bloody booty that honeys
The gentle beams of an endless day
Comes from humanity's delicate garden
With its flowers of intelligence its perfume of beauty

LE POÈTE

Le Christ n'est donc venu qu'en vain parmi les hommes
Si des fleuves de sang limitent les royaumes
Et même de l'Amour on sait la cruauté
C'est pourquoi faut au moins penser à la Beauté
Seule chose ici-bas qui jamais n'est mauvaise
Elle porte cent noms dans la langue française
Grâce Vertu Courage Honneur et ce n'est là
Que la méme Beauté

LA FRANCE

Poète honore-la
Souci de la Beauté non souci de la Gloire
Mais la Perfection n'est-ce pas la Victoire

LE POÈTE

O poètes des temps à venir ô chanteurs
Je chante la beauté de toutes nos douleurs
J'en ai saisi des traits mais vous saurez bien mieux
Donner un sens sublime aux gestes glorieux
Et fixer la grandeur de ces trépas pieux

L'un qui détend son corps en jetant des grenades
L'autre ardent à tirer nourrit les fusillades
L'autre les bras ballants porte des seaux de vin
Et le prêtre-soldat dit le secret divin

J'interprète pour tous la douceur des trois notes
Que lance un loriot canon quand tu sanglotes

Qui donc saura jamais que de fois j'ai pleuré
Ma génération sur ton trépas sacré

Prends mes vers ô ma France Avenir Multitude
Chantez ce que je chante un chant pur le prélude

THE POET

Then vainly did Christ come among men
If rivers of blood border the kingdoms
And even Love as we know is cruel
That's why we must still consider Beauty
The one thing on earth which is never evil
She bears a hundred names in the French language
Grace Virtue Courage Honor and she's always
The same Beauty

FRANCE

Poet honor her
Have concern for Beauty not concern for Glory
And let Perfection be your Victory

THE POET

Poets of times to come you singers
I sing the beauty of all our sorrows
I've caught her likeness but you'll know far better
How to give sublime meanings to glorious actions
How to fix for eternity the grandeur of these pious deaths

One uncurling his body hurling grenades
Another eager to shoot feeds the gunfire
Another with arms swinging carries buckets of wine
And the chaplain pronounces the divine secret

I interpret for everyone the sweetness of those three notes
Flung by an oriole cannon when you are sobbing

Then who'll ever know how much I mourned
My generation's holy death

Take my poems France Future Multitude
Sing what I sing a pure song the prelude

Des chants sacrés que la beauté de notre temps
Saura vous inspirer plus purs plus éclatants
Que ceux que je m'efforce à moduler ce soir
En l'honneur de l'Honneur la beauté du Devoir

17 décembre 1915

Of those sacred songs the beauty of our age
Will inspire in you purer more brilliant
Than those I force myself to modulate tonight
In Honor's honor the beauty of what has to be done

December 17, 1915

Chef de Section

Ma bouche aura des ardeurs de géhenne
Ma bouche te sera un enfer de douceur et de séduction
Les anges de ma bouche trôneront dans ton cœur
Les soldats de ma bouche te prendront d'assaut
Les prêtres de ma bouche encenseront ta beauté
Ton âme s'agitera comme une région pendant un tremblement de terre
Tes yeux seront alors chargés de tout l'amour qui s'est amassé dans les regards de l'humanité depuis qu'elle existe
Ma bouche sera une armée contre toi une armée pleine de disparates
Variée comme un enchanteur qui sait varier ses métamorphoses
L'orchestre et les chœurs de ma bouche te diront mon amour
Elle te le murmure de loin
Tandis que les yeux fixés sur la montre j'attends la minute prescrite pour l'assaut

Platoon Commander

My mouth will have the ardors of Gehenna
My mouth will offer you a hell of sweetness and seduction
My mouth's angels will throne it in your heart
My mouth's soldiers will take you by assault
The priests of my mouth will cense your beauty
Your soul will tremble like land in an earthquake
Your eyes will be freighted with all the love that has gathered in men's eyes since the beginning
My mouth will be an army against you an incongruous jarring army
Protean like a magician who keeps changing his shape
The choirs and orchestra of my mouth will tell you my love
It murmurs to you now from far away
Meanwhile I stare at my watch and wait for the moment when we begin the assault

Tristesse d'une Étoile

Une belle Minerve est l'enfant de ma tête
Une étoile de sang me couronne à jamais
La raison est au fond et le ciel est au faîte
Du chef où dès longtemps Déesse tu t'armais

C'est pourquoi de mes maux ce n'était pas le pire
Ce trou presque mortel et qui s'est étoilé
Mais le secret malheur qui nourrit mon délire
Est bien plus grand qu'aucune âme ait jamais celé

Et je porte avec moi cette ardente souffrance
Comme le ver luisant tient son corps enflammé
Comme au cœur du soldat il palpite la France
Et comme au cœur du lys le pollen parfumé

Sorrow of a Star

A fair Minerva is the offspring of my skull
A star composed of blood crowns me forever
Reason lies low and heaven lies over my head
Where for so long Goddess you maintained your rule

And so it's not the sorest of my troubles
This near fatal wound which turned into a star
But the secret sorrow that nourishes my fever
Is greater than any soul could dissemble

And I transport this ardent suffering within me
As the glowworm transports his flaming body
As in the soldier's heart throbs his country France
And in the lily's heart the pollen's fragrance

La Victoire

Un coq chante je rêve et les feuillards agitent
Leurs feuilles qui ressemblent à de pauvres marins

Ailés et tournoyants comme Icare le faux
Des aveugles gesticulant comme des fourmis
Se miraient sous la pluie aux reflets du trottoir

Leurs rires amassés en grappes de raisin

Ne sors plus de chez mois diamant qui parlais
Dors doucement tu es chez toi tout t'appartient
Mon lit ma lampe et mon casque troué

Regards précieux saphirs taillés aux environs de Saint-Claude
Les jours étaient une pure émeraude

Je me souviens de toi ville des météores
Ils fleurissaient en l'air pendant ces nuits où rien ne dort
Jardins de la lumière où j'ai cueilli des bouquets

Victory

A cock is crowing I dream and branches wave
Their leaves resembling poor sailors

Winged and whirling like false Icarus
Blind men gestured like ants and
Admired their reflections on the rainy sidewalks

Their laughter lumped in grape clusters

Don't leave me again murmuring diamond
Sleep gently you are home everything here is yours
My bed my lamp and my helmet with a hole in it

Precious glances sapphires cut near Saint-Claude
    The days were a pure emerald

I remember you city of meteors
They flowered in the air among those sleepless nights
Gardens of light where I gathered nosegays

Tu dois en avoir assez de faire peur à ce ciel
Qu'il garde son hoquet

On imagine difficilement
A quel point le succès rend les gens stupides et tranquilles

A l'institut des jeunes aveugles on a demandé
N'avez-vous point de jeune aveugle ailé

O bouches l'homme est à la recherche d'un nouveau langage
Auquel le grammairien d'aucune langue n'aura rien à dire

Et ces vieilles langues sont tellement près de mourir
Que c'est vraiment par habitude et manque d'audace
Qu'on les fait encore servir à la poésie

Mais elles sont comme des malades sans volonté
Ma foi les gens s'habitueraient vite au mutisme
La mimique suffit bien au cinéma

Main entêtons-nous à parler
Remuons la langue
Lançons des postillons
On veut de nouveaux sons de nouveaux sons de nouveaux sons
On veut des consonnes sans voyelles
Des consonnes qui pètent sourdement
Imitez le son de la toupie
Laissez pétiller un son nasal et continu
Faites claquer votre langue
Servez-vous du bruit sourd de celui qui mange sans civilité
Le raclement aspiré du crachement ferait aussi une belle consonne

Les divers pets labiaux rendraient aussi vos discours claironnants
Habituez-vous à roter à volonté
Et quelle lettre grave comme un son de cloche
A travers nos mémoires
Nous n'aimons pas assez la joie
De voir les belles choses neuves
O mon amie hâte-toi

You must be tired of startling the sky
          Let it stifle its hiccup

It's hard to imagine
How stupid and stolid success can make people

     At the institute of blind young men they asked
     Haven't you a blind young man with wings

Oh mouths men are looking for a new language
One the grammarians can't label

For the old languages are so close to death
It's really from habit and cowardice
That we still use them for poetry

But they're like sick people they lack volition
My God we'd soon get used to muteness
Pantomime works well enough in the movies

     But let's insist on speaking
     Let's waggle our tongues
     Send out postilions
We want new sounds new sounds new sounds
We want consonants without vowels
Consonants that explode voiceless
     Imitate the sound of the spinning top
Bubble a sound that's nasal and prolonged
Click your tongue
Use the muffled noise of someone rudely munching
The breathy rasp of spitting would also make a fine consonant

Also the various labial farts would make your words blare
Get used to belching at will
And what letter cuts like the clang of a bell
     Across our memories
We don't love intensely enough the joy
Of seeing beautiful new things
Oh my dear make haste

Crains qu'un jour un train ne t'émeuve
Plus
Regarde-le plus vite pour toi
Ces chemins de fer qui circulent
Sortiront bientôt de la vie
Ils seront beaux et ridicules

Deux lampes brûlent devant moi
Comme deux femmes qui rient
Je courbe tristement la tête
Devant l'ardente moquerie
Ce rire se répand
Partout
Parlez avec les mains faites claquer vos doigts
Tapez-vous sur la joue comme sur un tambour
O paroles
Elles suivent dans la myrtaie
L'Éros et l'Antéros en larmes
Je suis le ciel de la cité

Écoutez la mer

La mer gémir au loin et crier toute seule
Ma voix fidèle comme l'ombre
Veut être enfin l'ombre de la vie
Veut être ô mer vivante infidèle comme toi

La mer qui a trahi des matelots sans nombre
Engloutit mes grands cris comme des dieux noyés
Et la mer au soleil ne supporte que l'ombre
Que jettent des oiseaux les ailes éployées

La parole est soudaine et c'est un Dieu qui tremble
Avance et soutiens-moi je regrette les mains
De ceux qui les tendaient et m'adoraient ensemble
Quelle oasis de bras m'accueillera demain
Connais-tu cette joie de voir des choses neuves

Be afraid that someday a train will no longer
Thrill you
Look at it faster for your own sake
These railroad trains that circulate
Will soon vanish from our lives
And become beautiful and ridiculous

Two lamps burn before me
Like two women laughing
I bow my head sadly
Before that ardent mockery
Their laughter spreads
Everywhere
Speak with your hands snap your fingers
Beat against your cheek as if it were a drum
Oh words
In the myrtle garden they follow
Eros and Anteros weeping
I am the sky of the city

Listen to the sea

The sea moaning far away and crying alone
My voice as faithful as a shadow
Wants finally to be life's shadow
Wants oh living sea to be faithless like you

The sea that has betrayed countless sailors
Engulfs my great cries like drowned gods
And the sea in the sun upholds only shadows
Flung by birds with wings outspread

The word is sudden and it's a God that trembles
Draw near and sustain me I regret the lifted hands
Of those who together adored me
What oasis of arms will welcome me tomorrow
Do you know the joy of seeing new things

O voix je parle le langage de la mer
Et dans le port la nuit les dernières tavernes
Moi qui suis plus têtu que non l'hydre de Lerne

La rue où nagent mes deux mains
Aux doigts subtils fouillant la ville
S'en va mais qui sait si demain
La rue devenait immobile
Qui sait où serait mon chemin

Songe que les chemins de fer
Seront démodés et abandonnés dans peu de temps
Regarde

La Victoire avant tout sera
De bien voir au loin
De tout voir
De près
Et que tout ait un nom nouveau

Oh voices I speak the language of the sea
And in the harbor the darkness the last taverns
I who am more headstrong than the Hydra of Lerna

The street where my two hands are swimming
With subtle fingers searching the town
Runs off but who knows if tomorrow
The street were to become motionless
Who knows where my road would lie

Consider that railroads
Will go out of fashion we'll abandon them in a little while
Look

The Victory above all will be
To see clearly at a distance
To see everything
Near at hand
And may all things bear a new name

La Jolie Rousse

Me voici devant tous un homme plein de sens
Connaissant la vie et de la mort ce qu'un vivant peut connaître
Ayant éprouvé les douleurs et les joies de l'amour
Ayant su quelquefois imposer ses idées
Connaissant plusieurs langages
Ayant pas mal voyagé
Ayant vu la guerre dans l'Artillerie et l'Infanterie
Blessé à la tête trépané sous le chloroforme
Ayant perdu ses meilleurs amis dans l'effroyable lutte
Je sais d'ancien et de nouveau autant qu'un homme seul pourrait des deux savoir
Et sans m'inquiéter aujourd'hui de cette guerre
Entre nous et pour nous mes amis
Je juge cette longue querelle de la tradition et de l'invention
De l'Ordre et de l'Aventure

Vous dont la bouche est faite à l'image de celle de Dieu
Bouche qui est l'ordre même

The Pretty Redhead

Here I am before you all a sensible man
Who knows life and what a living man can know of death
Having experienced love's sorrows and joys
Having sometimes known how to impose my ideas
Adept at several languages
Having traveled quite a bit
Having seen war in the Artillery and the Infantry
Wounded in the head trepanned under chloroform
Having lost my best friends in the frightful conflict
I know of old and new as much as one man can know of the two
And without worrying today about that war
Between us and for us my friends
I am here to judge the long debate between tradition and invention
　　　　Between Order and Adventure

You whose mouth is made in the image of God's
Mouth that is order itself
Be indulgent when you compare us

Soyez indulgents quand vous nous comparez
A ceux qui furent la perfection de l'ordre
Nous qui quêtons partout l'aventure

Nous ne sommes pas vos ennemis
Nous voulons vous donner de vastes et d'étranges domaines
Où le mystère en fleurs s'offre à qui veut le cueillir
Il y a là des feux nouveaux des couleurs jamais vues
Mille phantasmes impondérables
Auxquels il faut donner de la réalité
Nous voulons explorer la bonté contrée énorme où tout se tait
Il y a aussi le temps qu'on peut chasser ou faire revenir
Pitié pour nous qui combattons toujours aux frontières
De l'illimité et de l'avenir
Pitié pour nos erreurs pitié pour nos péchés

Voici que vient l'été la saison violente
Et ma jeunesse est morte ainsi que le printemps
O Soleil c'est le temps de la Raison ardente
Et j'attends
Pour la suivre toujours la forme noble et douce
Qu'elle prend afin que je l'aime seulement
Elle vient et m'attire ainsi qu'un fer l'aimant
Elle a l'aspect charmant
D'une adorable rousse

Ses cheveux sont d'or on dirait
Un bel éclair qui durerait
Ou ces flammes qui se pavanent
Dans les roses-thé qui se fanent

Mais riez riez de moi
Hommes de partout surtout gens d'ici
Car il y a tant de choses que je n'ose vous dire
Tant de choses que vous ne me laisseriez pas dire
Ayez pitié de moi

To those who were the perfection of order
We who look for adventure everywhere

We're not your enemies
We want to give you vast and strange domains
Where mystery in flower spreads out for those who would pluck it
There you may find new fires colors you have never seen before
A thousand imponderable phantasms
Still awaiting reality
We want to explore kindness enormous country where all is still
There is also time which can be banished or recalled
Pity us who fight always at the boundaries
Of infinity and the future
Pity our errors pity our sins

Now it's summer the violent season
And my youth is dead like the springtime
Oh Sun it's the time of ardent Reason
                                        And I am waiting
So I may follow always the noble and gentle shape
That she assumes so I will love her only
She draws near and lures me as a magnet does iron
            She has the charming appearance
            Of a darling redhead

Her hair is golden you'd say
A lovely flash of lightning that lingers on
Or the flame that glows
In fading tea roses

But laugh laugh at me
Men from everywhere especially men from here
For there are so many things I dare not tell you
So many things you would never let me say
Have pity on me

Commentary

Note: Works by Apollinaire referred to in the commentary are identified by the abbreviations listed in the first section of the bibliography.

Critical works listed in the bibliography are referred to by the name of the author or, when more than one work is listed, by the name of the author and the date.

Full references are given for works not listed in the bibliography, except that articles in *La Revue des Lettres Modernes,* Série Guillaume Apollinaire (Minard, 1962 to date), are referred to by the abbreviation *GA* followed by the volume number.

LIENS

First published in the avant-garde review *Montjoie* (April 1913).

The italic type suggests that the poem is a kind of preface making a general thematic statement, valid for the section "Ondes" if not for the whole volume, about the poet's dual allegiance to the modern world of "simultanist" consciousness on the one hand, and to the elegiac introspective stance of his earlier poetry on the other. When one remembers that *Montjoie* was one of the most aggressively avant-garde reviews, declaring itself "contre tout sentimentalisme dans l'art et la vie" [against all sentimentalism in art and life], it would appear that Apollinaire, by publishing in that journal, was deliberately distancing himself from the more strident modernism of his contemporaries.

A nice ambiguity attaches to the central metaphor of chains: while the shackles of the past have to be cast off (l. 6) the new links that symbolize the dynamic world of the future are joyfully accepted (ll. 8-17). The assault of the modern world on the senses is suggested through clamorous sound (l. 1) and complex visual patterns (ll. 8-17), while the urgent tempo of the new sensibility is reflected in the rhythm and the syntax, with its rapid sequences of phrases, many of them verbless. Apollinaire sometimes referred to this style as "telegraphic."

Lines 2-3. Suggest the simultaneity of both space and time in the modern world. Bells have been ringing for centuries and thus concentrate past time in themselves, as well as sounding out to one another over frontiers.

Line 12. Bridges between countries swarm with people of every tongue. The vertical made horizontal occurs also in "Les Fenêtres": "Les Tours ce sont les rues."

Line 13. *Pontifes* is here taken in the etymological sense of "bridge builder." Spiders by their creation of webs are therefore seen as symbolizing the creation of new links among peoples.

Line 14. A sexual image made more explicit in the "Onzième Poème Secret" (*Poèmes à Madeleine, OP*, p. 635), where the play on *Pontiffe* also occurs:

Je jetterai un pont entre toi et moi un pont de chair dure comme le fer un pont merveilleusement suspendu
Toi Architecte moi Pontiffe et créateur d'Humanité

[I will throw a bridge between us a bridge of hard flesh a marvelous suspension bridge
You the Architect I the Bridge Builder and creator of Humanity]

Lines 18-24. Although lines 18-23 seem to sum up the theme of the poem as a celebration of the bright new world of the senses, there is a sudden volte-face in the final line which dramatically qualifies the poet's attitude. Far from having turned his back on melancholy and elegiac introspection, he declares himself to be as deeply attached to them (and so to what *Montjoie* called sentimentalism) as to extrovert delight in the modern world. The real theme of the poem thus becomes one of divided sensibility, and the ambivalence of the metaphor that provides the title is reaffirmed. Although the poet himself presents the two sides of his personality as being in conflict, however, the judgment of the reader may be that they make for a complex and rewarding whole (see introduction, p. 1).

LES FENÊTRES, page 26

Published for the catalogue of a one-man Delaunay show in Berlin in January 1913 and, in the same month, in *Poème et Drame*, Vol. II. A corrected proof of the catalogue, exhibited at the Galerie Louis Carré, December 17, 1946-January 17, 1947 (and reproduced in Vriesen and Imdahl, p. 48), shows revisions not indicated in the Pléiade edition. The corrected proof is also reproduced in *Omaggio ad Apollinaire* (Rome: Editions Ente Premi Roma, 1962), pls. 4, 5.

According to André Billy, "Les Fenêtres" was a collaboration, at the Crucifix bar in the Rue Daunou, between Apollinaire, René Dalize, and himself (*Avec Apollinaire: Souvenirs inédits* [Paris and Geneva: La Palatine, 1966], p. 97); according to the Delaunays, as recounted by Robert Goffin (*Entrer en poésie* [Bruxelles, a l'enseigne du chat qui pêche; Paris, Poésie 48, 1948], p. 159), the poem was written in the artist's atelier and alludes to various objects in the studio, including the sea urchin and the yellow shoes. Adéma and Décaudin resolve these conflicting statements by concluding that the poem may have been sketched out at a café table as a group effort, then composed by Apollinaire at the Delaunays (*OP*, p. 1079). Whether its point of departure be scraps of café witticisms or an atelier backdrop, all such external matter is digested in the finished poem, which is an undoubted creation of the poet's. (This same point is made by Adéma, pp. 209-210). Indeed, it was one of Apollinaire's favorites, an example, in his own mind, of new poetic experiments "pour simplifier la syntaxe poétique" (*TS*, p. 48, quoted in *OP*, p. 1079).

For six weeks in November and December 1912, Apollinaire had been living with the Delaunays. In November *Les Soirées de Paris* published an article by him which consists mainly of quotations from the painter's conversation, notably his observations about complementary colors; that article in turn led to a German version, published in December in *Der Sturm*, with an introduction and a conclusion by the poet (Adéma, p. 210). A phrase in the conclusion is particularly significant: "La simultanéité, c'est la vie-même, et quelle que soit la succession d'éléments dans une œuvre elle mène à une fin inéluctable, la mort, tandis que le créateur ne connaît que l'éternité" [Simultaneity is life itself and whatever be the succession of elements in a work of art, that work leads to an inevitable ending, death, while the creator knows only eternity] (*OC*, IV, 279). The statement as a whole indicates Apollinaire's relationship to his friend's theories: he finds in them, or imposes on them, echoes of experiments in structure and of ideas about the artist's role which had been shaping his own poetry as far back as "La Chanson du Mal-Aimé" or even "Le Larron" (*Alcools*).

Collage, anonymous voices, fragmentation, juxtapositions between space and time, are not new in Apollinaire's work, but in "Les Fenêtres" we find these techniques pushed to an extreme and implicitly associated with the painter's theories on simultaneity. (Lockerbie has, in addition, pointed out parallels with Picasso's early cubism [*GA* 5, pp. 8-11].) More convincing, as an indication of Delaunay's relationship to the poem, may be the role of color words in lines 1 and 34; always chosen by Apollinaire for their rhythmic and emotional effects, they are, in the opening line of "Les Fenêtres," directly related to Delaunay's ideas about color and about nineteenth-century color theories (Greet. But see also Lockerbie, 1967).

"Les Fenêtres" seemingly depends almost entirely on external elements for an evocation of the world: objects, fragments of conversation, puns. The poet seems atypically absent from his own poem, except at the end when he shares in or takes over the painter's powers and the poem itself becomes a window opening onto new forms and colors. The notion that the poem derives exclusively from external stimuli, however, has not as yet been satisfactorily clarified. Lockerbie points out the poet's presence in the conscious arrangement of images and rhythmic effects (*ibid.*, pp. 11-18). In addition, some lines can be interpreted as memories with a private emotional resonance for the poet or as references to the art of poetry.

The title, for example, suggests both the function of a poem and the title of a series of paintings by Delaunay. From an evocation of color recalling those paintings (1) flutter images of birds, tropical, legendary (2-3), introducing the theme of the making of poetry, a melange of myth and modernism (4-5), a mixture also of external phenomena, memories, thoughts directed toward the present and future, in short, an Apollinairean world. Fragmented lines may evoke Delaunay's atelier or his art (1, 10-11, 17-19); the same and other lines may be interpreted as snatches of conversation overheard by the poet; and the role of place-names or of adjectives derived from place-names (8, 24-26), 31, 33, 35) clearly denotes an effort at literary simultaneity. It is, however, Apollinaire's own overwhelming reaction to a painter's work, and not that work as such, which dominates this poem as well as the other two major poems for painters in "Ondes"—"Un Fantôme de Nuées" and "A Travers l'Europe"—and, in each instance, contemplation of another's universe leads him back into his own. Here, the poem expresses a lyrical apprehension of space and time—and becomes a triumphant form of simultaneity.

Line 1. A poetic transformation of the kind of nineteenth-century color theory Delaunay attacked (discussed by Imdahl, in Vriesen and Imdahl, pp. 78-80). According to Eugène Delacroix and Michel-Eugène Chevreul, red and green are complementary colors, whereas red and yellow form a dissonance and should not be juxtaposed; thus, according to Chevreul's color wheel, yellow "dies" en route from red to green. The opening line has ironic overtones, since Delaunay's own theory of color simultaneity embraces any combination of colors in the spectrum (Greet). Despite these conceptual implications, colors float, mingle, dissolve melodiously on a plane far removed from the conflicts of painter-theorists.

Lines 2-7. The style of these lines, while not so rhythmic and sonorous as that of line 1, can hardly be called prosaic when one considers the role of phonemes in lines 2-3, the imagery in lines 2-5, the mysterious terminology of line 6, and its control over line 7. Line 2 offers an immediate appeal to faraway places, which later on becomes at once more dominant and more precise. The unspecified rain forest is, perhaps, in Brazil, since *ara* is the Brazilian word for "macaw." These large noisy birds provide an amusing link with the opening line, since they are bichrome; they come not only in blue and yellow, red and blue, but—significantly—in red and green. They are associated, in turn, with the pihis of lines 3-5. In "Zone," published a month earlier in *Alcools*, Apollinaire had included a couplet on the fabulous Chinese pihis who, yoked like Siamese twins, share one pair of wings; there they form part of a poetic flight of fancy. An association between a magical bird of some kind and telegrams emerges in calligraphic form in "Voyage" (*OP*, p. 199). In "Les Fenêtres" pihis are associated with poetry, with telegrams and telegraphic style, and they suggest also a gourmet's delight, perhaps "pihi pasty" (Apollinaire was a great gourmet), as well as the poet's more ethereal delight in surprising, elliptical juxtapositions of words and sounds and his disregard for the earnest reader who seeks a thread of continuity.

The first of several abrupt transitions (6-7) exemplifies that telegraphic style, already linked to poetry in lines 4-5, which, in his letter to Madeleine, he praises because it offers "des ressources auxquelles l'ellipse donnera une forme et une saveur merveilleusement lyrique" [resources to which ellipsis will give a wonderfully lyrical form and savor] (*TS*, p. 48). "Tramatisme géant" may be a disconnected observation like those that follow: someone with a physical eye disorder seen in the crowd of a big city. For J. Clark, *traumatisme* suggests the color red (p. 105), but the correct meaning of the word is that of a condition resulting from a trauma, that is, a shock, not an injury. One can say that the pihi, the telegram, the concept of a world linked by modern communications, a face glimpsed in a city crowd, is a source of shock, or that there is no source. In any event, most probably the poet is playing with language in action: the word itself, *traumatisme*, is traumatic; it appears elliptically and shocks the reader.

Lines 8-9. Two disconnected observations of a type familiar to readers of "Zone." The aesthetics of such details is expressed in "Souvenirs." *Turinaises* is the first of a number of references to places which finally will link the old world and the new, the poet's past to his present and future. Tenses become increasingly significant. At the beginning of the poem the future tense is implied in what is possibly a question (2) and suggests teeming possibilities of invention in the poet's brain (4-5). Line 8 might refer to either present or past but, in the context of line 9, it probably refers to the past. The use of the past, in line 9, is significant because it fuses two possibilities —a fragment of conversation and a fragment of memory.

Lines 10-13. The image of the window, here and at the end of the poem, evokes the series of window pictures by Delaunay, possibly one painting in particular. The use of the future (10), present (11), and imperfect (12) creates a sense of temporal simultaneity. Spatial simultaneity may be stressed by the ambiguous *tu*: if the opening window is comparable to the evolving poem, "you" who draw back the curtain can be at once poet and reader, as well as some unspecified "you" in the general scenery of memories, happenings, conversation. A variant in the corrected proof, "Araignées les mains," indicates clearly an image of *spider hands* spinning light and implies that from the hands themselves comes the light they spin. One thinks of an artist whose medium is paint rather than words. From the light created in line 12, the whole of line 13 seems to emerge. A variant in the catalogue, "Pâleur d'insondables" [Paleness *of* fathomless], opposes or equates beauty and paleness. In the final version, beauty, paleness, *and* color are in ambivalent apposition. Thus one sees how, when revising, Apollinaire tends toward ellipsis, mystification, discontinuity, through an increasing emphasis on juxtapositions per se.

Lines 14-16. Another interjection, in familiar language. The theme of time may have been triggered by the play on words in line 16. *Le Temps* and *La Liberté* were newspapers. Apollinaire playfully suggests that they were not clearly distinguishable from each other, although he was a contributor to *Le Temps*. The puns juxtapose journalistic and poetic effects: at once ephemeral, banal objects, limited by time and space, and abstract but very suggestive concepts, they may also comment on the underlying theme of artistic creation, if time in which to create is seen as a kind of freedom.

Line 17. Much has been written about this line. On one level it may conjure up objects in Delaunay's atelier, but its evocative power has other sources. There is a shimmering light effect that picks up similar effects elsewhere. The juxtaposition between suns and sea urchin creates primarily an impression of a sphere with rays emanating from it and whose yellow color is being eclipsed by blackness. *Lotte,* in *Poème et Drame,* was *les bottes,* "boots." According to the corrected proof, the word underwent a series of changes from *les bottes* to *les lottes* to *Lotte.* The dominant impression created by these changes is that Apollinaire wanted to avoid the image of boots (probably because of the shoes in l. 18) but that he liked the sound of the word. A secondary impression is that he was attracted by the possibility of adding to the unexpected assortment of marine life: gastropod, echinoderm, and, at last, a fish. Finally, to drop the definite article and capitalize all four nouns heightens the mystification by treating them as place-names —or absolute ideas. Clark refers to an ingenious theory that *Lotte* the "turbot" is sacred to the moon-goddess Tamis (p. 109). In this way he finds references to circles in all four images, and thus to Delaunay's *Formes circulaires* and his *Discs.* One might counter that *lotte* comes from *lota* which is also Hindu for a globular water jug and thereby circular (*Grand Larousse*). The only likely reference in this line to Delaunay's paintings, however, is *multiples Soleils* (some of the *Formes circulaires* were *Soleils*). The search for a secret rationale linking these images is in the symbolist tradition and thus runs counter to the aesthetic, based on ellipsis and surprise, which dominates the poem.

Lines 19-24. Line 19, probably inspired by one of Delaunay's Eiffel Tower paintings, is immediately given an "op" effect (see also Lockerbie, *GA* 5, p. 13) by the translation of vertical into horizontal. In the same way the three-dimensional *puits* "wells" are transposed into two-dimensional *places* "city squares" and then back to three-dimensional "hollow trees." This double vision, recurrent in Apollinnaire's poetry, is particularly evident in poems inspired by paintings and is usually accompanied by a double use of language (see note to "Un Fantôme de Nuées"). Here, the pun on *puits/puis* "wells/then" links a point in space to a point in time and emphasizes visual impressions and a neutral tone of voice. By contrast the same pun, ten years earlier, in "La Tsigane," has an effect of lyricism and condensed ambiguities.

Lines 24-26. *Câpresses, Chabins, Chabines* are terms used in the Antilles (mentioned in l. 35) to describe the descendants of mixed marriages between Negroes and mulattoes (Pascal Pia, "Apollinaire aux Antibes," *Quo Vadis* [July-September 1954]). Just as towers and wells suggest hollow trees, so the *Câpresses* suggest lines 25-26, as though they were an afterthought of the poet's. There is a verbal play on *Chabins* and *le chabanais,* "noise" or "racket." *Des airs à mourir* is a phrase containing several plays on words. The *Chabins* sing, literally, "killing" songs, or sing one "to death." There is a play too on *mourir,* taken in the sense of *mourir d'amour* "to be dying of love"; that expression, which has obvious sexual overtones, in its literal sense suggests a violent love among exotic peoples.

Line 27. Apollinaire delights in onomatopoeia, both in *Alcools* where the cries of birds and animals are heard, and in *Calligrammes*, where the principal sounds are those of war. Here, *l'oie* "goose" becomes the trumpeting cry of geese on their way northward and evokes enormous mysterious migrations.

Line 30. This line has caused much comment. An image of faceted surfaces is seen simultaneously as reflecting light and also providing at least an illusion of depths. Not only is it associated with poem, poet, the globe itself, as well as the city lights of Vancouver and the glitter of the hurrying train, but it is nourished by the northern snows and crystalline snowflakes implicit in the preceding passage.

Lines 31-32. Apollinaire's modernism differs from that of his futurist friends by its lyricism. Trains always fascinated him. Here the image of the train emphasizes the flight of time. In the corrected proof a variant reads: "Où le train blanc de neige et doré de feux nocturnes a fui pendant l'hiver." The phrase "gilded with night lights" emphasizes the lit windows and shower of sparks from the locomotive, while the past tense and the phrase "during the winter" situate the train in time. In the final version the night lights are less localized and can refer more freely to moon and stars; the action, too, is liberated by its transformation to the present tense and by winter's personification as a huge pursuing force.

Lines 31-34. The switch from a Canadian city to Paris accentuates a parallel between the train fleeing winter and the fading out of the color yellow. And this fading of yellow may be related to the setting sun. Thus line 34 has more dynamic associations than when it first appeared as line 1. The refrain that changes meaning with its context is a favorite technique of Apollinaire's.

Line 35. This line was written in, on the corrected proof, with the third city as Lyons, not Hyères. The list of modern cities (ending with the exotic Antilles which brings us back to the songful *Chabins*) stresses simultaneity of place. The place-names are spread out over two continents and, by implication, the world. In the final version the list evokes once more the ephemeral by the puns *Hyères/hier* "yesterday," and *Maintenon/maintenant* "now," although one can say too that the worldplay stresses a temporal simultaneity prepared by the changing tenses of the poem. The original austere modernism of line 35 is softened by the puns, so that, like the image of the trains, it gains in lyrical effect. Apollinaire's poems inspired by the war were to reveal an increasing transformation of modern objects into poetically charged material.

Lines 36-37. Delaunay's own observation that color is the fruit of light (Vriesen, in Vriesen and Imdahl, p. 41), transmuted in the poem or perhaps originating in it (that is, Delaunay may have picked up the metaphor from

Apollinaire), becomes a comment on both painting and poetry and a final focusing on the present moment. Apollinaire seemingly resolves conflicting color theories by offering Delaunay and us an orange: it harmonizes with both red and yellow and it embodies light, an element essential to painters and poets. On a deeper level the whole poem, with its colors, its noises and voices, its far-flung lands, leads, in the last lines, to an intensely lyrical invocation of the poem—perhaps also of a painting—as a window opening onto life.

References

Clark, J. G. "Delaunay, Apollinaire et 'Les Fenêtres,'" *GA* 7, pp. 100-111.

Greet, A. H. "Rotsoge: A travers Chagall," In *Apollinaire et la peinture.* 8th Apollinaire Colloquium. Stavelot, 1975. In press.

Linkhorn, R. "'Les Fenêtres': Propos sur trois poèmes," *French Review,* XLIV, 3 (February 1971), 513-522.

Lockerbie, S. I. "Le Rôle de l'imagination dans *Calligrammes.* Première partie: 'Les Fenêtres' et le poème créé," *GA* 5, pp. 6-22.

———. "Qu'est-ce que l'Orphisme d'Apollinaire?" In *Apollinaire et la Musique.* Les Amis d'Apollinaire. Stavelot, 1967.

Vriesen, G., and M. Imdahl. *Robert Delaunay: Light and Color.* New York: Abrams, 1967.

Zurowski, M. "'Les Fenêtres' d'Apollinaire," *Kwartalnik Neofilologizny,* 6 (1959), 17-21.

PAYSAGE, page 30

First published in *Les Soirées de Paris* (July-August 1914) under the title "Paysage Animé," along with "Voyage," "Cœur Couronne et Miroir," and "La Cravate et la Montre." All four poems illustrate the deliberate return to a more figurative and rhythmical type of picture poem, following the appearance of Arbouin's article (see n. 5 to introduction).

Apollinaire had plans to publish these four poems, together with "Lettre-Océan," in mid-1914 under the title "Et Moi Aussi Je Suis Peintre," but the outbreak of the war frustrated his intention. At that stage the poems were still called *idéogrammes lyriques.* Possibly the term was dropped because, even with the addition of *lyriques,* it suggested too strongly the communication of ideas rather than of emotion: this was precisely the criticism leveled at "Lettre-Océan" in Arbouin's article. The term *calligrammes* suggests a more spontaneous and free-flowing procedure of composition, closer to instinctive emotion (cf. the use of *calligraphie* in "L'Inscription Anglaise").

It could refer also to the calligraphic pleasure the poet experienced in making them, although only a few were maintained in their original manuscript form in the published volume.

A satisfactory reading of "Paysage," as of all the calligrams, has to see the poem as an integrated whole rather than as a succession of separate entities. The main difficulty here lies in the ambiguity of the shape beginning *amants couchés ensemble*. . . . As graphic form this particular design might suggest a single human figure, either standing with arms outstretched or lying on the ground spread-eagled. The text, on the other hand, speaks of lovers lying together, but if the word *membres* is taken to be grammatically in apposition to *amants* (the most likely construction in French), the further implication is that the lovers are the poet's own limbs and that they will be separated. Some critics have understood this to be an allusion to the failure of love, visualized in the poet's own body, and thus see the shape as the poet himself lying disconsolately on the ground—possibly even dead. The most logical reading of the poem, in this case, would be to begin with the house and proceed in a clockwise direction to end with the spread-eagled shape. The theme would clearly be the loss or death of love, which casts a shadow over a landscape that is shown in the other texts to be full of birth and promise. The use of a landscape setting to express, by contrast, the personal distress of the poet has many other parallels in Apollinaire's poetry, not least in "Voyage," composed at exactly the same time.

But it seems equally possible to interpret the same graphic form in a different way and visualize the poet as disentangling himself from his lover, then rising to salute the surrounding landscape, rejuvenated by love. In this case it would be natural to read the poem from the bottom of the page up. The theme would rather be the projection of love as a force that emanates from the lovers and spreads through the landscape, making everything come to fruition in an almost magical operation (hence perhaps the original title). In this interpretation the graphic shape would form a double visual image—almost like a slow dissolve in a film sequence—picturing first the lovers on the ground and then the poet standing with upraised arms. It is interesting to note, as far as the latter shape is concerned, that in the poem "Les Profondeurs" (*OP*, p. 607) Apollinaire drew two similar figures with arms raised to express aspiration toward the future. Equally relevant is the fact that, in *Calligrammes* generally, rising smoke is identified with reverie and aspiration (see "Fumées" and "L'Inscription Anglaise" where the smoke of a cigar is specifically mentioned). The cigar and its smoke could thus be seen as an entirely appropriate linking device between the poet or the lovers and the landscape symbols at the top of the page (Lockerbie, 1977).

Other interpretations are possible and do not necessarily depend on reading the images in a fixed sequence. Even in a freer reading the designs interrelate both graphically and verbally, pointing to greater complexity and subtlety of feeling than might be immediately apparent. Scrutiny reveals many other detailed felicities: the simple but evocative verbal text, the pleasing diversity of shape among the four designs, the elegant lettering of the house (where the use of the question mark for smoke may be an unconscious recall of a Dufy illustration for one of Apollinaire's own poems, "La Sauterelle" in *Le Bestiaire*, *OP*, p. 19). Not least, the breakup of words into syllables in the design of the house gives fresh impact to the new combinations, increasing the amount of wordplay and verbal echoes that come into the reading.

References

Boisson, M. "Les auto-portraits d'Apollinaire." In *Lecture et interprétation des Calligrammes.* 9th Apollinaire Colloquium. Stavelot, 1977. In press.

Lockerbie, S. I. "Forme graphique et expressivité dans les *Calligrammes.*" In *ibid.*

Tournadre, C. "'Ondes' ou la musique des formes." In *ibid.*

LES COLLINES, page 32

First appeared in *Calligrammes.* For long "Les Collines" was assigned a prewar date, in spite of Scott Bates's intuition in his pioneer essay that the poem was written after Apollinaire's military experience. It was shown to have been written 1916-1918, according to manuscript evidence, by M. Poupon (*GA* 6, pp. 121-123).

The manuscript at the Bibliothèque Littéraire Jacques Doucet is a collage of stanzas written in different inks on pieces of paper and then pasted onto the page. Some of the glued papers correspond in appearance. Several stanzas are written on the page itself. The glued paper resembles the graph-type paper found in French notebooks and indicates that the poet kept a small notebook by him, as he had done in the past, in which to jot down verses.

The variations in ink and paper indicate that the poem was composed over a period of time. These variations include the following: purple ink on brown paper and green paper; black ink on brown paper, white paper, green paper, the page itself; brown ink on the page itself. Stanzas written on the page rather than on glued notepaper would seem later in date and thus establish a way of tracing the evolution of the poem, by the color of ink, but this is one of a number of false clues. For although there are some corrections of purple ink in a more recent black ink, one scrap of brown paper containing two stanzas begins in black ink and changes to purple, while the title of the poem is written firmly in purple ink. What the manuscript does reveal clearly is that the strata of words, lines, entire stanzas, jotted down in different inks on an assortment of papers, are of primary importance in accounting for various changes of theme, mood, point of view, for the mixture of times evident even in stanza 1, and for the poem's role as a microcosmic poetic diary reflecting the narrative quality of the entire book.

The appearance of the manuscript suggests that at first the poem arranged itself in groups of stanzas, and that the overall structure of those groups came last to the poet's mind (but see M. Davis, 1973, p. 159). Some definite groups include stanzas 1-3; 4-7 and 8-11 (these two groups probably together); 22-23; 25-27; 29-31 and 32-35 and 36-39 (these three groups probably together); 40-43; 44-45. In the same way there appear to be definite breaks or pauses in the composition of the poem between stanzas 3 and 4, 13 and 14, 24 and 25, 27 and 28, 39 and 40, 43 and 44. It seems evident, as Adéma observed (in conversation, 1977), that the manuscript's composition was piecemeal and prolonged. This type of composition is seen frequently in Apollinaire's poems, although never so complexly as here, except perhaps in the play *Les Mamelles de Tirésias.* But whereas *Tirésias* may have taken shape over many years, the time lapse for "Les Collines" is much less, perhaps two years.

If the poem was written after Apollinaire's return from the front, why is it placed in "Ondes"? In *Alcools,* Apollinaire's latest poem "Zone" serves as preface; but *Alcools* makes no claim to a chronological presentation. *Calligrammes,* on the other hand, may be read as a notebook of the poet's before, during, and after the war. "Les Collines," in its place as the fourth poem, is structurally significant; it provides a bridge from the poet's delight in his new spontaneity, expressed in "Ondes," to the grave tone of the last two poems, "La Victoire" and "La Jolie Rousse," where a principal theme is the poet's assumption of a new identity in that modern world which is about to emerge from World War I. (See also Bates, pp. 38-39.)

"Les Collines" has been interpreted as a kind of experimental public prophecy. For Bates it has a Promethean tone. There can be noted throughout, however, as S. I. Lockerbie points out (pp. 88-89), a conflict between the compulsion to play a Hugolian role and the need for a personal, somewhat plaintive, lyricism. "Les Collines" may be associated not only with Baudelaire's "Les Phares" and the idea that artists, poets, and musicians have prophetic powers, but also with *Vitam Impendere Amori* (1917) and even certain of Chagall's paintings (*OP*, p. 1080). Futurist objects, echoes of the war, and, above all, nostalgia for the poet's lost youth are as dominant as the theme of the poet's role in the modern world. Lockerbie demonstrates that, in spite of intellectual preoccupations which find their parallel in "L'Esprit Nouveau et les Poètes" and other critical writings, "Les Collines" remains, because of its tone, imagery, and fundamental structure, one of the finest examples of the *poème-promenade* or *poème-méditation.* The structure and the contrasting themes possess aesthetic implications; like those of "La Chanson du Mal-Aimé" (*Alcools*) or of "Zone," they indicate the continued, if submerged and transformed, appeal of symbolism for Apollinaire and, at the same time, growing preoccupation with a spiritual quest. Perhaps most interesting to the modern reader is the fusion of that quest with personal anxieties.

Stanzas 1-3. In this enigmatic opening scene of conflict and confrontations, the poet seems, at first, practically absent and the airplanes, originally, were empty: "deux avions vides" [two empty airplanes] (ms. Doucet). The dehumanized aeronautical combat above Paris (1-2) places the beginning of the poem at the time of World War I.

The Stendhalian colors, red and black, may refer to spiritual conflicts, manifest in early poems like "Le Larron" (*Alcools*), dominant in the prewar "Zone," and, to some extent, resolved during the war, when Apollinaire resumed attendance at mass (see *LL* and *TS*). Like the image of the Christ-plane in "Zone," these airplanes may also be a reminiscence of medieval Rhenish paintings. The solar plane of line 5, flaming eternally like the phoenix, is distinct from the two temporal airplanes. For J. Burgos, the solar plane is the poet (see note to stanza 20). For J. Levaillant, it represents the heights of space, as death or the unconscious represents the depths; in between, the poet, like Icarus, pursues an erratic course of ascents and plunges (*GA* 8, p. 52). For Levaillant, the spaces of the poem intermingle the objective and the subjective. For Lockerbie, it is more a question of time and space, while the motif of the poet's wandering reflects his yearning to be everywhere at once, a state he may reach only after periods of hesitation, doubt, and suffering (p. 89).

One does not know, for certain, which airplane is red or black in line 3 and which is compared to Lucifer or the archangel (9-10). But past and future, Order and Adventure, damnation and salvation, are suggested in an antithetical manner by the two: they relate the poet's own situation to that of the cosmos with typical Apollinairean immodesty. Particular and universal confrontations between *ma jeunesse* "my youth" and *l'avenir* "the future" (6-7) juxtapose a tone of personal nostalgia, which dominates many of the poems in *Alcools*, and the prophetic voice of the grandstand poet. Poetry as prophecy fascinated Apollinaire, beginning around 1908, and was probably inspired by Picasso's experiments at that time. The public tone of voice emerged later, during the war.

The lack of alignment in stanzas 1 and 2 between the two airplanes and what they represent sets up, in the third stanza, a new series of confrontations which are not parallel, although the terminology of line 11 and the repeated *Ainsi* appeal to our sense of logic. The confrontation may be seen as expressionist, in that the images express a state of mind without naming or symbolizing it. (For the possibility of Apollinaire's exposure to German expressionism, see note to "A Travers l'Europe.") Ambiguity results from a continual shift in focus as well as uncertainty of reference. In the lines, "ce que j'aime/Mon amour" (13-14), an old vein of personal lyricism—past loves as a source of poetic nourishment—seems attacked by what the poet sees as the future of poetry, that is, his present passion for prophetic poetry. One of Apollinaire's unexpected likenesses to Valéry is seen in the image of the tree that is given a voice by the same wind that destroys it (14-15).

Stanzas 4-5. The first of a continual series of breaks or shifts in thought which give the poem the air of a soliloquy interrupted by outer reality or irrational trains of thought. We seem, suddenly and briefly, to emerge into the present: it is early morning in Paris (an unusual hour for a nocturnal poet but perhaps indicative of habits learned as a soldier); *douceur* "sweetness" suggests the springtime. Paris singing her song, in line 20, contrasts with the shrieking tree of line 15. The song itself introduces stanza 5 which seemingly begins with a nostalgic question (21), answered with a visionary's faith in future glory (22). *Jeunesse* and *avenir*, however, recall the image of the fighter planes—one has fallen, the other flames (an ambiguous description: if a plane, it may be shot down; if the future, it may flame in glory). In line 22, as in the second person singular of the imperative *vois* (16), it is not clear to whom *tu* refers; the poet may well be addressing himself. The musical flow of line 21, undermined by ambiguities and the notion of a Pyrrhic victory, is interrupted also by syntactical devices in lines 22-23. After the airplane of the future downs the poet's youth (and perhaps is downed in turn), his public voice takes over (23-25) and introduces the following section.

Stanzas 6-12. In praise of great men and of an era of promise which Apollinaire sees as imminent. The heroes of modern times include scientists and poet-prophets. Or (see introduction, p. 1) Apollinaire is urging the latter to make themselves worthy of inclusion among "the hills." In any event, he stresses the likeness between scientific discovery and poetic invention, finding in them a common creative source, as do more recent thinkers. The image of prophets as high hills, elaborated in lines 26-30, is reminiscent of Baudelaire's "Les Phares." Interesting is the Apollinairean juxtaposition between future and past; compare *Alcools*, where, in "Cortège," almost the opposite statement is made: "Près du passé luisant demain est incolore" [Near the shining past tomorrow is colorless].

The Psylli of lines 33-35 were, according to Herodotus, an ancient race of snake charmers in Libya who vainly with their magic fought the south wind which was drying up their wells (Bates, 1967). The poet conceivably compares himself to the magicians of the Psylli and their inevitable fate: he, in contrast, is an "Ornement" limited by time and space, but enduring through his poetic art (but see M. Davies, 1973, p. 160). Line 32 echoes a paradoxical notion of time, or of the human being within time who simultaneously passes by and endures, which has already been expressed in *Alcools*, notably in two poems of 1912, "Cors de Chasse"—"Passons passons puisque tout passe / Je me retournerai souvent" [Let us pass on since everything passes / But I shall often turn again]—and "Le Point Mirabeau"—"Les jours s'en vont je demeure" [Time draws in I remain]. Or one can say that in *Alcools* the past seems irrevocable, but in a sense the poet achieves victory over it, whereas here in stanza 7 of "Les Collines" a feeling that the human spirit will still prevail introduces the glimpse of a machinelike age offered in the following stanza.

Parallel syntactically to this invocation of the past is the heralding, in stanza 8, of a possibly menacing future. The notion of machines becoming men or mastering the world of men (36-37) recalls the science fiction of Wells or Kapec. The nonhuman landscape of jewels and gold (38-39) is reminiscent of Baudelaire's "Rêve parisien" or Mallarmé's "Hérodiade." A metallic sea will give birth to new forms of life and a new Aphrodite, a process of dehumanization like that envisioned in "Le Brasier"; or, after a mechanized age, the sea will, once more, mother familiar forms of life including man.

In spite of the human vulnerability intimated in stanzas 7 and 8 (by the vanished Psylli and the threatening robots), the opening of stanza 9 celebrates man as the most evolved in earth's great chain of being, a theme common to Apollinaire and to Valéry. The image of man flying higher than the eagles reminds one of Apollinaire's hero, Icarus; as in "Zone," Icarus suggests the triumph of human inventiveness and, as in "La Victoire," the threat of an Icarian plunge (44). Like Ixion in *Alcools*, and perhaps replacing him in the poet's mythology, Icarus is a persona of the creator. The ambiguity surrounding his achievement and his fate is prolonged throughout the stanza which refers not only to man's soaring flight but to a possible downfall. Line 42, "C'est lui qui fait la joie des mers" [It's he who makes the seas exult], has at least two interpretations. One is stressed by an association between the phonemes in *mers* "seas" and *mère* "mother" (40), which underlines ancient and modern ideas of the ocean as the source of life. Thus man is the ocean's crowning achievement. More subtly, human consciousness creates or enlivens what it sees. The latter notion is not unlike Valéry's description of himself as "Tout entouré de mon regard marin" [Surrounded by my sea gaze]. "The shadow and the dizzy spleens," which man dissipates in his moment of glory (43-44), remain a part of him, a bridge between (lucid) "Mind" and (poetic) "dream" (45), and, as implied by the adjective *vertigineux*, a possible source of downfall. This passage is comparable to

Valéry's evocations of the unconscious in "Le Cimetière marin." Even the antithetic positioning of *l'esprit* and *le songe*, "mind" and "dream," is like Valéry (one may think of M. Teste and Mme Emilie). Although *ombre* (44) may, in context, suggest the unconscious or some other inward source of dreams, and even mortality, it suggests also a play on meanings: when an object flies upward, or when it falls into the water, its shadow vanishes.

The theme of human consciousness as prime creative source, which first emerges unambiguously in stanza 9, dominates the two subsequent stanzas. That age of magic heralded in stanza 10 seems closely related to an era of scientific progress which Apollinaire sees as resulting from World War I. The *prodiges* (48) are inventions, poetic as well as scientific, so new that they have not been anticipated by poets or philosophers. The word *fable* (49) is used in the same sense, in "L'Esprit Nouveau et les Poètes," when, comparing the myth of Icarus to the invention of the airplane, Apollinaire observes: "la fable précède la réalité" [myth precedes reality] (see also Bates, p. 37).

Consciousness and its different levels are finally described in precise terms (51). The whole of stanza 11, in fact, recalls once again Valéry ("Aurore"). There is a seemingly explicit reference to Freud (compare L. C. Breunig's discussion of Apollinaire's possible contact with Freud's ideas, *GA* 7, pp. 213-215) and a possible anticipation of Breton's early theories. There are, at the same time, implicit parallels with the essay "L'Esprit Nouveau": the notion of psychological research, the desire that poets and scientists participate in the new spirit, and two ideas fundamental to Apollinaire's aesthetics: that all reality is grist to the poetic mill and that the greatest surprise lurks in a future that lies within us. If the concept of a layered consciousness seems related to Freud, to surrealism, and to Apollinaire's own prose writings of 1917, the image of consciousness as a container of peopled landscapes seems shaped by memories of Mallarmé, Verlaine, and Laforgue.

Stanza 12, separate in the manuscript from the preceding stanzas, functions as a transition or résumé and was probably composed later as a conclusion to this section. The hills or prophets are compared to *savants* "scientists," with the reservation that the former will know the precise things the latter think they know. Apollinaire may compare the knowledge of observable phenomena and laboratory techniques with prophecy and the poetic technique of surprise. At the hands of the poet-prophet, surprise (especially the unexpected juxtaposition of images) might well transport us everywhere, by jolting us out of accustomed ways of thinking; in that sense, the prophecy or vision communicated by surprise would conquer both space and time. This notion, expanded in stanzas 37-42, anticipates the emphasis that Breton places on surprise, in his 1924 Manifesto.

Stanzas 13-15. These stanzas mark one of the abrupt changes that characterize "Les Collines." The concept of desire as man's principal motive power (61), however, seems an aspect of Freudian thought and a development of themes in the preceding section. Insofar as love of a woman inspires the poet to a vision beyond love, Apollinaire joins, once more, his painter friend Chagall. The vocabulary in stanza 13 is related to that of "La Jolie Rousse" (*légère, flamme,* in l. 63) and also to that of the visionary poems of 1908, "Le Brasier" and "Les Fiançailles" (*ardeur, éclait,* in l. 65), while *ardeur* functions as an ambivalent key word in the war poems. Through this mixture of associations, lines 63-65 present an image of present liberation, associated, in typical Apollinairean manner, with exorcised sorrows of the past. Stanzas 13 and 14 comment on a notion implicit in the 1908 poems, which evolves in the war poems and becomes a key theme here and in "La Jolie Rousse," that suffering ennobles both the poet and his poetry. The word "suffering" is used in a special sense, as are "willpower" and "desire." We tend to associate desire with the unconscious, willpower with consciousness. Apollinaire not only states, in stanza 15, that the latter, *sa volonté* (l. 73), has unexpected energies but his description of energy, *quelle force* (l. 74), explicitly links willpower to *la grand force* which, in stanza 13, he identifies as desire. In fact, both what Apollinaire calls suffering and what he calls willpower are inextricably linked to his notions of desire and of human consciousness.

Stanzas 16-19. Another abrupt change or new beginning, which Davies attributes to the "cyclical" structure of the poem (1973, p. 161). There may be an association of ideas between the theme of human consciousness and the image of helpful ghosts (76), but there is a marked shift from a general concern with humanity to the assertion of one man's poetic identity. Stanzas 16 and 17 are drenched in memories of Apollinaire's own poems. There are echoes from *Alcools,* particularly from poems of the Rhenish period. Ghosts mingle with the living in "La Maison des Morts"; time and the generations of men are like a circle in "Les Colchiques." The ring as a circle of time or infinity, and the association of circular time with ghosts, are reminiscent once more of "La Maison." In "Les Collines," the syntax would indicate that, because of spirits from the otherworld (the Latin word *manes* is significant, denoting chthonian gods as well as ancestral spirits and individual souls), nothing begins or ends; ghosts of the past, and perhaps of the future, haunt the poet. Stanza 16 builds up to an effect already existent in "Zone": the destruction of a sense of time, particularly of time past, followed by a visual image, at once object of meditation and symbol of time and space, which centers on the present. And indeed, in contrast with the atmosphere of the past, veiled by the present tenses of stanza 16, present and future seem evoked in stanza 17. The landscape of lines 81-82 evokes at once paintings (Chirico's city squares or Delaunay's windows) and Apollinaire's own verse (the crossroads of an early poem from *Alcools*, "Merlin et la vieille Femme," or the city landscape of "La Victoire" and that poem's desolate atmosphere of war). Lines 81-82 provide also a backdrop for the poet's entrance as a magician who, like the harlequin in "Crépuscule" (*Alcools*) or the acrobats in "Un Fantôme de Nuées," may be inspired by creations of the early Picasso. Again reminiscent of Picasso, in his role as *homo ludens*, is the phrase *faire des tours* "to play tricks," which describes art as a game. A more fanciful reading "to make towers" (the verbal play may well have triggered or been triggered by the preceding *carrefours* and *places*) refers probably to Delaunay once more and to Apollinaire's highly contrived poems about him. Thus the poet, against a background of his painters, plays out his own part, magical like theirs, and ambiguous also. For, necessary to his performance is a "dead" talisman. Is this mysterious image a mystification appropriate to a magician? Or is it a reference to the ring on his finger, to his friendship with Picasso (see note to stanzas 30-31), to the scar left by his wound and all that it represents for him, to that poetic identity that takes on character in the two stanzas that follow?

Jacqueline, Apollinaire's widow, chose stanzas 18 and 19 to be engraved on his tombstone. Almost at once, in line 88, not only the poet's future death is invoked but his present purification, a state linked to a mysterious past experience (ll. 89-90) which seems the concrete expression of a mystical vision. One may also interpret lines 89-90 as the words of a survivor of trench warfare and brain surgery who attempts to communicate his experience of life and death to noninitiates. Increasingly (ll. 91-95) a mixture of concrete and abstract verbs exteriorizes the poet's inner life. Also something like a progress in perception is indicated by the verbs: the touching or feeling as of a blind man (cf. the blind and winged poet of "La Victoire"), the exploring (*j'ai scruté*) which is also a kind of seeing, and, finally, the weighing—these unassertive verbs paradoxically assert the poet's claim to authority. They indicate different aspects or levels of insight or vision and also suggest that the poet as carpenter, potter, craftsman, is working with his hands to shape his poem so that he may face death with equanimity.

Stanzas 20-23. The theme of the poet as visionary leads to a renunciation of his past. In stanza 20, liberated from worldly considerations, he flies like Icarus, like an airplane, a Chagallian figure, or, according to J. Burgos, an eagle (*GA* 8, p. 158), which the latter identifies with "l'éternel avion solaire" of stanza 1. The sudden familiar style that emerges in line 97 is ambiguous: farewell, life and ghostly encounters; or, and more probably, farewell, poetry of youth with its talk of ghosts and wonders. Lines 99-100 may express a new awareness of Apollinaire's autobiographical poetry as a means of playing out his emotions. What seems a renunciation of past poetic techniques is based, curiously but typically, on a *dédoublement*, itself an old Apollinairean technique which he does not renounce.

The farewell to youth becomes an explicit refrain in stanzas 21-22. There is a flavor of *Vitam Impendere Amori* ("O ma jeunesse abandonnée") and, significantly, in line 101, an echo of *Alcools:* "jasmin du temps" recalls "Odeur du temps brin de bruyère" [Fragrance of time spray of heather] ("L'Adieu"). Quotation of his own works is a way of evoking the past and an old habit with Apollinaire. The technique of naming what one rejects (learned perhaps from Lucretius or Cicero) continues with a parade of memories. After the earliest, that of Rome at carnival time, the memories fuse. Stanza 23 may prolong the description of the Mediterranean; however, childhood in Monte Carlo, and (perhaps) the Lenten burning of the King of Fools over the water, may, instead, dissolve cinematically into scenes from the year he spent in the Rhineland: snowy skies, pine forests, white branches like cherubim wings, Christmas trees, his love for Annie Playden. The memories are linked to celestial imagery and perhaps to a feeling of flying as the artist's way of expressing universal harmony which could have its source in more recent memories of Chagall's paintings. Indeed, by the time one reaches the end of stanza 23 it is a little hard to know whether the poet still repudiates the past or whether memories have fused, in lines 114-115, with present visions.

Stanza 24. Whether gently or abruptly, the refutation of youth leads the poet into the present moment, where he pauses, briefly aware of himself, enclosed within time, as within this stanza, experiencing another *dédouble ment*. The basic idea of double identity, in which one not only observes oneself but becomes what one does, is derived in part from Western notions of Eastern thought (cf. Emerson's "And I the hymn the Brahmin sings"). Inevitably, considering Apollinaire's own sources, one thinks of Baudelaire and his hookah. If Baudelaire's concern is to communicate an experience with drugs, Apollinaire attempts to describe a purely mystical experience, although he had dabbled in drugs with Lou (See note to "La Mandoline l'Œillet et le Bambou"). There is also a curious parallel with Valéry's "Jeune Parque" who is part serpent. The image of serpent or flute is a combination of oriental and romantic ideas, imposed upon classical imagery and expressed with a certain phallic flourish typical of the poet, as are the increasingly erotic overtones of serpent, flute, and whip.

Stanzas 25-27. The poet takes up, once more, the theme of prophecy. His vision of a kind of balance (the middle age of the world) expresses also his own present feelings about himself, in his late thirties. Here, at the center of the poem, one becomes vividly aware of other motifs that have gradually assumed importance in preceding stanzas: time, youth, suffering, death, the unexplored regions of consciousness. Not only is there a cluster of key words in stanza 25 but there appears also a new word, *la bonté*, which colors subsequent stanzas. One meaning of *la souffrance* may be a passive experience of God which leads to *la bonté*, an active participation in the divine love, as poet-prophet. In line 125 the possibility of knowing the future assumes Faustian overtones. Forbidden knowledge, in the eyes of the medieval church, carried with it the penalty of death and even the death of one's soul. Such a reading closely allies visionary to scientific insight. A simpler reading is that a vision of the future is so intense that, before the new age of heroes, it would have been unbearable.

Increasingly the theme of prophecy takes on a personal coloring. Preoccupations with friends and lovers underlie the exaltation of man's image. Line 126 is almost identical to a line in "La Jolie Rousse" ("c'est le temps de la Raison ardente") which is, in part, a reference to Jacqueline. Line 128 has biblical associations with the seven years (actually twice seven years) Jacob served for Rachel. There may also be, in lines 129-130, beneath the humanistic concept, a reference to Picasso whose divinity is elaborated in *Les Trois Vertus Plastiques*.

As the prophecy becomes more enigmatic, it becomes more concrete. The discovery of other worlds (131) is already ambiguous (are they external? internal?). Does the mind that languishes yearn for these new worlds or for its own fruit? Or has the poet situated in some new world his timeless landscape where one contemplates an object and even tastes it before it appears or ripens? In any event, stanza 27 renders vivid the state of pure consciousness which precedes poem, prophecy, scientific idea.

Stanza 28. The poet returns to present time, but his mood has changed since his last return, in stanza 24. Now he proclaims not only "L'Esprit Nouveau" (136) but his own uniqueness. For Bates, the Promethean tone of the poem becomes testy in these lines (pp. 34-35). It is possible, however, that they are a commentary on line 136, that is, that they exemplify the spiritual state he has just referred to, the confidence (which Apollinaire was far from feeling, as a steady mood, at any time) that, in the future, the true poet's mind will rejoice in a unique harvest. Line 140 may express a conscious, exalted impudence, reminiscent of the poet's youthful tone of voice in "Vendémiaire" (*Alcools*). If stanza 28 is seen as a conclusion to the three preceding stanzas, the four together suggest a creative meditation followed by a short-lived feeling of jubilance. In that case, a section on prophecy ends, in a sense, with the drunkenness of the prophet who, like the sibyl, no longer knows what he says.

Stanzas 29-33. Five stanzas dominated by the theme of past sources of inspiration: some are discarded, some are lost; others, recalled piecemeal, only augment a present awareness of discontinuity. The break between stanzas 28 and 29 anticipates a first kind of discontinuity—the image of the murdered woman in her ship. Floating on the water like the Maid of Astolat, she suggests a mixture of symbolist and Pre-Raphaelite or art-nouveau visions of the Middle Ages. She is the beauty of the past which has charmed Apollinaire for so long and which he now renounces (not for the first time) by poetically evoking it, in the manner of Plato, Lucretius, Saint Augustine.

Another past source of nourishment seems offered him in stanza 30 by imagery reminiscent of the 1908 poems, "Le Brasier" and "Les Fiançailles"; not only is there an image of purification by burning but the giver of the flame may well be Picasso who was a major inspiration to the poet (cf. *Le Poète Assassiné*). The image of the torch in line 150 again suggests Picasso (cf. *Les Trois Vertus Plastiques*) as well as, to a lesser degree, the Christ of "Zone" and perhaps the poet himself.

There continues to be much discussion about stanzas 30-31. Particularly ambiguous is stanza 31, depending on whether one attaches it more closely to the preceding stanza or to 32, as do most critics. If one takes lines 151-152 as a continued invocation of Picasso (see also Bates, 1967, p. 147), they imply a lessening of friendship between Apollinaire and his friend (suggested also in *Le Poète Assassiné*); otherwise, they probably constitute an invocation to the poet's self. On the one hand, there is the theme of the friend who inspires and transforms (stanza 30) and subsequently withdraws (stanza 31), so that the poet is thrown on his own resources. On the other, the theme of a friend is set against the theme of a withdrawn, lost self. The notion generally held is that Apollinaire speaks uniquely of himself in stanza 31. In a conversation with Adéma in 1974, that interpretation was rejected; however, Apollinaire's biographer was positive that line 152 was not an apt description of any of Apollinaire's friends. But one might read line 152 expressionistically, as a description, not of another person's temperament, but of Apollinaire's feelings about a loss of friendship (just as, in his poems on painters, he describes his own reactions, not their paintings). In addition, the *profondeurs incolores* vividly evoke the muted colors and unlimited boundaries of early cubist paintings by Picasso and Braque.

In any event, the theme of the poet's solitude may lead, in stanza 32, to memories of other times of solitude. Or the stanza may describe a return from meditation, which takes the form of a new experience of *dédoublement.* Curiously, in the middle of the stanza, time comes to a halt. Solitude cannot be mastered, or the other self does not complete the return but still wanders *là-bas* "there"; the poet's memory seems to stop recording and to stick in a groove.

At the same time, as the poet, now totally alone, faces the present once more, in stanza 33, his happy/unhappy state can be expressed only through imagery from a past he has jettisoned. His mind is filled with echoes from

Alcools: lines 161-162 recall "La Chanson du Mal-Aimé" and "Marie" and, consequently, the unhappy loves of the past; lines 163-165 recall, in turn, "Le Brasier" and "Cortège" and, consequently, the poet as visionary, triumphant over human weakness. He passes from an earthbound to an airborne stage (the latter recurs in other poems): line 165 no longer has any orientation in terms of gravity, since *sol* (as in other poems) suggests *soleil* "sun" as well as "earth."

Stanzas 34-35. A résumé and repetition of the poem's didactic side, with echoes of "L'Esprit Nouveau." The stating of an intention to have visions and to suffer, however, intervenes between us and any sensation of immediacy. Only line 175 exemplifies direct experience and also perhaps synthesizes memories that reflect earlier poems about passion and poetry: in particular, "La Chanson," the Rhenish poems, and "Marie."

Stanzas 36-42. The long sequence of "surprises" with which the poem culminates may be considered as prophecy in action and also, in the light of the preceding stanza, as a kind of automatic writing. The poet begins anew, as in stanzas 24 and 28, with the present moment (stanza 36) in which he recalls a past that he will relate in subsequent stanzas (37-42). Emerging from a prophetic frenzy he starts to comment on his experience in concrete terms. He remembers what he felt and sang *là-haut* "above," when he hovered in an ecstatic fit, once more like a Chagallian figure. If lines 176-178 are pretty straightforward, lines 179-180 are ambiguous: as he writes up his vision, he seems to reenter it: possessed by huge forces, he likens himself to a tree quickened by the wind. As in stanza 3, one thinks of Valéry's "Au Platane." The words *balance* and *cheveux* may suggest angelic attributes for the wind, reminiscent of tree imagery in "Les Sapins" (*Alcools*).

According to manuscript evidence, the two groups of stanzas 37-39 and 40-42 seem to have been written at different times. Syntactically all seem an expansion of lines 177-178, "what I have felt/And what I sang up there." Ph. Renaud has reproached Apollinaire for only talking, in "Les Collines," about what he'll do and not doing it (1969, pp. 449-454). However, like *Les Mamelles de Tirésias*, which was put into final shape at about the same time, "Les Collines" and, in particular, these stanzas are related both to contemporary cubism and to a not yet formulated surrealism. There is much, too, that hearkens back to "Ondes."

As a whole, stanzas 37-39 seem concerned with the trivia or oddities of life—its surprises, when glimpsed from an unexpected angle. Stanza 37 has a fragmented effect, in part caused by its many monosyllables, in part by the imagery composed of dehumanized juxtapositions, which resembles that of "Lundi Rue Christine" (one of the experimental poems of "Ondes" which affected the early Eliot), and even passages in *Alcools*, notably from "Crépuscule" and "Le Voyageur." It is not only a surprising still life (cf.

Bates, p. 32) which has surrealist—or presurrealist—overtones, but it may be an explicitly cubist still life, with its seemingly ordinary objects situated in space by the image of the table and treated in an extraordinary manner. Thus, the gloves are "dead," as if they had once lived, and the people resemble monstrous objects. The pun on *s'avale* "swallows himself," or of a horse, "has a low belly," gives rise to the visual deformations of lines 184-185 which evoke what a cubist painter does to the human figure. It is no coincidence that here and in *Les Mamelles de Tirésias,* when evoking a cubist style, Apollinaire indulges in puns and deadpan humor. Cubist painters delighted in both (especially Picasso, Marcoussis, Juan Gris). The top hat, like that of a vaudeville magician, offers us surprises of its own, and the run-on line (181-182), while it emphasizes the prosaic opening, surprises us on another level. Line 183, too, surprises by its imagery. Its fantasy prepares the bizarreness that follows, while death, first suggested by the funeral top hat, dominates the stanza, permeating the images of gloves and suicidal lady and suggesting the category of the painting that the stanza becomes—for the figures themselves prepare to be subjects in a *nature morte* (literally, a "dead nature"). There is a breakdown of the frontiers between life and death, between life and a painting or a poem, which recalls the early "Rhénanes" and the later "Ondes."

In stanza 38 space has become more complex, moving from two dimensions to three or four. The dance takes place *au fond du temps* "in the depths of time"; there, movement, time, and space intermingle. The death motif continues but, instead of characterizing what the poet sees, it characterizes his action. He has killed the handsome orchestra leader who, like the lovely murdered lady, seems to represent a kind of beauty—in his case, since a conductor sets the tempo, perhaps ideas about order—and therefore he must be done away with by the modern poet. Even more heroic or helpful is the poet's peeling of an orange which becomes a fireworks display, an act that is perhaps presented with a tinge of humor since it fits in with his role as a magician. The poet's gift of an orange to his friends is surely his poetry; its description as a taste sensation or as ephemeral fireworks recalls the war poems as well as the ending of "Les Fenêtres."

In stanza 39 space is abolished and there is a shift to future time. The emphasis on the theme of death continues. All now are dead. But all who? Does the poet dismiss the oddities he created in stanza 37 and the friends he evoked in stanza 38? Or those who attempt to lead the dance? And who is the *maître d'hôtel*? Is he the poet? Is he death? And the unreal champagne? We seem, for a moment, to enter the world of Jules Laforgue who incorporated in his poems philosophical games. As interesting as the champagne itself is what it is compared to: the foaming of a poet's brain, evokes, above all, Apollinaire's trepanation. There is an effect of dismissal in the analogies created between the nonexistent or evanescent images of unreal champagne/foam of snail/foam of poet's brain and a mutually belittling effect in the incongruous juxtaposition of the maitre d' who pours drinks while a rose is singing. Or one can say, to the contrary, that the stanza rises to an affirmation over death, that the image of the poet is linked to that of the eternally singing rose whose image sends one back to "Zone" and to a remembered moment of repose, or to "Le Brasier" and the Dantean rose of paradise, and, at the same time, forward to the end of this poem.

After the series of endings and beginnings which, in stanzas 37-39, suggests the structure of a dream, we begin over again, in stanza 40, with a more logical structure, based on three "numbers"; *nombre*, like the top hat of line 181, evokes the world of vaudeville or circus and, implicitly, a fraudulent magic. Each turn is presented by some one who performs the impossible. The first is the slave with his sword (cf. "Les Sept Épées" in "La Chanson du Mal-Aimé"). The manuscript version of line 196, "L'empereur tient son épée nue" [The emperor holds his sword bared], is, because of the possessive adjective, overtly phallic and, because of the rank of the actor, revealing of Apollinaire's attitude toward love. But after the poet's emendations, the sword is no longer uniquely a phallic symbol, as in "La Chanson"; it is a more general creative force suggestive of violence, gigantism, creation from destruction, even a cesarean birth somewhat like that evoked in "La Petite Auto." The slave is not, like the emperor, in control of the power he wields, but is caught up by it. Yet, whether slave or emperor, he recalls the subjection that Apollinaire associates with love and a fusion between sexual love and poetic powers.

The second number is the chauffeur driving a car, a modern image curiously anticipatory of a Man Ray drawing in *Les Mains Libres*, illustrated with a prose poem by Éluard, "Le Tournant" [The Turn]. The idea is quite similar: around the turn is the magical, the nonhuman, the forbidden. The chauffeur's position, in Apollinaire's poem, is ambivalent. Is he in control of his machine, like the emperor, or subjugated, like the slave? Basic ideas of "L'Esprit Nouveau"—newness, surprise, truth—are suggested by the universe on his horizon which he pursues vainly and which remains virginal, unlike the pregnant universes of stanza 37.

The third number combines the traditionally poetic resonances of the first number with the modernism of the second. *Dame* suggests a middle-aged woman or a court lady (mysterious and lovely) of the Middle Ages. Seemingly *l'ascenseur* is one of those old wrought-iron French elevators one can look into or out of. A dreamlike atmosphere, or dream logic, imposes itself, and an almost surrealistic magic of the machine. Inevitably, because of the relation of "Les Collines" to the poems in its proximity, there is an association between the lady in the elevator and, in the following poem "Arbre," the description of Dame-Abonde, the magic woman in a tramway, and the poet's ride in an elevator where, at each stop, he glimpses marvels. Here the two images seem to have fused: the poet and the tram are absent; it's the mysterious lady who rides in the elevator; and the elevator (like sword and steering wheel) has assumed magical properties of its own. Or (more likely) these properties emanate from her.

The two sections 37-39 and 40-42 seem to balance and complement each other; the first celebrates the poet's role, the second, eventually, the role of the mysterious female—Muse, Mother Nature, Rimbaud's witch? There may be an echo of the ancient conflict between Merlin and Vivien which haunted Apollinaire in his youth, or of later conflicts, like that in *Les Mamelles de Tirésias*, between the procreative husband and Thérèse/Tirésias—in sum, those conflicts relating to women which played so large a role in the poet's life.

All these stanzas are based on surprise, "le grand ressort nouveau," according to "L'Esprit Nouveau et les poètes," but they are only "little" secrets, as Apollinaire indicates in stanza 43, that is, tentative examples of his new aesthetic. One reading of lines 214-215 is that they describe the invasion of the individual by an overwhelming vision. Their tone is close to that of other late poems, "La Victoire" and "La Jolie Rousse." The concept, however, of an opposition between multiplicity and unicity—particularly the fragmentation of human life in contrast with the absolute idea—is already a preoccupation in "Ondes" and before.

Stanzas 44-45. The final two stanzas resume major themes of "Les Collines" and, perhaps inevitably, provide thematic oppositions, between *la souffrance* and *la bonté* and, notably, between life's ephemeral charm and its central mystery. Stanza 44 evokes suffering without naming the experience, by a lyric repetition of words and sounds ("pleure pleure et repleurons"). In a comparable way, the passing of time, never mentioned, is evoked by antithetical juxtapositions (crescent and full moon, moon and sun). The nostalgic evocation of sunlit joys in the past (220) may be read as a final farewell to youth, a return to it in memory (cf. "La Victoire": "Les jours étaient une pure émeraude" [The days were a pure emerald]), an introduction to the golden light and paradisaic imagery of the final stanza where a new repetition of resonant sounds, *d'or, doré, adorable,* transforms a mood of melancholy into one of repletion. The flame and the rose, to be found in some of Apollinaire's most beautiful poems, nearly always communicate a faint atmosphere of Dante's *Il Paradiso.* The image of perfume may recall to the reader Baudelairean visions of exotic or dream landscapes, although the emphasis here is on the rising perfume, not on what it inspires. The first version of line 224, which has *Qui* instead of *Que,* reads more easily, according to *OP* (p. 1080), but changes the meaning profoundly. As the line stands, with "rose" as subject of the verb, from the worshiped rose emanates a flame, our universe, and a perfume, the essence of the rose—its distillation, as in "Fête" (see note). Indeed, if one considers "Les Collines" as a finale to the war poems, the exquisite perfume may be the odors of sacrifice which please the gods. Or, in a more traditional context, the perfume may suggest the poem itself, as it vanishes.

Although Apollinaire is not bound by a logical structure, basic themes resound through "Les Collines" and return musically, with variations: the passing of time, human consciousness, the poet's own identity, his suffering, his ability to prophesy. The final images of rose, flame, perfume, which may all be found in mystical poetry, express the poet's final attainment of his vision, after the poem's long preparation. For the entire poem leads us through the poet's life by a series of nonchronological flashbacks relating to his memories and to his autobiographical poetry. Thus "Les Collines" embraces Apollinaire's concept of the poet in the modern world and an earnest attempt to evaluate his own life and works—a final attempt, as it turned out.

References

Bates, Scott. "*Les Collines,* dernier testament d'Apollinaire," *GA* 1 (1962), 25-39.

Lockerbie, S. I. "Le Rôle de l'imagination dans *Calligrammes,* " part 2, *GA* 6 (1967), 85-105.

Wells, P. " 'Les Collines': Lutte et triomphe d'Apollinaire," *Bulletin de l'Association Guillaume Budé,* 4th ser., XXVI, 4 (December 1967), 477-487.

ARBRE, page 48

First published in *Le Gay Sçavoir,* 1 (March 1913). Its reappearance in *Cabaret Voltaire* (June 1916) indicates the interest felt in the poem by the Dadaists.

The title suggests, among other things, a tree whose foliage or fruits of gold and silver grant one godlike powers, a tree hidden in a grove and guarded by a monster, a tree that is at once a cross and a gallows. The general sense might be that of an ambivalent quest offering both danger and a precious treasure. On the level of the poet's own preoccupations, the title may suggest the poem as a verbal structure and as a typographical shape, or as the interworking of thoughts, memories, associations which are its nourishment. Here again the general sense would be both of danger (since creation is always a risk) and of discovery. One may also find, after reading the poem, retroactive implications such as branches that wander, cross over, come to a dead end, like roads or railway tracks.

Unlike the title, the poem does not deal with the suggestiveness of a given image. It expresses the fragmentation of a personality by abrupt changes in tone, subject matter, even subjects of verbs, and it could be considered as an experiment in simultaneism.

Lines 1-6. In the first six lines the pronoun subject is transformed in almost every verse: you, they, I, you, I. Reminiscent of "Zone" is a blurring between the first and second person singular, between *tu* and *vous* (the intimate and usual forms of "you"), between outer and inner phenomena.

The relation of line 1 to line 2 is put in doubt by the lack of punctuation. You (the intimate *tu* may indicate that the poet addresses himself) sing in contrast or as an accompaniment to the music of phonographs. These may suggest the gay, noisy vitality of modern life (see "Éventail des Saveurs" and note), and the poem may begin with the poet in a happy social situation from which he proceeds to abstract himself through an anxious meditation: in that event line 2 would be the poet's inner voice. Or the gallop of phonographs may be related to past time, as "le galop des étoiles" is related to the future ("Le Brasier," *Alcools*). In that event they may play the assortment of real, imagined, and literary memories which make up the rest of the stanza and, especially, line 2 with its tuneful variation on a refrain from Villon (see note to "C'est Lou Qu'on la Nommait"). The blind men are perhaps vanished poets; they may symbolize uncertainty of purpose; they seem, as in "La Victoire" (see note), to have mysterious but profound significance for Apollinaire. If they are poets, their disappearance renders doubtful the stature of the singer in line 1.

The leaf in line 3 is one of the few images to remind one of the poem's title. Ph. Renaud (1969) suggests it might be plucked from a tree of knowledge (p. 341). To pluck a leaf, however, suggests a poetic gesture of love, in the romantic or symbolist manner (Hugo, "Adieu"; Verlaine, "Green"). Whether the single leaf be poem or woman or some aspect of knowledge, its importance for the poet lies in its lack of stability: it multiplies and becomes illusion (or "mirages").

Multiplicity versus unicity as an indication of deception within or without is not new; neither is the associated image, in line 4, of a crowd of rather hostile women ("Les Fiançailles" and "Zone" in *Alcools*, "Le Musicien de Saint-Merry," *Le Poète Assassiné*). But who is the formal *vous* "you" whom the poet implores to stay with him? Another person, his own poetic persona, the deity he seems occasionally to believe in?

Lines 5 and 6 seem to juxtapose different pasts, historical and personal, exotic and familiar, and to stress once more relationships between multiplicity and unicity. The building of the mosque at Ispahan, ancient capital of Iran, evokes a multitude of tiny mosaics which compose a single blue dome and a mosaic sky which offers an illusion of reality. The road near Lyons evokes in itself a single image, but the walk with another person (if *vous* refers to a friend or lover, or even a self, subsequently lost) may, like mosaic and leaf, offer an illusion.

Lines 7-10. In "Liens," sounds link space and time; here the clang of a vendor's bell, which belongs to the poet's past, is juxtaposed to a sound in future time—a sharp or shrill voice on the telephone making a transatlantic call. The imagery is futuristic; the self-conscious prediction is also futuristic. In Apollinaire's day the transatlantic cable was used uniquely for telegraphing. The word *aigre*, which Renaud (1969) considers descriptive of Blaise Cendrars's voice (p. 339), was most probably inspired by the technical difficulties then being experienced in setting up an underwater cable telephone system; specifically, the wide range of frequencies in the human voice were impossible to transmit over a long distance. They were equally impossible to transmit over radio waves; voices on the radio, even into the 1920s, were notably squeaky and shrill. The vocal deformations on recordings may also be an underlying source for Apollinaire's imagined voice of the future. As in "Les Collines" (see note), Apollinaire's prediction links poetry to science, conquering time as the latter conquers space; but whereas in "Les Collines" his prophecies remain obscure, here he speaks clearly of something that is bound to happen. *Toi* in line 9 probably refers to the poet. Europe and America, in lines 9-10, like Ispahan and Lyons in lines 5-6, link points in time and space to the poet's present time in Paris, as though he were at the center of a web of memories and presentiments. These four place-names also indicate spatial orientation, at least for the duration of a verse, and thus provide a momentary resolution in the midst of flux, as well as the ending to a stanza.

Lines 11-17. The image of the child fuses Apollinairean memories of the past, particularly his memory of the man who sold licorice water, with an evocation of the Christ child and his surroundings, as well as an evocation of Chagallian imagery (line 12). Line 14, in turn, brings into his mind Le Douanier Rousseau who had painted a portrait of him and Marie Laurencin in 1909 and who died in 1910. The epitaph Apollinaire had written for Rousseau, containing the line "Laisse passer nos bagages en franchise à la porte du ciel" [Let our baggage pass through the sky's gate], was engraved on Rousseau's tomb a month after "Arbre" was published (*OP*, p. 1146). The association of an Eastern landscape with his painter friend leads him to make a comparable and more complex association (which may begin in line 17) with a cosmopolitan poet friend, Blaise Cendrars, who had recently published a poem inspired by the train trip from Moscow to Paris, the "Prose du Transsibérien et de la Petite Jeanne de France." Cendrars specialists have interpreted the reference to Cendrars as an inadvertent acknowledgment of Apollinaire's indebtedness to Cendrars's modernism. Renaud suggests that, in this one poem, Apollinaire carries on a prolonged conversation with Cendrars (1969, pp. 337-339). The probability, however, is that he does precisely what the poem indicates: he thinks of several friends and their pictorial or verbal worlds and then reenters his own poetic universe.

Lines 18-22. The notion of art as an expression of almost simultaneous preoccupations of the consciousness on different levels is emphasized by the surprising interpolation of lines 18-19 before lines 20-22. Whippoorwill and badger are nocturnal, like many poets, and the mole works in darkness. The latter's labyrinthine creation, achieved blindly, may be compared to a creation of the unconscious—and to the kind of poem Apollinaire attempts here. The theme of night is surely calculated: a variant reading, in *Le Gay Sçavoir,* of line 18, "Engoulevent grondin blaireau," contains the *grondin,* or "gurnard," an odd-shaped fish with fingered fins for walking on the sea bottom, a place of relative darkness. *Engoulevent* offers the translator two options, "nightjar" or "whippoorwill," the one suggesting an English, the latter, an American, bird. The latter was chosen by the translator to emphasize the picturesquely cosmopolitan aspects of simultaneism which Apollinaire strives for in "Arbre."

The kind of cosmopolitan and sentimental poetry attempted by Cendrars in his "Prose du Transsibérien" is, in lines 20-22, compared with the entirely different ubiquity conceived of by Apollinaire which is based on the nature of the creative, remembering mind. The theme of the voyage per se, whether through memory or actual journeys, at this point becomes dominant. Apollinaire loves to identify with travelers to far places, with Annie Playden in "L'Émigrant de Landor Road" or "Annie" (*Alcools*), as with Cendrars. A variant of line 22 in the poem's first two appearances, *son revolver aimé* [his beloved revolver], suggests an erotic pleasantry, a kidding perhaps of Cendrars.

Lines 23-28. The mention of Leipzig may be inspired by Marie Laurencin's engagement to a German, and memories of her probably fuse with the image of the thin woman, masculine like Thérèse/Tirésias (23) and intelligent (24). The place-name's effect, however, is to stress the poet's ubiquity. And the thought of an intelligent woman is associated with legends (25) and the mysterious "Dame-Abonde" (26), that is, most probably, with women of fairy tale and myth, like the Celtic fairy women who haunt Apollinaire's early work. The poet seems to warn that one should not forget them, probably because they destroy men. He may urge us, too, in lines 25-28, not to forget the modern myths: the vision of supernatural events against a Parisian backdrop which forms the subject of "Le Musicien de Saint-Merry" and "Un Fantôme de Nuées." If line 25 is a warning against magic spells, the poet himself seems to fall victim to them immediately. *Dame-Abonde* is hidden, like a kernel of magic, in a prosaic setting; her very name suggests her power over her surroundings. The tramway (26), which dissolves dreamlike into an elevator (26), functions like the phonographs by setting imagery in motion and mixing modernism with magic, the present with memories. Whereas the phonographs are juxtaposed to unexpected images, seeming to launch them, the tramway and especially the elevator seem displaced in their surroundings, and the unlikelihood of their being where they are is stressed by paradoxes or contrasts on the verbal level (*Abonde/désert*) (*chasse/s'arrêtait*). Most significant, *je montais*, which constitutes the link between the two scenes, "I was getting on" the tramway or "going up" in the elevator, indicates the kind of blurring one finds in dream transitions and suggests the poet as a dreaming observer. The hunt that he observes, like Dame-Abonde, and perhaps emanating from her, evokes the medieval legends of which he warns us: if, as is likely, the hunt is linked to a dangerous woman, it suggests a story of disaster at a woman's hands, like Merlin's fate, or the Unicorn's, or the poet's.

Lines 29-33. The litany is vividly reminiscent, for English-speaking readers, of T. S. Eliot, who borrowed from Apollinaire more than once. There is an underlying association of images, springing from *pierres* "stones" (or "precious stones"), *multicolores* "many-colored," *ardents* "glowing," even *vaisseaux* "vessels," which creates a privileged setting for *ton image*. These can be seen as in contrast with the commercial associations of the shop-window, the street vendor's brasier, the place-names. "Your image" is most probably not the poet's own, as it is in "Zone," but a haunting memory of Marie. The poet invokes the image; subsequently, it dominates the landscape, floating between him and all other images he calls up.

Lines 34-37. Stanzas consisting of one line or, at the most, two, suggest silence: the poet moves from spoken to unspoken thoughts and back again. His thoughts are fragmentary and still cling to the same theme. The Norwegian ships (32) may suggest Finland, and the shipmates, the birches (34). Birches, like the carob trees in line 39, remind one of the poem's title, without clarifying it. The paleness and the cold of the north contrast with the preceding glowing imagery. Line 35 once more suggests the Creole, Marie. As in 34 there is a delicacy of outline, a suggestion of engraving or etching. It is at once a climax to the poem and a fading away. Lines 36-37 seem an even more open reference to Marie and to an immediate past event that might be a card from her in Spain, where she has gone with her lover (see note to "A Travers l'Europe").

Lines 38-44. As the poem ends, so does its universe. Spain may suggest to the poet a wind from the *couchant*, the "west" or the "sunset." And sunset may, in turn, suggest the redness of the extremely hard wood of the carob tree. Or if one thinks of an afterglow fading into twilight, the carob trees may indicate a world that is hardening, like metal. As in "La Chanson du

Mal-Aimé" (*Alcools*), the gods are in peril. It would seem that a new world is launched by, and within, the complaining poet, and that *ta voix* refers, this time, to his own voice. The number three recalls, among other things, his favorite magician Hermes Trismegistus. Whereas in "Vendémiaire" (*Alcools*) the death of kings is *trismégiste*, here it is the birth of new worlds which is based on the magic number three. Notably, however, "trois par trois" suggests two groups of three or thirty-three and the last stanza makes explicit a dominant preoccupation of the poem: the poet is growing middle-aged and will soon be thirty-three years old, Christ's age when he was crucified. It is hardly a coincidence that his friends, the cubist painters Louis Marcoussis and Juan Gris, were to play with the same number, thirty-three, in book illustrations for Apollinaire and another friend, Max Jacob.

"Arbre," with its long lines expressing broken or rambling or momentary thoughts and its fragmentary structure, juxtaposes different but not antithetical notions. The structure of the poem stems from that seemingly spontaneous association of ideas, plastic images, and even tunes, in other words, the soliloquy of the total consciousness which was Apollinaire's increasing preoccupation just before the war. Nothing is explained, but there are links between images and between stanzas. And there is a mood, largely composed of nostalgia for lost possibilities of happiness and expressed by the irony that tempers nearly all self-pity on the poet's part, underlined by a steadfast awareness of his own identity, from the opening *Tu chantes* (fraternally with others, against a background of modern canned music) to the final hopeful note for a new world overwhelming the poet's own awareness that the gods—meaning himself—are growing old. Alternatively, one could see the birth of new beings suggesting something as melancholy and ominous as the aging of the gods (see introduction, p. 1). In any event, "Arbre," the poem, expresses Apollinaire the man and the poet; it does not symbolize his condition, as does Valéry's "Au Platane," but is expressive of an individual consciousness dealing with the multitudinous phenomena of the modern world, in 1913.

LUNDI RUE CHRISTINE, page 52

First published in *Les Soirées de Paris* (December 1913).

The term "conversation poem" is a more accurate description of "Lundi Rue Christine" than of "Les Fenêtres." Whereas the latter poem heightens its snippets of speech with images of light and color, and with language in a high poetic register, "Lundi Rue Christine" restricts itself more severely to apparently random phrases of banal conversation. As the title indicates, the poem is also more strictly confined in time and place, being concerned with one given place (somewhere in the Rue Christine) on one given day. With the help of the title, the reader can legitimately interpret the series of unconnected phrases as representing the general buzz of small talk in some public place, which certain lines suggest more specifically to be a café. The creation of a kaleidoscopic sound picture of a scene in an ordinary Parisian setting is consistent with Apollinaire's desire to stand at the center of life and register what he called the "mysteries" of everyday reality. Writing only a few months later in his review *Les Soirées de Paris*, he advised poets that the way to renew their art was to follow the example of the realist novelists of the nineteenth century and simply record observations of what they saw and heard around them (*OC*, III, 884). But of course the realist novelists never contemplated reproducing their observations as a series of apparently arbitrary juxtapositions, with little continuity from one line to the next. The poem may share realism's fascination for moments of lived reality up to a point, but it departs radically from the mimetic model in the boldness of its innovatory structure.

The implications of this structure are far-reaching in the freedom of interpretation it leaves to the reader (see introduction). It focuses his attention on the text as a self-sufficient object, without any necessary referential function, and, by challenging him to discover significance and possible connections in the apparently gratuitous phrases, leads him to participate in the elaboration of possible meanings. The invitation to become involved is highlighted by the presence in the text of one or two lines that can be interpreted as ironic or teasing remarks addressed to the reader, inducing him to become more aware of the literary "game" and to take part in it. This interpretation is further encouraged by the formal arrangement of the text. Where logically an undifferentiated mass of phrases might have been expected, there is instead a division into verse paragraphs, creating a grouping of lines that seem to hang together around a common idea or situation and thus provide a stimulus to interpretation.

The affection that later innovators—the surrealists and others—had for the poem is understandable. In a lighthearted way it overthrows the concept of poetry as a special linguistic activity remote from ordinary uses of the language. It shows that poetry is potentially present in every manifestation of language, however inconsequential, if form and structure can bring the right quality of attention to bear on it. Equally it undermines the notion of the literary text as a fixed set of meanings and encourages an approach to it as an "open" system, full of latent possibilities that allow the creative participation of the reader.

Lines 1-4. These lines can easily be read as a self-contained scene—a criminal escapade is possibly being planned—making for an interest-catching opening. Line 2 mimics the language of "tough guys," which contrasts with the elegant subjunctive of line 3 (*maintînt*). Such shifts and clashes of linguistic register are an important part of the wordplay of the poem.

Lines 5-9. Line 5 may be descriptive of the café's interior, and line 6 could be a consequential detail, highlighted by the internal echo of sound between *patronne* and *poitrinaire.* The similarity of construction in lines 7 and 9 (both being future clauses with the pronoun *tu*) might suggest an element of continuity, which could be a group around one particular table. A friend of Apollinaire's, Jacques Dyssord, claimed that the poem was written in a café on the evening before Apollinaire left for Tunis—hence possibly line 9 (*OP*, p. 1081). The similarities between lines 7 and 9 emphasize the incongruity of line 8.

Line 10. This line may be read as a provocative comment aimed at the reader. It announces improvisation and challenges the reader to respond to it.

Lines 11-14. Line 11 seems another scene-setting detail, the pile of saucers being particularly suggestive of a café. The onomatopoeia of line 12 is reminiscent of the futurists' use of the device, being abstract rather than descriptive sound. The bright lively nature of the sound fits well into the colloquial context and draws attention to the auditory texture that is being built up. A racy colloquial style is particularly evident in the next two lines, which exhibit a colorful brand of "low-life" humor. They round off vigorously a paragraph that has a distinct gusto of its own.

Lines 16-17. Line 16 could be a passing remark, but it can also function as scene-setting, while line 17 might be another mocking comment intended for the reader.

Lines 18-24. There is a calculated dissonance between the formal address of line 18 and the savory insult of line 19, which is again in the register of low-life slang. The pithy tone is maintained by the scornful comment of line 20, but there is then a contrast with the overtones of gentility in the two following exchanges about ladies with furs. After these lively tonal variations, the paragraph fades out quietly with the two descriptive details of lines 23-24.

Lines 25-33. The imperfect tense of line 25 is the only one in the poem, suggesting a meal in progress. It may refer back to line 7 and forward to line 29, which might be a waitress's conventional remark when serving. As Renaud points out (1969, p. 317), lines 26-27 can be read independently, but taken together they are an unusually evocative description of a fountain at night. The other lines form a random sequence. The phrases are of approximately the same length and encourage a rapid rhythm of reading, but they clash rather than merge with one another. The final longer line (l. 33), with its mock-melodramatic note, is highlighted as a result.

Lines 34-36. Taken together the three lines have a punctuating function;

they draw attention to the changes of pace and rhythm in the poem as it proceeds. Within the set of three, the first two are similar in tone and conversational register, but there is a contrast with the change in length and grammatical function of line 36.

Lines 37-38. In the first edition, line 39 begins the final passage. In the Pléiade edition, line 39 stands alone. There the "framing" of lines 37-38 by single lines encourages a reading of them together and emphasizes their faintly insinuating overtones, as Renaud suggests (1969, p. 317). Invitations to inspect engravings and paintings are notorious for the double meaning they frequently have! Apollinaire's intention, however, may have been either more subtle or more straightforward, since he oversaw the first edition.

Lines 39-48. This final paragraph seems to cohere around references to travel (cf. l. 9). Lines 40-46 may be read as a sustained series of exchanges, not excessively disrupted by the interjections of lines 42 and 44, providing a smooth buildup to the climax formed by the two final lines. These two lines end the poem on an emphatic note. Line 47 humorously mimics a pedantic maxim, while *quinte major* has an enigmatic air of solemnity. *Quinte* "quint" is an archaic formula used in piquet for a hand of five cards in the same suit; *la quinte major* is comparable to a royal flush in poker. As such, it is an appropriate phrase to feature in a café scene, where games of cards are a regular activity, but the expression is unusual enough in contemporary French to suggest something more weighty. This impression is enhanced by the fact that *quinte* can also mean a musical chord, which leads the reader into thinking that the poem ends with an orchestral flourish. Tongue-in-cheek humor is thus maintained to the final line.

LETTRE-OCÉAN, page 58

First published in *Les Soirées de Paris* (June 1914).

"Lettre-Océan" is undoubtedly the most radical experiment in "typographical simultaneity," involving a greater subordination of the text to graphic form than in the other calligrams (see introduction, p. 1). The symmetry between the two parts of the poem demands that they should be seen side by side—as in the original *Soirées de Paris* publication—but unfortunately no edition has respected this arrangement.

The poem celebrates the global awareness of modern man through developments in worldwide communication, a theme that already had a central place in Apollinaire's modernism (see notes to "Les Fenêtres" and "Liens") and was further stimulated when his brother Albert went to Mexico in 1913. Correspondence between the two brothers provides some of the main leitmotifs, both verbal and graphic, of the text. The title refers, according to Schmits, to a letter posted at sea (presumably by Albert) via a passing liner. The frieze of undulating lines may evoke the ocean that separates the brothers, but it also suggests the telephone cables or wireless waves that bring them together. The postcard evoking events of the civil war in Mexico is reproduced illusionistically, like a cubist collage, and could well be a verbatim reproduction of a message actually received by Apollinaire (*Album Apollinaire*, p. 186, has a photograph of a postcard from Albert; other evidence of regular messages from Mexico are to be found in *A*, pp. 104-106, 145-148). Other phrases from postcards (*Jeunes filles à Chapultepec*) or more general exchanges between the two brothers are placed at intervals throughout the design, some being known to be biographically correct (there was an earthquake at Nice where the brothers lived *c.* 1887; Apollinaire was in Germany when Albert left in early 1913).

The graphic form suggests expanding consciousness in the two circular shapes that dominate the two pages. They represent, first and foremost, radio communication with radio waves departing in all directions from the transmitters in the Eiffel Tower (identified in the first circle by its geographical position, in the second by its height), making a strong visual illustration of the theme of the tower as the focal point of the universe (see note to "Tour"). Simultaneously the right-hand shape, with its concentric circles, depicts a Gramophone record, which was for Apollinaire an equally vital twentieth-century mode of expression destined to replace the written word. Finally, in the general context of "Ondes," the shapes cannot fail to evoke the radiating force of the sun, which stands in "Les Fenêtres" as the supreme symbol of a world united through dynamic energy and poetic vision.

The verbal content of the radio waves and the Gramophone grooves is not made up of messages in the ordinary sense but of random snippets of speech and sound. Implicitly what is being beamed to the world is a sound picture of the many voices of a great metropolis, making up the typical vox populi common to cities all over the globe. The status of the phrases in this respect is emphasized by the fact that, unlike the similar speech fragments of the conversation poems, they are often grammatically incomplete, being interrupted in midphrase or midword. Indeed, the first phrase of the whole poem (*Je traverse la ville*) conveys an intention to plunge into the life of the city.

As in the conversation poems, an impression of zest and colloquial vitality arises from the mingling of different types of phrase and the often amusing changes of tone and register. There are political slogans (*Vive la République; Vive le Roy; A bas la calotte*); slang expressions and sexual innuendos (*et comment j'ai brûlé le dur avec ma gerce; non si vous avez une moustache*); stereotyped utterances of policemen (*allons circuler*), railway guards ([*en voi*]*ture les voyageurs*), and bus conductors (*changement de section*); set phrases from restaurant menus (*À la Crème*) and newspaper advertisements ([*pro*]*priétaire de 5 ou 6 im*[*meubles*]). Also slipped in are references to acquaintances of Apollinaire's (Toussaint Luca, Dyssord who went to Tunisia to set up a newspaper, Barzun with whom Apollinaire was engaged in a literary polemic), and—a sly joke—two phrases from symbolist-type verse: *de vos jardins fleuris fermez les portes, Des clefs j'en ai vu mille et mille;* the latter comes from Apollinaire's own, much plundered, early poem "La Clef" (*OP,* p. 553). With the onomatopoetic sounds, this jangle of voices constitutes an effective sound texture, but it is one that could not operate without the support of the graphic form to provide a meaningful framework of interpretation for the reader. It is in this sense that there is a distinction from other calligrams.

Affinities can be found in the poem, on both graphic and verbal levels, with the work of the futurists, who had already experimented with exploded language and bold typographic designs. The practice of onomatopoetic sound was one of the hallmarks of their style, as was the use of typographical signs to condense syntax (mildly illustrated here by the plus sign). But the resemblances with any particular work are not extensive (one or two details only in, for example, Marinetti's "Turkish Captive Balloon" from *Zang Tumb Tuum,* which Apollinaire might have seen, or heard about, a month or two earlier in 1914). There are sometimes resemblances with works composed after "Lettre-Océan" (Carra's word painting *Interventionist Manifesto,* which uses some of the same words, seems to have come later in 1914). The principal distinction to be made is in the much greater sobriety of Apollinaire's design, which avoids the air of frenzy typical of futurist experiments. The whole poem is carefully built on a symmetrical arrangement, with calculated departures from it in the free positioning of certain elements. The two explosive shapes are also set into a frame of coherent, discursive language, which is read in the normal way. The final result is a combination of order and disorder. Random reading is possible in many of the parts, but the general structure is compatible with a process of reading which begins at the top of the first page and proceeds from left to right to end on the second page. In that the second circular shape is bigger and more explosive than the first, this direction of reading seems to lead to a natural climax.

References

Delbreil, D., F. Dinanman, and A. Windsor. "Lettre-Océan." In *Apollinaire et la peinture.* 9th Apollinaire Colloquium. Stavelot, 1975. In press.

Schmits, G. "Lettre-Océan," *Savoir et Beauté,* 44, nos. 2-3 (1964), 2691-2698.

SUR LES PROPHÉTIES, page 66

First published in *Les Soirées de Paris* (May 1914).

Under cover of an apparently levelheaded and rational analysis of superstition, Apollinaire is conducting an astute defense of an imaginative outlook on life. If superstitious beliefs are but a legitimate way of observing nature, then there is no real conflict between an empirical and a magical understanding of reality. Rather than demystifying superstition, the argument tends to favor a sympathetic exploration of all wider, nonrational forms of knowledge of the world. Prophecy and similar gifts of insight are within the power of all men, if they can be helped to shake off the effects of a narrow education. By implication the poet, by cultivating the gift of surprise, by exploring the curious, irrational, or singular aspects of life, can help to restore the power of vision in ordinary people. The poetics that correspond to this outlook are what Apollinaire called *surnaturalisme:* a flexible accommodation between reality and fantasy in his poetic approach to the world (see introduction, p. 1, n. 4).

The casual style and expression are essential features of this view of poetry. The language and the mode of address are those of ordinary speech, skillfully manipulated to range from almost prosaic inflections to passages of more sustained, but still relaxed, rhythm. This amounts to a recognition that if prophetic insight is widely shared, so, too, must be the language that the poet uses. The heightening of reality must grow naturally from a common area of experience and so use a language that is accessible to all men.

Such a conception of prophecy and poetic expression does not represent Apollinaire's final aesthetic position (see introduction). But the ability to reveal a *merveilleux moderne* at the heart of everyday life is an important aspect of his modernism, seen to advantage in "Le Musicien de Saint-Merry" and "Un Fantôme de Nuées," which broadly reflect the poetics being advocated here.

Line 9. Madame Deroy was a real fortune-teller who is also mentioned in *A* (p. 46). The references to actual acquaintances of the poet reinforce the impression of casual spontaneity of style.

Line 13. His own shadow plays a major role in Apollinaire's poetry (see note to "Ombre"). Here he reveals that his attitude to it is far from rational.

Line 17. The claim not to believe does not detract from the obvious sympathy the poet displays for fortune-telling and similar practices.

Line 20. Billy was a close friend of Apollinaire's and a fellow writer. Addressing the poem to him gives both a semiepistolary intimacy of tone and a clear hint that, however casual, these reflections amount to an informal *art poétique.*

LE MUSICIEN DE SAINT-MERRY, page 70

First published in *Les Soirées de Paris* (February 1914).

Few poems better illustrate the aesthetic concept of *surnaturalisme*, that is, a poetry that embodies a mythic vision of reality without ever losing touch with the immediacy of everyday life. The fable that forms the main thread of the poem is a projection of Apollinaire's fatalistic obsession with unhappy love. The abduction of a throng of women by the mysterious musician who is the poet's alter ego (l. 17) may be interpreted in various ways: as a wishful dream of power over women, as an exorcism of past unfaithful loves, or as a sad recognition of the impermanence of happiness. Whatever the interpretation, the elegiac overtones are unmistakable; they are further strengthened by the nostalgic memories of the past aroused by the setting in the old historical district of the Marais, in the heart of Paris.

Yet the wistfulness of the main theme is set in the context of the poet's willing immersion in the contemporary world. In the opening lines he proclaims himself as freed from introspection and able at last to confront external reality. In the central section of the poem his thoughts radiate out, in disconnected flashes, to the simultaneous activity that is going on all over the globe. The aim of the poem, therefore, is to create a simultaneous reality, embracing every aspect of the poet's relationship with the world and drawing together the conflicting trends of his poetic personality, the introvert and the extrovert, the confident and the fearful. A considerable unity of tone is thus achieved, reconciling the different modes of expression represented by the fluent narrative of the fable, the lyrical declamation of the opening lines, the nostalgic evocation of the past, and the simultaneous flashes of the contemporary world.

Lines 1-7. These lines may not originally have belonged to the poem (the technique of dovetailing disparate fragments is one frequently employed by Apollinaire), but they make a commanding opening because they affirm the poet's conscious control over the whole fiction that is to be unfolded. Although now ready to immerse himself in the external world (ll. 1-4), he still proclaims that this varied and multiple reality will be the projection of his own aspirations (ll. 5-7). The paradox can be explained by referring back to "Les Fiançailles" (*Alcools; OP*, p. 152), where Apollinaire longed to be able to create a poetic world that would seem to have an independent existence; that moment of superior achievement, fusing personal vision and reality, has now been reached. The delight expressed in wandering (l. 7) is significant of his outlook: throughout Apollinaire's work the theme of wandering is associated with contact with the external world.

Lines 8-31. The fabulous nature of the narrative quickly becomes apparent. While the familiar name for the Boulevard Sebastopol (l. 12) and the quiet arrival of the musician suggest an everyday scene in Paris (as does the accurate topography of the Marais district), an otherworldly note is injected by the featureless face of the man, by the mass of flies, a traditional sign of Beelzebub, and by the hint that he navigates between life and death. The abnormal syntax of line 9, which exists in a grammatical vacuum of its own, is a sign of dislocation of normality, giving prominence to the idea of death in *Passeur des morts* and in the strange neologism *mordonnantes*, applied to the women of Saint-Merry. The word might be a condensation of *mort* and *bourdonnantes* (death and buzzing), or alternatively it might mean death-dealing, which for M. Poupon would suggest that the women are prostitutes (*la petite mort* being a euphemism for orgasm).

The association of the musician with death does not have sinister connotations but casts him as a supernatural figure who transcends all limitations. (An earlier fabulous poem in *Alcools*, "La Maison des Morts," also suggests that the power to cross the boundaries of life and death confers invulnerability.) The musician achieves perfection not only in his effortless subjugation of the women (ll. 27-31) but also in weaving his spell through music, thereby assuming the persona of Orpheus, god of poetry as well as of music, and one of the alter egos that most often haunted Apollinaire's imagination. Far from being a simple echo of the Pied Piper of Hamelin, therefore, the musician takes on complex resonances and embodies some of the most powerful aspirations of the poet. Perhaps it is in this sense that he is also Ariadne (l. 14), guiding the poet and the women through a labyrinth of deep emotions to some kind of self-fulfillment.

Lines 32-53. The fluent narrative is disrupted by a series of abrupt juxtapositions, a technique that, here as elsewhere, seeks to create a synthesis of the diversity of life. Although a vivid variation of tone and color is thus introduced, a link with the main narrative is made when the flashes begin to articulate the poet's own thoughts. A degree of poignancy creeps in as he reflects on the general unhappiness of men and their longing to come together (ll. 44-47), and this poignancy modulates into a more personal distress with the glimpses of an unhappy relationship (ll. 48-53). Whether or not these lines refer to the end of the affair with Marie Laurencin, the effect is to "fade out" the diversity of life and raise the tone of the final fragmentary flashes to the same emotional pitch as the rest of the poem; the point of fusion comes in the images of upward movement (ll. 51-53), suggesting a soaring exaltation in pain.

Lines 54-61. The poet's thoughts, having radiated out into contemporary life and been brought back to their point of departure, are now carried back in time. The sublimated melancholy in the fable finds a natural outlet in nostalgic thoughts of the processions of the past in the historic old district, which are now lost in the recesses of time—as the women soon will be. The *cortège* is a central image in Apollinaire's work, evoking the tumultuous movement of life, but frequently, as here, the movement is tinged with sadness because it is receding from the poet, disappearing into the distance of space or time.

Lines 62-73. The intervention of the poet to address the women personally (using the intimate *toi*) reveals that they stand for all his own past loves and obsessions. Rather than being individually significant, their names are collectively evocative of the pastoral and amorous poetry of earlier centuries, and this, together with the rapt intensity of their movement to the tune of the flute, heightens the sense that they are dream figures of ideal love.

Lines 74-90. A deserted house fits into the conventions of supernatural tales, while the modern use of a historic building (ll. 77-78) evokes the special atmosphere of the Marais district, as a meeting point of past and present.

The final disappearance of the women creates a charged climax (ll. 81-86), the multiple repetitions expressing the awe with which the poet regards their total surrender to some force of passion beyond life itself. Typically for Apollinaire, the most poignant note in the climax is the forsaking of memory (l. 86), for him the most vital dimension of living. The presence of the priest (l. 88) marks the otherworldly nature of what has happened.

Lines 91-102. Although the poet is left alone with his melancholy, there is no collapse of tension or sense of defeat, for the poem is brought to a balanced and controlled conclusion. The throbbing sadness of the last lines is the same emotion that has been enacted in dramatic form in the fable, so that the final lyric statement of it is a satisfying summation of all that has passed. The poet also remains caught up in the swirling mass of life: reversing the departures of processions in the past, crowds now flock back to the scene of his meditation (*revenait* and *Il vint*, ll. 95-97, contrasting with *s'en allait*, l. 58), but this time they are twentieth-century crowds representing the contemporary world. The mood of the final section is, therefore, all-embracing: the poet looks inward to his personal sadness and backward to the past, but at the same time he sees the vitality and movement of life by which he is surrounded.

References

Bohn, W. "Apollinaire and Chirico: The Making of the Mannequins," *Comparative Literature*, XXVII, 2 (Spring 1975), 153-165.

Lockerbie, S. I. "Le Musicien de Saint-Merry," *Cahiers de l'Association Internationale des Etudes Françaises*, 23 (May 1971), 197-209.

Paz, O. "'The Musician of Saint-Merry' by Apollinaire: A Translation and a Study," *L'Esprit Créateur*, X, 4 (Winter 1970), 269-284.

Poupon, M. "Le Musicien de Saint-Merry," *Cahiers de l'Association Internationale des Etudes Françaises,* 23 (May 1971), 212-220.
Renaud, Ph. "Le Musicien de Saint-Merry," *ibid.*, pp. 181-195.

LA CRAVATE ET LA MONTRE, page 78

First published in *Les Soirées de Paris* (July-August 1914).

As with other poems, there is an anecdote about the composition of "La Cravate et la Montre" which has to be treated with caution. It was supposedly written when Apollinaire took off his tie in the offices of the *Soirées de Paris,* putting it on a table beside Serge Férat's watch (*OP,* p. 1083).

Since Apollinaire himself identified the flight of time as one of the major motivating forces of his poetry (*LM,* p. 72), it is clear that a watch, with the hands about to meet at the fateful hour of twelve, would be, for him, whatever the circumstances of composition, a powerfully suggestive symbol.

The poem is made up of four clear and explicit phrases, which provide the key for understanding, and twelve more fragmentary and enigmatic expressions, which demand interpretation. The statement in the tie shape speaks of the stifling effect of civilized society, with the implication, confirmed by the phrase forming the handle of the watch and the phrase on the right of the watch face, that if the pleasures of every passing hour are enjoyed to the full, a fuller, more rewarding life will be gained. But as the eye moves around the hours and their pleasures, time runs out; the hands move away from the confident statement that the beauty of life surpasses the sorrow of dying and the fateful hour approaches.

The clear statement of the theme, elegantly embodied in the simple graphic shape, is complicated by the more enigmatic phrases representing the hours. At one level, these are clever puns of various kinds to identify the hours, the key (provided by Chevalier and Bassy) being: heart = 1 o'clock (only one heart); eyes = 2, child = 3 (coming after mother and father); Agla = 4 (the fourth term of the mystic pentacle); hand = 5 (five fingers); Tircis = 6 (pun on *tire six* "strike six"); week = 7 (seven days); infinite = 8 (the mathematical sign for infinity stood upright); Muses = 9 (nine Muses); stranger = 10 (an unknown person is designated by X, the Roman ten); Dantean verse = 11 (eleven-syllable line); hours = 12 (traditionally twelve hours).

Over and above this clever game, however, these expressions can have many other connotations. They are to be distinguished from the fragmentary expressions of the conversation poems or of "Lettre-Océan" in being on a higher literary register and capable of carrying meaning in their own right. Particularly when brought into contact with resonant phrases like *la beauté de la vie passe la douleur de mourir,* they invite the reader to seek out their hidden suggestions. Thus even simple expressions like heart, eyes, and hand evoke the important role and the emotional overtones these parts of the body have in Apollinaire's poetry, and possibly in the imagination of every reader. *Les Muses aux portes de ton corps* similarly suggests the deep inspiration to be found in sensual love, even for readers who do not know the secret poems to Madeleine, to which the phrase alludes (*OP,* pp. 613-638). *Le bel inconnu,* a phrase from medieval literature, carries with it overtones from a long literary tradition, as does the reference to Dante's poetry. *Tircis* evokes not only the traditional lover of pastoral poetry, but also, through a further ribald pun on *tire six,* a cruder approach to love, contrasting with the tender associations of the pastoral image.

The play of meanings in the poem is thus extended, and thereby the tension is increased between the enjoyment of each hour and the inexorable movement of the hands around the clock. It seems unnecessary to postulate, as Bassy does, a clear-cut division between the hours before six, which are happy, and those after six, which are somber, or to assume that it is death that waits at 12 o'clock. But while the tension need not be so dramatically stark, the conflict between love of life and the flight of time is nevertheless the major theme. Moreover, this conflict arises from the interaction between graphic form and verbal text: without the visual interpretation of movement around the watch face, the contrast would be neither so obvious nor so eloquent. This dual mode of functioning is the hallmark of the calligramme.

References

Bassy, A. M. "Forme littéraire et forme graphique: Les schématogrammes d'Apollinaire," *Cahiers de recherches de l'Ecole Normale Supérieure,* 3-4 (1973-74), 189-194.

Chevalier, J. C. "La poésie d'Apollinaire et le calembour," *Europe,* 451-452 (November-December 1966), 59-76.

UN FANTÔME DE NUÉES, page 80

First published in *Les Ecrits Français,* 1 (December 5, 1913), and subsequently in *Le Nouvel Imagier* (1914-1918).

According to Scott Bates the title (1967, p. 158), suggests, on the mythological level, Hera, the mother of the centaurs, and Ixion, their father, who embraced her in the form of a cloud; for Apollinaire, Ixion is the poet embracing his vision and so creating poetry that, like the centaurs, has a hybrid nature, at once human and divine. A variant of the myth, which

Apollinaire was aware of, is that Zeus made a cloud which resembled Hera and in this manner fooled Ixion. Thus the title's mythological interpretation as poetic vision may also suggest the uncertainty of that vision. If one dismisses hidden erudite meanings, there are other possibilities, including the title as a description of what poetry is, or as an invocation of the world of the twentieth-century which, before World War I, seemed so full of possibilities. Or perhaps the literary imagery of the title, caused in part by the somewhat low frequency of *nuée,* is dissipated during that metamorphosis of reality into fantasy which shapes the poem; consequently the last line, whose imagery refers back to the title, assumes a more convincing allure because *nuage* is a word in common usage. In other words, what started as the poet's vision, announced obscurely, is to be shared by a world of ordinary people using ordinary words to express the extraordinary—a world where "Tout le monde est prophète" ("Sur les Prophéties").

According to André Billy, Apollinaire wrote the first ten lines as the beginning of a story and then "ne sachant plus que dire, il fit appel à son démon, et la nouvelle tourna en poème" [not knowing what to add, he invoked his demon, and the story turned into a poem] (*Apollinaire vivant,* pp. 53-54, quoted in *OP,* p. 1084). What seems to be Apollinaire's point of departure, however, here as elsewhere, is an everyday stroll in the street—and an encounter with the supernatural, comparable to what the surrealists later call "le merveilleux." Apollinaire's vision of the marvelous, however, is based on no arbitrary expression of the unconscious but on a calculated seduction of the reader. His style, accordingly, changes only gradually from the prosaic to the intensely poetic or exalted. Imagery stresses a metamorphosis of the everyday into the magical by a union between small and huge: weights lifted are transformed into cities (13-14); the bar joining the dumbbells becomes a frozen river (15). Gradually, the alliance shifts to one between concrete objects and the intangible or abstract; a cigarette is as bittersweet as life (16); spots on a carpet become a haunting melody (20-21). These metaphors are based on our ability to pass from the real to the imagined, from the concrete object to an indefinable but illuminating emotion. In contrast with what we find in "Les Fenêtres," simultaneity is offered, not as a way in which to approach the inhuman variety of the universe, but as a bridge between two kinds of human experience whose alliance can enrich our creative powers.

The title of the poem describes or defines not only poetry but painting (not to mention music, whose role in the poem Ph. Renaud stresses (1969, pp. 277-280). Apollinaire thinks of Picasso, in particular, whose imagery is evoked in *Alcools* as early as 1904, with "Saltimbanques" and probably "Crépuscule." Four years later, in *Alcools,* it is an awareness of the painter's genius and personality (and perhaps an attempt to rival "Les Demoiselles d'Avignon") which dominates "Le Brasier" and parts of "Les Fiançailles." Apollinaire's final word on his friend seems to have been said, somewhat bitterly, in *Le Poète Assassiné* and, more cryptically, in "Les Collines" (see note). Apollinaire's lyrical art criticism also frequently attests to the painter's presence in his imagination. The passages that one recalls, as one reads "Un Fantôme," are from an early essay, written in 1905, "Les Jeunes: Picasso, Peintre" (*OC*, IV, 65-68); they survive, however, in revised form, as part of a chapter in *Les Peintres Cubistes* (1913), and most probably were in Apollinaire's mind when he wrote the poem.

At any rate, in "Un Fantôme de Nuées," Apollinaire's major poem for the painter, written well after Picasso's cubist period had taken shape, it is the early paintings that the poet nostalgically remembers: creatures from the blue and rose periods seem to quit their canvases and stroll through the poet's text. The result is a prolonged juxtaposition of real and imaginary, as, beginning with a walk through Paris streets, the poet introduces us into a world of fantasy and dream which gradually and increasingly assumes the familiar characteristics of an early Picasso painting. As in "Les Fenêtres" and, even more, in "A Travers l'Europe," specific paintings come to mind, notably *L'Acrobate à la boule* and *Femme à la corneille* (Greet).

The principal color in this almost colorless poem is rose. There are two examples of harmony of similarity. In lines 19-21 not only do green and yellow harmonize but they express the obsessive character of the melody that to the poet-narrator suggests vague memories. In line 30 again two colors in close harmony have as their principal function an associative value: the theme evoked is clearly death. Thus, although colors may be used according to theories that were in Apollinaire's mind at the time because of conversations with Delaunay, they have the nonpainterly function of symbols. Apollinaire's use of color is also a comment on Picasso's paintings of impoverished, half-starved acrobats (31-35). Characteristically, he manages at least one pun based on color, *Peau-Rouge* "redskin" (71), which suggests both American Indians and the pink colors worn by Picasso's acrobats in paintings of the rose period.

An emphasis on a seeming objectivity is underlined by some of the variants found in *Le Nouvel Imagier;* in the final version, *ta vie* has become *la vie* (16), *Cher petit esprit* has become *Un petit esprit* (60), *tant d'audacieuse harmonie* has become *tant d'harmonie* (66). These changes, however, do not conceal the urgent appeal to the spectator within the poem and the reader outside the poem to share in the vision of the vanished child.

Lines 1-7. July 14th, Bastille Day, is comparable to our July 4th. Apollinaire emphasizes the passage of time, the disappearance of old customs—preparing for the miraculous disappearance at the end of the poem.

Line 11. The role of the audience resembles that described by Apollinaire in "Picasso, Peintre": "Leur spectateur doit être pieux, car ils célèbrent des rites muets avec une agilité difficile" [Their spectator must be pious, because they celebrate mute rites with formidable nimbleness] (*OC*, IV, 67).

Lines 22-28. The description of the organ-grinder and his barrel organ in terms of past and future introduces circular aspects of time, recurrent in Apollinaire's poetry (see note to "Les Collines"). His paradoxical appearance and the mechanical but plaintive sound of his music recall the poet's preoccupation with a similar contrast between the literary aura of the word *harlequins* and their actual features and character in "Picasso, Peintre": "des arlequins taciturnes ont les joues et le front flétris par les sensibilités morbides" [taciturn harlequins whose cheeks and brows are blighted—or branded—by a morbid sensitivity] (*ibid*).

Line 30. The old juggler's wearing of a color associated with a sickly young girl recalls a number of paintings, notably *Femme à la corneille.* The mingling of the two sexes in the juggler's appearance may relate, in the poet's mind, to the androgynous character he observes in Picasso's harlequins: "Des arlequins accompagnent la gloire des femmes, ils leur ressemblent, ni mâles, ni femelles" (*ibid*).

Lines 37-41. The second juggler, like the hanged man or the harlequin Trismegistus in the ghostly, shadowy world of "Crépuscule," is magical; he wears only his *ombre*, his "shadow" or, conceivably, his "ghost" (that is, his future, comparable to the accoutrements of the first juggler). He is also faceless, like the musician of St. Merry.

Lines 42-45. A return to the prosaic tone of the beginning and a contrast with the preceding impressionistic or nonrealistic descriptions. The vulgar appearance of the last juggler and the argument about money introduce a practical note, an impression of alternation between two worlds, which prepare the denouement.

Lines 58-59. The final description of the child acrobat, inspired by Picasso's *L'Acrobate à la boule,* gradually assumes magical proportions. Apollinaire sees in the sphere on which the child balances a cosmic significance: "le mouvement rayonnant des mondes" [the radiant—or radiating—movement of the worlds] (*ibid*).

Lines 59-63). The image of the child's transformation into a music of forms which destroys the organ music is clarified by Apollinaire's comment in "Picasso, Peintre": "Ces enfants . . . savent sauter et les tours qu'ils réussissent sont comme des évolutions mentales" [Those children . . . know how to leap and the tricks they achieve are like mental maneuvers] (*ibid.*, p. 65). The poet is obviously more sensitive to the visual arts (here, something akin to the dance) than to music.

Lines 71-72. The double vision of outer reality and inner surreality experienced by the spectators is stressed by the double use of language in the pun on *Peau-Rouge* and by the simultaneous evocation of wind in the leaves and the winglike shape of branches (see note on "Les Collines").

Lines 76-77. For Davies (1964, p. 237), the "miraculous child" represents the hidden orphic spirit which alone can illuminate the cloudy confusion of the century. For Bates (1967, p. 114), the ending communicates to the crowd the artist's "Ixion-like vision." The final lines, however, are open to a number of interpretations. In *Les Peintres Cubistes* Apollinaire adds to his early essay a description of Picasso's transformation from an artist inspired by a muse to one who painfully invents his own universe. That account of Picasso's abrupt switch in style and subject matter, on which Apollinaire was working at approximately the same time he wrote "Un Fantôme," may possibly be related to the final lines of the poem, in which Picasso's early sources of inspiration vanish and a world of amorphous shapes is invoked. The widening of possibilities for the painter would apply also to the poet and to the other spectators. One can say almost the opposite and arrive at a similar conclusion. At the end of the poem the spectators and the poet possess within themselves the essence of what they have just experienced, and they, in turn, are encapsulated not only in space but in time: as the child acts upon them, so they may act upon their, as yet, unshaped century.

Reference

Greet, A. H. "Rotsoge: A travers Chagall." In *Apollinaire et la peinture.* 8th Apollinaire Colloquium. Stavelot, 1975. In press.

CŒUR COURONNE ET MIROIR, page 88

First published in *Les Soirées de Paris*, 26-27 (July-August 1914), with the other calligrams from "Ondes."

Three calligrams—heart, crown, mirror—offer images of reflection, memory, and transformation, as well as an emblematic portrait of the poet. A reverse image of "Cœur" is to be found in *Vitam Impendere Amori* (1917), V, 6: "La flamme est mon cœur renversé" (*OP*, p. 161). The large black capitals indicate that one should read in a clockwise direction.

In "Couronne," the fall of kings is linked to the poet's role, as in earlier verse ("La Chanson du Mal-Aimé" and "Vendémiaire"). Apollinaire, who was fond of endowing himself literally with royal (or imperial) lineage, felt a kinship to the many kings who seemed to be dying out in his own time. On another level, he, as poet, is virtually a royal heir. Here again use is made of occasional oversize capitals: they suggest jewels or even the structure of the crown; the central capitals that downward read QUIA "because" underline the inevitability of a flow from kingship to poet.

In "Miroir," as in "Couronne," Apollinaire feels no modesty in asserting his poetic identity. A wreath of words encircles the name of the poet who is thus "living and real" in a Mallarméan sense; that is, the poet's name, by replacing his reflected features, suggests the absence of all the Apollinaires of every moment in time and, in their place, the presence of an ideal Apollinaire who dwells in the Absolute, beyond change. The typographical presentation has a three-dimensional effect which lends depth to the mirror and to the name floating within it. The mirror frame or wreath (as in the laurel wreath that, in ancient Athens, crowned athletes and poets) may also be seen as an aureole, and the words composing the aureole may be read as a playful reminiscence of Mallarmé's *angelisme:* "Je me mire et me vois ange! "

References

Bassy, A. M. "Forme littéraire et forme graphique: les schématogrammes d'Apollinaire." *Cahiers de recherches de l'Ecole Normale Supérieure,* 3-4 (1973-74), 161-207.

Lockerbie, S. I. "Forme graphique et expressivité dans les *Calligrammes.*" In *Lecture et interprétation des Calligrammes,* 9th Apollinaire Colloquium. Stavelot, 1977. In press.

TOUR, page 90

First published in *Portugal Futurista* (November 1917).

The Eiffel Tower and the great Ferris wheel, built for the Universal Exhibition of 1889, were symbols, for the modernist generation, of the technological triumphs of the modern world. The tower was one of the main themes of the paintings of Robert Delaunay, who also painted a series of canvases linking the tower and the wheel. This is no doubt why Apollinaire combined them in this poem, when he was asked to supply a text for a postcard to mark the Delaunay exhibition in Berlin in early 1913. The postcard is reproduced in Cailler (pl. 82) where it can be seen, however, that an inappropriate choice of painting was made to illustrate the poem, since only the tower is shown.

When published in *Portugal Futurista,* the poem was spread out laterally and vertically on the page (cf. *GA* 4, pp. 104-105, where the page of the review is reproduced). This arrangement was appropriate in that the theme of the poem is the global consciousness and universalist outlook shared by Delaunay and Apollinaire. The modern spirit embraces all points of the compass and all the pulsating energy of the natural world implied by the swelling ocean and the turbulent noises from the East. In this context the wheel that the tower addresses is not only its Parisian neighbor but, by implication, the cosmic wheel of the universe (cf. M. Poupon, *GA* 6, pp. 110-112). The tower thus becomes the pivot, or the still center, of the turning world. Delaunay had already implied this by writing on the back of his painting, *Tour—première étude* (1909), the phrase, "Exposition universelle 1889. La Tour à l'Univers s'adresse" [Universal Exhibition 1889. The Tower addresses the Universe].

References

Bergman, P. "A propos des 'Fenêtres' et de 'Tour,'" *GA* 1 (1962), 62-65.
Décaudin, M. "'Arbre' et 'Tour' dans *Portugal Futurista*," *GA* 4 (1965), 103-105.

VOYAGE, page 92

First published in *Les Soirées de Paris*, 26-27 (July-August 1914).

M. Poupon points out that the writing of the poem coincided with the marriage of Marie Laurencin and her departure on her wedding trip (*voyage de noces*) with her husband. So Apollinaire laments the flight of love, ambivalently comparing Marie's departure with Dante's journey to exile, or even with his imaginary descent into Hell (*GA* 6, p. 115).

There is much, therefore, in "Voyage" which is reminiscent of *Alcools*: not only the theme of loss of love, but also the association with that theme of a more general sense of transience, symbolized by the train disappearing into the distance. (Passing trains are used as early as "Rhénanes" to suggest the transitoriness of experience.) The evocative setting of a landscape at dusk, the graceful phrasing, the elegiac coloring of the language—all flow from these complementary themes and create the mood of reverie tinged with sadness which is typical of many early poems.

A new dimension, however, is given to the familiar subject by the graphic form. The spatial values of a landscape setting which do so much to enhance the themes in *Alcools* are here evoked by graphic as well as verbal means. This is not done by description: on the contrary, the typographical layout is, at best, a severely schematic depiction of a landscape. It is rather through visual interpretations of the form, and by a kinetic process of reading, that a sense of space is created.

Because of the normal direction of reading, and the size of the type, the reader puts the cloud and the train into the foreground and, by coming to the sky only at the bottom of the page, is led to project it in his mind as a distant backdrop to the scene, thereby introducing depth and perspective. The effect of spatial recession (and thus of unattainable remoteness) is reinforced by the multiple eye movements and the slow scanning of the page which are necessary to build up an impression of the stars. Within this elliptically three-dimensional framework, however, other spatial relationships are left vague. The cloud is not perceived in the same perspective as the sky and, therefore, is not "fitted into" it. The telephone pole and the telegraph are seen from still different points of view and cannot be situated at any precise points in the imaginary landscape. Rather than a "picture," therefore, what is built up is a mental construction of space which, though closely tied to the graphic form, still creates an evocative impression of distance and spatial perspectives.

The graphic form also interacts with the verbal text in more specific ways. The words composing the cloud and the telegraph may be read in different sequences, which highlights their imagery and verbal play. The black *C* in the sky amusingly depicts the moon, and the heavy lettering at the end of the train represents the locomotive. An important effect of the latter shape is to create a tension between the *verbal* suggestion of dying away (*meurt au loin*) and the *visual* impression of the train coming nearer. Given that the phrase that is thus highlighted and brought nearer (*tendre été si pâle*) is evocative of the beauty of summer, the result of the tension is to suggest a reconciliation of contradictory emotions: the sense of loss and transience is halted and balanced by a positive stress on the beauty of the natural world. For this reason, no doubt, the train shape forms the dominating center of the design. Ultimately, however, the same reconciliation is implicit in the whole graphic form in that it "arrests" and lays out for contemplation, in a controlled pattern, appearances that are described as evanescent.

References

Bassy, A. M. "Forme littéraire et forme graphique: les schématogrammes d'Apollinaire." *Cahiers de recherches de l'Ecole Normale Supérieure*, 3-4 (1973-74), 161-207.

Lockerbie, S. I. "Forme graphique et expressivité dans les *Calligrammes.*" In *Lecture et Interprétation des Calligrammes*, 9th Apollinaire Colloquium. Stavelot, 1977. In press.

A TRAVERS L'EUROPE, page 96

First published in *Les Soirées de Paris*, 23 (April 15, 1914), and in *Der Sturm* (May 1914).

Apollinaire's exposure to German expressionism took place, in part, under Delaunay's aegis. He was first in touch with *Der Sturm* in December 1912, and in January 1913 he visited the gallery in Berlin with Delaunay, who was putting on a show there, and gave a talk on "La Peinture Nouvelle." A year and a half later, *Der Sturm* published the poem.

In *Ma Vie,* Chagall has told the story of the beginnings of "A Travers l'Europe," underlining that spontaneity which Apollinaire so esteemed and which often seems so suspect in his poetry: "Je n'ose pas montrer mes toiles à Apollinaire. 'Je sais, vous êtes l'inspirateur du cubism. Mais, moi, je voudrais autre chose.' Quoi d'autre? Je suis gêné. Nous traversons le sombre corridor où l'eau goutte sans fin, où des monceaux d'ordures sont entassés. Un palier rond; une dizaine de portes numérotées. J'ouvre la mienne. Apollinaire entre avec prudence comme s'il craignait que tout le bâtiment s'effondre soudain en l'entraînant dans ses ruines. . . . Apollinaire s'assied. Il rougit, enfle, sourit et murmure: 'Surnaturel! . . .' Le lendemain, je recevais une lettre, une poème dédié à moi: 'Rodztag.' Comme une pluie battante, le sense de vos paroles nous frappe" (pp. 159-161). [I don't dare show my paintings to Apollinaire. "I know, you're the inspirer of cubism. But I want to do something else." What else? It's embarrassing. We cross the dark hallway where water drips endlessly and piles of garbage are lying about. A circular stairwell; a dozen doors with numbers on them. I open mine. Apollinaire enters cautiously as if he feared the whole building might crumble and drag him down in the ruins. . . . Apollinaire takes a seat. He blushes, snorts, smiles, and murmurs: "Supernatural! . . ." The next day I received a letter, a poem dedicated to me: "Rodztag." Like a pelting rain, the meaning of your words beats upon us.]

Obviously, from this passage, Apollinaire was deeply moved, both intellectually and emotionally, by Chagall's paintings. He related them to his own taste for a mixture of real and fantastic, that is, "le surnaturel," and also to his loss of Marie. The rapidity with which he expressed his enthusiasm, however, remains in doubt. The first title, according to the painter, was "Rodztag," literally "red day," and the poem was composed in a few hours. On the other hand, Adéma and Decaudin observe that the maquette at the Fonds Doucet is composed of a collage manuscript, "papiers découpés et collés"; only the first two verses are written on the page; the titles "Rotsoge" and "Prophétie et Vision" have been successively crossed out (*OP,* p. 1085). Bearing this conflicting evidence in mind, it seems reasonable to suppose that the painter received a first version which was subsequently reworked.

The final title is appropriate to Chagall's first trip from Russia to Paris. "Paris," he says in *Ma Vie,* "tu es mon second Witebsk." "A Travers l'Europe," as ambiguous a title as "Les Fenêtres" or "Un Fantôme de Nuées," suggests the cosmopolite character of both painter and poet. Another of the characteristics shared by the two artists is suggested in the second rejected title, "Prophétie et Vision."

Of Apollinaire's three major poems to painters, "Les Fenêtres," "Un Fantôme de Nuées," and "A Travers l'Europe," all in "Ondes" and all first published between January 1913 and April 1914, the last-named may be considered the culmination. Reminiscent of "Les Fenêtres" are several anchors in external reality: visual images from paintings by Chagall, references to objects in his studio, scraps of conversation. As in the earlier poem, abrupt transitions link divergent points in time and space. The atmosphere, however, despite stylistic differences, is reminiscent of "Un Fantôme," partly because of the dreamlike nature of Chagall's images. Chagall seems to have affected the poet more powerfully than any other painter except Picasso. Nostalgic memories mingle with an awareness of the present and anticipations of the future. The memories are often expressed by verses from "La Clef" (*OP*, pp. 553-555), a poem in the Stavelot notebook. The first quotation from "La Clef" establishes a pattern for other returns to the past and eventually for a fusion of different pasts concerned with loss.

Continual fluctuation between the poet's memories and what he sees in the painter's world provides a poetic structure: contemplation of Chagall's paintings sends the poet to his own past, at first to a time far distant and finally to a fairly recent past, to his loss, most probably, of Marie Laurencin. This theme of loss mingles with Chagallian motifs and leads the poet finally to a new awareness of his own identity. He examines past losses by the light of present experiences, transforms past loves into a sort of poetic and cosmic matter, and emerges victorious as creator and prophet. As a kind of prism also. For the fragmentation throughout "A Travers l'Europe," which accompanies the switchbacks in time, suggests the poet's assumption of a prismatic function: he breaks what seems to be one impression, as it pierces his sensibility, into reactions at different levels. Then, after the fragmentation of a total aesthetic experience, there takes place a second prismatic action, that of recombining or reintegrating the now separate elements into a new whole—which is the poetic vision resulting from the experience of recording the poem.

Apollinaire had recently absorbed Delaunay's theories on color (see note to "Les Fenêtres"). These theories, as much as the poet's impression of Chagall's paintings, seem to have determined his use of color words. "A Travers l'Europe" begins with a typical ambiguity, *Rotsoge*, a title that eventually became the first line. It may be a nickname for the red-haired painter, or it may have been inspired by his self-portrait (with red mustache and a red mask). *Rotsoge*, or "red trail," suggests too the wake of color left by a flying object in a painting and thus introduces not only a Chagallian vision but perhaps the painter himself in the guise of a new comet. The first line leads us directly to the second: besides its figurative meaning, *écarlate* literally changes the hue of redness, according to the laws of harmony, and plunges us into a Chagallian world of people with oddly colored faces. In Chagall's pictures, the main figure—painter, violinist, flying onlooker—usually has a green face (as in *Moi et le village,* 1911). Apollinaire seems to play one of his erudite games by turning the color wheel and substituting red for its complement green (Greet).

The third stanza contains a single verse, which concerns the color violet. Here the poet thinks of Chagall, rather than of Delaunay. For Delaunay, a single color has little meaning. For Apollinaire, the color violet has many meanings. In "Les Fenêtres" it suggests mysterious depths. In "Un Fantôme" it is associated with death. In "A Travers l'Europe" the poet seems to react to Chagall's use of the color in paintings about the mystery and the joy of love, such as *Le Mariage* (1910), where the bridegroom wears a lavender suit, or *La Promenade* (1913), where Bella the fiancée floats through the sky in a lavender robe; thus the color violet becomes for the poet *épouvantable* because it sets off his loneliness (Greet).

In the final stanza Apollinaire's adaptation of Delaunay's color theories merges with what can be considered as his own interpretation of expressionistic techniques. A painting that may have existed in Chagall's studio leads us into the poet's past. Lines 18 and 19, reminiscent of Chagall's prewar style and, in particular, of the *Marchant de betail* (1912), recall too Delaunay's technique of color fragmentation. Apollinaire's presentation of the colors is calculated in its effect: mauve and yellow are complementary; yellow and blue constitute a dissonance; and, although blue and green constitute a harmony of similarity, green and red, once more, are complementary. The emphasis (here, overwhelming) on complementary or opposed colors creates, according to Delaunay, an effect of intensification; in the poem, it is precisely at this point that the poet's memories become intensely emotional. It would seem that, whereas in "Les Fenêtres" Apollinaire plays around with color theories and in "Un Fantôme" he uses colors in his accustomed way as symbols, he becomes, in his poem for Chagall, more experimental and subtle. Keeping in mind a theory learned from Delaunay, he begins with a playful mystification; then, as the poem changes in atmosphere, he associates color more and more directly with a state of mind that is never explicit but is increasingly expressive of intense emotion. Thus his poem appears far closer to an expressionist vision than to those symbolist beginnings recalled by "La Clef" (Greet).

Lines 1-8. The movement of the first stanza proceeds from three lines evoking Chagallian motifs to a fourth line, expressive of the poet's nostalgia. Three fragments of a conversation, at once mysterious and cliché-ridden (5-7), lead us back to an evocation of the painter's world.

Line 2. The image of a biplane that becomes a hydroplane suggests colors of air and water (blue, violet, green) and themes (transformations, clouds, the flying couple, the painting that transports us into other dimensions) which Apollinaire may associate with Chagall. A less obvious theme suggested by the biplane/hydroplane is the bisexual nature of the painter. In Chagall's world one frequently encounters a couple who, like Apollinairean *pi-mus* or *pi-hi*, have some part of their anatomy in common. In *L'Hommage à Apollinaire* (1911-1912), Chagall had already portrayed the androgynous character of the poet's literary identity.

Line 3. *Ta maison ronde* refers to Chagall's studio, "La Ruche," on the round stairwell, which Apollinaire visited. The *hareng saur* which swims appropriately about Chagall's dwelling is probably a staple in the painter's larder at that time, as well as a subject of such paintings as *L'Homme au hareng* (undated, probably 1911) or *Le Saoul* (1911-12). The image of the herring swimming in an aquarium/atelier prolongs the mixture of elements and an absence of frontiers between external reality and dream which Apollinaire had immediately recognized as "surnaturel." (But s.v. "Rotsoge" in S. Bates, 1975, for another interpretation of lines 1-3.)

Line 4. A quotation from "La Clef" (c. 1900). The technique of introducing former sorrows and the symbolist language of his youth by juxtaposing a *vers de jeunesse* with present time has already occurred in *Alcools*. The reference to the past adds an obvious temporal dimension; it creates an illusion of objectivity by pulling the narrator out of the present moment; it gives the reader the impression that layers (or streams) of consciousness are simultaneously at work in the poet; and, not least in value for Apollinaire, the intrusion of an old mannerism jolts the reader by a clash in styles (notably between ll. 4 and 5). The verse announces a major theme of the poem. In reaction to the art and milieu of Chagall, the poet cries out for *la clef*, conceivably the key to Chagall's art, at least that key to art necessary to his own creations. *Paupières* "eyelids" can suggest the act of seeing but, for Apollinaire, the image usually suggests a girl. Thus already there is, implicit in the poem, an association between loss of poetic inspiration and the loss of a sweetheart, lost long ago at Stavelot or in the Rhineland, lost most recently with Marie. Implicit too is another characteristic shared by the two artists: their dependence on a woman. What "la fiancée," the faithful Bella, means to Chagall the painter, the Muse whose identity changes but whose nature seems always unloving means to the poet Apollinaire.

Lines 5-7. Anonymous voices intrude, with a typical turning from sentiment to humor. M. D. probably refers to Maurice Denis and to the religious world of his paintings. The verb *voir* may be taken, not only literally or in opposition to verbal communication, but as a visionary act encompassing all aesthetic creation.

Line 8 may offer an answer to the question posed in line 7. It is curiously launched by two numbers, seemingly concerned with precise statistics yet not related to anything precise and, consequently, dreamlike or, more appropriately, floating. They may suggest nothing at all, a flight upward, a hovering as in dreams, the respective heights of the Tower of Pisa and the Eiffel Tower (J. Manson, graduate paper, UCSB). The poet is playing games with us: 9 plus 0 equals 9; 3 plus 2 plus 4 equals 9 also. The man in the air recalls at once an image from "Zone" (the *joli voltigeur*) and a number of prewar paintings by Chagall. The transparently pregnant cow is purely Chagallian; Apollinaire may have seen *La Vache enceinte* (1913). The line as a whole evokes the painting *Paris, à travers la fenêtre* (1913), in which a man floats near the Eiffel Tower.

Lines 9-16. Three verses from "La Clef" open the second stanza, expressing loss, not only of love but of some contact with nature, and that mysterious melancholy one associates with postsymbolism. But Apollinaire does not linger on any one theme or mood. Thus line 12, while it echoes the verb *ouvre*, found in "La Clef," seems closer to a later poem of reminiscence, "Le Voyageur" (*Alcools*) (*Ouvrez-moi cette porte* . . .), whereas line 13 echoes the imperative mood of the preceding verse; at the same time it changes the tone to one of familiarity and surprise, and stresses once more the theme of seeing. Nostalgia gives way momentarily to the artist's task of working with materials drawn from daily life (14). The noting of curious detail one associates with Chagall, especially in his early paintings, and with Apollinaire, most evidently in the later poems (see note to "Souvenirs"). At this point (15), by means of a verse in Italian, "Once I heard someone say . . .," the theme of lost love and the problem of what constitutes poetic material begin to fuse. A voice out of a past even more remote than the memories of Stavelot, his first seven years in Rome, postulates an ambiguous question—"What do you want?"—a question that all his life the poet will find diffcult to answer. Instead of answering, he ends the stanza by imposing, through a typical distortion of pronouns, a formal distance between the adult Apollinaire and what he recalls of his child self in Rome or Monaco (16).

Line 17. In terms of inner time, the one-line third stanza probably has a density comparable to that of the eight-line stanzas preceding it. *Et toi*, an invocation to Chagall, suggests the intimacy of friendship, the implicit understanding between artists. Above all, the line suggests that the entire experience of the poem, elaborated in the final stanza, turns upon the magic gesture of the painter.

Lines 18-29. Contrasting with the long lines 2 and 8, which overflow with disparate images, lines 18 and 20 suggest the prolongation of a single image. They proceed through irregular alexandrines (based on the elisions of familiar speech) in lines 19, 21-22 to shorter lines and rapid changes in meter.

Line 23 can conceivably, if improperly, be read as an octosyllabic line. There is an increasing effect of syncopation which stresses an increasing fragmentation of emotion, as well as of visual images. This seemingly spontaneous if painful shorthand based upon private references recalls a state of mind celebrated in "La Chanson du Mal-Aimé" (*Alcools*), that of one who has been overwhelmed and betrayed by experiences which he is finally able to exorcise through his poetry.

From another point of view, the beginning of the final stanza exemplifies Apollinaire's attitude to painting as a subject for poetry. Although Chagall is the magician who stirs the poet's emotions, what matters is Apollinaire's aesthetic experience (which in his case is closely related to his private emotional experience) at the moment of looking around the painter's atelier, interrupted by chance external phenomena or by internal phenomena based on his own changing identity. Rapid changes of mood link humor to regret: Marie Laurencin may be *une charmante cheminée*, but, although the phrasing is light, touched with a humorous fantasy rather than with bitter irony, the theme is loss and emerges in the three lines of pathos which follow.

Lines 24-27. The impression of syncopated rhythm and fragmented feelings is prolonged into the first line of a final quotation from "La Clef." Line 24, in its original version, was octosyllabic, like the three it introduces: *Et la veilleuse consumée* [And the burnt-out night-light]. In these lines the theme of lost love is transformed into a stressing of the ephemeral (24, 25), which in turn becomes an affirmation of the present moment as the sole experience worthy of poetry. The change of tone, from loss to affirmation, takes place where an image of light is seized at a moment of intense glory, juxtaposing notions of finality—Marie or someone else has gone—and of poetic promise (26, 27).

Lines 28-29. The final articulate affirmation indicates that the whole passage is artistically contrived: an evolving ars poetica rather than a lover's sorrow is Apollinaire's essential preoccupation. In the last two lines, love, glorified and unchanging, as it already exists in "La Maison des Morts" (*Alcools*), in *les glaciers de la mémoire*, merges with Apollinaire's own poetic vocabulary and with images from Chagall's paintings. The image of the hair, always reminiscent of Marie, leads Apollinaire back to the world of Chagall and to a wider vision of the cosmopolitan poet. An echo of "La Chanson du Mal-Aimé" (*les tramways feux verts sur l'échine*) [tramways with green fires along their spines] reminds us that the poet is, above all, the singer of a modern world and only secondarily "le mal-aimé." The beloved's hair trailing across the sky above European cities, as, in Chagall's later paintings (such as *Fenêtre dans le ciel*, 1957), the beloved or the couple hover above a village at night, expresses the exalted vision of the artist, be he poet or painter. Marie like a goddess spreads her hair across Europe. At the same time, and a little in contrast, the poet, no longer as lover but as a spectator, stresses his vision of the modern world. Comparably, in later paintings, Chagall's man in the air often is not exalted but is simply the elevated observer of Paris or a village scene. Thus the poet returns from explorations of his own identity to the visual source of his meditation: undamaged, but transfigured and illumined by his aesthetic experience.

References

Chagall, Marc. *Ma Vie.* Stock, 1957.

Greet, A. H. "Rotsoge: A travers Chagall." In *Apollinaire et la peinture.* 8th Apollinaire Colloquium. Stavelot, 1975. In press.

IL PLEUT, page 100

First published in *SIC,* 12 (December 1916).

"Il Pleut" was written, in all probability, at Deauville in July 1914. Apollinaire mentioned it in a letter to Serge Férat on July 29, 1914, sketching out the shape of the poem on the page without, however, supplying the words (*OP,* p. 1085). One must doubt the statement of P. A. Birot, the editor of *SIC,* that Apollinaire attached little importance to the typographical interpretation of this and his other calligrams, being content to leave the responsibility to the printer (Themerson, p. 23). In fact, the manuscript reproduced in Themerson (p. 25) shows that the printer has remained very faithful to the poet's intentions.

The number of times the design has been imitated, or echoed, in the work of concrete poets, and even in graphic commercial art (Massin, p. 156), is sufficient testimony to its appealing visual quality. It is interestingly different in conception from two other typographical representations of rain (see note on "Du Coton dans les Oreilles"); possibly it evokes raindrops running down a window pane, as Décaudin suggests (*GA* 8, p. 239). Apollinaire might have conceived the idea of using slanting lines after seeing Boccioni's futurist paintings of 1911, *States of Mind: Those Who Go* and *Those Who Stay,* in which diagonal and downward moving lines are associated, respectively, with speed and sadness. But the poem is so different in tone and subject matter as to make this conclusion unlikely.

The first function of the lines as graphic form is to sustain and enhance the verbal music. Effectively the visual continuity turns each line into one long rhythmic unit, thereby emphasizing its musical potential. The emotion that is first heightened is an elegiac one reminiscent of Verlaine in the murmuring tone that is adopted, in the association of rain with vanished happiness and women's voices that are gone, and in the verbal play on *pleut* and *pleurent.* But the second and third lines quickly establish, in place of simple Verlainean melancholy, a more complex dialectic in which rain is also associated with the enrichment of new experiences and wholehearted involvement in the expanding modern world. These contradictory associations are fused together in the ambiguity of the final line, in which the verb *tomber* has the two meanings of "falling" and "falling away," that is, disintegrating. As in other poems in "Ondes," including "Liens" itself, the double attitude of Apollinaire toward the modern world, looking nostalgically back and eagerly forward, is nicely caught in the two strands of the poem.

In this light the graphic form might be seen as ambivalent also. Trickling raindrops may be expressive of sadness, but in the way they spread down and over the windowpane there is also a sense of adventure and exploration of space. The light undulating lines, as they push delicately down and out, reflect the poet's open attitude to experience and his desire to make new "encounters" in a new and expanding world. To this extent the graphic form anticipates the use in other poems of sinuous lines fanning out over the page ("Visée," "Du Coton dans les Oreilles"), as well as verbal expressions of a similar desire to "flow" out into space (notably in "Merveille de la Guerre").

Reference

Lockerbie, S. I. "Forme graphique et expressivité dans les *Calligrammes.*" In *Lecture et interprétation des Calligrammes.* 9th Apollinaire Colloquium. Stavelot, 1977. In press.

LA PETITE AUTO, page 104

First published in *Calligrammes.* The poem evokes Apollinaire's precipitate return to Paris on the eve of war, from Deauville where he had been on a journalistic mission with André Rouveyre. A prose piece, "La Fête Manquée" (*OC*, V, 704-706), commemorates the same journey.

Judging by a reference in an epistolary poem to Rouveyre dated January 14, 1915 (*OP*, p. 780), the first draft of the poem was not written until several months after the event. The manuscript also seems to establish that the central section (ll. 11-31) was composed at a still later date (*OP*, p. 1086). The conclusion to be drawn from the evidence is that, with increasing hindsight, Apollinaire sought to amplify the messianic view that the poem takes of the war. There is already an apocalyptic note in the earlier part (esp. ll. 5-10); it is considerably extended in the central section where the poet presents himself as a seer whose vision of the future is magnified by the momentous events he inwardly contemplates. The poem is an eminently fitting introduction to the entire war poetry, and the literary strategy that is pursued in it (see introduction, p. 1).

Line 1. It was on July 31, not August 31, that Apollinaire left Deauville. Some critics have seen in the change of date a conscious or unconscious reminiscence of a number of popular songs about war which begin in a similar way.

Lines 5-10. The images here suggest an impending cataclysm on a cosmic scale (an idea repeated in ll. 19-22) from which, however, some deep insight will emerge (l. 9).

Lines 14-16. Since Germany had not yet invaded Belgium by July 31, this allusion confirms a later date of composition (as does the reference to aerial warfare in ll. 21-24). Apollinaire is speaking from personal knowledge of the area around Stavelot in the Belgian Ardennes, where in 1899 he spent a long summer that was of capital importance in his development as a poet. Francorchamps is a town, and l'Eau Rouge a river, near Stavelot; *pouhons* is the local word for the mineral springs in the area.

Lines 25-31. The emphasis throughout the central section has been on the growth of Apollinaire's powers of vision through his ability to embrace within himself the vast dimensions of the coming conflict; hence he uses *je* rather than the *nous* of the first and last sections. At the climax of the development, the poet's privileged status as a seer is further reinforced, for the expansion of his consciousness allows him to see even further into the future and glimpse the fabulous new universe that will emerge from the war. As in "Merveille de la Guerre" (see note on that poem), the poet seems to draw from his vision a sense of ubiquity—a mythic sense of his self being universally extended throughout time and space—hence the feeling that the future is being unfolded "within his consciousness" (l. 25: *Je sentais en moi*).

This vision may not be without a somber side, as lines 29 and 30 may be seen as a hint that in the transfigured future powerful leaders will manipulate ordinary humanity, like sheep. There is a similar fear at the end of "Le Brasier" in *Alcools* (*OP*, p. 110), and, significantly, the manuscript had an additional line after line 28 which read: *Où l'humanité était une marchandise* [In which humanity was merchandise]. As in "Le Brasier," however, this equivocal note is subdued and does not fundamentally affect the state of visionary exaltation the poet attains.

Je n'oublierai jamais... The text of the calligram combines a mood of apprehension (*O départ sombre*...) and of anticipation (the blue of Lisieux, the gold of Versailles). Despite the constraints of the design the language is melodious, with internal echos (the three exclamatory phrases forming the body of the car) and verbal play (the two phrases forming the wheels are made parallel by forcing the first syllable of Versailles to double up as the preposition *vers*). The design is set off visually and rhythmically by the two long "framing" lines.

As graphic form, the shape is simply descriptive, without the visual ambiguities of other calligrams. It emphasizes the simplicity of the car (suggested in the text by *petite*), which makes it very different from the powerful, threatening roadsters dreamed up by the futurists as symbols of the new age. It is typical of Apollinaire that even in visionary mood he remains attentive to everyday reality.

Lines 36-44. Following on from the calligram, the closing lines adopt an effective simplicity of tone. The momentousness of the event is conveyed by the positioning of *Nouvelle* in a line of its own and by the neat paradox of the last two lines.

References

Clark, J. G. "La poésie, la politique et la guerre," *GA* 13 (1974).
Roques, M. "Aspects de G. A.," *Neophilologus*, XXXI, 3 (1947).

LA MANDOLINE l'OEILLET ET LE BAMBOU, page 112

On the galleys, three alternative titles are scored out. In each instance it is the third term of the title which varies, being first "Le Bambou Parfumé" ["The Perfumed Bamboo"], then "Le Mystère Odorant" ["The Fragrant Mystery"], and finally "Le Rêve" ["The Dream"]. These variants leave no doubt that the bamboo is an opium pipe; the conclusion can be drawn that the poem in all probability dates from the period in Nice, just before and after Apollinaire's enlistment, when he was smoking opium with Lou. Other writings from the same period which touch on the same theme are "Fumées" (see note), the first of the *Poèmes à Lou* (*OP*, p. 377) in which calligrams of a flower and the pipe reappear, but the mandolin is replaced with a fig, and a prose passage entitled "Le Sang Noir des Pavots (*OC*, II, 702-704 [The black blood of the poppies]) which offers points of comparison in ideas and vocabulary with the opium calligram.

The poem as a whole is concerned with sensation as a stimulus for the poetic imagination. Opium provides the most powerful sensations acting on the poet's consciousness, but the sense impressions associated with the mandolin and the carnation similarly lead him to reflect on their capacity to extend and refine his perceptions.

"La Mandoline" explicitly takes the form of a search for analogies to illuminate the poet's immediate sensations. The mandolin itself is metaphoric, being the first stage in the process of discovering a higher significance in the violence of war. The comparison of the trembling earth to music etherealizes the sounds of battle and the bullet tearing the flesh and makes them suggestive of a deeper insight (*la vérité*). This insight is then connected to the experience of love through a pun on the word *raison*. Reason, the characteristic of woman (cf. *la Raison ardente* of "La Jolie Rousse"), is related to truth but also to sound because it is *rai-son* ("ray-sound") or sound that, like light, has a penetrating quality. An analogical circle is thus described going from war to sound, to truth, to reason, to woman, and back to sound. One might say, on a prosaic level, that the poet is seeking to relate the exhilaration that he experiences in war to the delight that he feels in love, but the elliptical analogies spin out and refine this blunt thought into a series of more subtly interrelated perceptions. Graphically, the circular line of the musical instrument echoes the circular movement of thought, while its enclosed shape suggests the self-sufficiency of the aesthetic meditation that it represents. The mandolin contains within itself the violence of war—battles are at the center of its sounding board, and the projecting neck possibly recalls the shape of artillery pieces—but the auditory associations of the instrument transmute the violence into an experience of another order.

In "l'Œillet" the carnation is real rather than metaphoric and olfactory sensations are said to offer stronger stimulation to the mind than the auditory impressions dealt with in "La Mandoline." In this part, however, the poetic potential of the sensations is not so much explored through analogies as formulated in a general statement, which is made appealing and suggestive by the hint that the poet can already glimpse the laws that will bring about a great expansion of human consciousness. The large and stately design of the flower—the dominating graphic form in the poem—adds emphasis and dignity to the aesthetic pronouncement. The use of the plus sign to mean "more" perhaps evokes the concision of thought that will result from the new insights yielded by olfactory sensations; it may have been suggested to Apollinaire by a similar use of the sign in futurist poetry. In every other respect, however, the qualities of repose and ornamental beauty inherent in this design are to be distinguished from the frenetic dynamism of futurist graphics.

The most powerful sensations of all are those induced by opium. To convey the hallucinatory expansion of the mind produced by a compact substance in a confined space, the poet fashions a corresponding density of form, which releases lingering ambiguities of meaning. The ambiguities arise, in some measure, from the elliptical syntax, especially evident in the first line with the uncertain status of the noun *centre* and the adverb *y*. Cunningly, the calligrammatic design adds to the syntactical complications. While the three large circles in the drawing have the graphic function of representing the joints in the bamboo pipe, the first of them has also the verbal function of acting as an apostrophe to the beginning of both the first and second lines. If the first apostrophe has no disruptive effect, the second (*O univers*) becomes an exclamatory interjection, separating the noun *chaînes* from its participial adjective *infiniment déliées* and thus confusing the normal word order. Although the two other circles have no such obvious verbal function, nevertheless the graphic symmetry of the three *O*'s encourages a tendency to read them also as exclamatory interjections, thereby introducing further interruptions and uncertainties into the syntactical sequence.

Moreover, simply by dividing the lines visually into strongly separated segments, the three *O*'s tempt the reader to explore the possibilities of different combinations of the segments. No fully satisfactory alternative order emerges, but the hesitation is sufficient to reinforce the general process of interactive wordplay in the poem which is encouraged by the loosening of the syntax. One product of such tentative explorations is the hypothesis that *O* may be a disguised prepositional *au.* This idea is feasible for the first circle, making the initial phrase read "in the nose of the pipe"; it is not impossible for the second circle, which might be interpreted as a missing, or merely delayed, preposition for *centre,* which would then read: *au centre fourneau* "in the center of the bowl."

The dislocations, delays, and overlapping meanings inscribed in the syntax reinforce the final ambiguity in the poem, that of the image of chains of opium smoke. This image connects with other occurrences of spirals of smoke in *Calligrammes,* which always suggest moods of reverie and dreamy meditation. To these associations is added here an ambivalence arising from the contrasted words *déliées* and *lient* ("unbound" and "bind") which is reminiscent of a similar ambiguity in the metaphor of bonds or *liens* (see notes on "Liens" and "Il Pleut"). In one interpretation the loose, supple chains may be thought of as binding together fruitfully the more conscious faculties of the mind. In another, they may be seen as shackling and restricting the formal powers of thought and intelligence. Interestingly, in "Le Sang Noir des Pavots," it is the latter, pejorative view of opium which Apollinaire takes. The verb *lier* is used there in the favorable sense of "bind together," but it is so used of the intellect, whose powers are said to be "extinguished" by opium. The poem is not so categoric; it deliberately allows both interpretations to be entertained within the general accumulation of meaning in a highly suggestive work.

The unusual triangular arrangement of the three calligrams (which is reproduced at the wrong angle in most editions) does not necessarily have a specific significance in itself, but it helps to suggest the tight interrelationship between the sensations meditated on by the poet and, by extension, the importance of sensuous experience in his poetry.

FUMÉES, page 114

First published in *Calligrammes.* On the galleys the original title is "Fumée." The poem was presumably written soon after Apollinaire's acceptance by the artillery at Nimes.

Lines 3-4. A poet's credo, exalting the olfactory sense, is more fully developed in the preceding calligram "La Mandoline l'Œillet et le Bambou" (see note). These passages have, as an immediate source in *Alcools,* Apollinaire's meditations on the senses in the sixth poem of "Les Fiançailles," where they seem to mislead or limit his thought, and in "Cortège," where they expand the poet's imagination. Here, his images of smoke and flowers recall a line describing the sense of smell, in "Les Fiançailles": "La bête des fumées a la tête fleurie" [The beast of smoke has a flowering head].

The calligram of the pipe includes and stresses the word *Zone,* that is, the free area where tobacco would be available. Apollinaire's yearning for tobacco returns in several war poems and is a constant preoccupation in letters to Lou and Madeleine, both of whom sent him cigarettes.

Lines 6-15. As the poem proceeds it becomes ambiguous. Does the poet smoke a pipe of tobacco or does he, at least in memory, smoke opium, as he did with Lou in Nice? Does he describe an almost hallucinatory experience or daydream based on actual smoking or is he inspired by the visual image of smoke? Smoke, as a visual inspiration for daydreams of love and for poetry, returns in several war poems. Besides the apparent fusion of smell, sight, and reverie, there emerges, toward the end of the poem, a close association between love (and smoking or gazing at smoke) and the writing of poetry (and gazing at flames or his pages).

A NÎMES, page 118

First published, under the title "Le Dépôt" ("The Depot"), in *La Grande Revue,* 11 (November 1917), where it was dated December 1914.

Having enlisted on December 4, 1914, in Nice (where he had gone shortly after the outbreak of war), Apollinaire joined the 38th regiment of field artillery in Nimes on December 6. He underwent basic training and officer training at the Nimes depot until April 4, when he gave up his officer's course and asked to be transferred to a fighting unit.

Like the slightly later "2^{e} Canonnier Conducteur," "A Nîmes" conveys the state of mind in which Apollinaire undertook his military training. The mood is one of resolute enthusiasm, qualified—understandably, at this early stage—by occasional moments of emotional vulnerability (ll. 19-20), passing nostalgia for his prewar life (ll. 21-22), and restless impatience

(l. 27). The ready acceptance of a new existence is the predominating attitude, however, making itself felt in the deliberate simplicity not only of language but of form. The alexandrine, on this occasion, is stripped of its usual melodiousness and given something of the artless inflection of folk poetry. The arrangement in rhyming couplets contributes to this impression, but it also has the effect of giving each successive moment of experience its own particular plenitude. There is an even flow of time and activity, making a continuum in which the poet willingly submerges himself.

Line 5. The reference is to Apollinaire's passionate love affair with Louise de Coligny (Lou) begun in Nice and continued, during brief periods of leave, in both Nice and Nimes.

Line 15. The colloquial form *se mange* reflects the poet's immersion in the life of the barracks and the popular speech (and interests) of his fellow soldiers.

Line 20. The poet's use of *tu* in addressing himself has the effect here, as frequently in his poetry, of suggesting an intimate inner meditation—a dialogue between the poet and his innermost self.

Line 28. The *tour Magne* is a well-known monument, high on a hill in Nimes.

LA COLOMBE POIGNARDÉE ET LE JET D'EAU, page 122

First published in *Calligrammes.*

The poem was inspired by a drawing of doves sent to Apollinaire at Nimes in late 1914 by André Rouveyre. Strikingly revealing of the elegiac strain in his inspiration, the poem invests the age-old theme of *ubi sunt* with a new resonance. The strangely named *colombe poignardée* is the bleeding-heart dove (see note to "Refus de la Colombe"), which has a vaguely heart-shaped spot and a scatter of smaller spots on its breast, all brilliant red. Apollinaire plays on this peculiarity, and on the violent connotations of its French name, to suggest the cruel destruction wrought by time on love. Several of the girls named are known to have featured in his life, but the names also have general emotive value, evoking, with the dove image, the most tender and innocent kind of love.

It is revealing of the importance of friendship in Apollinaire's life that the sadness is no less haunting when he wonders what has become of his friends. All the friends named are artists or men of letters who were close to him, but with whom he lost contact, for a time, after his enlistment. The lines making up the fountain, in regular rhyming octosyllables (in the dove shape there is a mixture of six- and eight-syllable lines, with one decasyllable), are among the most melodious that Apollinaire wrote, and the incantation is maintained in the final part (the basin of the fountain) where the longer lines also divide into rhyming octosyllables (the line ends occur at *guerre/mer/guerrière* and at *maintenant/abondamment*). The imagery of the final two lines ends the poem on a particularly melancholy and death-haunted note.

The design, one of the most striking in the volume, testifies to Apollinaire's calligrammatic skill. The pictorial shape is achieved by sensitive layout and subtle changes of type. The capital *C* of *Chères* figures the bird's head and beak, and gradations in the type size depict the fanning of the tail. A discreet use of a question mark provides a plume oin the center of the spray of water. The black *O* suggests the drain hole in the center of the basin, which is pictured by heavier and darker type.

But beyond its pictorial function, and the support it lends to the musical flow, the design has a role to play as graphic form. In particular, where the verbal text describes the dove as simply being near the fountain, the design presents it in a hovering position above the water, in an outline resembling the traditional representation of the Holy Ghost. This depiction considerably reinforces the word *s'extasie* in the text, giving it the value of an ecstatic sublimation of pain, with overtones of divine suffering. Rather than representing only sad memories, the jets of water that rise toward the dove take on a force of aspiration and longing, which seems to strive toward an apotheosis.

Conversely, the collapse of each spray of water back into the pool assumes particularly somber implications. Water, whether stagnant or flowing, has associations with death throughout Apollinaire's poetry, nowhere more strongly expressed than in the obsessive image of glances drowning in water which features in "Le Pont Mirabeau" (*Alcools*) and elsewhere. It is significant that the image recurs here in the verbal text of the fountain (*Et vos regards en l'eau dormant/Meurent mélancoliquement*) and is reinforced by the graphic form. The oval shape of the basin suggests not only a pool with a gaping hole at the center—through which water and life can drain away—but also a staring eye submerged in the pool, exactly as in the verbal image. Simultaneously the capital *O* in the center of the eye pictures the other obsessive image of death which the line itself evokes: that of the bloodred sun sinking into the sea (cf. the famous image of "Zone" in *Alcools: Soleil cou coupé* [Sun slit throat]).

There is thus an interaction between verbal text and graphic form throughout the poem which adds considerable intensity to themes. The mourning of lost loves and friends is heightened into a conflict between apotheosis and death, expressed in the arrangement of the three shapes on the page and the echoing music and imagery of the language.

2^e CANONNIER CONDUCTEUR, page 124

First published in the opening number of *Der Mistral* (March 3, 1915), at Zurich, a futurist little magazine which appeared in neutral territory because of its international flavor. Apollinaire was still in touch with Marinetti and others of the group whose notions had intrigued him. The futurist aesthetic may have contributed to his use of modernistic images, that, in both verbal and visual forms, abound in this poem, but not at all to his ideas about the function of such imagery of the ultimate meaning of poetry (see introduction, p. 1).

Romain Rolland attacked this first issue of *Der Mistral* and, more generally, Apollinaire's generation for "le cubisme et toutes les maladies intellectuelles du temps." Concerning the poem he wrote: "Elle est écrit dans tous les sens, en rond, en rectangle, en losange" (quoted in *OP*, p. 1078) [It's written in all directions, a circle, a rectangle, a lozenge]. Apollinaire, in turn, attacked Rolland repeatedly for his political stand. On July 18, 1915, he wrote to Madeleine: "Romain Rolland fait de désagréables et très déplacées manifestations presqu'en faveur de l'Allemagne. Moi j'ai publié au mois de février à Zurich un poème intitulé '2e Canonnier Conducteur' qui ne laissait aucun doute sur mes sentiments anti-boches" (*TS*, p. 64) [Romain Rolland is making unpleasant and very uncalled-for demonstrations, almost pro-German. As for me, in February I published a poem in Zurich, '2e Canonnier Conducteur,' which leaves no doubt about my anti-Hun feelings].

The poem incorporates five calligrams, in the form of a trumpet (or, conceivably, a cannon), an infantryman's or artilleryman's boot, Notre Dame, the Eiffel Tower, and a cannon shell, in much the same way that cubist painters incorporate words into their pictures. The main difference may be that whereas the newspaper collage used by such artists as Juan Gris undermines words, Apollinaire's calligrams lend a mystique to the substitution of visual for verbal image which is reminiscent of Mallarméan poetics, where, inversely, there is a substitution of word for object (see note to "Miroir," in "Cœur Couronne et Miroir"). Mallarmé's word takes on an absolute character. Comparably, here, an object like trumpet or boot does not seem to have individual plastic characteristics but, in the poet's mind, to represent *the* trumpet or *the* boot. On the other hand, the actual words that form a calligram have not only a specific but a surprising or disconcerting application, so that plastic values and verbal values in no way overlap but indeed may give rise to tension (see introduction, p. 1).

Lines 1-3. A feeling of liberation and of comradeship with Apollinaire's fellow soldiers in the artillery (even an anticipation of dangers to be shared) is announced as a major theme of this poem and, perhaps, of the war poems generally.

The words of the calligram, which are to be sung to the notes of reveille, constitute one of a number of such songs, generally risqué, which the French soldiers composed for the different trumpet calls. In context, *La fameuse Nancéenne* assumes the role of the soldier's muse, appropriately a prostitute. The association between the whore of Nancy and Apollinaire's phallic calligram is a pleasantry as blatant as the soldiers' joke against themselves. The necessity of a vertical reading, within the horizontal shape of the calligram, especially at the beginning, can be seen as reinforcing the musical structure, the melody's prolongation by a kind of plastic onomatopeia, into a visual dimension. This complex exploitation of shape to evoke sound might explain why Apollinaire has the trumpet face to the left—misleading to those readers who are unacquainted with the couplets and their tunes. Or the orientation of the trumpet may be the result of the poet's conscious or unconscious desire to exploit the visual ambiguity of the shape which suggests not only a trumpet, but a phallus, a cannon, even a syringe for treatment of VD. Here, as elsewhere, whatever the poet's intentions, the poem has its own identity and an independent relationship to the reader.

Lines 4-11. Fragmentary observations are made by the poet as he rattles by on the gun carriage. The hard realities of war mingle with the new soldier's pride and with a picturesque animation of objects reminiscent of his prewar poetry. In the same way old and new words commingle: *par mont par val* is reminiscent of the early "Merlin et la vieille Femme"; *l'avant-train, le porteur, la serviette-torchon, la sacoche,* introduce a new world. The *sous-verge,* the "off horse," is one (of a pair) which is not being ridden. The word *sac* may be read as a pun: primarily "kit bag," but also "pillage." Thus the foot soldier, an immediate object of pity, is an eventual source of fear. Such a reading, however, may be seen as psychologically unconvincing, given Apollinaire's mood.

The three calligrams of the commonplace but necessary boot, the most revered of French cathedrals, and the Eiffel Tower (whose evocation could constitute a joke at that time) are in unexpected juxtaposition. Boot and Eiffel Tower are large. Notre Dame is small. The first two shapes have humorous connotations. Notre Dame does not. A comparable tension may exist among the three verbal statements. As in the first calligram, the actual words seem to have their source in an association of ideas. The rainy march endured by the soldiers gives rise simultaneously to visual images and anonymous voices which translate their mood as one of humor, nostalgia, and hope. The boot may be spurred and may belong to the poet, not to an infantryman. In that event, the first voice is surely Apollinaire's, and all three voices may register increasing notes of excitement. If the boot represents the complaint of a foot soldier, the voices are in more obvious contrast —plaintive, nostalgic, defiant.

Lines 12-27. Detailed fragmentary observations mingle with the recurring theme of transformations, as Apollinaire increasingly glorifies the soldiers. His intoxication with a new language is revealed in his repetition of the word *fantassin* and the mythology he associates with it which is enriched by such unspoken verbal analogies as *fantasque, fantastique, fantasmagorique, fantoche, fantôme.* (But cf. *TS*, p. 35, where he writes to Madeleine on June 4, 1915: "... les artilleurs rient des Fantassins, ... le terme de Fantassins est une injure entre cavaliers") [the gunners laugh at the foot soldiers, ... the term foot soldier is an insult among troopers]. He thinks of the myth of Cadmus, also of Zola's *Germinal.* As in "Cortège" (*Alcools*), *sol* is a pun on "soil" and "sun." The foot soldiers become as magical as the dragon's teeth that were sown by Cadmus and sprang from the soil in the guise of an army. An officer, already associated with the North Star, becomes a blue angel (blue because of his French uniform). Picturesque images mingle with eloquent lines on victory; the latter escape a traditional rhetorical cast by their dependence on realistic detail; the modernistic image of aiming the guns returns in many poems, for example, in "Reconnaissance" (see note). These five lines (23-27) may be read as a culmination of, or, because of their rhetorical tone, as a contrast with the rest of the poem; in any event, they sum up the poet's attitude in "Étendards," before he has been in battle.

The final calligram of the cannon shell, in its verbal aspect, evokes literally a paradoxically beautiful bird of prey. The adjective *rapace,* which may also refer to an agent, at once volatile and catalytic, used in blasting (and probably in firing guns), may have been used in military terminology to designate a cannon shell (C. Tournadre, *GA* 13, p. 74, and *Glossaire*). If so, Apollinaire seizes on this fact to make a metaphoric use of the term here (where the *rapace* sings like a real bird) as elsewhere (see note to "Saillant"). Paradoxical also are the plastic values of this calligram: the poem ends, after a somewhat grandiose passage on victory, with the image of a shell in flight, about to explode—or it may be stationary, lying on its side; in any case, it is deadly. If read as an excited affirmation, the final calligram indicates the poet's admiration of a powerful engine of war and, more generally, an attitude toward war itself (and the war to end wars) shared by an entire generation; it is illuminating above all in regard to Apollinaire's aesthetics in the face of war: the remarkable compulsion he felt to turn war into poetry. It is also the first of a series of transformations of bullets, shells, guns, into singers and songs that are mortal in both senses of the word.

The noises of war, suggested at the end of the poem, are an intense expression of fugitive but violent emotion and underline the acceleration of life as it is experienced at the front, in later poems. The poet longs for a more immediate experience of war, as immediate as his feeling, at the poem's beginning, of fraternity or unity with his fellow soldiers.

VEILLE, page 130

Sent to André Rouveyre from Nimes on March 13, 1915, in a longer version (*OP*, pp. 1087-1088), with a recurrent refrain, "t. du c." (*trou du cul*, literally "ass hole," which possibly refers also to canteen tobacco, as does *gros cul* in "A l'Italie").

Lines 1-8. The first two stanzas are built either around one of the tuneless tunes to which Apollinaire composed his poems (Adéma) or around a traditional song, "Marlbrouck s'en va-t-en guerre" (M. Davies, 1964, p. 256). According to Scott Bates, line 2 is inspired by the refrain to a bawdy song, set to the tune of "Marlbrouck," while *Champignon* and *Tabatière* are fin de siècle slang terms for penis and backside (s.v. "Troudla" in S. Bates, 1975). In line 6, *Mars*, associated with hope, constitutes a pun on the month of March, overture to spring, and the war-god Mars, lover of Venus; the same associations had been made in the "Aubade" to "La Chanson du Mal-Aimé" (*Alcools*). The image of *papier quadrillé* in line 8 refers to the notebook paper, resembling graph paper, which Apollinaire used in noting down his poems; one can see examples in collage manuscript pages of the *Calligrammes* galleys (see note to "Les Collines").

Lines 9-10. Two long free-verse lines juxtapose the length of the road, the hugeness of the poet's cloak, the duration of the night watch.

Lines 11-20. The visual effect of the line divided into nine monosyllabic units may suggest a pencil, a strip of sky glimpsed through trees, a moonbeam; perhaps the image of a pencil dominates because the verb "to write" which ends the poem characterizes the poet's role and retroactively enhances the meaning of the title. The verb tenses set up contrasts or relationships which continued to preoccupy Apollinaire in his poetry during and after his military service. The one past tense is associated with notebook paper and its fixed or rigid patterns (7-8); the present is, with few exceptions, associated with movement and unfinished action; the future is used only with reference to the unknown (3-4). Here the tone is optimistic. The past contains, not lost loves, but what one has written. The present is at once fleeting and immortalized by the creative act. The future is more hopeful than threatening: there seems little doubt in the poet's mind but that he and his friends will come back.

OMBRE, page 134

First published in *Calligrammes.*

According to Philippe Soupault (*OP,* p. 1088), the poem was written at his request, in about three hours, on a visit to Apollinaire. If that is so, it must date from 1917 at the earliest and therefore appears out of chronological order, no doubt to present a premonition of the serious side of the coming conflict and so add a note of gravity to this early section. (A similar tactic was followed with "Les Collines" in respect to the first section.)

The shadow as a projection of the poet's innermost self is a central image in Apollinaire's poetry, particularly in *Alcools.* Here, by incorporating the shades of his dead comrades into his own shadow, he extends the connotations of the image to include not only sorrow and fraternity but also—since the dead now live through his projected light—a discreet celebration of his own powers as a creator who gathers into himself the identities and aspirations of all men who have preceded him.

Line 3. An image that as often with Apollinaire, is intuitively suggestive rather than immediately intelligible. Perhaps the condensation of many memories of past friends into one (the idea pursued in the following lines) evoked the hard, compact shape of the olive, which is the fruit of long years of growth. But the analogy could also be through taste. Experience of life is frequently conveyed, in Apollinaire's poetry, through the senses (cf. the use of *saveur* in "Éventail des Saveurs" and elsewhere): here the experience of capturing time through memory is suggested as being sharp and pungent, like the taste of the olive. (In "L'Adieu" in *Alcools,* time is experienced through another sense, as a perfume: *l'odeur du temps* [*OP,* p. 85].)

Lines 7-17. The theme of the poet's assumption of the identities of his comrades is strongly expressed. While they are now powerless in death (ll. 11-12) he has the gift of vision that can make them live on in his poetry. This does not imply a diminishing of his comrades—on the contrary, they are given their full weight of human dignity in the solemn word *Destinées*—but is rather an expression of a proud sense of poetic sovereignty. (The concept of the poet as the heir to the whole of humanity is also the theme of "Cortège" in *Alcools.*) The lines are made especially appealing through the evocative imagery of movement (7-8, 10, 17) typical of Apollinaire's particularly visual imagination.

Lines 18-21. Four short lines of similar length and rhythm bring the poem to a quiet close, into which creeps a note of sadness. Apollinaire is suggesting not only sorrow for his dead comrades, but also an underlying personal anguish that frequently accompanies the shadow image in Apollinaire's poetry, insofar as the shadow is the projection of an elusive, unknowable dimension of the self.

C'EST LOU QU'ON LA NOMMAIT, page 138

First published in *La Grande Revue,* 11 (November 1917), in "Poèmes de Guerre et d'Amour," and dated February 8, 1915, the day on which it was sent to André Rouveyre.

The octosyllabic quintain is one of Apollinaire's favorite stanzas, which he claimed to have revived. It is used, notably, in "La Chanson du Mal-Aimé" (*Alcools*). Common to both poems—and to other love poems where the poet is unhappy—is the complaint of being poorly loved, as well as the familiar themes of the cruel mistress and the eventual vindication of the unfortunate lover by history, which will recognize him as a poet. Again, as in poems to Annie and Marie Laurencin, Apollinaire suddenly assumes a lofty poetic pose, a statuesque awareness of mortality and glory (not without irony), an attitude reflected perhaps by Cocteau in *Le Sang d'un poète* and expanded in Apollinaire's own prewar novella, *Le Poète Assassiné.*

Line 1. *Loup* is a pun on the nickname of Louise de Coligny-Chatillon whom Apollinaire met in September, after his arrival in Nice.

Line 7. *Toutous* are *chiens* "dogs." The same simile occurs in "La Chanson du Mal-Aimé" ("Je suis fidèle comme un dogue / Au maître . . ."), but there he vaunts his own fidelity, while here he claims that girls are no longer faithful.

Line 13. On the galleys, "soldats . . . empires" are both lowercase.

Lines 16-22. Apollinaire sees himself immobilized in an eighteenth- or nineteenth-century wood engraving, not unlike, in style, woodcuts that Derain and Dufy provided for him, respectively, in *L'Enchanteur Pourrissant* (1908) and *Le Bestiaire* (1911). At Épinal, the capital of Vosges, on the Moselle, flourished for over a hundred years, beginning in 1750, the house of Pellerin, probably the most famous center of popular prints. Georgin, their best "imagier," contributed, by his woodcuts, to the Napoleonic legend. Apollinaire may well have in mind old prints of "le petit caporal."

Lines 24-25. The echo of Villon in the last two lines may have been launched by an actual quotation, "Neiges d'antan" [Snows of yesteryear], in *La Grande Revue* which evolved to "Soldats d'antan" [Soldiers of yesteryear] in the galley proof, to "Soldats passés" in the published edition.

CASE D'ARMONS, page 143

This section of the volume has an unusual history. The poems it contains were all written at the front between April and June 1915 and were made up into a small volume which was privately printed, on ordinary jotter paper, by the battery duplicating machine. Only twenty-five copies of this cyclostyled edition were produced; they had small drawings and designs on various pages which were not reproduced in the printed edition. The intention was to sell the edition privately and donate the proceeds to soldiers from the battery who had lost their homes through enemy invasion.

The title itself is no less intriguing. It is a technical term designating a compartment on ammunition carriages, in which personal effects were stored (C. Tournadre, *GA* 13, p. 67). The unusual term was no doubt emblematic for Apollinaire of his new life in the artillery, where he had to learn many such new words. Perhaps it suggests also a treasure store of poems.

LOIN DU PIGEONNIER, page 144

The original edition of "Case d'Armons" was dedicated "Au p'tit Lou," an affectionate term for Louise de Coligny, involving a pun (because of the masculine gender) on *loup* "wolf." (Cf. "C'est Lou Qu'on la Nommait.")

Le pigeonnier was Apollinaire's word for his apartment on the top floor of 202 Boulevard Saint-Germain, which he lent to Lou on her visits to Paris. Here, because of the amorous hints in the poem, it clearly has the connotation of "love nest." The image of the eel winding its way to its nest (using the bilingual pun *se love* which particularly appealed to Apollinaire; see 'L'Inscription Anglaise") is obviously amorous. On a private level, this image probably evokes Lou's adventures with another lover who was also in the army and whom she went to visit in his camp in the east of France. But, in the context of the poem, the image functions equally well as an expression of the poet's own erotic longing for Lou, repeated in the phallic image of the 75-mm gun. *Malourène* is a word that features in an enigmatic sense in "La Chanson du Mal-Aimé" (*Alcools*), but here it becomes a gallant compliment to Lou (*Ma Lou Reine* [Lou My Queen]). *Canteraine* seems coined on the kind of words found in old country stories and songs. The conjunction of the two terms adds a tender note to the phallic image.

This relatively happy love fits into the general mood of well-being conveyed by the rest of the poem, a mood characteristic of Apollinaire at this stage of the war. The magic sanctuary of the wood (see introduction) is suggested by the capital letter in *Forêt,* the carefree songs of the soldiers within it, and the transformation of 305-mm shell bursts into innocuous sprays or sheaves. In this context the barbed-wire constructions (six-sided constructions, *Xexaèdres* being a misprint for *Hexaèdres* in the original calligram) are also mysteriously protective. The use of disconnected phrases recalls the simultanist technique of "Ondes," demonstrating, as it did there, the poet's confident, all-embracing awareness of his environment.

The calligrammatic design is less figurative than prewar uses of the form, the disconnected phrases being placed on the page to form an abstract, purely visual pattern. The design is given coherence, however, by the strong shapes of the two long lines, which convey associations on different levels. Richter points out that the sinuous line could picture the long, winding line of trenches going from the English Channel to the Alps. By extension both lines can be seen as having dynamic connotations, evoking the poet's consciousness extending into space in both vertical and horizontal directions. At the same time, on a semifigurative level, the two lines come together to form, first, the rough outline of a heart and, second, the even more appropriate image of a harp, the sign of Orpheus, symbolizing the poet's ability to transform and elevate his war experience through song.

References

Lockerbie, S. I. "Forme graphique et expressivité dans les *Calligrammes*." In *Lecture et interprétation des Calligrammes.* 9th Apollinaire Colloquium. Stavelot, 1977. In press.

Richter, M. "Loin du Pigeonnier." In *ibid.*

RECONNAISSANCE, page 146

In "Case d'Armons," dedicated to Madeleine. Also published in *La Grande Revue*, 11 (November 1917), in "Poèmes de Guerre et d'Amour," and dated April 1915. First versions of the poem, differing slightly, were sent on May 11, 1915, to both Madeleine and Lou.

The title is a pun on a military maneuver and platonic recognition. The poem carries out the title's intention; symbolist techniques, Apollinaire's earliest poetic language, express the imagery of modern technological warfare, to which he is just becoming exposed, and his desire to rise above—or quite simply to escape, through superposition of romantic memories upon a woodland landscape—the violent atmosphere of a war whose full horrors he has not as yet experienced.

Letters of that period to both Lou and Madeleine mention the sounds of gunfire, near misses from German shells, the propinquity of the trenches to his forest, and, in contrast, the sky as glimpsed through the forest trees. In a letter to Lou, dated May 5, 1915, he writes: "Je t'écris dans une clairière de notre forêt. Je ne vois au-dessous de ma tête que le ciel. . . . Le mugissement sourd des canons lointains est le clapotement des liquides intérieurs causé par la revolution de . . . notre terre autour de son axe . . . je ne vois plus que le ciel qui est peut-être aussi mon amour pour toi. . . . Je fais galoper mes pensées" (*LL*, p. 345) [I am writing you from a forest glade. Overhead I can see only sky. . . . The muffled boom of distant cannon is the surge of underwater liquids caused by the spin . . . of our earth upon its axis . . . I no longer see anything but the sky which is also perhaps my love for you. . . . I am making my thoughts gallop]. The association of sky with emotion, the use of the verb *galoper*, the impression that the boom of distant cannon is soporific, and a general transformation of war experience into agreeable poetic imagery anticipate the poem. The notion that Apollinaire is rising above dangers, perhaps excited by them but in any event compelled to transform them into poetic images (which here smack of escapism and elsewhere seem a direct translation of the conflict), is vividly perceived in a letter to Madeleine, also dated May 5 (*TS*, p. 18).

In the original twenty-five copies of "Case d'Armons," illustrated with odd little drawings, "Reconnaissance" ends with something approaching a calligram. The last line is broken into four lines:

Tirent mes songes
vers
les
Cieux

After these appear six lines resembling the Morse code, the first of them growing out of a prolongation of the final letter of the text. The dots and dashes of varying size also evoke the sound of gunfire. Apollinaire juxtaposes the polarities, abstract and concrete, of the poem: he seems, in his role as painter, to stress the evanescence of military action (or to transcend it and make it symbolic of another kind of aspiration) and, in his role as poet, to embody the eternal Idea within the word *Cieux*, which was capitalized in the original version. Even in the truncated effect of the final version, these notions seem valid: the *T*'s of *Traverse* and *Tirent* are set apart typographically, directing our attention to the verbs and to angles, whereas *cieux*, with a small *c*, seems to fade away into the Absolute.

S P, page 148

The title stands for "Secteur Postal" (postal sector), an essential feature of the address of every soldier. It has no direct connections with the content of the poem but is generally evocative of military life. The dedication is to the fellow soldier who helped to print "Case d'Armons" (see the dedication of "Visée").

Except for the first stanza, the poem is in the form of a calligrammatic design of an artillery piece firing toward the sky. The detonation is suggested by the onomatopoetic *pan pan; perruque,* according to C. Tournadre, may refer to camouflage of the gun (*GA* 13, p. 74), but it also has an onomatopoetic effect. The barrel and the upright of the gun are made up of truncated extracts from a military manual, instructing on antigas procedure. It is the first primitive type of gas mask that is being described, consisting of protective spectacles and a mouth pad impregnated with bicarbonate of soda (C. Tournadre, in *ibid.*, p. 70). The technique is slightly reminiscent of cubist collages, with a humorous effect stemming from the irreverent treatment of elaborate and prosaic instructions. The base of the gun refers to the warning to avoid wetting the mask and suggests that the only risk for the poet's mask will be from his tears of laughter. This sense of fun, together with the tone of the introductory stanza, which is a lighthearted imitation of a popular refrain, makes the whole poem expressive of Apollinaire's vigorous and good-humored involvement in his soldierly duties in the early stages of the war.

VISÉE, page 150

Sent to Madeleine on June 10, 1915. The dedication is to the wife of a fellow soldier who helped to print "Case d'Armons."

"Visée" is a poem that reveals, both verbally and graphically, the imaginative enlargement of the war experience in the poet's mind. The title refers to the action of aiming with the *triangle de visée,* the instrument employed to determine the position of enemy artillery (Apollinaire frequently used the instrument as an observer; "Lueurs," in *Poèmes à Madeleine, OP,* p. 618, notes the method in detail). The upward (and downward?) arc described by the instrument and possibly the raking fire of the machine guns evoked in line 2 may have suggested the graphic form. The introduction of elegantly curved lines into the design, however, makes it expressive of more than a simple functional action and of more than violence; it becomes, rather, a visual metaphor for the projection of the poet's thoughts into the space of the battlefield (cf. the use of sinuous lines elsewhere—as in "Il Pleut" and "Loin du Pigeonnier"—to express expansion into space).

At the verbal level there is similarly a strong meditative emphasis. The literary technique is one of evoking the simultaneous impressions and reflections of the poet through a free assembly of "autonomous" lines, which can be read in either direction or in any order. The language is dense in overtones and allusions, suggesting the imaginative complexity of the thoughts aroused in the poet by the conflict in which he is engaged.

Line 1. A terse evocation (in the "telegraphic" style of his modernism) of Apollinaire's physical location: among the horses of the mounted artillery, on the borders of northern France.

Line 2. A whole process of fabulation of the battlefield is condensed into this line (and occurs also in others). The machine guns are turned into fairy-tale objects, spinning legends.

Line 3. The use of *hypogées* (underground burial chambers) to evoke the soldiers' dugouts has ominous associations. Optimism overcomes fears of death, however, in the assertion that liberty is waiting in these subterranean tombs ready to spring forth.

Line 4. As in "Il Pleut" and "Du Coton dans les Oreilles," rain is associated with music and the poet's aspiration toward the world around him. The harp image carries the additional connotation of the poet's awareness of his poetic function (see "Loin du Pigeonnier" and note to l. 7 below).

Line 6. The visionary mood of the poet is clear in this line, discovering in instruments of war portents of a reality that transcends them (cf. l. 3), here the future itself, the most central of Apollinaire's values in *Calligrammes.*

Line 7. The metaphor here possibly arises from a pun that can be found in a letter to Lou (*LL,* p. 231): "reçu aujourd'hui télégramme, petit poisson bleu des ondes télégraphiques" [received today the telegram, little blue fish of the telegraphic waves]. The sinuous suggestive power of language, as Apollinaire thought of it, is conveyed by the image, whatever its origins. (The sinuous shape of certain lines of the poem could reflect the same conception on a graphic level.) The thought of language amidst experiences of war reveals Apollinaire's awareness of the poetic act in which he is engaged.

Line 8. There is an echo, in this line, of the modernist vision of "Ondes," where cities feature as an important part of the global consciousness of the modern world. Here also there is the suggestion that the poet's vision is radiating out, beyond the battlefield, to cities throughout the world and the secrets of life to which they hold the key (cf. *l'avenir secret* of l. 6).

Line 9. The gas mask (kept in a blue canvas holder, the same color as the soldiers' uniforms), like other military implements, was quickly absorbed into Apollinaire's private mythology and given mysterious overtones. Donning the mask, notably in the tale "Le cas du brigadier masqué (in *Le Poète Assassiné,* in *OC,* I), dehumanizes the wearer and makes him supernatural. (There may be an analogy here between the *brigadier masqué* and the featureless face of the musician in "Le Musicien de Saint-Merry.") The beginnings of that idea are present in this line, where the soldier is compared to God who hides his face behind the blue sky.

Line 10. The two contradictory experiences of war for Apollinaire are evoked in this line: a stoic effort of endurance through which personal salvation will be achieved and a sense of loneliness and spiritual emptiness such as is revealed in "Dans l'Abri-Caverne." The generally confident tone of this poem suggests that here, at least, the poet has satisfactorily overcome inner doubts. In both "Visée" and "Échelon" the word *ascèse* has overtones of calmness and strength (hence *paisible*) which it loses in the later poem "Exercice" (see note on "Exercice").

Line 11. Severed hands were an obsessive theme in *Alcools*, but the image here seems poignant rather than one of dread, perhaps standing as a symbol of the martyred youth of France. Stories in the front line of atrocities committed on children by the enemy may have inspired the image.

Reference

Lockerbie, S. I. "Forme graphique et expressivité dans les *Calligrammes.*" In *Lecture et interprétation des Calligrammes.* 9th Apollinaire Colloquium. Stavelot, 1977. In press.

1915, page 152

This phrase was originally included in a longer poem sent to Lou (*OP*, p. 479) with a similar layout. In extrapolating from the original context, Apollinaire has simply changed some letters to capitals and enlarged the whole design. The phrase thus becomes an example of the "autonomous" line promoted to the status of a poem, a technique already employed in "Chantre" (*Alcools*). Whereas "Chantre" was enigmatic, however, "1915" is a sonorous statement of the poet's admiration for his fellow soldiers. The images suggest a range of opposing qualities possessed by the soldiers—fragility and indestructibility, innocence and passion (from the red of the precious stone), humility and splendor—which make them the personification of the poet's love for his country. The resonance of the phrase gains considerably from the bold plastic values of the posterlike display, which enhance the impression it makes as a complete poetic statement.

M. Boisson reads sexual allusions into the design and the imagery (see Boisson, "Les Auto-portraits d'Apollinaire," in *Lecture et interpretation des Calligrammes*, 9th Apollinaire Colloquium, Stavelot, 1977 [in press]).

CARTE POSTALE À JEAN ROYÈRE, page 154

This poem, like "1915," seeks to communicate through plastic values, but it uses a more elaborate visual code which may have been partly inspired by memories of cubist collages. The handwritten text, on a facsimile of a postcard (of the kind issued to the troops for free correspondence), conveys the impression of a message straight from the front line. But the fragmentary reproduction of the card, the bold layout of the text, and the figurative instruction scrawled over the postmark transcend the conventions of realism and make the total composition a statement of the poet's confident patriotism. This quality is particularly highlighted in the phrase *on les aura*, expressing a sturdy and aggressive determination to win, which was a byword among the troops before being immortalized in a speech by Pétain in 1916 (Esnault, p. 575; cf. *LL*, p. 297).

The intriguing signature *Lul* probably refers back to one of the more mysterious poems of *Alcools*, "Lul de Faltenin," where it seems established, after much scholarly debate, that the name has a phallic reference. Since "Lul de Faltenin" was published in a review directed by Jean Royère, its use here could be a private joke—a hypothesis that may be supported by the fact that, in the original edition of "Case d'Armons," it seems a later addition, in a different ink (as is *on les aura*).

SAILLANT, page 156

The poem is dedicated to a collector of modern paintings with whom Apollinaire became friendly in 1914 and with whom he corresponded during the war. See *Correspondence de Guillaume Apollinaire 1: Guillaume Apollinaire André Level*, Bibliothèque Guillaume Apollinaire, 9 (Minard, 1976).

The terse "telegraphic" style of Apollinaire's modernist experiments is used here to convey the many simultaneous impressions crowding into his mind when he comes under enemy artillery fire. The situation being evoked is almost certainly that experienced by Apollinaire as an *agent de liaison* when, on horseback or on foot, he had to carry orders and information between the echelon in the rear (see note on "Échelon") and the forward gun positions. These duties required him to cross open country exposed to enemy fire. A letter to Lou (*LL*, pp. 278-279; see also the poem to Lou entitled "Agent de Liaison," *OP*, p. 433) deals with the experience, describing the swift gallop through a wood with shells crashing into trees, sending leaves flying into the air. In "Saillant" everything is accelerated and the stream of consciousness made more complex: the poet not only registers the explosions but dreams of love, delights in the sights of nature that catch his eye, records (wistfully?) the signs of normal life continuing only a short distance from the front line (l. 18). More significantly—and typically—visionary touches heighten and transform the scene; the war zone becomes a beautiful scarred kingdom, and the mysterious shepherd of line 12 introduces mythic overtones. The abrupt juxtapositions of the telegraphic style encourage the reader to make his own synthesis of these diverse impressions, as do the spatial elements of the typographic layout.

Line 1. Evokes the swift gallop of the poet toward the front line, carefully watching for signs of danger and only slightly uncertain about the direction ("Agent de Liaison" mentions various direction signs that he had to look out for).

Lines 2-4. The sight of a cavalryman on foot coincides with the first explosion of an aerial torpedo. The dragoon has possibly lost his horse and weapons after an attack, or he could be from one of the dismounted cavalry regiments that fought on foot.

Lines 5-8. The explosion blasts leaves and branches from the trees—hence the comparison to a broom sweeping away greenery. The broom seems to have a private meaning for Apollinaire and Lou (l. 6), but it now takes on a new significance in this strange new environment. The comparison of the shell to a bird of prey (cf. "2^e Canonnier Conducteur") is one of several signs of the imaginative heightening of the experience in the poet's mind. The marginal positioning of the reference to an ear of corn is both aesthetic and evocative of the rustic setting. Apollinaire took great pleasure in the plants and flowers of the countryside in which his battery was stationed (see "Échelon"), but he introduces this natural observation in a way that emphasizes the deliberate construction of the poem as an artistic montage rather than as a conventional description.

Lines 9-10. Another natural observation. Apollinaire had a particular affection for the little grass snakes that were numerous in the area. A letter to Lou (*LL*, p. 401) describes a similar sight of a snake rearing up when touched. *Pif* at the end of line 10 is an onomatopoetic rendering of the explosion that is described in line 11 as opening up a large, clean crater.

Lines 12-15. The shell is likened to a shepherd, as the earlier one was to a bird of prey. Shepherds leading mysterious flocks are always supernatural, godlike figures in Apollinaire's poetry (see "La petite Auto" in this collection and "Le Brasier" in *Alcools*). Any disquieting associations such a figure may have are tempered here by the indication (l. 13) that love is among his flock. A swastika features in a poem Apollinaire sent to his *marraine de guerre* (*OP*, p. 643) where he himself described it as signifying gentle happiness ("la douceur bienheureuse," *LM*, p. 54). The swastika is also a symbol with an ancient history, and it is no doubt this symbolism, combined with the visionary quality of the whole episode, which prompts the general evocation of the legendary past (l. 14) and of the night song of the toad; although Apollinaire was fond of the cry of the toad in real life (see note to l. 18), the past tense in line 15 seems to suggest a conjuring up of a mythic night scene of great beauty.

Lines 16-17. Verzy was a village in Apollinaire's sector where champagne was made. Lou is being tersely compared to the sparkling wine. (A more elaborate metaphoric use of the wine is made in "Le Vigneron Champenois.") *Le capiston* was the soldiers' word for a captain. The lettering and the layout possibly imitate a slogan scrawled on dugout walls and elsewhere. Again, the device emphasizes the deliberate montage construction of the poem.

Line 18. In a letter to Lou of May 2, 1915 (*LL*, p. 340), Apollinaire speaks of a barge he had seen passing on the nearby canal, with two girls on board combing their hair, and he describes the nostalgia with which he watched them disappear into the distance. The isolation of the line at the end conveys some of the wistfulness of, and makes an ironic contrast with, the war scene, similar to that in some classical paintings where, in a context of catastrophe, a more ordinary activity is going on. In the same paragraph of the letter the poet speaks of the night song of the toad in highly evocative language: "la nuit il y a un crapaud qui fait tinter sa note pure et claire comme le clair de lune épars sur les champs de bataille" [at night a toad sings his pure, clear song like moonlight playing on battlefields].

In "Case d'Armons" the poem ended at line 15 with a line of drawings along the bottom of the page which included two toads (saying "Lou"), an opium pipe, a sword, a bottle of champagne. Toad, sword, and champagne can clearly be found in the poem; the missing opium pipe may be the private significance of *balai de verdure.*

GUERRE, page 160

First published in *L'Elan,* 8 (January 1916).

As it evolves, "Guerre" is in some respects a prophetic poem, written at a period when prophetic art was the province of poets and painters. Among Apollinaire's friends, Giorgio de Chirico, in his portrait of the poet, "prophesied" the poet's head wound, and Max Jacob, in several prose poems of *Le Cornet à dés,* claims to have prophesied World War I.

Lines 1-3. The style of the opening lines, which imitates military jargon, contrasts with the rest of the text to an extent that may be seen as ironical. For, in fact, the poet is not the dry observer he seems; he is emotionally involved in the "horrors of war" and the promise of the future. Here and in other poems, an echo of military orders or military manuals can be seen as turned against itself with ironic or simply humorous effect (see also C. Tournadre, *GA* 13, p. 75). In "Guerre" a military style is juxtaposed to the poet's own voice which swells eloquently to take over in line 6. What amounts to a dialogue may be set up (as, for example, in "S P"), but the tonalities are far more complex: lines 1 and 2 are separate, incomplete fragments belonging to military vocabulary; in line 3, the poet intervenes within his own collage to say "we're firing toward," before quoting military language. It should be noted, too, that in Apollinaire's war poems sounds become increasingly important not only as evocations of an atmosphere of conflict but because their very nature stresses the poet's evolving awareness of the intense, short-lived present moment. At the beginning of "Guerre," one of the poet's early poems written at the front, the gunners' only orientation in a confused world where nothing is familiar is an echo or the memory of shots (the noise of enemy fire is removed to the past tense).

Lines 4-5. An invocation of the soldiers and their surroundings humanizes the landscape of war, humanizes the poet also, in contrast with the impersonal, remote style of the beginning which resulted from the poet's seeming detachment. Syntactically, line 4 might amplify *On* of line 3, but lines 4 and 5 together indicate a flow of thoughts rather than of sentences.

Line 6. A change of tone from the neutral description of lines 1-3 and the restrained pathos of lines 4-5 is emphasized by *'donc,* a paradoxical or at the least puzzling adverb since semantically it indicates that the opening lines are the source of the grandiose development. Regarded, however, as analogous to a musical direction, it indicates a change not only in tone but in tempo: the fragmented style of lines 1-5 abruptly gives way to the eloquence of swelling sentences.

Line 10. The word *aviatique* is untranslatable. A neologism in French, it may be based on *Aviatik,* a German biplane (see also C. Tournadre, *GA* 13, p. 74). The English "aviatic" would limit Apollinaire's meaning.

Lines 11-21. One's first impression of blind men in a dehumanized landscape is set off from the poet's vision of a future worthy of heroes. The evocation of the senses (18-21) as a way of seeing beyond appearances spiritualizes the vision which at first is expressed mainly in material terms. In 1915 Apollinaire could still be optimistic not only about the war to end all wars but about the war as source of progress toward an age of science and science fiction.

MUTATION, page 164

The form is reminiscent of Apollinaire's ironic use, in *Alcools,* of folk song ("La Loreley," "Les Cloches"). The refrain, as well as the repeated grammatical construction, gives an impression of parallel verses, but the images are, on one level, not parallel. The poet, perhaps perched on a wagon as gunnery driver, passes three tableaux where people act out scenes of grief, war, and peace, and three more where objects evoke war (twice) and (once), on a trivial level, frustration. People and objects are seen engaged in transient motions; glimpsed briefly by the poet as he is swept onward, they seem irrelevant and haphazard. On another level, the scenes do seem parallel. They reflect the poet's experience of the war as a haphazard flux, a kind of variant on simultanist vision, already evoked in "2[e] Canonnier Conducteur," where, as probably here, he sees all from a high mobile vantage point. (Passages from the letters to Lou [pp. 304, 340] describe scenes both fleeting and static, which he glimpses from his forest encampment.)

Whatever the poet's vantage point, the scenes make an ironic, perhaps mysterious, commentary on his own "mutation" into a soldier. The contrast between the tableaux and the poet-soldier's experience is underlined by the use of the imperfect in the former, which here, as in "Mai" (*Alcools*), suggests a prolongation and eventual fading of a single transitory act or state rather than a repetition. The contrast between outer and inner weather is underlined also by the structure: a long decrescendo followed by a surprise ending. There is a switch in tenses which implies a summing-up, even a kind of finality, and a last appearance of the refrain which, to the contrary, suggests a prolongation of the situation. The new soldier's declaration, after his evocation of a world where all is transitory, that everything in him has changed "except my love," is ambiguous—perhaps earnest, perhaps playful.

ORACLES, page 166

The speaker initially is no doubt Lou. Apollinaire sent her both a ring and a whistle, and this is presumably her reply from Paris; note the reference to metro and taxis (see "Madeleine," in which a reply to the poet also features). On the other hand, it is more likely to be the poet who intervenes in lines 9-10 with a rapturous exclamation, prompted by the loving message from Lou but embracing the whole new experience of war in which he is engaged. His euphoric state of mind, at this particular period, makes him ready to elevate simple objects—the ring and the whistle—to the status of oracles, foretelling future bliss.

The literary strategy of the poem is to attempt to convey these happy exchanges with straightforward simplicity. After the opening statements (ll. 1-4) on a fairly formal tone, ending with an unusual comparison, the tone modulates into one of colloquial intimacy. The use of *tu,* the breakup of lines 6 and 7, and the ending of the sentence with the preposition *avec* (a familiar feature of the spoken language) suggest the excited delight of the recipient and prepare the reader for the stronger outburst of pleasure in the following exclamation. The two detached phrases at the bottom of the poem are respectively a term of endearment for Lou (which according to Bates,

1975, has erotic significance) and instructions for measuring her finger. They form a verbal and visual coda, rounding off the idea and calling attention to the deliberate spatial arrangement of the poem.

14 JUIN 1915, page 168

The date and the details of the first three lines suggest a note scrawled quickly during a troop movement, probably at night. Apollinaire's battery changed sectors about this time (see *TS*, p. 39; there is a gap in the letters to both Lou and Madeleine). The intended recipient could be the poet's mother, to whom the poem was dedicated in the original edition of "Case d'Armons." Epistolary details are one of the leitmotifs of this section (see "Carte Postale à Jean Royère," "Oracles," "Madeleine," "Venu de Dieuze"), giving a distinct flavor of the poet's daily life at the front, in which correspondence played a role of great importance. A note of pathos (a slight reminiscence of Verlaine?) is introduced in line 4, but it is dissipated in the rest of the poem which assumes the more elevated tone of a patriotic meditation. The *Marseillaise* of the sculptor Rude (1784-1855), one of the famous sculptures decorating the Arc de Triomphe in Paris, depicts the departure of the revolutionary volunteers in 1792 to fight for the newly formed French Republic (it was praised by Apollinaire in a prewar critical article; see *CA*, p. 285). In itself the pointing sword of the leading volunteer is an eloquent symbol of patriotic fervor, but it becomes doubly so when the poet imagines it appearing as a constellation in the sky (an idea perhaps inspired by the constellation Orion, part of which is supposed to represent a sword). In the final lines (11-15), however, the poet reflects that this symbol is too traditionally heroic to help him in his concentration on the here and now. Although this device cunningly ensures that the poem does, in fact, benefit from the rhetorical overtones of the image that is being dismissed, the attempt to forgo rhetoric in favor of simplicity (although not always successful) is part of Apollinaire's literary strategy in *Calligrammes*. This poem itself, like "Oracles," seeks to be a direct and simple understatement.

DE LA BATTERIE DE TIR, page 170

Published also in *La Grande Revue*, 11 (November 1917), in "Poèmes de Guerre et d'Amour," and dated May 1915.

Images of sparkling light, from a diamond necklace, suggest the endurance and indestructibility of soldiers as well as gunfire at night. At the same time other themes contribute to a paradoxical concept of endurance and mortality. The diamonds are not a true source of light; thus the verbs *chatoie* and *éclosent* first describe light that changes (because composed of reflections playing on a faceted surface), then light (again in context, reflected) which is newly born. In contrast with these optical illusions and with the theme of birth, the invocation *O Roses* suggests at once fragile young blossoms that will soon fade and the theme of military glory (see note to "Vers le Sud"). Finally, the word *Étincelles* refers to an incandescent and true source of light, which is even shorter-lived than roses. These images ring changes upon what can be considered as the essence of heroism: endurance in the face of death.

Lines 2-3. The Negros Islands, evoking, through a play on *Negros*, exoticism of place and race, are in the Philippines. The other place-names, distant in time rather than in space, suggest ancient, mythical sources for the soldiers: the drowned continents, the much-sought-for country of gold, the mysterious lands to the north of Greece.

Lines 9-10. *Arc-en-terre* is not a neologism but a rainbow formed on the ground by rain or dew (C. Tournadre, *Glossaire*). There is an opposition between *l'Arc-en-terre* and *l'Arc-en-Ciel.* The imbalance between lowercase *t* and capital *C* points up a distinction between terrestrial humanity and the celestial Absolute which flatters the former (as in Valéry's "Je suis le défaut dans ton grand diamant") [I am the flaw in your huge diamond]: only the ephemeral human being can consciously choose the eternal heroic stance; the heavenly rainbow, an ancient sign of hope (God's promise to Noah), is less potent than the earth's rainbow of mortal heroes idealized by the poet.

ÉCHELON, page 172

Here one sees the allegorical process by which the wood where Apollinaire's battery was stationed is transformed in his imagination into a place of sanctuary (see introduction). The echelon, in artillery terms, was the rear position, some way behind the gun emplacements, where the horses and the reserve ammunitions were kept (Meyer, p. 118). The fighting is thus remote: the white wound of the trenches is in the distance (l. 6) and Death dangles at the edge of the wood (ll. 10-14) where the danger begins. The poet can enjoy the small beauties of nature around him, both flora and fauna, and give himself up to his private joy of collecting samples of flowers and other curiosities (l. 20). Nevertheless, although danger is distant, it can be heard, and although Death is on the perimeter, it can be seen. The proximity of danger and Death no doubt explains why, despite the sense of protection, the tone of the poem is more measured and calm than that of certain others, and why the poet is gravely conscious of war as a trial and endurance (*Ascèse*, l. 3).

Line 2. According to Claude Tournadre, there is a play on words here, *crapauds* and *crapoussins* being soldiers' terms for German bombs, as well as meaning toads (*GA* 13, p. 72).

Line 5. Another protective shelter reinforcing the general associations of the wood.

Line 7. The simple naming of the sky, with the use of a capital letter at *Ciel*, suggests its peaceful connotations.

Lines 8-9. There is a yellow variety of poppy, but it is more likely that two types of wild flower are evoked here.

Lines 10-14. The evocation of Death is ambivalent, the alluring beauty of her body contrasting with the sinister implications of hanging. it is perhaps a reflection of the poet's mixed fear of and fascination with what waits outside the wood. The phrases in the margin of this stanza suggest the simultaneity of the poet's awareness: he hears antiaircraft fire in the distance, sees around him familiar equipment typical of his military life, and observes the world of nature. *Sac à malice* and *La trousse à boutons* refer in the first instance to the soldiers' pack and pouch for needle, thread, buttons, and the like, but C. Tournadre thinks they are also familiar terms for the gas-mask container (*ibid.*, p. 70).

Lines 15-17. In a poem in which observations of flora and fauna are numerous, it is fitting that the poet's patriotic thoughts should be inspired by a flower, no doubt the wild rose. *Halète* could simply refer to the physical exhaustion of the fighting troops, but it may also evoke the effects of gas attacks (Tournadre, in *ibid.*, p. 70).

Lines 18-20. The spacing out of the last three lines ends the poem on an equable note of pleasure in birdsong and peaceful pursuits of collecting natural specimens, in the security of the wood.

VERS LE SUD, page 176

First published in *Nord-Sud* (February 1918), with "Océan de Terre," and dated April 3, 1915.

Here, and in other poems, variations are rung upon words that become key images in *Calligrammes*, endowing the book with a special kind of structure, loosely comparable to that created by classical drama's use of key words and key images (for example, in Euripides' *Bacchae*, the various implications of *thyrsus* are revealed only gradually). The chronological appearance of *Calligrammes*, which seems to narrate one man's reactions as he survives from day to day through a world war, is deceptive. The displacement in the volume of specific poems (such as "Les Collines" and probably "Ombre") and the discreet avoidance of chronology within specific sections not only slant the narrative but indicate that words and images link poem to poem and, to some extent, control the order of poems within a given section, even throughout the book. These key words and images contribute to the drama that is unfolded and to its eventual denouement, or revelation ("La Victoire," "La Jolie Rousse").

Line 1. *Zénith* is a word in the general literary vocabulary which also belongs to military language.

Line 3. Given the context of the surrounding poems (such as the immediately preceding "Échelon"), the limitless gardens no longer have the same symbolist resonance they would have had in a poem about Stavelot, or even around 1908 when, in "Le Brasier" (*Alcools*), Apollinaire attempts to describe a mystical apprehension of the infinite. They suggest also a new perception in his consciousness of the vastness of space, stimulated by the war. There are, in letters to Lou and to Madeleine of the period, numerous references to the gardens dug by the soldiers and artillerymen near the trenches or within the wood.

Line 4. What may seem an echo of *Alcools* has also a specific orientation to the war. Apollinaire may remember, from his own early poem "Le Larron" (*Alcools*), another, far more fantastic and sheltering wood, with its *crapauds que l'azur et les sources mûrirent* [toads that azure and pools ripen]. At the same time, *crapaud* as slang for a German shell (C. Tournadre, *GA* 13, p. 72) carries over from "Échelon," although the poet thinks primarily of toads in the wood. The association of the toad's call with tenderness and with azure is to be compared with an observation in a letter of May 2 to Lou (*LL*, p. 340), where his note is linked to purity, moonlight—and the battlefield: "la nuit il y a un crapaud qui fait tinter sa note pure et claire comme le clair de lune épars sur les champs de bataille" [at night there's a toad sounding his pure clear note like moonlight scattered over the battlefield]. Since both *crapaud* and *crapoussin* were slang for kinds of shells, it would seem, not only from "Échelon" but from another line to Lou, June 4 (*ibid.*, p. 430), that Apollinaire wrote, with conscious ambiguity, of their songs: "les crapauds et les crapoussins chantent une seule note, qui est comme la topaze brûlée de ton regard" [toads and baby toads sing a single note which is like the burnt topaz of your eyes].

Lines 6-10. In contrast with the poems directly inspired by military life which precede and follow, this poem recalls the melancholy lyric tone of parts of *Alcools*. On the other hand, images in neighboring poems, of a more warlike nature, contribute to the general aura of those in this poem, though not to a specific meaning. Consequently some words simultaneously evoke the poet's past and his present experience. Here *roses* suggests primarily the pleasure of love, and also the brevity of love and youth, as in early poems (see "La Cueillette," *OP*, p. 318). But because of other poems, primarily in "Case d'Armons," the image has an added resonance and creates a blurred impression, compared with that created by subdued puns (see note to "Chant de l'Horizon en Champagne"). In "De la Batterie de Tir," two poems before, the soldiers defending France were, somewhat ambiguously, invoked as *O Roses*. In "Échelon," the preceding poem, France is *O rose toujours vive*, recalling both the mystical rose of "Le Brasier" and the immortalized, if fading, tea roses of "La Jolie Rousse." In "Fête" and in poems from other sections, such as "Tourbillon de Mouches," the rose suggests love, perhaps death, and overtones of military glory. The latter notion is notably evoked in "Visée" which launches the image in "Case d'Armons." Thus, consideration of a single postsymbolist image suggests that even a minor poem like "Vers le Sud" has importance when one is considering Apollinaire's use of a language seemingly outworn, but, in reality, renewed by the positioning of poems in *Calligrammes* and by the overall environment of war.

Again, a series of alliterations reminiscent of *Alcools*, *rossignol* (for the nightingale singing in the woods of Champagne, reminding Apollinaire of love, see *LL*, p. 376), *rosier*, *roses*, builds up to a pomegranate image which, without explicitly punning, contains complex undercurrents associated with the war. The untranslatable pun on *grenade/grenadier* "pomegranate/pomegranate tree" and "grenade/grenadier" appears in the subsequent two sections of *Calligrammes*, where it works overtly as a pun ("Les Grenadines Repentantes," "Chant de l'Horizon en Champagne," "A l'Italie"). Here only one meaning is exploited. Although the poem was dated, in *Nord-Sud*, the day before Apollinaire left Nimes for the front, in an earlier version the tree hung with hearts was a *citronnier* "lemon tree," reminiscent of a similar image in "Les Fiançailles" (*Alcools*). The substitution of *grenadier*, whether it took place at Nimes or later, indicates an awareness of the poetic richness, for a collection of war poems, of vocabulary with military overtones.

LES SOUPIRS DU SERVANT DE DAKAR,
page 178

Sent to Lou on June 11, 1915.

Contrasts and parallels between military life and life in an African village contribute to this portrayal, unique for Apollinaire, of another psyche than his own. Such a lyric evocation of primitivism recalls paintings and poetry by two of his friends, Le Douanier Rousseau and Max Jacob. The original version sent to Lou was not divided into sections. Additions and minor revisions in "Case d'Armons" and *Calligrammes* have refined the text.

Lines 1-6. At first there is a contrast between an industrialized world at war and a joyous primitive world. In line 1, *cagnat* is gunners' slang for a tent or a dugout. (See C. Tournadre, *GA* 13, p. 69, for brief discussion of term.)

Lines 7-33. The description of the village in Dakar begins and ends on the theme of the white man's wars that touch on the lives of the villagers. When they were bringing the Gold Coast under control, the British fought against the Ashanti and finally subdued them in the 1890s. Lines 7-9 probably refer to that war. The enlistment of one native tribe against another would be a nice example of the unnaturalness of colonial wars, set off against conflict between the natives as a natural phenomenon, in lines 42-46.

The thematic structure is emphasized by the addition in the final version of line 33, which underlines, in contrast with the three lines on the Ashanti and the English, three lines on the French at Arras.

Exoticism is underwoven by themes of sexuality, violence, and magic. In the original version and in "Case d'Armons," the theme of sexuality was more marked; incestuous overtones may have led up to the *atroce amour* which was then the end of the poem. The attitude of the speaker, however, is innocent; and it is amoral in the sense that he is outside the bounds of the white man's morality.

Again, the theme of violence is innocent (in contrast with the violence of the white man in World War I). The twenty-year-old speaker may recall, in lines 19-20, his initiation into manhood when he learned man's principal role—that of killing another man. The fact that the boy killed his enemy is not stated, although in the original version the implication was clearer; it is veiled by images of magic.

What matters in his memories and in this section of the poem is the magical side to things, and that is brought out by Apollinaire, in part through a combination of imagery and verbal play around the word *nègre*, as descriptive of race or simply as the color black. There is confusion between the silver head and the reflected moon (22-24)—or perhaps a superimposition of one upon the other—and a subsequent confusion between silver head and real moon (25-26). The color silver may be linked to the paleness of death, the color of moonlight, a frenzy or a magical power granted by the full moon, but not the color white to which it seems in opposition. Through the repetition and varying of refrains, a victory dance is evoked whose fast rhythm is slowed by lines 28-29. The image of the boy in the cave—hiding in ambush before the kill?—transforms the mood: the dancer becomes invisible, the silver head also. The latter becomes *une tête de nègre,* "a Negro head," "a head that is black," which cannot be described in the night become moonless, and yet the three images of silver head, moon, and Negro head are intimately related, as Apollinaire points out in a line added in "Case d'Armons": *Similitudes Paleurs* (30). "Resemblances Pallors" functions, structurally, as the center of the poem, indicating the analogies through which the poem works. Unlike the adjective silver, which seems to have a secret meaning set apart from the white man's world, pallor suggests all the different palenesses which, superficially, resemble one another, from the paleness of death to that of the white man who has imposed new patterns on the boy's life, which only superficially resemble the old.

Lines 34-68. The third passage alternates between past and present. There are increasing interventions from the white world: the bishop, the administrator, the final recruitment. The analogies become increasingly false: between the gunners' dugout and the village hut, between the war and memories of a hunt or of fighting other tribes, between the illusory enchantment provided by the spectacle of night bombardment and that far from illusory magic created by the boy's own people which still possesses him. Line 54, *on m'a blanchi du coup* may be considered one more play on *nègre* or as a comment on Apollinaire's own experience of being a French soldier, but not a French citizen. Line 60, *bobosses:* in one of his learned expositions on the meaning of words, Apollinaire writes Madeleine on June 4, 1915: "*Bobosses* est une sorte de diminutif attendri de *fantabosses* (*fantabosses* signifie sans doute *fantassins* à bosses—à cause du sac . . .) qui était un terme comique . . . [utilisé par] les artilleurs" (p. 35) [that is, untranslatable gunners' slang for soldiers who because of their kitbags look humpbacked]. The last five lines (64-68), added in a final recasting of the poem for publication, remind one that Apollinaire's experience of the front lines dates mainly after the poem's picturesque first version. The image of the exploding eye, or of fierce staring eyes bursting out of the darkness all over the sky, is probably the most painful, or violent and nightmarish, of a series of key images in *Calligrammes* built around exploding shells. Apollinaire may evoke here not only the destruction of war but a kind of destruction at work in the boy. What happens in these final lines is not a discovery of likenesses that reaffirm the boy's manhood but a painful discordant fusion of conflicting ways of life; the white man's way seems to overwhelm and dissipate that resolution of dark and horrible with joyous and innocent aspects of a primitive life which makes up the poem.

TOUJOURS, page 184

Published also in *La Grande Revue*, 11 (November 1917), in "Poèmes de Guerre et d'Amour," where it is dated May 1915.

"Toujours" can be read as one of Apollinaire's prophetic poems. It reveals his old love of science-fiction imagery and is related thematically to the eternal circle of the generations and of phoenixlike loves characteristic of *Alcools*.

Lines 1-2. The paradoxical opening heralds "L'Esprit Nouveau et les Poètes," Apollinaire's lecture given at the Théâtre du Vieux-Colombier on November 26, 1917. There, in prose, he is more explicit: progress, which is limited to the manipulation of external phenomena, exists on the level of scientific invention; newness, which man can find within himself, exists, apart from progress, in science and especially in art: "Il [le nouveau] est tout dans la surprise" (*OC*, III, 906).

Lines 3-8. Don Juan, on an endless voyage, seems in his turn a paradoxical figure, when one confronts him with his probable source in *Les Fleurs du Mal:* no longer world-weary, Apollinaire's hero, with a Gidean curiosity, enamored of comets and ghosts alike, seeks new phenomena in the universe of himself. There he discovers powers of the imagination which anticipate "Les Collines." Whether or not Don Juan be a persona for Apollinaire, the images of *planètes* and *nebuleuses* are, in all likelihood, prompted by the starry nights, the flares and shells and gunfire described in *Lettres à Lou* (see esp. pp. 265, 342); thus the war experience of the poet seems transposed into an inner dimension. The image of Don Juan, in turn, may have been inspired by the overtones, erotic for Apollinaire, of stars and nebulas (going back at least to "La Chanson du Mal-Aime") and of flares and gunfire (passim in the war poems).

Lines 9-17. Stanzas three and four pose a way of reconciling Order and Adventure which, once more, is paradoxical: a fusion between the transience of all things and the immortal creative act which, as it creates, at the same times sweeps away previous structures and boundaries. The poem ended, in "Case d'Armons," with an anticipation of a surrealist notion (ll. 13-15); subsequent to the spring of 1915, and before the autumn of 1917, Apollinaire added the final two lines which can be taken as an optimistic statement on Pyrrhic victories or as a vision of the creative energies to be found in war.

FÊTE, page 188

Published also in *L'Elan*, 10 (December 1, 1916). Sent to Lou in September 1915.

These lines indicate a poet's way of enduring life at the front. Erotic daydreams provide a distraction, whether he is taking momentary shelter in his forest, which still survives bombardment, or contemplating the fireworks of war; both kinds of solitude present him with illusory images of beauty or peace which conceal a menace and furnish no real escape.

The English translation has not preserved the regular form of the French poem which underlies the experimental typography: four quatrains and one quintain contain octosyllables rhyming alternately, with the exception of the final repeated rhyme in *oz* which stresses the central image of the poem. That image, as so often in the war poems, has its point of departure in reality: springtime flowers in the poet's wood (*LL*, April and May 1915, passim). The connotations of *rose* evolve from erotic to aesthetic, within the poem, and seem a final commentary on the role of that image in this section (see note to "Vers le Sud").

Lines 21-23. *Mortification* has become, in French, a rare term for dying tissue (gangrene). Apollinaire may have this meaning in mind as an indication of the other side of the coin: his forest offers only temporary shelter from the threat of death. In any event, rather than the usual figurative meaning, common to both languages, concrete parallels to a spiritual mortification preoccupy him: the whipping of flesh, or of roses (*LL*, pp. 423-424), which for him has an erotic, not a religious, connotation; and, specifically, the beating of roses prior to their maceration. There is conceivably, in the context, a blurring of linguistic distinctions between *mortification* and *macération*, and thus a fusion of the two steps in the manufacture of perfume by shredding and then steeping flowers in liquid. A similar image occurs at the beginning of the stanza (ll. 19-20). The ideas of metamorphosis and of refinement through exposure to an alien element (as well as the images of *alcools* and *parfum*) are directly related to Apollinaire's attempt to turn war into poetry and himself into a new kind of artist.

MADELEINE, page 192

Like "Carte Postale à Jean Royère" and "Venu de Dieuze," this poem is conceived as an overall plastic composition, with visual symbols assuming as much importance as the words. It represents the early stages of Apollinaire's correspondence with Madeleine. The handwritten script, as in the other pieces, marks the personal nature of the exchanges. Most of the communications emanate from the poet, but Madeleine's reply, in the shape of an envelope, forms the centerpiece of the composition, nicely balanced by a drawing and a verbal phrase on each side.

Although Madeleine lived in a suburb of the city of Oran in Algeria, it pleases Apollinaire to imagine her in an Arab village, with all the associations that setting conjures up of romantic love, far from civilization, in an exotic climate. As decorative motifs the star and the heart fit well into an implied oriental setting, where such emblems are common. The language of love that they speak is also decorous and courteous. The poet dares only to identify openly his memories (of their brief meeting, no doubt), but the heart shape, and the verbal allusion to songs of another kind, are a plain hint of stronger feelings. Madeleine's reply, despite using the formal *vous*, has an equally obvious tone of intimacy (*votre petite fée*). A bolder note is introduced into these innocent exchanges, however, by the final design at the bottom of the page. If the phallic significance of guns for the poet may not be immediately apparent in the crossed cannon of the artilleryman's badge, Madeleine was no doubt meant to understand the erotic significance of the phrase in Arabic which flanks them (see Chevalier, *GA* 1, p. 41). The rose is also a flower that has private erotic meaning for Apollinaire (see "Lou Ma Rose" in *Poèmes à Lou, OP*, p. 475).

The eroticism has been toned down in the final text, in that the "other songs" of the heart shape were originally described in the version sent to Madeleine as *moins douces* [less gentle]. But enough remains to allow the reader to perceive the combination of gallantry and discreetly veiled passion, adding to the piquancy of a text that is already original and inventive in its graphic conception.

LES SAISONS, page 194

Sent to Lou in a slightly different version, as part of a longer poem, on May 11, 1915 (see *OP*, p. 455). First published separately in *La Grande Revue*, 11 (November 1917).

A carefree mood of content runs through the poem, as the poet looks back on a succession of happy days in both peace and war. *Saison* is one of the key words of Apollinaire's vocabulary in the figurative sense of a major moment of experience in the poet's life. Sometimes it stands for a period of trial and difficulty and has grave associations, but here the use of the word in the plural suggests a smooth continuity between the seasons and thus a feeling in the poet of being at one with time and the universe. The mood is sustained by the flowing rhythm of the stanzas, by the jauntiness of the refrain, and by the use of the poet's own name in the third person, turning him into a kind of folk-song hero. (A similar use of "Gui" occurs in Apollinaire's letters; see esp. *LL*, p. 334.) Only in the final stanza does the happy tone falter, and then not sufficiently to undermine it completely.

Lines 1-4. Prewar happiness on the beach is evoked in this stanza. The poet's vivid recollection is suggested by the syntactical dislocation and sudden switch to the present tense in line 2.

Line 8. The use of *artiflot,* a slang term for artilleryman, adds to the jauntiness of the refrain. The fact that the refrain is in the past tense puts it in harmony with the recapitulative nature of the first three stanzas. Its overtones may be different on its last appearance, however.

Lines 10-13. The first lines of stanzas two, three, and four are punctuated by the unusual use of a capital letter at the seventh syllable. This helps to underline the rhythm and, in the first two instances, stresses the continuity of tone. In the fourth stanza, on the contrary, it emphasizes the significant break in continuity. Again the change of tense in line 11 highlights the happiness by bringing it into the "historic" present. The humorous implication that the shells are mimicking the stars (l. 12), and the reference to the night movements of the artillery (l. 13), evoke the explosions and bustle of war but drain them of horror.

Lines 19-22. The use of *vagues* (19) suggests an unbroken stretch of happy days, merging into one another in memory. It is a frequent device of Apollinaire's to address himself in the second person singular (21); this mode of address often has pathetic effect, but here it adds to the tone of relaxed pleasure, as does the adjective *invraisemblables.* He was busily engaged at this time in making rings from shrapnel.

Lines 28-31. The change to the present tense in this stanza is quite different from earlier uses. With the blunt intrusion of *La guerre continue* we are brought up to the time of writing, in the real present, and we see the poet reflecting that long months have passed (l. 29) with no end to the war. There is thus a certain contrast between the final stanza and the rest of the poem, which also colors the final appearance of the refrain: the happiness that is evoked there is implied to be a thing of the past. There is no radical disenchantment, however, for line 30 pictures the poet still within the shelter of the wood, with all the overtones that this image has in "Case d'Armons"; and his listening to the song of a star (l. 31) suggests his continued involvement in poetic activity, with all the awareness of the wider universe, and all the ability to transcend his immediate environment, which such involvement gives him.

VENU DE DIEUZE, page 198

From "Case d'Armons" to the proofs of *Calligrammes* the poem's makeup underwent considerable changes. It is, in fact, not precisely a calligram, but it exemplifies a broader conception of plastic composition (see introduction,

p. 1), appealing to both visual and auditory senses. The changes indicate that Apollinaire, as his interest in plastic expression evolved between 1915 and 1918, wanted a more complex design than he had started with.

If the size of the calligraphy indicates sound and emphasis, the first *Halte là* is louder than the second and emphasizes the adverb, "halt *there*," giving a sense of dramatic urgency to the opening. In the same way, the question *Qui vive* is less loud than the sturdy *France* which takes up a whole line. Comparably, but almost opposite in technique, when the poet—or the message—gives the password, the handwriting becomes faint, like a whisper, but swells from *Claire* to *Éternel.* Beneath this hyphenated line, the musical notation, with the *forte s'allontanando* "loud [but] dwindling," and the marginal statement to the right seem to belong, not to the password, but to something that happens at that moment, setting off the second part of the poem, probably the explosion of a shell as it lands in the swampy forest. The marginal part corresponds to the technique of simultaneous impressions used in several poems to convey the totality of war experienced by the poet. In particular, the juxtaposition between the world of the forest and the encroaching world of war occurs also in "Saillant" and "Échelon" (notes to both poems). But here the emphasis is not on a disjointed kind of simultaneity. Rather, the impressions form one coherent statement evoking the effect of the shell, scarring trees and frightening the waterfowl. The final part of the poem evokes the resurgence of forest life after the explosion—noises, movement, and color.

Dieuze is a town in the region of the Moselle where Lou was, at one point. If Apollinaire met her there, the poem describes him coming back to his billet. Otherwise, and more likely (Adéma), it is the description of a message from Lou, en route to the poet and undergoing a playful version of military ritual.

The first part of the poem evokes sentry duty and, in the proofs of *Calligrammes*, the soldier's hobby of making rings (described in "Les Saisons"). Apollinaire frequently asks Lou in his letters for her ring size. Madeleine proves far more receptive to the notion. The password itself becomes an ambiguity, *Le Mot*, the Word of all words; it is phrased like a telegram and includes such keywords as *Cristal* (which occurs in "Guerre," another prophetic poem of this period); structurally it introduces several simultaneous moments of different kinds of lyricism or excitement: a musical notation, the marginal, parenthetical *funambule* "tightrope walker" or military slang for "shell," the plaintive, slangy song.

G. V. C. was the Gardes des Voies et Communications who defended bridges and railways from enemy spy action. This passage, now placed in the margin, originally, in "Case d'Armons," came after the song.

M' quiot' fille is local patois for "my little girl" (Tournadre, *Glossaire*).

Mouqu', properly *mouque,* "fly," is used in the familiar expression, *enn' mouqu' dans d'huile,* which may mean, in opposition to the preceding line, *un pauvre type* "a poor drip," even "a useless lover."

The closeness between poet-soldier and poem-experience at the top of the page changes as one reads downward. The poet's embroidery on the password and his fantasy about the forest are interrupted by an anonymous but doubtless real voice singing a funny song about the disappointments of love. The song leads him momentarily into real or imagined fragmentary scenes, whose linguistic ambiguity suggests not only the forest but, conceivably, an erotic urge in nature. The last three lines are perhaps already prepared by the *hennissements* of the artillery horses Apollinaire loved so to ride and which he describes in letters to Lou. *Hennissements* might also refer to the beginnings of trumpet calls. One can find a continuity between the swelling tone in the evocation of nature and these last three lines—a continued escalation of the enthusiastic mood. On the other hand, the last lines may turn abruptly upon the word *Amour* and mark an unexpected distancing of the writer from his material, indicated by a gradual enlarging of the letters, emphasizing *Patrie, Le général,* and the entire final line. Thus the passage may be taken, on the one hand, as sabotage, mystification, music making (in the manner of Satie, perhaps), or simply as wholehearted praise of Apollinaire's general who becomes a symbol of French virtue and devotion to duty.

The stature of Apollinaire's general is exalted by the classical references, most obviously by the second. Fabius could be one of a number of military Romans in the Fabian family. The two best known are Fabius Maximus, a general in the Samnite Wars, and Fabius Cunctator, the general who fought against Hannibal. Probably Apollinaire was thinking of one of these. If the name of Fabius represents military glory, that of Antisthenes may indicate a way to its achievement. Antisthenes was the Greek founder of the Cynic school of philosophy, which is based on the Socratic principle that happiness is found in the practice of virtue and on Antisthenes' own conviction that the free man must be unhampered by desires. Antisthenes' ideas may indicate not only the life Apollinaire seems to imagine for his own general but, in fact, the life that he himself attempted to lead at the front. In early April he frequently wrote Lou (April 4, 8, 9, 11) of his desire to be faithful to her. Finally, on April 14, he swore a vow of chastity: "Quel bonheur de n'être plus dominé par l'amour charnel, de n'être plus la proie d'un désir, de se dominer soi-même enfin, afin de dominer un jour les autres" [What a joy no longer to be mastered by carnal love, or a prey to desire, [but] at last to be master of oneself, so as, one day, to master others]. It is a moot point, of course, how long such a mood could last, with Apollinaire, but his patriotism and his desire for a true love seem never to have wavered. Thus the end of the poem may sound like a trumpet call, restoring order and voicing the soldier-poet's aspirations.

LA NUIT D'AVRIL 1915, page 202

Sent to Lou (to whom it is dedicated) in a significantly different version, as part of a longer poem, on April 10, 1915 (see *OP*, p. 429). First published separately in *L'Élan*, 9 (March 1916).

The poem is no doubt placed last in "Case d'Armons," out of chronological order, because it is a summation of the full range of contradictory emotions experienced by Apollinaire during his first months in the war zone: the newfound excitement of danger, the sweet sadness of disappointed love, the consolation sought in erotic dreams, the celebration of life and hopes for a radiant future. The revisions to the original version considerably increased the suggestive power of the poem. Several key images were rendered more elusive and appealing, and the introduction of irregular spacing, in place of the regular five-line stanzas of the original, brought in effective changes of pace and rhythm.

Lines 1-6. The conception of the forest as a refuge within which warfare becomes something exciting and enchanting—a gay ball—is particularly obvious here. Even sudden alerts (l. 5) do not break the spell. The "word" of lines 4 and 5 is the military password, which for Apollinaire has overtones of an open sesame; the description of it as fatal, therefore, signifies mystery rather than anything more sinister (cf. the password of "Venu de Dieuze" and the references to secrets in "Visée" and "Loin du Pigeonnier"). In Apollinaire's letters the word *mystère* is used of the battlefield (see esp. *TS*, p. 281).

Lines 7-10. The disappointed love for Lou is evoked in a concentrated series of images. The poet's heart is compared to a star that is both lovelorn and out of orbit (*éperdu*), seeking that perfect harmony with time and happiness which, in the previous poem, was conveyed by the word *saisons*. The constant analogy between stars and shells in the war poetry generates the further image of the heart as an exploded shell, whose violent explosion has used up the poet's vital feelings (likened to ammunition) which will, however, be replenished from deep inner resources (l. 10). It is impressive here to see military analogies (ll. 8, 9) being blended with an older strain of imagery coming from *Alcools* (l. 10) in which the innermost self is expressed through the eyes and given overtones of divinity.

Lines 12-14. The deep attachment of Apollinaire to elegiac poetry is openly expressed in lines 12-13. After sending Lou the poem, he wrote to her in a letter: "Mais je ne déteste pas que l'Amour me fasse parfois souffrir.

C'est là une source intarissable de poésie" [I do not mind suffering from Love occasionally. It is an unquenchable source of poetry]. Line 14 expresses the same idea in another dense and deeply felt image. Immersion in water is an obsessive image of death for Apollinaire (see note to "La Colombe Poignardée et le Jet d'Eau"), but here the conjunction of *souffle* and *nage* suggests that the poetic self (*souffle*) willingly immerses itself in the fatal current of dying love and that it will be buoyant (*nage*), drawing nourishment from the experience.

Lines 15-17. The pleasurable nature of suffering means that there is no real contradiction between melancholy and fervent patriotism. It is an example of oscillation (already seen in l. 10) between attitudes that are of equal significance and strength.

Lines 18-19. The swing back to melancholy is given hallucinatory force by the image of rain and dead eyes. It may have been inspired by the fact that *pleuvoir* and *pluie* were used by the troops to refer to falling shrapnel (see Tournadre, *GA* 13, p. 72). But it is also consistent with the whole imagery of eyes in Apollinaire's poetry, drowned glances signifying death (see "La Colombe Poignardée") and the vitality of life being projected through the eyes (see l. 9).

Lines 20-22. It is almost second nature for Apollinaire to identify himself with unhappy or wandering heroes of legend. Ulysses (l. 20) already occurs as a persona in "La Chanson du Mal-Aimé" (*Alcools*) and here conjures up the idea of exile in an inhospitable land, which follows convincingly from lines 18-19. The consolation sought in a remorse so warm and comforting that it becomes an erotic dream (ll. 21-22) shows not only that feelings and emotions form interconnecting complexes in Apollinaire's work, but also that they are profoundly willed (see ll. 12-14).

Lines 23-26. These lines were not in the original version. The addition shows the poet's desire to end on an affirmative note. The disarticulation of lines 23-25 helps the buildup to a climax.

LA GRÂCE EXILÉE, page 208

This poem and the six that follow form a sequence intended to illustrate, in verse, drawings by Marie Laurencin; the series was to have been called "Le Médaillon Toujours Fermé." Although Marie had made for Apollinaire at least one drawing, *La Semaine Sainte à Grenade* (Cailler, pl. 97), before he composed the poems, she seems later to have let the project drop. Possibly the *Portrait imaginaire de G. A. en Canonnier* (pl. 96) was also one of the series. "Le Médaillon" was sent to Louise Faure-Favier, as intermediary, to be forwarded to Marie, on August 20, 1915. It was sent also to Madeleine, on September 3, 1915.

The seven poems were published in *Mercure de France*, 433 (July 1, 1916), together with "Chant de l'Horizon en Champagne," under the title "Lueurs des Tirs." With the later addition of seven more poems, this group, so entitled, became a section of the final volume.

All seven poems consist of octosyllabic quatrains, and all but one, of two stanzas. All recall symbolist language, themes, and imagery interwoven with a vocabulary evocative of military life: in "La Grâce Exilée," for example, rainbow, flag, exile.

Although "Le Médaillon" conceals references to the situation between Apollinaire and Marie Laurencin, for Poupon it is Madeleine's portrait also (*GA* 6, p. 115); for André Rouveyre, Lou is a hidden image. Poupon relates imagery in "La Grâce Exilée" specifically to Marie's marriage with her German painter and to her subsequent move to Spain for the duration of the war; he concludes that in Apollinaire's eyes she had lost integrity: "à la place des écharpes magiques qui entouraient la bien-aimée, nouvelle Iris ou nouvelle Vierge Nimbée dans son arc-en-ciel, il a choisi le drapeau tricolore, il a remplacé la colombe par le coq gaulois" (*ibid.*, p. 115) [instead of magical scarves worn by the beloved, a new Iris or a new Virgin haloed in her rainbow, he chose the tricolor, he replaced the dove by the Gallic rooster]. The tone of the poem, however, seems affectionate, not resentful, and the change in imagery may indicate simply that the empty place left by his rainbow girl is now filled by devotion to the tricolor (thus a substitution rather than a replacement). An illuminating study of metamorphosis of imagery throughout the sequence has been made by Davies (*GA* 13, pp. 76-98).

LA BOUCLE RETROUVÉE, page 210

See note to "La Grâce Exilée." The tone of voice expresses vivid and painful awareness of loss rather than the generous acceptance indicated in "La Grâce Exilée."

Lines 4, 11. The role of *le destin* evokes Apollinaire's fatalistic attitude toward his love for Annie Playden, ten or a dozen years before his difficulties with Marie. As nearly always, in moments of despair, his various memories of love mingle to form a kaleidoscopic present.

Lines 5-6. Most of Apollinaire's artist friends lived in Montmartre and threw wild parties which he and Marie attended together (Davies, 1964, p. 141). He moved to Auteuil in order to be near Marie and lived there for nearly three years, 1909-1912, until their final break.

Lines 9-12. The lock of hair appears in the title as a concrete object, then, in the opening lines, as a memory, and it finally assumes ambiguous identity on both levels, just when it seems to slip entirely from the poet's grasp. Although "found," it signifies, by the end of the poem, what has been irretrievably lost. The final stanza transforms the mood of nostalgia into one of fatalistic melancholy, for, in its association with *automne, tomba* "fell" implies disappearance and death; and, in the same way as the poet's memories and keepsakes, *notre destin* will vanish into oblivion with the fading day. The poem itself ends, in symbolist fashion, with the verb *finir*. Thus there is, for the moment, no hope of future phoenixlike loves or poems.

REFUS DE LA COLOMBE, page 212

See note to "La Grâce Exilée."

The tone of voice becomes increasingly bitter, losing the graceful melancholy of "La Boucle Retrouvée."

Line 1. *Annonciade* is an old form of *Annonciation.*

Line 2. If *Passion* refers to Christ's passion, these first two lines at once evoke and deny the promise offered by the Nativity and accept only the notion of the Crucifixion. If *Passion* means the passion of love, there is still, implied by the context, an undertone of suffering.

Line 3. *Sade* means "nice, kind, charming," but also, in all probability, a pun is intended on *sade/Sade*, which stresses the recurring themes of deception and needless cruelty and avoids the seeming tautology of *charmante* and *sade*. In context, line 3 is savagely ambivalent: if the poet thinks of *Passion* as the suffering of Christ or as his own doomed love, its description as "charming" is ironic; if he links *charmante* and *sade* to line 4, one reading is that an escape from unhappy love through "renunciation" has been a pleasant relief (but see Poupon, pp. 120, 124, for another interpretation of this stanza).

Line 5. The *colombe poignardée* or "bleeding-heart dove," found in the Philippines, is a small shy pale bird with a brilliant large red spot on its breast, resembling a wound, and neighboring flecks of red, like drops of blood. There is a contrast in both the appearance and the name of the dove between painful violence which can only end in death and gentle peacefulness, between destructive cruel forces and hope of salvation through love, even through faith. (See note to "La Colombe Poignardée et le Jet d'Eau.")

Line 6. *Refus* "refusals" could describe the action of either lover, or refer back to "renunciation," or be an attribute of love itself which plays no part in human betrayals.

Lines 7-8. The plucking of the dove's feathers, which suggests the poet's bitter (and ruthless) harvesting of his experience, or perhaps the attempt to kill his lost love, is counterbalanced by the bird's transformation into an image outside time and beyond bitterness; the memory of past love becomes, in the final line, the poem one has just read. Like "La Boucle Retrouvée," the poem ends, in symbolist fashion, with a verb that suggests an ending: *tu fus* "you were [and are no longer]." Yet the poet consciously transforms his suffering into poetry, not without a note of triumph in the closing lines which links this poem to other and grander triumphs over the cruelty of women, such as "La Chanson du Mal-Aimé" (*Alcools*) or "A Travers l'Europe."

LES FEUX DU BIVOUAC, page 214

See note to "La Grâce Exilée."

In the first version, the fires are *mourants* in line 1. By postponing the image of dying fire until the final line, the poet changes the direction of the poem, so that in the first stanza he may evoke dreams and, only in the second, disillusionment.

The dominant image of the campfire evokes Apollinaire's life in the forest (see introduction, p. 1) as he describes it in letters to Lou and Madeleine, and his reveries there, inspired by smoke (usually by cigarette smoke but in "L'Inscription Anglaise" by smoke from the campfire and from a cigar) or by glimpses of sky through the trees.

The structure, which consists of following up a deceptively enchanting reminiscence by its disintegration, or by its transformation into a mood of bitterness, recurs in the sequence (notably in "L'Adieu du Cavalier"). In contrast with the preceding poems, which are uniquely concerned with the poet's feelings, this poem evokes in the first stanza a real place, a shelter from that war which has been so discreetly announced in "La Grâce Exilée" but which gradually takes over "Le Médaillon." Only in the second stanza does a memory of suffering emerge. Here, at the center of the sequence, the landscapes of the poet's war and of his unhappy love are in equilibrium.

LES GRENADINES REPENTANTES, page 216

See note to "La Grâce Exilée."

Apollinaire described this poem as "une allusion" to Marie Laurencin's "dessein merveilleux," entitled *La Semaine Sainte à Grenade* (Cailler, pl. 97), of two ladies in Spanish dress, looking mournfully from a high window (see also Poupon, *GA* 6, p. 114).

Built around a pun on *grenade* which occurs in the third line of each stanza and is stressed by other wordplay, the word *grenadines* in the title suggests, above all, the women of Granada, one of whom is addressed in the second stanza as *Infante;* in the context of the poem, it may also suggest a creature that has given birth to something monstrous and repents of it or, more simply, Marie, now in Spain, whom the poet imagines as repenting that she left him (*ton seul péché,* l. 2).

Lines 1-4. After its first allusion to the city of Granada, *grenade* reappears in an ambivalent context, suggesting first a pomegranate and subsequently a hand grenade which changes into an *œuf coché.* The primary meaning of *coché* would be the deep clefts, for gripping, incised into the egg-shaped grenade. Then, since it explodes and produces smaller elements, the second sense of *œuf coché* "fertile egg" is introduced.

Lines 5-8. The egg gives birth to *coqs* "roosters" and, possibly if not probably, to *coques* "shells," if Apollinaire had in mind the English pun on shell. Thus there is a faint possibility that "Listen to them sing" suggested to him also "Listen to them whine overhead." The last two lines contain a double play on words: the fruit is touching sentimentally; the bomb touches us physically in our horrible gardens of war (the soldiers' gardens are mentioned in letters both to Lou and to Madeleine; see note to "Vers le Sud"). A magical object, at once fruit and bombshell, changes into an egg; this, in turn, like the golden oranges in the fairy tale which concealed enchanted canaries, hatches out a crowing cock. The imagery can be seen as circular: one is offered a hurled grenade, an egg, a bird, an exploding grenade. The emphasis is on metamorphosis; the image of the weapon, although its shape is stressed, is blurred by the changes it undergoes. In the same way one might add that what emotion underlies the poem is blurred also—or unstable; more simply, the poet's bitter nostalgia for a past love has undergone a sea change and become a warrior's fierce love of country and, even, of the atmosphere of war. For Poupon, however the plays on *grenade* suggest Apollinaire's resentment, while the ambivalent *Grenadine* and *Infante* reveal his scorn (*ibid.*, p. 115). Perhaps. It is more likely that worry about a woman's integrity does not preoccupy Apollinaire; primarily, he is proud of his own involvement in the war. Comparably, in this part of the sequence, the landscape of love gives way almost entirely to the landscape of war.

TOURBILLON DE MOUCHES, page 218

See note to "La Grâce Exilée."

The title is ambiguous. If associated with death and rotting corpses on the battlefield, it indicates an ending beyond the ending of the poem, perhaps anticipating the final poem of the sequence. Apollinaire's letters to Lou and to Madeleine, as he moves north after leaving his forest at the end of June, complain increasingly of flies. The phrase *Les tourbillons de mouches* occurs in a poem to the latter (*OP*, p. 615). He is obsessed with flies on the battlefield and the stench of corpses buried in the trenches. In a letter to Lou, clouds of greenish flies are associated with heightened daydream and a hypnosis provoked partly by the heat in which he sees knights in armor approaching (*ibid.*, p. 473).

The faintly medieval flavor of the time slips in this and the following poems may have been encouraged by the faintly medieval aspect given to Apollinaire in Marie Laurencin's *Portrait imaginaire* of the poet, dated February 7, 1915 (Cailler, pl. 92). A mixture of times (medieval, ancient, modern) is evoked in the first stanza by *Un cavalier* (l. 1), *cette flotte à Mytilène* (l. 3), *Le fil de fer* (l. 4). Or one may, more interestingly, consider them as involuntary time slips which are already a part of Apollinaire's universe in *Alcools* ("Cors de Chasse").

Line 3. "That fleet at Mytilene" refers to the rebellion of the Isle of Lesbos against Athenian rule in 428 B.C., its submission in 427 to an Athenian fleet, the vote of the assembly at Athens that all the townsmen of Mytilene should be put to death, and the subsequent reversal of that judgment which led to a trireme's being sent to Lesbos and dramatically arriving just in time to save the lives of the people of Mytilene. Whether *cette flotte* suggests conquest and massacre or unlooked-for salvation is not entirely clear. For M. Davies it suggests the latter, reinforces the image of the girl, and contrasts with that of the barbed wire in line 4 (*GA* 13, p. 94). If the poet remembers his history precisely, he thinks of a threatening fleet, not of a single trireme. In any event, the ambiguity of the line is reinforced both by context and by syntax. Lines 1, 2, and 4 are statements; after the affirmation of line 2, line 3 hangs in the air like an ambiguous question to which line 4 furnishes an equally ambiguous answer.

In contrast with the present tense, which binds together the different times evoked in the first stanza and draws in the reader, three different past tenses put a certain distance between reader and text in the second stanza and even within the stanza, between lines 5-6 and 7-8. *Rose* and *ardente* are key words relating to the whole of *Calligrammes*. *Rose* has several associations which change with the context (see note to "Vers le Sud"); here its primary meaning of love has overtones of military glory. *Ardente* retains a comparable ambivalence; its primary function of intensifying amorous desire is faintly undermined by association in other contexts with military desire and the actual flames of combat (see "Chant de l'Horizon en Champagne"). *Rose, soleil, bouche,* all seem in happy contrast with the imagery of stanza 1, but they carry an undernote of menace: the rose will fade, the sun will set, the mouth will grow old or fickle; or perhaps these things have already happened, since they are set in the past. In the final two lines the theme of love may reach its most intense expression in this sequence of poems. Line 7, however, introduces ambiguities that differ in tone from those in line 5 and darken the mood. *Mais* "but" emphasizes the uncertainty emanating from these lines. A feeling of doubt is stressed by the twofold function of *quel* "what," at once exclamatory and interrogative. Even more dubious, as an evocation of happy love, the term *errante* may mean "wandering" in both a literal and a figurative sense, implying at once propinquity and distance: the suggestion of a mouth's caress brings the lover close to the girl; the anticipation of uncertainty as to where he may wander recalls line 1 and places an irrevocable distance between the two, emphasized by the use of the pluperfect tense in line 8 which evokes a remote past. Thus, both stanzas seem to start in a major key and to end on a question whose answer is probably not a happy one.

L'ADIEU DU CAVALIER, page 220

See note to "La Grâce Exilée."

Here is a new merging of the themes of love and war, anticipated by the preceding poem. In both, all bitterness toward Marie, as well as Marie's presence, seems to have vanished. The girls in both poems seem to represent woman as the poet would like her to be.

Lines 1-4. The poem opens with an ironic line, often quoted out of context. M. Zurowski (*GA* 8, pp. 38-39) offers, as a possible source of the title and the general attitude of the poem, an ironic Polish song, "Comme c'est joli à la guerre." The verbal play *Ah Dieu/Adieu* launches a series of less obvious levels of irony which point up the futility of both love and war. The incongruous epithet *jolie* triggers line 2's misleading description of life at the front, which leads into an equally misleading description of what one does there. The hobby of making rings, as a way to pass the time between military engagements, is described in more detail in "Les Saisons." The first three lines, which seem a direct expression of the narrator's feelings, partly because of the present tense (1, 4) and the perfect (3), which leads into the present, are delicately undermined by line 4 where the switch from *Je* to *vos* (both probably referring to the narrator) indicates a change to a more distant attitude. The sighs suggest boredom, inner emptiness, a yearning for life and love. The wind represents an environment that offers no escape from one's dilemma, only its augmentation. The rhythm of the first stanza, slowed by syntax and sound, evokes the experience of endless waiting, as if time had stopped.

Lines 5-8. The second stanza, in contrast, moves quickly. It is seen from outside by the narrator who no longer participates in the action. After line 5 the verbs are in the past: those in lines 6 and 7 are in the historic past, connoting finality; that in line 8 is in the imperfect, suggesting a prolonged or repeated action. Irony continues, mainly in dramatic form: the *Adieu* turns out to have a literal meaning for the lovers; military glory and excitement are deceptively invoked in line 5; the verb *disparut* (6) seems but is not a neutral word; the lover died *là-bas*, not in a real place but an indefinite no-man's-land. These lines also evoke, like the time slip in "Tourbillon de Mouches," a medieval past which joins with the present before the determining fact of war: death, far off, unexpected, and unprepared for. A final irony may be seen in the girl's laughter, laughter as an alternative to tears, as an expression of surprise, or as a way of facing up which may come close to hysteria or madness. (For an illuminating discussion of Apollinairean laughter see Breunig, 1969, pp. 37-38.) The last phrase, [*le*] *destin surprenant*, has at least two implications: fate that is "surprising," as in "La Boucle Retrouvée," and fate that "takes by storm" and overwhelms not only the lover and the girl, but perhaps also the poem, the sequence, and the poet. The image of overwhelming destiny is a key to the title "Le Médaillon Toujours Fermé": we have had a series of glimpses into the locket, but each time it has shut once more, and now it may be engulfed with the poet and his memories or, more probably, as a work of art, it remains, closed, enigmatic, beyond the reach of human destinies.

LE PALAIS DU TONNERRE, page 222

Sent to Madeleine on October 11, 1915. Published in *La Grande Revue*, 11 (November 1917), in "Poèmes de Guerre et d'Amour," where it is dated August 1915.

Le palais du tonnerre of the title is, like *l'abri-caverne*, a dugout.

Lines 1, 6. An ambiguous term for the trenches is *boyau*, literally "gut," a key word in *Calligrammes* (see note to "Vers Le Sud"), returning in such poems as "Désir," "Il y a," "Merveille de la Guerre," and linking these poems which are all inspired by the terrain of the front lines. In some poems the double meaning is made very clear ("Désir," "Il y a"). In others there is a blurred quality, an undercurrent of simultanist vision ("Merveille de la Guerre"); or the *boyau*, as here, may be associated with invisibility ("Il y a," "Chant de l'Horizon en Champagne"). In "Le Palais du Tonnerre" there is no enemy presence, no consciousness of the past, but an awareness of the monotony of war, its aggrandizement of space and time, and a reaching forth to the future and to a new ars poetica. The poet's vision is emphasized by the endless length of the trenches which he must surmount. His manipulation of images and of wordplay (which is latent in this text, notably *boyau, fusées, funambules, ardeur*) expresses associations and concepts, particularly an ebb and flow between hostile external phenomena and his warm internal world; thus ambiguous words and images stress that transformation of reality which is the dominant concern of the poem: it is through war itself that the poet has a vision of the wonder which he bequeaths to posterity.

Lines 1-21. Apollinaire seeks to impose meaning on the war by humanizing the protective space of the dugout which becomes, thematically, a continuation of the wood. From the beginning, animism of objects contributes to the humanization of the seemingly dehumanized landscape. Humans have carved a nook in the heart of war, and their accessories are humanized also. Inanimate fixed objects in the external world seem to slide away, to escape, an illusion that stresses the anguish and hidden desires of the soldiers. The verbs *fuir, meurt, recule, avance, s'en va, passe, tombent,* evoke movement. Other words, *humide, en hâte, fantôme, creux, blanchâtre, vieillesse,* suggest not only movement but old age, death, total disappearance. In contrast with the trench is the freshly dug shelter of line 9, an expression of man's modern aesthetic in which an alliance between the Baudelairean word "new" and Apollinaire's concept of "old" or "antique" has replaced the outworn term "beautiful." Within the dugout there is security, an atmosphere of domesticity. If the description of the trench slips from the level of reality to that of a ghostly fantasy (ll. 6-7), the description of the dugout moves abruptly from the level of precisely observed detail (ll. 10-11) to one of abstraction. *Vieillesse* (l. 12) may suggest inner unease. On the other hand, it is a familiar phenomenon and, in the context, reassuring. Even more reassuring, after an evocation of blue sky and dreams, the dugout itself dissolves gradually into chalky clouds (l. 21), suggesting the ethereal quality of dreams and aspiration. Indeed the image of *craie* "chalk" comes to symbolize the triumph of imagination over reality (cf. the end of "Dans l'Abri-Caverne").

Between the two appearances of the chalk image (ll. 12, 21), a mixture of realistic detail and psychological experience or symbol is elaborated, expressing not only dissolution or evaporation but also a longed-for reconciliation between multiple external phenomena and some inner sense of continuity, an old preoccupation of the poet's ("Le Larron" and "La Chanson du Mal-Aimé" in *Alcools,* "Le Musicien de Saint-Merry"). Fire in a makeshift fireplace symbolizes the soul because, paradoxically, it is so flickering, "si fugitif." A labyrinth of wires resembles memory. Piles of blue uniforms are like the sky.

Lines 22-34. In letters to Madeleine, Apollinaire expresses his pride in the arrangements of his camp, here adorned with shining shells and rich blue coats. His fantasy is often based upon a kind of impressionistic juxtaposition of images (like "flare" and "acrobat" in lines 22 and 24) which the younger French poet and theorist Pierre Reverdy would have found *juste*. In the case of "acrobat," the association with *fusée* is linguistic, since *funambule* can also mean "shell." The description of the gunners in action continues the techniques of the beginning, in particular, the mixture of realistic detail and psychological experience. The men are invisible, but the metallic objects—corrugated iron like a congealed, waterless river or the shelled "Japanese" landscape—are a combination of observed detail and subjective impression which prolong and intensify the transformation of a harsh military scene into a world of fairy tale.

Lines 21, 24, 35. Several variants indicate a conscious emphasis on motion. Line 21 originally read *stagne* instead of *flotte*; line 24, *fils de fer* instead of *trajectoires*; line 35, *une bougie petite comme une souris* omitted the dynamic image of the flame.

Lines 38-62. Apollinaire's main ideas, later set out in "L'Esprit Nouveau et les Poètes," are inherent, not only in the words *neuf* and *simple*, recurrent toward the end of the poem, but also in the key word *ardeur* which, although mentioned only in passing (l. 59), is rich in associations. Elsewhere it characterizes the soldier's courage; here it contributes to that modern beauty which the poet finds in war—in war, that is, as a human activity, nourishing to the creative mind. That aesthetic which the poet seeks, increasingly during 1915, to derive from war, is pointed to by one of the variants (l. 54): the original phrase, *si vieilles dans ce palais*, omits the idea, contained in *et si usées*, of habitation (or perhaps haunting)—a frequentation by men or by their imaginings, which humanizes the outer world and makes of it matter for poetry.

PHOTOGRAPHIE, page 228

Sent to Madeleine on October 13, 1915, after receiving a photograph from her on the 8th (cf. the hope expressed in "Madeleine"). First published in *La Grande Revue*, 11 (November 1917).

"Photographie" was, in its original form, a poem of only eight lines; the restructuring to create a larger number of much shorter lines obviously underlines the delicacy of tone and the finespun nature of the images. The use of different sense impressions in several metaphors is reminiscent of the symbolist technique of *correspondences*, perhaps brought back to Apollinaire's mind by some lines of Baudelaire's which he quoted to Madeleine on receiving the photograph on October 8. The ethereal quality of thought and feeling, however, is also entirely consistent with his attitude to Madeleine at this time (cf. "L'Inscription Anglaise").

Lines 6-9. The evocation of a garden landscape as an extended comparison is particularly typical of symbolism, as in Verlaine's "Votre âme est un paysage choisi."

Lines 10-16. Gently rising smoke (l. 10) and music (l. 16) are recurring images in *Calligrammes* for the expression of moods of reverie and delicate perceptions. They contrast with other images that connote a more vigorous enjoyment of sensuous experience.

Lines 17-19. The shadow is a central image in Apollinaire's poetry (see "Ombre"), suggesting the mysterious projection of the inner self. Here the image is given platonic overtones with the implication that the shadow only dimly reflects the radiant perfection of Madeleine's essential beauty.

L'INSCRIPTION ANGLAISE, page 230

One of the first poems sent to Madeleine, on May 28, 1915. First published in *Calligrammes*.

This poem has a still greater ethereality of feeling than "Photographie," the poet taking deliberate pleasure in the tenuous and delicate associations he is conjuring with. Again, this effect has been reinforced by dividing some long lines in the original into two. The conscious nature of the meditation, in which love becomes the theme for an exercise of the imagination, is characteristic of his relationship with Madeleine (see introduction, p. 1).

Lines 1-6. These lines recall Apollinaire's first meeting with Madeleine, in a train going from Nice to Marseilles, when he was returning from leave to his barracks in Nimes. The encounter is enhanced in his mind by memories of the Mediterranean landscape, to which his childhood in Nice and Monaco had made him deeply attached (see "Les Collines," ll. 101-115).

Line 7. The terse disjunctive nature of this line contrasts with the orderly syntax of the rest, injecting a note of urgency. It is an indication that, despite the meditative tone of the poem, sensations and sense impressions are real and vivid for the poet.

Lines 12-17. Here again (see "Photographie," l. 10) smoke expresses a mood of musing reverie. Similar images of rising movement, gentle or vigorous depending on the mood, are to be found throughout the volume, and they are no doubt to be connected with the use of sinuous or curved lines in the graphic form of the calligrams.

Lines 18-23. Apollinaire was fond of the little grass snakes of the area in which his battery was stationed. Their coiling habits had sensuous associations for him, which were reinforced by the happy coincidence that the French verb to describe their movements, *se lover* (to coil or writhe), lent itself to a bilingual pun (see "Loin du Pigeonnier").

DANS L'ABRI-CAVERNE, page 234

Sent to Madeleine on October 8, 1915. Published in *La Grande Revue*, 11 (November 1917), in "Poèmes de Guerre et d'Amour" and dated December 1915.

This poem may express a mixed reaction to the big battles in Champagne (September 22 and 25) and thus be concerned with battle fatigue, as well as with a psychological state of depression. The poet attempts to surmount his mood by an almost hallucinatory invocation of the beloved. The poem, in the context of *Calligrammes*, is the third of five poems inspired by Madeleine, and the variants in the original text relate the poem overtly to her. In general, the revisions indicate a change in focus from a soldier's amorous daydreams to a poet's meditation on beauty.

In the *Manuel d'infanterie à l'usage des sous-officiers et caporaux* (anon., (1921, pp. 427 ff.) may be found a description of *l'abri-caverne*, a dugout six meters deep: "enterré sous six mètres de terre vierge au moins" (also in Tournadre, *Glossaire*).

Line 2. The image, *un feu solide*, is not new. Apollinaire had already used paradoxes of this kind, which belong to the language of mysticism, to evoke a poetic vision of salvation (or destruction) in *Alcools: ce feu oblong* ("Cortege"), *le feu solide* ("Le Brasier"). Here the image of fire is linked to a momentary but overwhelming vision of his love.

Lines 4-7. Words of destruction and violence, *s'effrite, cassures, arrachés*, stress the gap between the dream and the reality. The image of *craie* "chalk" suggests instability, even menace, to a far greater extent than in "Le Palais du Tonnerre." One might say that the ugliness and the depression evoked here and the daydreams evoked in line 21 of "Le Palais," by the same image of chalk, illustrate the antinomies to be found in much of Apollinaire's poetry, for there is always another, and frequently an "opposite," meaning latent in the Apollinairean vocabulary, probably because the latter constitutes an attempt to describe emotional and intellectual man in the round.

Lines 8-28. In "Le Palais du Tonnerre" fragments of a clear sky are glimpsed. Here, the time is evening (ll. 8, 14, 15) and even the poet's mood is full of shadows. There is no sun or source of brightness within him. One thinks of the antinomies of light and shadow in *Alcools*. But the self-doubts of 1908, or the more usual theme, in *Alcools*, of lost love, has given way to a loss of identity. In contrast with the opening lines where the poet has the power to change reality (1-3), in contrast also with that mood of "gaiety" in which the war seems a "fantastic" spectacle, as Apollinaire repeatedly writes before September, the heart of the poem plumbs the depths of a new experience, a new form of emptiness which attacks, perhaps, Apollinaire's poetic imagination, and perhaps for that reason he clings to thoughts of his new love as a source of poetic nourishment. The objectivity that allows the poet to view his mood as a mood, and therefore temporary, also compels him to question his memory and his beliefs in a new way, and in particular to question that image of Madeleine which has become so necessary to him.

Line 18. The original verse read *Et imaginant ta nudité*. *Beauté* becomes a key word toward the end of the poem, and it is used here in an ambiguous transition between two levels of yearning or aspiration.

Lines 29-31. When the poem was published, these three lines, addressed to Madeleine, were omitted. In them, the image of chalk, *la craie*, was linked with the sadness experienced by the poet in the trenches:

Mais tu existes Madeleine ta beaute est réelle
Je l'adore
Malgré la tristesse de la craie et la brutalité
incessante des coups de canon

This ending indicates that loving and to some extent erotic daydreams were increasingly the poet's escape from war's "horrible" reality, an impression borne out by other poems and by the letters to Madeleine. Daydreams contribute to the theme of a wider spiritual aspiration, a need of the whole being to find a source of belief in life.

FUSÉE, page 238

Sent to Madeleine on October 9, 1915, in a longer version from which several lines have been deleted. First published in *Calligrammes*.

As in "Chef de Section," "Simultanéités," and other poems, the ardent longing for Madeleine is expressed in the language of war. The daily realities of Apollinaire's life color all his thinking to the extent that even an artillery bombardment becomes an expression of (partly disguised) erotic feeling. His passionate thoughts are interwoven with the more accidental and incongruous impressions of the front line which are also part of his daily life —an application of the technique of simultaneity. The effect created is of an all-pervasive atmosphere in which love and war are inextricably mingled in the poet's mind.

Lines 5-11. The thoughts and observations in these lines (and in ll. 18-20) are less disjointed and abrupt than the juxtapositions of earlier poems ("Saillant" or "Échelon"). They resemble the more ordered flow of consciousness of "Il y a," but since they are more restricted to the immediate scene than those of that poem, they are even more easily assimilated. Along with small picturesque details (that of l. 7 having potentially dramatic implications of a dead or dying man to be recovered from no-man's-land) there are typical observations of the wild life of the front line (ll. 8-9) and an example of the superstitions (ll. 10-11) that Apollinaire cultivated assiduously as a mild form of the *merveilleux.* (See "Sur les Prophéties." Apollinaire also wrote an account of the superstitions in the front line; see *OC*, II, 540-547.)

Lines 12-17. The artillery is completely absorbed into the poet's amorous dreams, its warlike purpose forgotten. The god that presides over the war (l. 17) is clearly Eros, flanked by cherubim.

Lines 18-24. The sound of tractors (l. 19) perhaps comes from the outside world of normal activity continuing in the midst of war (see the last line of "Saillant") and thus provokes a moment of nostalgia for a stable, safe existence now lost in the past (l. 20). The contrast drawn between past and present is ambivalent, however. The underlying connection is the implicit phallic analogy between the tall chimneys and the guns. While the purer, nobler sexuality of the past is evoked wistfully, the more aggressive virility of the present is clearly attractive to the poet. Hence the poem ends on a note of celebration of the virile energy of war, idealized, however, by the religious overtones of the final line.

DÉSIR, page 242

Sent to Madeleine on October 6, 1915. First published in *La Voce* (January 1916) and then in *La Grande Revue,* 11 (November 1917).

Initially the poem seems to echo "Fusée" in expressing amorous longing through metaphors of war. It is quickly apparent, however, that there is a fuller awareness of the ominous realities and discomforts of war, which leads to a greater complexity of tone and feeling. The whole poem is colored by the circumstances it evokes: the mounting of the major attack of September 25, preceded by a long artillery barrage. This explains why the "desire" of the title is progressively less directed at the woman of the poet's thoughts as the poem proceeds. Individual desire is replaced by a more general aspiration, on the poet's part, to imagine and project himself mentally toward the areas behind the enemy lines, which the attack is aimed to conquer. Despite the equivocal note of lines 24-26, this aspiration has none of the lightheartedness of "Fusée"; instead, it builds up to a somber and apocalyptic view of the attack as a long night of labor, from which something will be born, but only at the cost of suffering.

Lines 1-8. The two types of desire, one remote and one in front of the poet, are identified twice over, with some suggestion (ll. 7-8) that attention will be concentrated on the immediate, less personal, one. *La butte du Mesnil,* like the *Main de Massiges* (l. 22), was a position in the battle zone which was bitterly contested.

Lines 9-11. The sense of frustration here will disappear gradually as the artillery barrage gathers in intensity and the tone of the poem swells accordingly.

Lines 12-20. The menacing sounds of war build up. At the same time a glimpse is given (ll. 13-16) of the misery and discomfort of the long night for both poet and troops. The Decauville, a light railway named after its inventor, was used to move ammunition and supplies to the trenches.

Lines 21-33. The poet's frustration is less obvious at this point; it is no doubt canalized into the activity of firing the guns. The tone of lines 24-26 is that of an astonished detachment at the "irreverence" of his behavior in firing on trenches with such prestigious names, but this quickly yields to the more solemn tone of the final lines building up the vision of an awesome crescendo of violence. In the metaphor of a woman in labor (l. 32) there is implicit promise and hope, but the main emphasis is on the masculine violence that precedes childbirth (ll. 28, 33).

CHANT DE l'HORIZON EN CHAMPAGNE, page 246

Sent to Madeleine on October 27, 1915. Published in *Mercure de France,* 433 (July 1, 1916), in "Lueurs des Tirs" with "La Médaillon Toujours Fermé."

The first of the two songs was sent to Madeleine on October 23, the second, on October 25, and the poem in its entirety, two days later. The inclusion of texts already written is a familiar process, as Adéma and Décaudin observe (*OP,* p. 1094), particularly in major works. They express varying moods or voices of the poet, often with ironic effect, and here stress his manifest desire to create a poem—or myth—capturing the total experience of war.

Line 1. The adjective *verruqué,* for *verruqueux* "warty," does not occur elsewhere, according to C. Tournadre's *Glossaire.* The appearance of the same phrase, "l'euphorbe verruquée," however, in letters to Lou (p. 473) and to Madeleine (p. 96), might indicate that the name either was not invented by Apollinaire or, if it was, that the invention was probably inadvertent.

Lines 6-17. The free-verse sprawl of the opening lines (1-5) suggests the endless horizon and introduces the first of the two songs. The songs are set off from the horizon's monologue by their traditional form, octosyllabic quatrains with alternate rhymes. The first song mixes symbolist vocabulary and techniques with modernistic detail and idiom. The original title "Le Brancardier" and the occasion (the poem was written for a wounded poet friend, Leo Larguier) are absorbed into an introductory line of free verse. Religious imagery in lines 6-9 is set off from the war imagery of the rest of the song and may refer to Larguier's poems; certainly the phrase *la blessure / Du soldat de Promission* (8-9) seems to refer to him, as well as to Christ. The word *Promission* is found only in the phrase *terre de Promission* (Tournadre, *Glossaire*); that association has influenced the English translation. In lines 6-7, Mallarméan images of *le sol blanc* "white earth" and *azure* (here a verb), juxtaposed to the verb *saigne* "bleeds," not only contribute to the religious symbolism but evoke the patriotic tricolor. In contrast, the second stanza (10-13) comments on background noises, trivial or menacing, and on the light of night bombardment, gives a sardonic twist to someone's slangy remark, and evokes gas masks. The vocabulary also creates a contrast with that of the first stanza; it is neither literary nor religious. *Miaule* describes battle sounds in Apollinaire's letters, as early as his first letter composed to Lou in the forest, whereas *lueur* is one of his two favorite words when evoking for Lou and Madeleine the spectacular side of night combat. *Masque* is one of a group of technical words, *cagoule, gaz asphyxiants,* or *lacrymogènes,* recurrent in a few poems and letters. *Masque* changes meaning with its context. Here the image of the gas mask suggests stoicism and anonymity (13) and, perhaps above all, madness (14). *Fou rire,* "uncontrollable laughter," has menacing overtones because of the literal meaning of *fou,* "insane." What hides beneath the mask? The same preoccupation returns in "Océan de Terre," the poem immediately following, but suggests a different answer. *Blancheur* (15) undoubtedly refers to the trenches (it is used in this manner passim in the letters to Lou and Madeleine). Again, "Océan de Terre" takes, as its point of departure, the chalky whiteness of the trenches. Both there and here, a real situation feeds fantasy. The song's ending anticipates the poem's ending. War becomes a way of life for everything, even for the dove of peace.

Lines 18-21. In contrast with the stage setting of lines 1-5, which briefly indicate landscape, narrator, audience, and subject of first song, the second passage is lengthy and ambivalent. The narrator is, at first, unidentified: *Je*

(18) might link the poet to the horizon, while the subsequent identification of *Je* with trench and forest (19) reinforces the idea of ubiquity. Immediately thereafter, *Je* is the bullet with its whining threat (20-21). These various voices, on one level, all emanate from the poet or indicate an extension of the poet's self; on another level they contribute to the variety of roles played by the horizon.

Lines 22-30. The horizon's voice assumes its own distinct tonalities. The soldiers, evoked as costumed characters in a drama, are compared to creatures, land, and water. Their summoning suggests some higher level of significance in which the frenzy of war is ultimately meaningful because a nonhuman entity—the horizon—orders it (see introduction, p. 1). The army's role is thus poeticized. Here, more strikingly perhaps than elsewhere, destructive implications are excluded by the context, as the warrior and his weapon are evoked in terms of colors and textures which recall the natural world, perhaps even a nature deity, and which create an atmosphere at once menacing and poetically nourishing.

Lines 24, 26. Apollinaire's favorite color blue (passim in the letters to Lou and Madeleine) occurs here in *bleu-de-roi, bleu-horizon,* adjectives that ally the soldiers to royalty and to the supernatural horizon. Although *bleu-horizon* is the standard adjective of color used to describe the French army uniform before 1916-17, its occurrence, especially here but also in letters to Madeleine, indicates Apollinaire's interest in its poetic possibilities.

Lines 29-30. The continual metamorphosis through imagery leads to a metamorphosis through wordplay. A passage containing a number of plays on words is launched by the equivocal *fusée,* "spindle, rocket, fuse" or a "vocal run or ripple of music." *Fusée* is a recurrent ambiguity in *Calligrammes,* where we are continually made aware of the evanescent light from gunfire and rockets. It is rarely used as a pun but usually is limited by its context to one meaning. It exemplifies the structural use of key words, for the changing contexts and changing associations that link *fusée* at different times to the poet's love, to his sense of identity, to his art, have a cumulative effect (referring backward as well as forward through the book). Here, because it is in apposition to *fantassins, artilleurs, grenadier,* the term suggests not only theatrical light but, more important, a heroic image of the poet-soldier, which is amplified by the confusions generated around *grenadier.* At once pun and metaphor, *grenadier* evokes a tree that tosses its arms like a man and a man who is rooted to one spot like a tree (one thinks of Valéry's "Au Platane"—the associations are quite different, but the point of departure is almost identical, as with other images the two poets share). The phrase *pommes de pin* suggests the oval shape common to pinecones, pomegranates, and grenades, and may, as a phallic image, stress the virility of the soldier. The sound of *pin* anticipates a pun on the horizon's identity.

Lines 31-37. The image of the man-tree launches a host of verbal ambiguities. The *alidades* (31) are part of an angle-measuring instrument used in the artillery to determine the position of the enemy (see note to "Visée"). Apollinaire personifies them, as though they were the gunners. In the French, there is a conscious distinction between *des trous*, physical "holes," and *les profondeurs*, metaphysical "depths" (32-33), suggesting that Apollinaire continues to see war as a promoter of progress.

The ambiguities of *je fais la roue* (35) are several. Their main effect is to establish the horizon as an immense new deity on a level with elder deities such as Pan. The verbal play evokes also notions that may seem discordant but still do not undermine the central imagery. Rather, they play a synthesizing role, adding once more to the structural unity of *Calligrammes*, from its prewar beginnings, when Apollinaire felt himself to be at the height of his powers, to a moment of poetic expansion during the war. Thus, *roue* "wheel" can mean "the Ferris wheel," as it does in the prewar "Tour," or, *la roue de loterie* or *de fortune* "the wheel of chance," on a physical or emblematic level. *Je fais la roue* may mean "I spread my tail" (for a bird), "I swagger" (same gesture for a man), "I wheel about" (for soldiers), "I turn cartwheels" (in anticipation of the horizon's attitude, at the end of the poem). These meanings, and others, stated or implied, underline the all-encompassing role of the horizon. Whichever possibilities one accepts, the result is a blurring of distinctions; the horizon, already invisible, loses its identity as horizon and become analogous to slightly discordant notions anticipating the chaos of the ending: the circle of the horizon as Ferris wheel or wheel of change; the horizon itself as divine peacock, seducer, soldier, acrobat, artist.

The alliterative *pin. Paon, Pan* are linked also by assonance, whereas the relation of *pin* (30) to *Paon, Pan* (35, 37) is an example of paronomasia and *Paon, Pan* form a pun. The wordplay not only may have an onomatopoeic function (for Apollinaire, *pan!* evokes an exploding shell [*LL*, p. 279]), but it underlines the more fantastic aspects of the horizon who is a mystic peacock, invisible, possibly demonic, a singer like the poet and, like him, surely a poet. The capitalization of *Paon,* like the reference to the oracles, underlines the association between the modern deity and the old god Pan. Apollinaire assuredly had in mind the orphics' interpretation of Pan as the All and the mysterious announcement of his death when Christ was born.

Lines 38-47. The image of wine and wine country suggests blood also (38). The associations of wine with blood and with Dionysiac orgies (where the blood of a living creature is the most precious wine) are dwelt on at length in "Vendémiaire" (*Alcools*). They recur, more explicitly than here, in "Le Vigneron Champenois" (see l. 8 and also note). There too the identity of the speaker is blurred. Here line 43 can be read as a transition between the horizon's satisfaction and the pathos felt by the poet-observer. There is an abrupt change, at this point, from exultant grandiose invocation to the noting of small events. The haughty hiding of identity by German officers (44) contrasts significantly with the naive but confident assumption that God and everyone else recognize a poor man, through his first name, cried aloud (47). *Bon Dieu,* although an oath, also suggests an intimate relation between the wounded soldier and his God. In this line, which is probably an actual memory, the religious overtones of the saint's name contribute to that ennobling of the French soldier which is a major theme in the poem.

Lines 48-75. The original title of the second song, "Classe 17," may have given rise to line 41, which originally read *classe 17,* and subsequently *classe 15,* before it finally became *classe 16. Classe* refers to the annual quota of recruits. The first part of the song sets the scene in the familiar landscape of Apollinaire's letters: the constant sound of the cannon, the white chalky sea of the trenches, the flora and fauna which represent continuity and, for the poet, a shelter in the face of war. The touch of pathos, evoked by the soldier's youth and the fleeting youth of the girls back home, avoids sentimentality because of imagery and wordplay which stress the aspiration of the final lines.

The military term *cagoule* "gas mask" (63) originally, and still, signifies a monk's hood and cape, as well as the head covering, with eyeholes, of a penitent. In a letter sent to Madeleine on September 15, 1915, Apollinaire is reminded by the word of his early childhood in Rome and his fear of the hooded monks at funerals (*TS,* p. 141). Because it has a technical meaning in modern warfare, its relationship to the song's traditional lyricism is at once discordant and appropriately medieval, reminiscent of other Apollinairean juxtapositions, in *Calligrammes,* of modernistic imagery with accepted poetics or with time slips. Or one can say that *cagoule* suggests the enforced chastity that soldiers and monks share.

Lueurs des Tirs, "blazing of the guns" (translated in the title of this section as "flash of gunfire"), replaces the muse of poetry, Mnemosyne (or Memory), for the soldier. Accordingly, in the last six lines of his song, it is not the memory of a girl which inspires him. Although *ardeur* and *ardente* link war to love, the beauty of women has given way entirely to the beauty of war. *Ardeur* describes both the soldier's eagerness for battle and the battle's flames. The word *ardent,* along with its family, is a recurring ambiguity in *Calligrammes,* associating, literally, flames and, figuratively, love of women, patriotism, valor, poetic aspiration, with the soldier's lot. Here the play on words stresses a series of transformations. The heat of battle is characterized by gunfire and exploding shells; these in turn evoke a gigantic goddess on the horizon, a burning (*ardente*) muse. The song seems to emanate from the actual fighting, an idea that is at odds with the postsymbolist style and suggests, rather, expressionist ideas (see end of poem and note to "A Travers l'Europe").

Lines 76-82. There is a transition from *Il* "he," the soldier, to *Moi* "I," the horizon. The horizon is perhaps a persona of the poet, particularly at the beginning of the poem. If, however, one does not consider the horizon a poetic persona, it becomes an expression, or personification, of the atmosphere of battle as perceived by the poet-soldier: a feeling that does not coincide with external reality but has become externalized, or objectified, and, as a violent vision of an irrational world, can be compared, throughout the poem, with techniques of German expressionism before World War I. (Once the war starts, Apollinaire's letters from the front are anti-German and make scathing references to his former literary and artistic acquaintances.) Although line 79 asserts *je combattrai pour la victoire,* in the final lines the horizon seemingly becomes chaos, violence, and death, the pure and pointless manifestation of war. On another level it may signify the coming of a beneficent future which will transform everything totally, as in Rimbaud's "Après le déluge." Again, one may think of the final mood as ambivalent: the war is a pointless submersion before which one feels awe because the cataclysm is larger than Good or Evil; it is an amoral demonic force that sweeps through, upsetting everything; the chances that it purifies as it goes are small.

OCÉAN DE TERRE, page 252

Published in Pierre Reverdy's *Nord-Sud,* 12 (February 1918), and dated December 1915.

Dedicated to Giorgio de Chirico (who later, in 1930, illustrated a limited folio edition of *Calligrammes* with lithographs).

Victor Martin-Schmets has discovered four alexandrines that may be a first version of the poem (*GA* 5, pp. 101-102):

Le poète
Je suis comme un palais bâti dans l'océan
Les fenêtres mes yeux donnent sur le néant
Des poulpes vont grouillant en place des murailles
Leur triple coeur bat à grant [*sic*] *coups dans les batailles*

[I am like a palace built in the ocean/Its windows my eyes face nothingness/Octopuses go swarming instead of high walls/Their triple heart throbs with huge heartbeats in battle.] Those verses were followed by the beginning of another line: "Et leur bec cogne aux vitre" [sic] [And their beak knocks at the windows].

The octopus is a favorite image of the poet's. Apollinaire probably learned of its peculiarities at Monaco when he was a schoolboy. A passage in "Zone" (*Alcools*) recalls a boat trip and fish watching in the Mediterranean: "Nous regardons avec effroi les poulpes des profondeurs / Et parmi les algues nagent les poissons images du Sauveur" [Terrified we see in the depths octopuses / And fish the Savior's symbols gliding through seaweed]. In *Le Bestiaire* (1911), fish are already identified with Christ and the octopus is represented as a frightening image of the poet. The triple heart (4) repeatedly intrigued Apollinaire who felt affinities with the creature. Squids, octopuses, and cephalopods, generally speaking, have one main heart and two lateral hearts, one at the base of each gill. In addition, three curious habits, frequently observed and exploited in his poetry by Apollinaire, characterize the octopus. It ejects a black liquid as camouflage (11). With a paralytic digestive saliva, it paralyzes its victim and digests it externally (although it can also ingest). The radula inside the parrotlike beak is a rasp with teeth, which moves over a fulcrumlike seesaw, to chop pieces of food or shells. Thus the beak, mentioned in "Océan de Terre" (4, 16) and in "Le Poète," is menacing; and the sucking of blood, referred to in "Le Poulpe" (*Le Bestiaire*), where the octopus is a persona of the poet, "Suçant le sang de ce qu'il aime" [Sucking the blood of what he loves], probably results from Apollinaire's firsthand observation of the octopus seemingly sucking its victim.

Line 1. The image of the ocean, like that of the octopus, dominates the poem. It derives from the chalky, churned-up nature of the battlefield, often mentioned in letters to Lou and to Madeleine, which eventually evoked for Apollinaire a frozen sea. In "Le Poète" the house is underwater, or surrounded by water, and is identified explicitly with the poet. In "Océan de Terre" the poet probably thinks of himself as the house that he has built, or he may think of the dugout that shelters him, which is the main image of two preceding poems in this section, "Le Palais du Tonnerre" and "Dans l'Abri-Caverne."

Line 2. The escape of self through the eyes is a recurring theme (see note to "La Nuit d'Avril 1915"), sometimes exalted but here somewhat ominous. There is also a suggestion in this image of the flowing trenches which anticipates the imagery of the following poem ("Merveille de la Guerre"), where the theme of the expanding self is glorified: "j'ai coulé dans la douceur . . . J'ai creusé le lit où je coule" [I have flowed into the sweetness . . . I have hollowed out the bed where I flow]. On the other hand, the house with the rivers flowing from it suggests the poet, weeping from German attacks of tear gas (increasingly mentioned in the letters), and at the same time resembles the silhouette of the octopus.

Lines 3-4. In "Le Poète" the octopuses replace the high defense walls around the house, engage in battle, probably on its behalf, but their knocking at the windows seems a threat as much as a friendly signal. In "Océan de Terre," because of the rapid buildup of visual analogies in the opening lines (among house with its rivers, weeping poet, flow or twist of the trenches, octopus shape), the octopus is more complexly suggestive. His beak and bulbous eyes recall the gas mask used in World War I and thus his image may evoke the poet's fellow soldiers who, as he writes Madeleine, don their gas masks during an attack and, instead of taking cover as do the artillery, emerge to confront the enemy with hand grenades and guns. Like the octopuses of the poem, with beating heart, they "swarm all over the walls."

Lines 5-6. *Maison humide* suggests the damp dugout and the human being whose physical nature is largely compounded of water. In contrast, *Maison ardente* suggests both an ardent nature and the image of a house on fire, like the poet-pyre in "Le Brasier" (*Alcools*) or like some of Magritte's musical instruments flaming along the seashore. The poet as an isolated house is a dominant theme in Chirico's lithographs for *Calligrammes*, as are some of the visual analogies already mentioned (Greet, 1978, p. 11 and pl. 7).

Lines 7-8. A new contrast. *Saison rapide* suggests the swiftness with which time passes and the immediacy of death. *Saison qui chante* suggests the poet-soldier, singing but imprisoned by time. (Cf. Dylan Thomas's lines on his own mortality written some thirty years later, after another world war: "Time held me green and dying/Though I sang in my chains like the sea.")

Lines 10-13. In "Le Poulpe" the ink thrown about by the octopus and the blood it sucks are set in opposition. In "Océan de Terre" the ink has given rise to an untranslatable pun, *ancre/encre*, "anchor/ink" (10-11), and also to a dreamlike soliloquy with its honeysuckle image (12), which might be suggested by smoke twisting upward from a bombardment (Adéma). Another member of the cephalopods in the Mediterranean, flying squid, may have inspired the image of the airplanes (9-11) which not only, birdlike, lay eggs (or bombs) but probably also, squidlike, cast the anchor (or ink). Lines 10-11 stress the impression that the scene is to some extent underwater, with airplanes at once like boats casting anchor and like squid squirting ink downward.

Line 15. Among images that evoke the no-man's-land of the front lines (the airplanes, the octopuses swarming over the walls), most notable is the digging of one's own grave, a vivid image of the dugouts which, as Apollinaire writes Madeleine, were often in part composed of corpses, both French and German.

Line 16. The reprise and development of a line from the preceding poem "Chant de l'Horizon," "Sur cette mer aux blanches vagues," exemplifies the evolution of key images and the positioning of poems throughout the book. The octopus, which can change color at will, is almost indistinguishable from the landscape. The recurrent color words, *Pâles, crayeuses, pâles,* evoke the pallor of death and reinforce the image in the preceding line. There is an implicit association, suggested first in lines 2-3, and again here, between the shape of the octopus and the long twisting trenches of the front lines, described in letters to Madeleine toward the end of November, when Apollinaire transferred to the infantry. There is also a faint possibility that the image of chalky waves evokes two kinds of habitat for the octopus (if he is associated with soldier and gas mask), a chalky ground, dug up in waves, and also *la vague,* the fumes of tear gas, here chalk-colored because of the dusty nature of the country.

Lines 17-18. A fusion of earth, water, and even air is stressed by the metaphor of the ocean.

In "Le Poulpe" and "Chant de l'Honneur" the poet identifies himself with the octopus; in "Océan de Terre" the octopuses are outside. Visually, in all probability, a fusion between sheltering gas mask and what Mikhail Sholokhov has called the "monstrous" zigzag of the trenches, the octopuses may be, on one level, hostile toward the house and the poet; on another level they may represent a fraternal alliance, far removed from the sadistic loves of "Le Poulpe." Analogies between poet and house, between ocean and battlefield, between octopus and trenches/house/gas mask, contribute to an atmosphere where, paradoxically, visual patterns impose an order upon a world that is torn up, and things seem to correlate and harmonize in the midst of man-made confusion.

MERVEILLE DE LA GUERRE, page 256

First published in *La Grande Revue,* 11 (November 1917), where it was dated December 1915. No manuscript of the poem was known until recently, when P. M. Adéma published the copy of a draft he found in a notebook used by Apollinaire between September 1915 and 1916. His conclusion is that the poem was written between December 19 and 23, 1915, during Apollinaire's second tour of duty in the front lines (*GA* 13, pp. 99-104).

The pyrotechnic beauty of flares in the night sky, which impressed many writers who saw service in the trenches, here inspires one of Apollinaire's most determined attempts to maintain an optimistic attitude toward the war. The depiction of the flares as dancing girls, in the opening lines, sets a tone of lighthearted fantasy, which is then carried over in some measure to the conceit of the battlefield represented as a banqueting hall (ll. 12-24). The potential horror of this image of the earth as a cannibalistic ogre is muted by the degree of defensive irony implicit in the fantasy. By playing of the fanciful notion on a feast, the poet can jocularly pretend to ignore the grim reality underlying it.

Horror having thus been subdued, his self-confidence can soar in the final section, where he imagines himself attaining a state of ubiquity through participation in the total experience of war. The imaginative process here is very similar to the drive to attain a global consciousness which characterized his prewar modernism. In both instances the poet feels his awareness being infinitely expanded through the magnitude of the experiences that inspire him, and this produces a mythic conception of the self as universally present throughout space.

But, however fervently Apollinaire's exalted state of mind is expressed, there are signs that it is precarious. Repeated references are made to the incompleteness of the experiences that the poet is imagining. The beauty of the flares is transient, and they are not sufficiently numerous to be totally meaningful (ll. 9-10, 12-13); the sky, therefore, does not fully relate to the awesome spectacle being enacted on earth (ll. 21-24). Even more significant is the final admission that full ubiquity has not yet been achieved (ll. 39-43). All these reservations point to a state of tension in Apollinaire's mind, stemming from an inability to bend reality totally to his will. But, by the same token, this tension shows that the poem, rather than being a complacent glorification of war, as has sometimes been alleged, is the product of a determined struggle to make the war experience a significant and fulfilling one.

Line 5. The appropriate comparison of the flares to comets takes the form of an allusion to the legend of the Egyptian princess Bérénice, a lock of whose hair is supposed to have formed the constellation of stars called the Coma Berenices. But through the Racinian tragedy the name Bérénice also stands for the ideal of pure love, and, by pluralizing the name, Apollinaire gracefully invokes all the women of his dreams. (Compare with the enumeration of women's names in "Le Musicien de Saint-Merry" and "La Colombe Poignardée.") Perhaps it was this invocation in the plural, however, that led him to insert in line 4, as a prudent afterthought, a direct reference to Madeleine which was not in the original draft.

Line 6. The image of dancing girls is already present in a much earlier letter to Madeleine (September 2, 1915) in an extended comparison of a night bombardment to an opera (*TS*, pp. 114-115).

Line 16. The mouths here are the trenches. The image of the earth as a carniverous ogre occurs elsewhere in even more sinister form in poems where the trenches are personified as lascivious and voracious females (see, for example, "Chant de l'Honneur" in *Calligrammes* and "La Tranchée" and "Les Attentives" elsewhere [*OP*, pp. 304, 466, 636]). The horror here, however, is played down by the deliberately casual tone of the following lines.

Line 25. The poet's movement through the communication trenches (the *boyaux*) becomes an intimate fusion with the earth and an expansion to its outer limits, remarkably conveyed by the images of flowing water which suggest a natural, irresistible, and all-pervasive process. (It is significant that *j'ai coulé dans la douceur de cette guerre*, the most highly charged expression in the passage, combining the ideas of liquid ease and the transfiguration of war, was a later addition to the original draft.) The mythic nature of the process is underlined by the miraculous signs of divinity which accompany the poet's progress (l. 26) and by his proclamation of himself as the founder of a new future (ll. 29-30).

Lines 31-38. It is interesting to note that Apollinaire toned down the original draft of this passage, making the language less grandiloquent. "La fable de Guillaume Apollinaire" became more simply "l'histoire" and "Dans les espaces stellaires / Dans les glaces antiques dans les soleils incandescents" [In the stellar spaces / In the age-old frozen wastes in the incandescent suns] became the more restrained line 37. The building to a rhetorical climax through the repeated *dans* undoubtedly gains from the simplification of the language.

Line 39. The repeated "*Mais* ce serait plus beau" (9, 12, 21) is varied to "*Et* ce serait," no doubt to echo the "Et" of the preceding line, but the sense is the same. To be distinguished from this string of conjunctions, which convey frustration, is the *Mais* at the beginning of line 25 which, on the contrary, asserts the poet's achievement in imposing his vision on the war.

Lines 42-43. There is a hint, in this admission, of the inner emptiness experienced in "Dans l'Abri-Caverne." It is not, however, so radical a form of disenchantment: it qualifies rather than dissipates the poet's elation.

EXERCICE, page 260

Sent to Madeleine on November 22, 1915, just before Apollinaire's transfer to the infantry. First published in *Calligrammes*.

Short, simple, in language metrically regular and melodious, *Exercice* reveals the growing seriousness of the late war poems in the effective tension between the limpidity of form and expression and the starkness of the theme.

For one group of combatants, the stress of war is seen to have broken all impetus toward the future (see Hubert, *GA* 7, p. 197). Twice over, first figuratively (ll. 4-5) and then explicitly (ll. 9-10), talk of the past is identified as a retreat from the future and thus as an acceptance of impending death. The key word *ascèse*, which in "Case d'Armons" stood for resolute endurance (see notes on "Visée" and "Échelon"), now suggests stoic preparation for the inevitable. The title word similarly takes on an ominous ring, with the revelation of its full sense being reserved for the very last line: the exercise is not only a military training, but also a training for death.

The poet, however, is not part of the graphic little scene he is painting. The verbs, in third person and imperfect tense, indicate that he is an omniscient observer. This role produces a further fine balance in the poem between compassion and detachment. Although vividly aware of the destructive effect of war on the human spirit, the poet himself, by implication, has not been broken and his faith in the future remains entire.

A l'ITALIE, page 262

First published in *La Voce*, 17 (November 15, 1915).

Italy did not immediately enter the war on the side of the Allies. She declared war on Austria-Hungary in April 1915 but delayed hostilities against Germany until August 28. Apollinaire's poem, begun in early August 1915 and written especially for an Italian journal, was his impassioned attempt to persuade Italian opinion to join in the fight alongside France. His personal affection for the country in which he was born, and his many connections with Italian artists and writers, were factors that must have encouraged him in his plea.

As an exercise in public persuasion (the original title was "Cri à l'Italie" [Cry to Italy]), the poem is straightforwardly discursive in form and bears many marks of the conventional rhetoric of war poetry. Apollinaire, however, seeks to combine the high-flown tone with a direct and personal style of address, in language often infused with colloquial vigor and enlivened by graphic evocations of the surrounding battlefield. While the enemy may be depicted in conventional terms as a brutal oppressor, the Latin virtues presented as the defense of civilization against the foe—irony, wit, good sense, laughter, joie de vivre—are heralded precisely because they represent the spirit of unconventionality and nonconformism. The poet's call to arms, therefore, rests on his demonstration that fervent patriotism is a natural attitude of all those who prize robust individuality of outlook.

Lines 1-5. The "confessional" details in the opening lines give the poem the tone of a personal message coming straight from a combatant in the trenches.

Lines 14-16. It has been speculated that there is a literary reminiscence here (A. Fongaro, *GA* 11, p. 154). Even without knowledge of the source, the heroic connotations of the resurrection of the oppressed slaves of former ages to fight against Germany are obvious.

Lines 41-45. The intermittent evocations of the battlefield inject a note of reportage, reminding the reader that the poet is speaking direct from the war zone. Here the strange beauty of war is dwelt on (cf. "Merveille de la Guerre").

Line 52. A line to which the words *démerdards* and *se dégonflent* give a strong colloquial flavor (cf. l. 64 with the still more unusual slang term *occase* for *occasion*). The intention is clearly to temper rhetoric with rough gusto.

Line 54. *L'électricité en bâton* is possibly a humorous acknowledgment that the blockhouse has only candles rather than electricity (C. Tournadre, *GA* 13, p. 74). It may also be a reference to battery torches which were used at the front. In September 1915 Apollinaire thanked Billy for sending him a torch (see *Avec Apollinaire: souvenirs inédits* [Paris and Geneva: 1966], La Palatine, p. 105).

Line 56. The reference is to an earthquake in Sicily in 1908. It is thought of as having destroyed the fabulous Sirens and Scyllas which had a favorite place in Apollinaire's imagination. The same idea is to be found in "Vendémiaire" (*Alcools*).

Lines 57-58. Colleoni was a famous soldier of fortune of the fifteenth century (his equestrian statue by Verrocchio is considered one of the finest of the Italian Renaissance). The red shirt evokes Garibaldi. In both cases the Italians are being urged to follow the example of their great warriors of the past.

Lines 67-68. Italy had entered the war against Austria-Hungary mainly with the motive of acquiring the Italian-speaking territories beyond its frontiers.

Line 85. A reference to Lou, despite the fact that the poem was sent to Madeleine.

Line 87. The waves are of poisonous gas; gas attacks were frequent in Apollinaire's section of the front line.

Line 96. *Rosalie* was soldiers' slang for the bayonet (Esnault, p. 471).

LA TRAVERSÉE, page 272

Sent to Madeleine on October 1, 1915.

In the catalogue of a Derain show, October 1916, entitled "Voyage" and dedicated "A. M. P." [to Madeleine Pagès].

Inspired, according to Adéma and Décaudin (*OP*, p. 1097), by Madeleine's letter about her trip home from France to Algeria.

Precious vocabulary (*tendres*, *Palos* for "Spain") and precious imagery (notably in ll. 2 and 8) set off the one modern military image, *sous-marins* "submarines," menacing in "Il y a," sent to Madeleine the preceding day, but ambiguous here where their role is not clearly defined.

Generally, in simpler love poems, such as "La Traversée," Apollinaire plays with precious concepts and language, while literary preciosity is transcended in the more energetic and serious poems to loved women, such as "Le Médaillon Toujours Fermé," and the longer poems to Madeleine (see introduction, p. 1).

Several techniques are veiled by the precious style: the first one is associated with Renaissance art; the others, with nineteenth-century French poetry. Like images of villages resembling eyelids or hearts hidden among the lemon trees, which appear in "Mai" and "Les Fiançailles" (*Alcools*), the image of a girl's eyes as sailors guiding a ship suggests anamorphotic drawings where human faces and figures are concealed in the landscape. In the first stanza the poet's fantasies and feelings control a supposedly external decor. In the second, a reverse process takes place: external imagery is internalized, and the invasion of the poet's soul is heightened by a kind of synesthesia. All these techniques reappear in surrealist art and poetry of the 1920s and 1930s.

The plays on words conform to the general preciosity of the poem; they offer no element of surprise or incongruity but stress the amorous flavor of the language, as in *Port-Vendres* [Porto Venere], literally "Port-of-Love." Two puns occur in the last line; like Apollinaire's puns in *Alcools* they have a structural function (Greet, "Puns in Apollinaire's *Alcools*," *Wisconsin Studies in Contemporary Literature* [1965), pp. 309-315; *Alcools*, ed. Greet, 1965, passim in notes) and contribute to a multiplicity of meanings, comparable to the notes of a musical chord, an image that is evoked in the last lines. There is an implicit pun on *chœur/cœur*, "chorus/heart." Enclosed in the same letter to Madeleine, another short poem, "L'Espionne," written in a similar style, plays repeatedly on the image of the heart. The word *ardent*, a recurring ambiguity (see note to "Chant de l'Horizon en Champagne"), here evokes primarily love of a woman and of poetry, but, coming so soon after "Océan de Terre" and "Chant de l'Horizon," it may also, like other key words in *Calligrammes*, be considered as a subdued pun whose sunken meanings depend on surrounding poems. Thus "La Traversée" can be considered, to some extent, as an exception, in *Calligrammes*, where wordplay and, in particular, puns and subdued puns function as structural key words, most strikingly in the major poems (Greet, 1970, pp. 298-306).

IL Y A, page 274

First published in *Calligrammes.*

Sent to Madeleine, September 30, 1915. A prototype seems to have been written to Lou in a train on the preceding April 5.

"Il y a" consists of a list, not unlike later ones invented by surrealist poets and made popular by Jacques Prévert, reminiscent also of medieval inventories of the beloved. In surrealist inventories, there is often a confrontation within a line of verse, leading to a vision of the absurd or of the surreal, whereas medieval inventories are usually a simple listing. Apollinaire's inventory is of what surrounds the poet—in outer reality and in his memory (but see also R. R. Hubert, *GA* 7, pp. 197-198, 201). There is a confrontation between lines or groups of lines, as the poet thinks of Madeleine far away (1, 3, 13, 20-21, 25), or observes the landscape of war around him (2, 4-6, 9-10, 14-15, 18-19, 23, 26), or fuses the two themes with thoughts of her letters or snapshots or of a souvenir he has made for her (7-8, 11, 22). Gradually concrete imagery gives way to abstractions, as other notions come increasingly into his mind concerning other levels of existence, at the front or in other parts of the world, all governed by space and time, which contribute to the complexity of the ending (12, 16-17, 24, 27-30). The juxtapositions seem controlled by a flow of consciousness, more natural, less contrives (or less interrupted), than in the conversation poems. They suggest the increasing ubiquity of the poet and a kind of simultaneous consciousness by syntactically very simple means, and by words and images which one finds also in the letters to Madeleine.

Line 1. A reference, as in "La Traversée," to Madeleine's journey home.

Line 2. The unexpectedly antiromantic image of "maggots" in a traditionally poetic context exemplifies Apollinaire's occasional surprising resemblance to T. S. Eliot. One thinks of the latter's famous lines: "Evening is spread out against the sky/Like a patient etherized upon a table." The same combination of terms, *saucisse* and *asticot*, occurs in a fanciful description of planes fighting, in a letter to Madeleine of October 11 (*TS*, p. 202), which seems to have been inspired by the line in "Il y a."

Line 3. The submarine threatens the ship of line 1, as in "La Traversée."

Line 6. The play on words, *boyau*, "trench" or "gut," is obvious. Apollinaire speaks as a soldier and a poet, slashing at the enemy and at a literary tradition.

Line 7. In the first version, the line read "une lettre de Madeleine." The poem was accompanied by a complaint that he had not received her daily letter.

Line 8. The image of snapshots anticipates "L'Espionne," the poem he sent to Madeleine the following day.

Lines 9-10. Originally, between these two lines about the realities of the battlefield, occurred the line: "Il y a une jeune fille qui pense à moi à Oran" [There is a girl in Oran who thinks of me]. The alternation stressed a preoccupation with love which is lacking in the final version where love, instead of being in opposition to the soldier's duties, becomes part of a total vision.

Line 12. The theme of the superhuman spy mingles with that of the equally superhuman and invisible horizon (as in "Chant de l'Horizon en Champagne"). Originally, after *invisible*, the line read: "comme le bleu horizon dont il est vêtu . . ." The image of the blue horizon indicates an association in Apollinaire's mind between the symbolist color "azure," with its metaphysical associations, and the soldier's blue uniform. (See also, for the color *bleu horizon*, note to "Chant de l'Horizon en Champagne.")

Between lines 12 and 13, originally, were the following lines: "Il y a Vénus qui s'est embarquée nue dans un havre de la mer jolie pour Cythère / Il y a les cheveux noirs de mon amour" [There is Venus who embarked naked in a port of the lovely sea for Cythera / There is my love's black hair]. The first of these lines is thematically close to "La Traversée." The second is probably a seed of the poem "Fusée," sent to Madeleine nine days later. Apollinaire frequently invokes his love's black hair in letters to her.

Between lines 13 and 14, originally, was the following line: "Il y a des Américains qui font un négoce atroce de notre or" [There are Americans who are engaged in a dreadful traffic with our gold]. It may have been omitted, in the final version, because of American intervention toward the end of World War I.

Lines 14-17. The increasing ubiquity of the poet appears focused on places where dwell people he thinks of—his brother Albert in Mexico and Madeleine in Algeria. TSF is the abbreviation for *téléphonie sans fil*, "wireless telephony."

After line 21 (the recurrent phrase *mon amour* functions as a thematic refrain), line 22 read originally: "Il y a un encrier que j'avais fait pour Madeleine. . . ." The inkwell made for Madeleine is mentioned several times in letters to her. In the final version, the inkwell, formed from part of a flare, belongs to the poet and suggests a poetry based on the tangible effects of war. *Fusée*, a key word whose primary meaning is "rocket" or "flare," is often associated with some aspect of poetry (Greet, 1970, pp. 302-303).

Line 25. This new return to the theme of poetry originally read: ". . . avec douceur vers Madeleine."

Line 30. The original ending, "et par-dessus tout il y a le soleil de notre amour" [and over everything is the sun of our love], was changed to the final mysterious version (but see Hubert, *GA* 7, p. 198): "the art of invisibility" is an ambiguous phrase, at once menacing and inviting. It suggests that in modern war one fights without seeing the enemy; that killed, one becomes invisible; that the boundaries between the dead and the living have broken down; and, if one takes the creation of this poem about a soldier caught in a modern war as an example of *l'art de l'invisibilité,* that the war has sharpened our awareness of memory, of dreamlike realities, of the complexly layered human consciousness at work noting the visible things of the world, only to render them abstract, diffused, to a point of expansion or evaporation which approaches invisibility.

L'ESPIONNE, page 278

Sent to Madeleine on October 1, 1915, along with "La Traversée."

Like "La Traversée" (see note), this poem is an exercise in literary preciosity which recalls the one meeting between Apollinaire and Madeleine and refers obliquely to snapshots she sent him. These are mentioned in the letter enclosed with the poem.

The allegory can be seen as derived from medieval allegories of love where the characters represent aspects, often conflicting, of a single personality. Traditional motifs of court poetry are the lady as a besieged fortress and the lover as a fragmented psyche which spies on and eventually invests her.

The title has modern military overtones. One of the most intriguing aspects of the poem is the feminine portrayal of the spy who personifies the poet's faculty of memory. *La mémoire,* in French, is feminine in gender. Mnemosyne, the Greek for memory, is traditionally the Muse of poetry. In addition, memory, as a female attribute of the poet, recalls Apollinaire's view of his own identity as bisexual (see note to "A Travers l'Europe").

In the second stanza Apollinaire plays openly with *rime riche,* in *déguise/guise* and *vainqueur/cœur*; their homophonic elements contribute to the preciosity of the poem.

The spy's execution, in the third stanza, is a little startling, if one imposes on the poem the logic of real situations. It would seem that the heart and love are ungrateful employers. Once the heart possesses the lady, however, there is no more need for a spying memory. Perhaps more significant, the execution takes place at (or after) the end of the poem, which was inspired by a memory and now supplants it. Minor poems written in a precious manner may be considered as temporary escapes from the harshness of life at the front. On the other hand, "L'Espionne" and "La Traversée," like nearly all Apollinaire's poems, are each inspired by a real event which had meaning for the poet.

LE CHANT D'AMOUR, page 280

Published in *Nord-Sud*, 10 (December 1917).

Sent, in a different version, to Madeleine on December 7, 1915 (*OP*, "Le . . . Poème Secret," p. 657), after his transfer on November 20 to the infantry. Apollinaire had now been exposed to continued fighting in the front-line trenches since November 28.

The poem is based on the poetic stratagem of a list, not unlike the lists in medieval poetry. In the original version, lines 6, 7, and 12 had erotic implications: Jason cries out, because he finds the Golden Fleece (which, for Apollinaire, symbolizes the female sex). The swan sings his dying song because he is seduing Leda. Line 12 was overtly phallic: "Le tonnerre des artilleries où la forme obscène des canons accomplit le terrible amour des peuples" [The thunder of the artilleries where the obscene form of the cannons accomplishes the terrible love of nations]. The sequence and the number of lines also change enormously; for example, line 13, which offers a kind of resolution for a poem of sonnet length, was originally line 11 in a poem of twenty lines.

Most significant, the original version superimposed a vision of war's chaos upon an amorous fantasy devoted to Madeleine. In the final version, by line 4, the reader becomes aware that Apollinaire's hymn to love is, primarily, a hymn to the heroism he sees around him and to the madness, pain, and screams of terror which are its components.

AUSSI BIEN QUE LES CIGALES, page 282

Sent to Madeleine on February 12, 1916. First published in *Calligrammes*.

Arminel Marrow suggests that the cicada could symbolize the soldiers in general and the poet in particular. Its nympha lives underground, like the soldiers in their dugouts. It shows its tenacity and courage by tunneling to the surface and by squirting urine at its enemies. It rejoices in the sun and, like the poet, sings.

Apollinaire, who was knowledgeable about insects, may well have known these facts. (He mentioned in an earlier letter to Madeleine his admiration for the entomological studies of Fabre, observing that these taught him about as well as insects [*TS*, p. 209].) The analogy could also have been inspired by the fact that, according to two commentators, *cigales* in military slang signified shrapnel (Bates, 1975; Tournadre, *GA* 13, p. 73). In enjoining his comrades to imitate the insect, therefore, he urged them to energy and effort in battle. There is a disparaging reference to the laziness of his fellow soldiers from the Midi in a letter to Lou, which might explain this exhortation (*LL*, p. 271). The repetitive nature of the text, ringing the changes on a limited number of phrases, is appropriate for such hortatory purposes; it may also suggest the monotonous piercing song of the insect.

The graphic form, at a primary level, is emblematic, even if the shape seems to represent a grasshopper rather than a cicada. This ambiguity may merely be the result of a common confusion between the two insects, or perhaps Apollinaire preferred the more angular form of the grasshopper because it allowed a higher degree of stylization. It is noticeable that, compared with two manuscript versions (one in *L'Esprit Nouveau*, 26 [1924], the other in *TS*, p. 329) in which the insect's front leg was curved, and there was a revolver shape clearly outlined at the bottom of the page, the design in the final text has been tightened up into a rectilinear, gridlike shape, with a compact and almost abstract pattern of lines which is pleasing in itself. These revisions testify, at the least, to Apollinaire's keen sense of graphic values as important components of the picture poem in their own right.

At a second level, however, the graphic form may have other associations. In particular, this dense pattern of lines may be read as a subtle visual reference to the topography of the poet's daily life in the war zone, which was similarly dominated by a mazelike pattern of lines—those of the trenches through which he had continually to find his way. (The presence of a revolver shape in the manuscript shows how strongly he had the war in mind.) Such an interpretation is encouraged by the metaphoric connection between the poet and the cicada and, equally, by the kinetic act of reading itself, for the layout of the text imposes on the reader a zigzag progress through the poem, with some hesitation at various intersections where it is not immediately obvious which direction to follow next. The repetitive nature of the text here fulfills another function, that of turning the poem frequently back on itself and thus reinforcing the impression of a labyrinth with no clear opening until the very last line. This hesitant and uncertain progress through the text highlights the implied analogy with the tenacious burrowing of the cicada toward the sunlight, which is itself metaphoric of the laborious marches of the soldiers through the miles of trenches, borne on by the hope of ultimate joy in victory and peace. The final line serves all the more effectively as the "exit" from the maze as it is a simple, straight line and sentence, couched (for the first time) in the future tense and culminating in the word *soleil*. The relief of emergence into the sun is emphasized by the capitalized phrase which serves to confirm, once the pattern has been grasped, the ultimate goal toward which the maze leads.

There is thus, in this as in all the calligrams, an interplay on more than one level between the graphic and the verbal elements, to produce a text that can have different layers of meaning.

Reference

Marrow, A. "Form and Meaning in Apollinaire's Picture Poems," *Australian Journal of French Studies,* V, 3 (1968), 295-302.

SIMULTANÉITÉS, page 284

Sent to Madeleine on October 14, 1915. First published in *Calligrammes.*

The title announces the poet-narrator's capacity to act and observe as a soldier while experiencing the feelings of a lover. It refers, too, to the simultaneous presence in his consciousness of an image of the distant lover and the immediate sensations of war. The poem, however, is not primarily concerned with the simultaneity of external phenomena, expressed through poetic structure, to be found in "Ondes" (see introduction, p. 1).

Lines 1-3. Concerning the striking image of the noise of war in the front lines, R. R. Hubert (*GA* 7, p. 198) has noted the rapport between the thunder of cannon and the beating of hearts. A comparable image dominates in Part I of Baudelaire's "Chant d'automne." The sound of the cannon is also mentioned with growing frequency in the letters to Madeleine, especially after Apollinaire joins the infantry. A phrase dated December 2, six weeks later, describes an experience that may have triggered the poem: the Germans bombard "avec une force telle que le cœur remue à chaque tonnerre" (p. 278) [with such force that one's heart turns over with each thunderclap].

Line 2. *Vagues* "waves" is an image evocative of the bursts of sound from the cannon (1). At the same time, the juxtaposition *vagues tempête* initiates an image of stormy waters, common to several of the major battle poems ("Chant de l'Horizon en Champagne," "Océan de Terre," "Du Coton dans les Oreilles").

Lines 2-3. At the center of this first stanza the *simultanéités* are already suggested: the continuing boom of the cannon, likened to a less antihuman, more natural, background noise of waves or a storm, aggravates the poet's inner feelings about love, closeness, separation, and, significantly, intensifies his ennui, an ambivalent word, literally "boredom" but also ranging through various states of fatigue and depression to a Baudelairean vision of the futility of life. Sounds of war in *Calligrammes* usually express the poet's emotion, ranging from excitement through reverie to, as here, a kind of weariness. Weariness with life at the front becomes a theme with variations in the letters and poems toward the end of 1915.

Line 4. Here the poet's ennui, for the moment inescapable, becomes totally identified with external noise. The boundaries between inner and outer worlds break down.

Lines 5-8. Prisoners are mentioned in other poems ("Chant de l'Horizon,"

"Il y a"). That visual observation is almost immediately submerged by background noise, now seemingly less loud than at the beginning but increasingly overwhelming, to a point that it may, like swarms of flies on the battlefield, become a hypnotic source of daydream within the poem (see note to "Tourbillon de Mouches").

Line 9. In "Chant de l'Horizon" the wearing of a *casque* symbolizes military involvement. Hubert has observed that when the soldier of "Simultanéités" takes off his helmet, he has "la tête libre." Whether or not such a reading is valid for Apollinaire, the notion of liberating one's imagination by doffing one's hat is recurrent in later twentieth-century French art and literature, from Magritte's bowler-hatted men to such writers as Prévert ("J'ai mis mon képi dans la cage / et je suis sorti avec l'oiseau sur la tête") [I placed my cap in the cage / and I left with the bird on my head]; dependence on the hat for even incomprehensible verbal communication or for the thinking of even incomprehensible thoughts is Beckett's ironic variation on the theme. For Apollinaire, the helmet may have a latent symbolism but seems less linked to flights of fancy than does the gas mask.

Lines 10-12. A nostalgia for French gardens with their heraldic lilies and roses, and with jasmine reminiscent of the Midi, anticipates Aragon's "Les lilas et les roses," composed near the beginning of World War II ("Je n'oublierai jamais les jardins de la France / . . . Et vous bouquets de la retraite roses tendres / Couleur de l'incendie au loin roses d'Anjou") [I'll never forget the gardens of France / . . . And you nosegays of the retreat tender roses / Color of the distant conflagrations roses of Anjou].

Line 13. For the persona of the soldier wearing his gas mask and thinking of love, as well as for associations with the image of the mask and with the ambiguous term *cagoule*, see notes to "Chant de l'Horizon" and "Océan de Terre." Concealed behind his gas mask the soldier finds a shelter in which to create his fantasies.

Lines 14-16. His thoughts turn into a dream. The dark hair is Madeleine's; he arrives at a pier, by ship, probably at Oran where she is waiting, if it is she. The sea he crosses is dark and shadowy like her hair, like his dream itself, like the ocean or watery elements he conjures up in other poems (see line 2), only quieter. The correspondence between the sea and Madeleine's hair is evoked in a letter of October 19: "tes cheveux noirs se déroulant comme les vagues de la mer quand souffle la tempête" [your black hair tumbling like waves of the sea when the storm blows] (*TS*, p. 221). *Vagues, mer, tempête,* words in the letter which relate not only to her hair but also to the water and storm image of stanza 1, suggest that the soldier's whole dream may be spun from, or overlies, the landscape of war.

Lines 17-20. Increasingly there is a disconnection from war's reality, a disconnection even from continuity of images within the poem. The nut tree as the poet, and its fruit as his kisses, occur in "Signe" (*Alcools*), where the same verb *gauler* suggests that someone, perhaps the wind, is shaking the tree. In "Signe" the poet is weary of old loves. In "Simultanéités" the nut tree keeps its mystery but suggests a confident state of mind. It seems once more an image of the poet, but it could also be Madeleine, serenely unaffected by the turmoil he is experiencing. If the tree is the poet, there is an abrupt switch to the image of the girl listening to a bird, perhaps the magical bluebird in disguise who sings in "Un Oiseau Chante" (sent to Madeleine three days later), at any rate, an innocent image of youth and gaiety. The twitter of the little bird (Apollinaire chooses the onomatopoeic *gazouiller*) indicates how far removed the soldier's dream has become from the noise of battle.

Lines 21-29. In the final stanzas the soldier breaks out of his dream, freed now from his original ennui and from that invasion of his identity which had sent him inward. He is prepared by his dreamlike meditation on love to fuse inner and outer worlds in a new manner; his vision of Madeleine helps him to humanize the spectacle of war, love itself, and, as usual, his own poetic identity.

As in the second song of "Chant de l'Horizon," the principal theme is the poetic imagination at work, with images that suggest a comparable intensity of life and with a comparable vocabulary. Whereas in "Chant de l'Horizon" a lack of memories compels the soldier to transform the spectacle of battle into a muse of poetry, in "Simultanéités" love's memories are linked both to war and to poetry. The nostalgic soldier sees images of love around him on the battlefield. Ephemeral phenomena are juxtaposed to memory or to a persistent ideal: the heart's searchlight signals to its twin which flashes from the beacon; gunfire blazing through the night evokes Madeleine's eyes. The poet's yearning is thus transformed into a vision that approaches the surreal in its anamorphotic superimposition of a human face on a landscape. In addition he implies by juxtaposition a metamorphosis of the real: the military beacon becomes a blossom and then, perhaps because it is a beckoning or pulsating signal, it becomes the poet's memories which are replaced, in turn, by the actual presence of Madeleine's black hair.

In lines 21-24, *ardeur* suggests both the yearning of the two hearts and the searchlights moving across the sky. *Clarté* plays a similar role in lines 27-29, uniting the crackling gunfire to a lucidity inspired in the poet by the spectacle of war and the memory of Madeleine's eyes. Each of these ambiguous words, which are key words in *Calligrammes*, humanizes and poeticizes the harsh reality of war by underlining fantastic resemblances and by imposing transformations. The alliterative, assonantal coinage *phare-fleur* and the ambiguous *clarté*, in the final stanza (25-29), contribute to a synthesis of present and past, as well as of love and war, whose function is to comment on the soldier's total experience as an individual with memories and feelings caught up in an impressive overwhelming disaster, and his power as poet to impose order on the chaos around him. (This humanizing and ordering of the inhuman and chaotic, which is inevitable, perhaps, in a war poem, seems part of that thirst for total experience discussed in the introduction, p. 1).

DU COTON DANS LES OREILLES, page 288

One of the most ambitious of the war poems. Apollinaire may have started planning it on January 29, 1916 (*TS*, p. 314, speaks of a "long poem" he would like to write about the war). It was finally begun on February 10 and finished on February 11, but it was subsequently revised for publication in *Calligrammes*. (The original text is in *TS*, pp. 322-326, with a photograph of part of the manuscript).

The modernist techniques of "Ondes" are used here to create a visual and aural montage of the noise and confusion of battle. The chaotic mental impressions of a soldier engaged in war are conveyed by the marked discontinuities between the various disparate fragments which are abruptly juxtaposed, and by the often radical changes of tone and register from one stanza to the next.

Despite the apparent confusion, however, the poem has a strong underlying coherence. Unifying elements are to be found in the repetition of two leitmotiv phrases and in the introduction, at one point, of a "stage direction" advocating the use of music, a device deliberately calling attention to a controlling hand at work in the overall elaboration of the structure. A narrative progression also becomes discernible as the poem unfolds, the earlier stanzas being concerned with an artillery barrage, which is then left behind as the poet advances toward the infantry trenches. This poem may be read, at the simplest level, as describing a return to the trenches after a period in the rear, the movement thus being through space. More profoundly, it can be seen as encapsulating Apollinaire's whole war experience, covering his transfer from the artillery to the infantry, and therefore giving the poem the fuller coherence of an odyssey that traverses time as well as space.

Not least, the poem is held together through its sound and rhythm. In a manner that is reminiscent of Laforguian music making, Apollinaire plays with multiple variations on rhyme and meter to build up a distinctive sound texture. From all the internal modulations, harmonies, and dissonances emerges a strong rhythmical movement which runs through the poem, suggesting the inevitability with which the events of war sweep onward, and yet at the same time artistically channeling the flow and demonstrating the poet's control over disorder.

Tant d'explosifs... A striking calligrammatic interpretation of an artillery bombardment. The expressiveness of the design is reinforced by the futuristlike emphasis in the typography (one of the rare examples of this in *Calligrammes*), with the use of large type and punctuation signs to suggest violent explosions.

On closer inspection, however, the graphic values are not exclusively violent. The three oblique lines that might be supposed to represent the trajectories of shells in fact rise in a gradual and indirect way which suggests a more *meditative* projection into space, similar to that expressed on a verbal level at the end of "Reconnaissance" (cf. the poet's fascination elsewhere with rising smoke; the lines might indeed be smoke rising from a bombardment). To this extent the plastic values, like other elements in the poem, reveal an individual mind and sensibility at the heart of the confusion, asserting themselves by reflection on it (Lockerbie).

Line 5. The first of the sharp changes in tone and register: the solemn mood of the preceding lines (in regular octosyllables) is punctured by this wry, colloquial interjection. The underlying fatalism of outlook, however, remains the same.

Line 7. This first leitmotiv phrase obviously imitates a call sign on the field telephone. The term may have caught Apollinaire's imagination because there was a wood in the battle zone called La Truie (Tournadre, *GA* 13, p. 73); in *TS* (p. 277) he commented to Madeleine on the picturesque names of reference points on the map.

Les Cénobites Tranquilles. The design represents a sign that, according to Esnault (p. 578), was frequently fixed by soldiers to the entrance to their dugouts. The sign is an ironic reference to the enforced chastity of the soldiers, but it is also a lewd pun since it can be read as "Laissez nos bites tranquilles" [Leave our pricks alone], which conveys the same idea in a cruder manner. The jocular nature of this pun contrasts with the more serious tone of the lines evoking the sentry, who seems a mysteriously symbolic figure (perhaps similar to the enigmatic *matelots* of "Le Voyageur" in *Alcools*).

Lines 15-21. the poignant symbolism of the wild poppies on the battlefields is caught in the first two lines. The mood of the somber question in line 16 is subtly transposed, in the rest of the stanza, into a grimly ironic key, for the apparent humor of an unnamed soldier frenetically becoming drunk on water can be seen as an attempted escape from the horrors of war which the poppies innocently symbolize. The vigorous colloquialisms of the language heighten the dissonance between tone and meaning.

Lines 22-30. In "Ondes," Gramophones stand for the bright gay cheerfulness of modern life (see "Arbre," l. 1, and "Lettre-Océan"). Their silence suggests that the happy days of peace are gone, an idea repeated in the "mangled songs" of line 30. The notion of absence of music thus provides the "frame" for the stanza, within which violent explosions of light show what has replaced it. In the condensed image of line 23, bullets form a rapid stream of light like the light beam of a film projector, and in the rest of the stanza the eruptions of light suggest a cosmic upheaval. It is indeed an environment from which harmony has been banished.

Lines 31-38. This stanza begins with isolated snatches of conversation (cf. the conversation poems of "Ondes") and modulates into a popular jangle, perhaps even nonsense verse. The stanza functions largely, therefore, as part of the sound texture of the poem and mixes in a lighthearted, inconsequential note. The Star of Benin was a decoration for colonial service. Coincidentally (?) Apollinaire's nickname for Picasso was *l'Oiseau du Bénin.*

Lines 41-42. The first appearance of the second refrain: the phrase refers to gunners protecting their hearing from the deafening explosions of their guns. The tone is still lighthearted here, as is shown by the poet's casual attitude to a gas attack and by the mimicking of the popular pronunciation of the pretentious Christian name, Désiré.

Lines 43-48. A more serious, mysterious mood is created in this stanza. Among the violence and confusion, some insight or experience of beauty, beyond his power to define, is given to the poet. But it is ephemeral, borne away in the general transience of war, which is symbolized by the artillery dashing off to new positions and by the rapid fading of the explosions. (So universal is the transience that soldiers and explosions seem to become identified in line 48.)

The image of line 47 is enigmatic. Bearing in mind the importance of wordplay and sound play in the poem, it may well have been generated principally by the rhyme sequence *nom/canons/fanons* (*fanions* in the next stanza is a variation within the same chain). Perhaps the whale evokes the encompassing night (a night scene is implicit in lines 22-30 and in the rain sequence) and the vertical rows of whalebone in its mouth were suggested by the explosions of light rising in the night sky; in that case the artillery dashing off to new positions are still "inside the whale" and will merely find elsewhere the same fading explosions and the same transience.

Ecoute s'il pleut... An interlude of great musical beauty, in which the rain becomes an expression of the poet's compassion for his fellow soldiers. The hoped-for merging of soldiers with the horizon suggests not only fellow feeling, but also a wish to see men magnified by their traumatic experiences and becoming part of a larger dimension. The horizon carries here, therefore, the same hint of a mythic vision as in certain other poems (see notes on "Chant de l'Horizon en Champagne" and "Le Vigneron Champenois").

The verbal music of this passage is the result of elaboration through at least three different stages. The process can be followed through "Les Neuf Portes de Ton Corps" in *Poèmes à Madeleine* (*OP*, p. 621) and the manuscript of *TS*, the point of perfection not being reached until the final version in *Calligrammes*.

The typographical layout is interestingly different from that of the two other rain calligrams. In "Il Pleut" the light, tremulous lines of the rain are at once more figurative and more exploratory of space, whereas the emphatic, slanting lines of the poem to Louis de Gonzagne-Frick unquestionably depict the depressing rain of winter (*OP*, p. 797). In contrast, the elongated, vertical lines of this passage suggest the calm, sustained tempo of the gently falling rain, and thus they are expressive of the poet's emotional identification with the scene.

Lines 60-68. Leaving behind the artillery positions (cotton wool in the ears is no longer necessary: ll. 72-73) the poet advances to the front line. The farewell of line 61 suggests a decisive stage in his progress, which becomes symbolic of his journey through the war. The *pare-éclats* (protective mounds of earth along the trenches, called elephants because of their shape), the weather vane (to warn of wind direction in case of a gas attack), and the periscope were all familiar features of the front line referred to in *TS* (pp. 275, 281).

Lines 78-80. *La vague* is the wave of gas; an attack is being launched. The cellars of ruined villages in the front line were used as shelters. The telephone call in lines 74-75 is presumably a warning being passed back (Tournadre, *GA* 13, p. 71), whereas the earlier calls were communications between the artillery and their forward observers.

Note that the marked rhythm of the previous stanzas is now allowed to wind down. The poem ends arhythmically to suggest the real, uncomfortable daily life of the trenches, made up of physical discomfort and sudden alerts.

Reference

Lockerbie, S. I. "Forme graphique et expressivité dans les *Calligrammes*." In *Lecture et interprétation des Calligrammes.* 9th Apollinaire Colloquium, Stavelot, 1977. In press.

LE DÉPART, page 300

Sent November 19, 1915, to Madeleine and to Jeanne-Yves Blanc, Apollinaire's wartime *marraine*. First published in *Nord-Sud*, 8 (October 1917).

The poem is written in the same general style as "Le Médaillon Toujours Fermé," "La Traversée," and "L'Espionne." In the accompanying letter to

Madeleine, Apollinaire describes its making and his thoughts about it: "J'ai fait aujourd'hui un petit poème mélancolique dans le cimetière boche. Je te l'envoie mais cette mélancolie simplement poétique ne nous concerne pas en tristesse quoiqu'elle concerne nos baisers et je pensais en le composant au retour du poéte blessé et à sa rencontre avec sa femme" (*TS*, p. 263, quoted in *OP*, p. 1100). [Today I wrote a melancholy little poem in the German cemetery. I enclose it, but the melancholy which is quite simply poetic does not concern us as a real sadness although it does concern our kisses and I thought as I wrote it of the wounded poet's return and of his meeting with his wife.] The wounded poet is Blaise Cendrars whom Apollinaire imagines returning to his wife from the front. It is not the first time that a melancholy cemetery is the setting for Apollinairean creation. At least three poems in *Alcools*, largely Rhenish in inspiration, "L'Adieu," "La Maison des Morts," and "Rhénane d'automne," suggest that graveyards and the making of poetry were associated for the young poet. In a setting of war, a graveyard full of fresh corpses as a parenthesis or shelter for the creating of poetry would seem unconsciously ironic, although Apollinaire is attracted by the German graveyards at the front and describes them to Madeleine, before and after writing "Le Départ." The poem itself, however, contains no reference to a graveyard or to Cendrars. The avoidance of specific detail and the final title of the poem would indicate that the poet sought to change and enlarge its meaning.

In Madeleine's copy the title "Sous la neige" was crossed out and "En silence" was written in; in Jeanne-Yves Blanc's copy, there was no title; finally, in *Nord-Sud*, the poem was entitled "Le Départ."

Among the variants, the *purs pétals* of *Nord-Sud* were at first *blancs*, "white," suggestive of the symbolist origin of the poem. More interesting is the history of line 4. On the same day Apollinaire sent to Madeleine the personal "Comme tes mains sur mes baisers" and to Jeanne-Yves Blanc the noncommittal "Comme des mains sur des baisers." The version in *Nord-Sud* changes the narrator's point of view, "Comme ses mains sur tes baisers." In *Calligrammes* there is a final return, slightly modified, to the first version. The point is that line 4 does not have much meaning beyond indicating a feeling of sympathy for all meetings and farewells between lovers. In context, however, line 4 has a special function. The relationship between images in lines 3 and 4 is paradoxical—that is, one would expect snow on petals to be analogous to kisses on hands, rather than to hands on kisses. This reversal, as also the ambiguity of *brisés* "broken" in line 2 and the underlying image of severed hands in lines 4-5, points to the tentative expression of a kind of discontinuity, more modern than the style of the poem would suggest.

LE VIGNERON CHAMPENOIS, page 302

Written shortly after Apollinaire's arrival in the small town of Hautvilliers where his regiment was dispatched for rest and training. Sent to Madeleine on February 7, 1916. First published in *Nord-Sud*, 9 (November 1917).

If the image of wine is used as a metaphor for both soldiers and artillery in the poem, it is not only because Apollinaire was stationed in the heart of the champagne country. More important is that fact that wine, and the related imagery of alcohol, have, throughout his writings, magical and Dionysiac associations that are appropriate to the theme of the poem. These associations can be seen at work in the central section (ll. 12-17) where a mythic night scene is conjured up which is reminiscent of such poems in *Alcools* as "Nuit rhénane" and "Vendémiaire." In the translucent darkness (compare "Tout l'or des nuits" of "Nuit rhénane") the vine grower is magnified into a mysterious and allegorical figure, with no mouth, although he sings, and, although bent over the vines, receding (and growing?) to merge with the horizon. It would seem that, as in "Chant de l'Horizon en Champagne," this figure is a larger-than-life deity who presides over the war from a standpoint beyond the notions of death and destruction. In the bountiful vision of such a deity the artillery can appropriately be likened to a sparkling, explosive wine, for it represents a manifestation of vitality and exuberance, transcending its death-dealing function to become an expression of the life spirit.

The Dionysiac vision, however, is sketched in, rather than being fully developed. The vine grower's song (assuming that it embraces lines 6-11 and 18-22) is couched in ordinary human tones rather than in those of an incantation. The charm of the poem is that it moves easily between hints of a mythic dimension and a more spontaneous and casual utterance, reflecting the soldiers' pleasure at a brief respite from war. There is a pleasing warmth and informality of expression in details such as the bustle of arrival, the exchange of greetings, and the soldiers' relaxation from duty (lines 1-7, 18). The laconic reference to what the morrow may hold (line 22) maintains to the end a lightness of touch which is typical of the poem in its entirety.

CARTE POSTALE, page 306

Sent as a postcard on August 20, 1915, to André Rouveyre.

That a brief poem whose dominant preoccupation is with the poet's relation to ephemeral phenomena should be inscribed on a postcard is hardly accidental, although it may seem paradoxical to the reader aware of the antinomies suggested here. Like circles within circles in *Alcools,* there are in *Calligrammes* mortalities within mortalities. The poem emphasizes differing spans of time, for the poet's life encompasses the summer's day and the day is far longer than that shot of gunfire which, as in other war poems by Apollinaire, is compared to evanescent flowers. Since the poet meditates on the ephemeral, one tends to think of ephemeral aspects of life, especially considering the concrete context of the postcard and also the larger context of war. Thus, one reading of this little poem would suggest that not only is life more transient than we can quite comprehend it to be, but the essence of the present moment finds expression in a phenomenon so brief that it seems over before we have really grasped it.

Yet, as so often with Apollinaire, another and opposite reading is equally, or perhaps more, valid, and most certainly intended by the poet who speaks so contentedly and with such appreciation of things dying. It is not the *canonnade* that matters but Apollinaire's naming of it and his creation of analogies. For Renée Riese Hubert (*GA* 7, p. 199), in poems such as "Carte Postale" the present paradoxically loses its ephemeral character. She finds in the poem "cette volonté de dépasser l'immédiat. . . . Alors que le jour, la floraison, les coups de canon sont voués à une vie sans lendemain, le poète s'efforce d'arracher quelques mots ou une pensée à cette menace universelle de disparition" [that fixed intent to go beyond the present. . . . Although the day, the flowering, the cannon shots, have no tomorrow, the poet struggles to snatch a few words or a thought from the universal threat of engulfment]. On the linguistic level, a comparable process may be seen at work. The poet builds up, through words associated with what is rapidly vanishing, or faintly perceived, our acceptance of the final line: *meurt* (l. 2), *floraison* (l. 3), *à peine* (l. 4), *éclatante* (l. 5), *Se fane* (l. 6). If, thematically, *Se fane* returns to *meurt* in a symbolist circle, still the whole is firmly controlled by the first words: *Je t'écris;* the act of writing is counterbalanced, but not submerged, by the final disappearance into the past: *avoir été.*

ÉVENTAIL DES SAVEURS, page 308

First published in *Calligrammes.*

One of the most interesting of the calligrammatic poems, in which the formal qualities of the layout combine with the terse allusiveness of the phrases to produce a composition that seems meant to intrigue.

A manuscript reproduced in Cailler (pl. 65) bearing the longer title of "Éventail des saveurs de guerre par l'oeil et le doigt jusqu'à la bouche" [Fan of flavors of war through the eye and the finger to the mouth] indicates a concern with parts of the body and the senses. This concern is still evident in the final text, but slight changes in typographical layout, and the shortening of the title, result in a greater degree of ambiguity, both verbal and visual. In the manuscript, notably, the calligram "Mes tapis de la saveur . . ." was clearly laid out in the shape of a lady's fan. This arrangement not only gave a literal as well as a metaphoric sense to the word *éventail,* but also identified this calligram as the starting point of a prescribed order of reading, which was then spelled out by the longer title, with what amounted to a one-to-one relationship between each shape and the object it evoked. With the substitution of a more ambivalent shape for the fan in the final text, and the shortening of the title, the prescribed sequence disappears: the emphasis in the new title falls on *éventail* in its purely figurative sense of "scale," "gamut," or "spectrum," and most, if not all, of the individual calligrams are left freer to acquire associations with more than one object.

Taking these changes into account, the final text could be described as a set of free variations on the theme of sensuous enjoyment, particularly the enjoyment that arises from the poet's thoughts of love. There is, indeed, a strong similarity between the language and ideas of the calligrams and those of the secret poems to Madeleine and Lou, which are essentially exercises in sensual evocation. Hidden meanings in both verbal and graphic forms are, therefore, to be expected. Apollinaire had an irrepressible appetite for erotic double entendre which was never more freely deployed than in compositions that are relatively lighthearted and playful, as in this poem.

Attols singuliers . . . A similar reference to atolls (in the form of a roughly circular calligram) occurs in "Le Troisième Poème Secret": "attols singuliers de la guerre" [strange atolls of the war] (*OP*, p. 624). Possibly the image was inspired initially by the ring-shaped craters and shell holes scattered over no-man's-land like atolls over the ocean (the war zone being compared to the ocean in several other poems, notably "Océan de Terre"). Here the image is complicated by being combined with the different visual shape of the revolver, a free association of different pictures of war in the poet's mind. At a primary level of meaning, therefore, this calligram refers to the war, the attitude encapsulated by both shape and verbal statement being one of virile enjoyment, as is expressed in numerous other poems.

In the secret love poem, however, "atoll" seems also to have an erotic meaning. At the end of the immediately preceding "Deuxième Poème Secret," Madeleine's pubic hair is described as a tropical submarine garden of coral and underwater plants, and this imagery recurs in the third poem, associated with the atoll calligram. Bearing in mind the phallic significance of the revolver, as of the cannon, generally in *Calligrammes* (see "Fête" for the revolver and "Fusée" for the cannon), there seems little doubt that the conjunction of the two images (one verbal and the other graphic) has a disguised sexual meaning.

Des lacs versicolores . . . A simple but expressive evocation of the lover's eyes, in which the shape provides one term of the metaphor, and the words the other. The image of eyes as lakes, which is common in love poetry, occurs also in "Le Deuxième Poème Secret." (See also "Souvenirs.") The graphic form, which was a regular oval in the manuscript, is more expressive in the final version because the slight curve suggests the corner of the eye.

1 tout petit oiseau . . . This calligram conceals a sexual joke, which involves both visual and verbal punning. On the verbal level, *queue* is a common slang term for penis, so that the placing of a tail on a bird is an obvious reference to intercourse. A. Fonteyne (*Apollinaire prosateur* [Nizet, 1964], p. 184) suggests that Apollinaire might have found the joke in Virmaître's *Dictionnaire d'Argot-Fin-de-Siècle,* where *oiseau* is given the more precise sense of "maidenhead," which it also seems to have here: hence the appropriateness of the verb *s'envoler,* that is, flying off in the sense of disappearing, no longer existing.

To this the graphic form adds a pun of its own. Whereas in the manuscript the shape appeared to represent a finger, in the final text it resembles the wings of the bird waiting to receive the tail. But the same shape can suggest open legs, and the placing of the tail in the middle then becomes a visual allusion to intercourse. A very similar calligrammatic design in the *Poèmes à Lou* (*OP,* p. 474) is specifically identified in this way.

Mes tapis de la saveur . . . The shape given to this calligram in the final text might be that of an open mouth, thus making the graphic form echo the verbal text. But since it is tipped slightly to the right (whereas the drawing in the manuscript was perfectly horizontal) it might also suggest a schematic ear. This latter reading—of an ear shape whose text is concerned with the mouth—is encouraged by the fact that the calligram at the bottom of the page presents exactly the opposite view: by its position on the page and its horizontal alignment this drawing seems more clearly to resemble a mouth, but its text is concerned with the sense of *hearing*. Such an effect of verbal-visual chiasmus (ear shape/mouth; mouth shape/ear) would not be inappropriate in a poem that is an exercise in the intermingling of sensations.

But whether mouth, ear, or simply a pleasing abstract shape, the typographical layout gives emphasis to a text that evokes elliptically the multiple satisfactions that can be achieved through the mouth. The first phrase suggests all the refinements of the sense of taste, which play an important role throughout *Calligrammes* (in occurrences elsewhere of the word *saveur*). Beyond the pleasures of the palate, the mouth is further privileged by Apollinaire for its sensual role in love (see "Chef de Section") and, above all, for being the organ of speech and poetic utterance (see "La Jolie Rousse" and "La Victoire"). The second phrase of the text could refer equally to the inchoate sounds of love and to that extension of poetic language through the use of nonverbal sound which is called for in "La Victoire" ("O bouches l'homme est à la recherche d'un nouveau langage") [Oh mouths men are looking for a new language]. The final phrase, while evoking the beauty of the lover's mouth, must also be a celebration of the heightened—celestial—powers of expression with which the mouth is associated, the key word, *azur*, being doubly highlighted by the graphic form.

Ouïs ouïs le cri... A thrice-repeated "Ouïs" occurs in "Le Troisième Poème Secret," urging Madeleine to hearken to sounds expressing the poet's passionate desire. Here the sounds are perhaps more generally symbolic of the noise and vitality of modern life (the first three sounds—the cry, footsteps, and the phonograph—occur with such associations in "Ondes"; see "Liens" and "Lettre-Océan"). The last two sounds mentioned—the aloe and the flute—may, however, have erotic overtones. According to two authorities (Bates, 1975, pp. 60-61; M. Poupon, *GA* 6, p. 117), this is true of *le petit mirliton* in "A Travers l'Europe." As far as the aloe is concerned, it is a plant of phalliclike growth, associated with hot countries and mentioned in the Psalms for its sensuous properties. A bursting sound may possibly accompany the scattering of seed, a feature of plant reproduction that could have sexual overtones.

SOUVENIRS, page 310

The first four poems were sent to Madeleine, after an unprecedented month of sending her no poems, on March 10, 1916. Included also were several "Inscriptions." In the letter accompanying them Apollinaire wrote: "J'ai fait aujourd'hui (ce matin) quelques petites poèmes pr peintres. Il y avait longtemps que je n'avais plus rien fait" [Today (this morning) I made up some little poems for painters. It's been a long time since I've done anything at all]. A major reason for silence was that his regiment had been out of the front line for more than two months and was engaged in intensive maneuvers and long marches from one sector to another. Hence he had little time to himself and suffered from fatigue (*TS*, pp. 318, 320, 321, 334, 337-338). The poems may have been inspired by a few days' break in routine. Indeed, the following day, he sent one more, the last before his return to the line on March 14. Three days later, on March 17, he was wounded.

The poems sent to Madeleine were numbered I to IV and entitled "Poèmes pour Peintres." They were published in *SIC*, 7 (July 1916), with the addition of the fifth poem, and were then numbered I to V. The new title, "Poème," indicates that Apollinaire wished to point out their structural unity. In *Calligrammes* the numbering was removed and the poems are printed as stanzas of one poem. The final title, "Souvenirs," seems to associate memories and the "paintings" of the first title. That association had already been made in "Ondes" in the poems about painting (see esp. note to "A Travers l'Europe"). The juxtaposition of the poems may not have been based, originally, on an association of ideas or themes, but rather on their conception as a group of similar formal experiments, in which a combination of precise detail and sketchiness leaves much to the imagination. This approach bears a structural likeness to some of the calligrams, notably "Éventail," which immediately precedes "Souvenirs."

Each of the stanzas or poems presents at least one surprise. Each appeals to our visual sense, but the musical imagery of the second and fourth stanzas creates an impression of alternation between the visual and the auditory.

Lines 1-3. "Souvenirs" and "Éventail" are linked not only by structure but by imagery, notably the initial *lacs/attols*. In French there is a second meaning for *nègre*, "dark brown in color," as well as the etymological meaning "black." Apollinaire seems aware of all these meanings and to play on them as he does in "Les Soupirs du Servant de Dakar" (see note), evoking a kind of magical primitivism one associates with his friend Le Douanier Rousseau and which is reinforced by the image of the forest and abruptly undermined by the image of the [white] shirt, symbol of an urban civilization. A few days before, he had visited Rheims and this first poem, as well as the others, may describe a scene near or in the city. Again, he may recall a landscape in the war zone, lakes muddy from the winter rains, a wood, laundry spread out to dry during a brief moment of sun. Or—but not likely in the context—this first poem may be a somewhat precious description of a woman's face.

Lines 4-6. A harmonium is, roughly, a small church organ. In his letter Apollinaire describes to Madeleine the partly destroyed cathedral in Rheims and mentions a pretty church which might have inspired this evocation of the mouth singing above the organ and the voice composed *d'yeux*, or *Dieu*. The pun on "eyes/God" is untranslatable. But whether the voice is linked to God or to the eyes of worshipers, the elliptical style suggests a wordless, profound experience, whereas the waiting about of the *petites gens*, the "humble (or common) people," contrasts by its flat style.

Lines 7-9. The old lady may be in the church, since she has the foot warmer with her (the weather, according to the letters, was cold). *La bouillotte* can be a foot warmer, a rubber hot-water bottle, or even a teakettle of sorts. Originally line 9 read "Une femme qui a une gorge épatante" [A woman with a gorgeous bust]. The change may have been determined by the structure of the other poems, all of which pivot, in some way, by means of the last line, so as to comment on what precedes; within each poem there is continuity. The final version of line 9, which contains an unpleasantly vivid image of death, develops the theme of mortality implicit in line 8, although, in the larger context of Apollinaire's experience at that time, it may be inspired by a memory of rotting corpses in the trenches. The images of corpse and rat enhance the picture of a homely old lady sitting in a pew, warming her feet on an elegant foot warmer, or at home, boiling water in a blue kettle. Indeed, all these vignettes affirm a sense of the continuity of daily routines, devoutly or contentedly carried out—little fragments of the poetry of life which continue to be spontaneously invented, even at the edge of war.

Lines 10-13. These lines are sometimes quoted as an illustration of Apollinaire's aesthetics or of the kind of realism developed in "L'Esprit Nouveau": the juxtaposition of life's unexpected or incongruous aspects; simplicity as a way of expressing the complexities of experience. Here an everyday act and a trivial song furnish the basis of an ars poetica, but the song is not really trivial: *chantant*, like *chanson*, is traditionally associated with poetry and with the immortality that poetry bestows, whereas *opéra* suggests that combination of different arts to transmit the spectacle of life which Apollinaire will elaborate in the Prologue to *Les Mamelles de Tirésias*. Apollinaire suggests that his muse is nourished by something glimpsed or overheard, a fragmentary vision of spontaneous action. The essential act, however, as in "Carte Postale," is the creative act of the poet who records the poem, here, significantly, in a familiar style.

Lines 14-15. The last poem was added, in *Calligrammes*, probably as a question, or questions, which the poet does not choose to answer directly, Is *tu* the poet, or the reader, or, more probably, both? Is the king an envoy of God? And would a Second Coming, a new death, change anything, within these vignettes of daily life or in the world of violence beyond them? That last question, or something like it, with the marked change in the degree of seriousness it brings about, seems the point of these "souvenirs," if a point is needed.

L'AVENIR, page 312

Sent to Madeleine on March 11, 1916. Apollinaire's regiment was now in reserve, prior to moving back to the front line on March 14. There are references in preceding letters to the fatigue of long marches, and in the letter enclosing the poem he confesses to having little to say, being in a state of "enervating waiting" (*TS*, p. 341). First published in *SIC*, 4 (April 1916).

The poet's response to the apprehension of waiting and his "almost insurmountable need for sleep" (same letter) is to seek fortitude in a stoic retreat within the self. In this respect the title of the poem might, at first sight, seem ironic. The future, a dynamic concept in other poems, is now something to which he apparently closes his mind. The first priority is spiritual survival, and to this end attention is strictly confined to the present (l. 12).

Concentration on the immediate environment and the immediate tasks in hand does not prevent dreams of love (l. 6), but whereas in other poems ("Chevaux de Frise," e.g.) the poet allows his thoughts to fly off to a more ideal landscape for love, here the elements of the idyllic setting are brought firmly within the narrow limits of his present situation and are reduced to the essential. The rose, the fountain, and the bee—symbols of summer and happiness—are isolated from their normal context and translated to the wintry scene of the war zone, but they are seen with such force in the mind's eye that they become as tangibly present as the snow and the straw.

Yet it is the implication of the poem that by this "implosive" effort of the imagination the poet will be able to transcend his situation. The title is not, after all, ironic. This seems the sense of the final stanza in which the physical presence of the hands holds the key to the bleak present, to the dream world, and to the future alike. By a stoic effort of the will, and a wholly inner meditation, the future can be won. The extreme simplicity of statement is appropriate to the theme. Whereas in "Exercice" the condensed form has a musical potential that is deftly exploited, here the short lines are rhythmically irregular and without the support of rhyme. The amelodic effect thus achieved defeats the reader's expectations of harmony and (together with the repeated imperatives, *Soulevons, Regardons,* etc.) underlines the severity of the poet's effort at mental concentration.

Line 7. *Gabions* are wicker baskets filled with earth and used for protection in the trenches. Interestingly, this line originally read "Les deux tours sont là" [The two towers are there], and it was accompanied on the printer's proofs by a sketch of a seaport, with sailing ships and two towers or similar buildings (cf. *Album Apollinaire,* p. 286). If, as seems likely, the reference was to a Mediterranean port, and thus to memories of Apollinaire's leave spent in Algeria with Madeleine, the textual revision can be seen as further evidence of a desire to eliminate direct thoughts of the outside world.

UN OISEAU CHANTE, page 314

Sent to Madeleine on October 17, 1915, in a longer version (nine stanzas) with variants in all but what is now the first stanza (*TS,* pp. 216-217). First published in *Calligrammes.*

The first version of "Un Oiseau Chante" requested a letter from Madeleine and also anticipated a meeting between lovers. The published version is a poem about metamorphosis in which changes are rung on a series of images: from a girl's soul to a singing bird; from a singing bird to the bird of love to the girl; from the bluebird to the blue heart of the girl; from blue love to a blue heart. In order for images to change into other images, the poet continually shifts his meaning, as when *amour* means, in line 13, "love" in the figurative sense and, in line 14, "sweetheart." There are also mysterious juxtapositions, unexplained analogies, and, in this seemingly simple song, sudden leaps into the elliptical. The most striking example, however, of deceptive openness is probably the term "blue" which has obviously shed its usual meaning.

Blue has two principal associations for Apollinaire: the color of the soldiers' uniforms, notably *bleu horizon*, inspires imagery in several major poems, among them "Le Palais du Tonnerre," "Chant de l'Horizon en Champagne," "Il y a." Blue is also Apollinaire's favorite color and a key word in letters to Madeleine: she has a *cœur bleu* (*TS*, p. 205); she is his *amour bleu* (p. 256). Most revealing is a comment from an early letter, dated June 4: "La superstition du bleu nous réunit exquisement et quand j'imagine votre cœur je le teinte de bleu" [The superstition of blue unites us and when I imagine your heart I color it blue] (p. 35). In other letters blue is associated with daydreams and with faithfulness. In addition to the poet's private associations with blue and to its use in an intimate language between lovers, an overt symbolism is attached to the bluebird of fairy tale. In "La Tzigane" and "Les Fiançailles" (*Alcools*), the bluebird sheds his feathers, suggesting unhappy love or disillusionment. Here, to the contrary, he triumphs.

Lines 21-24. A brief but vivid description of the spectacle of war which so enchants the poet replaces five stanzas on love. Line 20, in the published version, launches imagery evocative of a threatening beauty. Lines 21-22 possibly echo Victor Hugo's last stanza to "Booz endormi," with its rhetorical question and its images of harvest and stars, but here there is gunfire and, instead of a divine reaper, a sower who is the enemy. The original final stanza began with an evocation of a lovers' meeting: "Tu m'ouvriras les bras et puis / Tu me répéteras je t'aime" [You will open your arms to me and then / You will say over and over I love you]; in the context of these verses, the last two lines were an affirmation concerning the future. In the published version, the last stanza may be read as juxtaposing the risky splendors of military action, the ennui of the soldier (or, to the contrary, an unnaturally rapid passage of time), and the soldier's love. Thus the ending seems no longer so hopeful as it did when the poem was first sent to Madeleine: the bird's song has faded away; the elliptical style echoes the staccato sounds of machine-gun fire; the days go by to the rhythm of the guns; the image of the heart has become an ambivalent, somewhat fragile, symbol of love and also of life. The threatening reality that emerges toward the end of the poem contrasts with the fantasy of the preceding stanzas and yet provides one more example of metamorphosis. As in other poems ("Carte Postale," e.g.), the poet's power to transmute realities dominates all other themes.

CHEVAUX DE FRISE, page 318

Sent to Madeleine on November 18, 1915, just before Apollinaire's transfer to the infantry. His battery was now in an advanced position in the front line, occupying former German trenches in a sector scarred by intense fighting. Snow had fallen on November 14 and still covered the battlefield. First published in *La Grande Revue*, 11 (November 1917), in "Poèmes de Guerre et d'Amour."

This poem is one of the most fully developed examples of the use of love poetry, not as an escape from the reality of war, but as a means of investing it with significance and maintaining the poet's power over it (see section on the war poems in the introduction and notes to "Simultanéités" and "Un Oiseau Chante"). For a more dismissive view of the poem see Ph. Renaud (1969).

As M. Davies points out (1964, p. 275), the rapturous tone, the note of almost religious fervor and supplication, are strongly reminiscent of the style of the Psalms. Apollinaire refers more than once, in his letters, to the Song of Songs, specific terms of endearment for Madeleine (*la belle Africaine*, e.g.), no less than the general passionate nature of his vocabulary confirm the strong influence exercised by the biblical texts. Rhetorical flow is of the essence of this style: hence the many devices—accumulation, repetition, deft changes of rhythm, internal echoes, innumerable assonantal variations (rather than strict rhyme)—which are deployed to give the free verse a sweep that matches the ecstatic nature of the theme.

The flow is, however, controlled and channeled by a series of metamorphoses, based on wordplay and parallelisms in imagery, which form the basic dynamic pattern of the poem. The first transformation results from the opposition between the scarred trees of the battlefield and the flowering tree in the poet's heart and leads, through the associated contrast of dead and blossoming flowers, to the major metamorphosis of the barbed-wire defenses into real horses. (*Chevaux de frise*, literally "Friesland horses," were so called because this type of defense, resembling a large "sawhorse" covered with barbed wire, was invented during the Dutch war of independence as a protection against enemy cavalry.) The punning here is felicitous, resting not only on the central term *chevaux* but also on a subsidiary play between *barbe* and *barbelé*. Moreover, the metamorphosis is extended by the hint of a further transformation of the horses into sea horses, being carried on the waves of the Mediterranean toward Madeleine, thus working into the pattern of imagery the recurring associations of the sea which play a large part in other poems.

A dynamic progression, consciously elaborated, thus carries the poet's thoughts over the ocean to Madeleine and justifies the prolonged celebration of her charms in lines 27-40. The echoes of the Psalms are most pronounced in this section, but much of the language and imagery with erotic overtones is also central to Apollinaire's own vocabulary (*colombe, rose, Panthère, lys*; see Bates, 1975, for some of these). Also typical is the Pentecostal image of the Paraclete descending (ll. 30-33) to confer the gift of speech on the poet.

Here a deep-seated need in Apollinaire to associate the poetic gift with miraculous powers is gracefully turned into an amorous compliment, for in this instance it is Madeleine's beauty that works the miracle.

The final transformation occurs with the return to the battlefield in the last lines, which is essential, for it shows the poetic and psychological strategy of the whole poem being fulfilled. The cold, stark scene of the opening lines is now transfigured in the light of the flare, significantly compared to a blossoming flower and then to gracefully falling tears (possibly a further hint of the Pentecostal theme, but at all events an image of emotional fulfillment, supported by the careful dying away of the rhythm). By a deliberate effort of the imagination, therefore, the forbidding face of war has been humanized and the poet, by implication, has drawn from his meditation the power to dominate reality and make it meaningful.

CHANT DE L'HONNEUR, page 322

First published in *Calligrammes*. Dated December 17, 1915.

Marc Poupon (1967, p. 113) describes the reader's surprise when he or she comes upon this rather didactic poem. He attributes its "éloquence pompeuse" to the influence of Alfred de Vigny's *Servitude et Grandeur Militaires*, a book Apollinaire read for the first time in February 1916 (see letter to Madeleine, February 25, *TS*, p. 335). As Poupon observes, the date December 17 indicates quite precisely the time period involved, but not the poet's mood, and he points out two important shifts in emphasis: Apollinaire substitutes for Madeleine an allegorical Beauty and he seems remote from the scenes of destruction that surround him. He concludes that, since Apollinaire had little time in February, "Chant de l'Honneur" was written after the poet was wounded and hospitalized in Paris—and before he regained his sense of humor (and, one might add, his usual ambivalence). One might add, too, in support of this perceptive dating of the poem, that the few poems Apollinaire found time to write in February ("Du Coton dans les Oreilles," "Aussi Bien que les Cigales," "Le Vigneron Champenois") differ sharply in tone from this poem by their sense of immediacy, their humor, their transformation of military events into lyric fantasy; that they were all sent to Madeleine; and that this poem alone, in which the poet takes himself so seriously, was supposedly held back.

Lines 1-9. The introductory lines are not at all typical of the war poems, which tend to begin in medias res. They sound like a conceptualizing after the event. An Indian play entitled *Le Chariot d'Enfant* was translated by Nerval in 1850; one of the characters in the cast is a thief (see *Oeuvres complémentaires de Gérard de Nerval I* [Minard, 1959], p. 261-269).

Lines 10-11. These lines echo the last lines of "Le Palais du Tonnerre."

Lines 15-17. Here is probably a reference to the advance of French infantry (described in letters to Madeleine in November 1915) to invest trenches formerly occupied by the Germans.

Line 21. The *Butte de Tahure* (*TS*, p. 271) was taken just before Apollinaire joined the company that took it. He describes to Madeleine his pride in being in that company (*ibid.*). By December 17 he had spent eleven difficult days, November 29-December 9, in the trenches near Tahure.

Line 22. For the three hearts of the octopus, see note to "Océan de Terre." Here the poet identifies himself with the octopus.

Lines 26-31. The images of shells and flares, of water, of the uncertain house, recall the major war poems.

Lines 55-61. Does Apollinaire anticipate the use of cinematic techniques (as he may in the prologue to *Les Mamelles de Tirésias*) in lines 55-57? The four lines that follow conjure up vivid scenes, as do lines 12-17, but in contrast with that passage, which develops one scene, they suggest the kind of commentary a camera can make as it shifts abruptly and noncommittally from one scene to another.

Lines 62-63. These lines seem a transition between the voice that simply remembers, without commentary, and that other self-conscious public voice, successfully used by some Romantic poets but which Apollinaire does not carry off very convincingly.

Lines 66-71. It is conceivable that Apollinaire, in writing these lines (as in the passage on beauty in lines 45-54), had in mind Vigny's exaltation of honor and also, in latent form, his own ideas about "L'Esprit Nouveau," in the sense that he attempts to embrace all his war experience through an expansion of the one word Beauty, giving it new meanings and undermining its traditional associations.

CHEF DE SECTION, page 330

First published in *La Grande Revue*, 11 (November 1917), in "Poèmes de Guerre et d'Amour," where it is dated March 1916. In fact, the poem is a revised version of "Le Quatrième Poème Secret" (*OP*, p. 631), sent to Madeleine much earlier, on October 19, 1915, when Apollinaire was still in the artillery.

Although the final version is more veiled in its eroticism than the original, the poem still conveys an urgency of physical desire which was an important part of Apollinaire's feelings for Madeleine and which was expressed in a much more explicit and unbridled way in the other "secret poems," not all of them yet published (see "Poèmes à Madeleine" and also "Poèmes à Lou" in *OP*). The equation that is established here between the martial aggressiveness of the soldier and the virile nature of his desire leaves no doubt that Apollinaire saw the sexual urge as a natural compensatory reaction to the horrors of war. For this reason, no doubt, he felt justified in adding to the earlier version the new final line, which (together with the date in the *Grande Revue* publication) implies that the whole poem was inspired by combat in the front-line trenches. Although that was not literally true, it is true that after his transfer to the infantry Apollinaire experienced still more powerfully the reaction with which the poem is concerned, as certain letters graphically demonstrate: "L'horreur tragique, horrible, obscure du corps à corps dans les tranchées, les boyaux, les entonnoirs augmente ma volupté à t'aimer" (*TS*, p. 293) [The horrible, tragic, murky horror of the hand-to-hand fighting in the trenches and shell holes increases my voluptuous love for you].

The structure of the poem is effective, probably owing something to the celebratory style of the Psalms (see note on "Chevaux de Frise"). The repetition of similar phrases in a steadily mounting sequence (supported by the religious imagery of ll. 3 and 5) produces an effect of ecstatic devotion. Any risk that the military metaphors might inject a note of brutality is dispelled by the softening of the tone brought about by imagery in other registers. There are more idealistic overtones in the longer verset of line 7 and in the images of lines 9 and 10: the magician or enchanter, one of the oldest of Apollinaire's personas, carries implications of clever and subtle weaving of spells rather than of brutal conquest. Significantly the climax of the enumerative sequence, in the penultimate line, is one of total quietness and gentleness, underlined by the verb *murmurer* and the switch to the present tense.

The most cunning structural effect is that brought about by the last line, for it gives all the preceding lines the status of thoughts running through the poet's mind as he prepares for the attack. The sexual urge is thus given psychological validity by the situation, and the mounting intensity of the poet's desire is seen to be a fervent aspiration toward life in the face of possible death.

TRISTESSE D'UNE ÉTOILE, page 332

First published in *Calligrammes.*

On March 17, 1916, Apollinaire was wounded in the head by fragments from an exploding shell. He was sent from the trenches back to Paris to the hospital Val de Grâce and from there to the Villa Molière where he underwent a trepanation operation on May 9. One of his nurses was Jacqueline Kolb, "the pretty redhead," whom he married on May 2, 1918, six months before his death. Already, before his operation, probably on May 7, 1916, he had written to Madeleine: "Je ne suis plus ce que j'étais à aucun point de vue et si je m'écoutais je me ferais prêtre ou religieux" (*TS,* p. 349) [I'm no longer in any way what I was and if I listened to myself I'd become a priest or a monk]. After his operation he wrote her twice more, in August and September, gently putting her off and requesting various notes and books he had sent her. In the last letter, September 16, 1916, he concludes, "Mes compagnons de guerre sont presque tous morts. Je n'ose même pas écrire au colonel pr [sic] lui demander des détails. . . . Tout cela est assez macabre et devant une aussi horrible évocation je ne sais qu'ajouter. Je t'embrasse. Gui." [My comrades in the war are nearly all dead. I don't even dare write the colonel to ask for details. . . . The whole thing is quite macabre and, faced with such a horrible evocation, I don't know what to add. I embrace you. Gui.]

The tremendous change from the wartime Apollinaire, healthy, buoyant, enjoying the feeling of soldierly brotherhood, to a wounded man who has almost died, who has lost many of his friends in the war, and who is subject to melancholy is revealed in the imagery of "Tristesse d'une Étoile." Probably this poem and "Chant de l'Honneur" were the first to be written after his operation, before he regained the health that made possible "Les Collines," "La Victoire," "La Jolie Rousse," and, most probably, the final version of *Les Mamelles de Tirésias.* Whereas "Chant de l'Honneur" is weakened by a kind of didactic pomposity, "Tristesse d'une Étoile" is, although a far better poem, derived from Romantic and symbolist sources, especially Victor Hugo and Baudelaire. The poet of adventure has, for the moment, fallen back on tradition ("Ordre"). As usual, however, his point of departure is his own experience, although here transformed by rhetoric. Thus the loss of friends who were killed in the war; his patriotism and his pride in his own suffering; the spiritual as well as physical change he feels within himself; the love that has lost its center in Madeleine and perhaps has already found its new and final center in Jacqueline—these somewhat conflicting feelings contribute to a conflicting mixture of images.

The title may hearken back to "Tristesse d'Olympio," announcing that a profound, even magisterial, sadness is the poem's subject.

Lines 1-2. The poet is at once Jupiter giving birth to Minerva and Christ wearing his crown of thorns. Line 2 also anticipates the scene in *Le Sang d'un Poète* where the poet shoots himself in the head and is crowned with laurel. Stars, for Apollinaire, when they are not a way of describing bombardment at the front, are often controllers of destiny. But when he himself is practically a star, he may well think of the magic talisman of the pentacle, as in "Le Brasier" (*Alcools*): "Ma tête mes genoux mes coudes vain pentacle." [My head knees and elbows vain five-pointed star.]

Lines 3-4. In lyric poems about himself Apollinaire often uses the term *la raison* in a special sense ("A la Santé," *Vitam Impendere Amori*) as descriptive of a phase in his own life which follows the phase of youth. Here he seems to indicate that the age of reason is over and that a new phase will emerge, or perhaps simply that for the moment he has lost footing. The loss of the goddess will be made good in "La Jolie Rousse," where reason returns in the guise of a pretty girl. So the loss of orientation may indicate, in part, an uncertainty in love.

Lines 5-8. This stanza seems directly inspired by Baudelaire's "La Vie antérieure" where a secret sorrow pursues the poet in all his avatars. Comparably, for Apollinaire, there is a mysterious correspondence between his wound and *le secret malheur*. The latter, which may have to do with the death of friends, the end of his love for Madeleine, an overwhelming fatigue at the war's being so drawn out, or other drains on his strength, seems essentially an awareness that he has been so changed by his experience that he feels a stranger among the Parisians who were not soldiers. The question is almost posed whether this unaccustomed feeling of alienation will inspire him as a poet: *mon délire* may be the feverish state of the creator or the ill health that still undermines him.

Lines 9-12. All these images have to do with love, on one level or another. To interpret them uniquely as an expression of patriotism seems arbitrary and limiting. Here *ardente*, a key word in *Calligrammes* (see note to "Le Palais du Tonnerre"), suggests primarily in all probability, the soldier's courage, but there are associations also with his desire for a muse, whether she be an emanation of battle or a real woman. The latter specific association, which takes over in "La Jolie Rousse" (see note), may be anticipated here. Again, the glowworm's body is ambiguously *enflammé:* the term is, on one level, a repetition on a more literal level of *ardente;* it suggests a painful love, but of what? of one's country, of poetry, of a woman? The overtly patriotic imagery of line 11 may be taken as a key to the final stanza and to the poem. It is, however, somewhat in contrast with the last line which, in spite of Apollinaire's evocation of French gardens in "Le Palais du Tonnerre," is, essentially, an erotic image. Thus the stanza in its entirety seems to describe various sides to love and, perhaps, to equate the passion in all its complexity to the poet's "secret sorrow."

LA VICTOIRE, page 334

First published in the first number of Pierre Reverdy's review, *Nord-Sud* (March 15, 1917). Apollinaire's contribution of a major poem to a new review seems a generous vote of confidence.

Not only the title but the whole poem has baffled critics, no two of whom seem to be in agreement (see, for example, M. Davies, *GA* 7, pp. 156-159; Ph. Renaud [1969], pp. 458-465; C. Tournadre). What is the victory? Is Apollinaire's tone of voice at times ironic? Is the poem an affirmation—or an aspiration? Probably no one mood prevails: we overhear the poet talking to himself, around and about the nature of art which, for him, must always be in a state of flux, if it is to reflect inner and outer realities. The continual shifts in his own point of view, which may appear contradictory, exemplify his concept of the poem as a living presence, changing from stanza to stanza and from line to line.

Lines 1-6. At the beginning, dreams are fused with memories, and the juxtapositions may be seen as anticipating surrealism. The first line introduces three levels of consciousness: *Un coq chante* may evoke a real noise, or perhaps a noise in the poet's dream; *je rêve* is at once a stage direction and an objective analytical comment; *les feuillards . . . à de pauvres marins* seems an image within the dream, with no outside reference, but it may refer to a scene outside the window. The syntax underlines this progression into the poet's world: after the simple declarative structure of lines 1-2 and the stanza break, line 3, with its Mallarméan technique of the floating line, may still refer back to the sailors, but as one proceeds, one sees that it also refers forward to the blind men. Comparably, after the effect of immediacy caused by the present tense in lines 1-2, the use of a past tense in line 5 implies that lines 3-5 describe what the poet has just been dreaming: the imperfect tense suggests a prolongation of the scene within the dream itself, or its lingering on afterwards in the poet's mind. Thus the reader is pulled by degrees into the poet's dream which seems to last for six lines, although these first lines may conceivably furnish a dreamlike setting for the whole soliloquy. The latter premise would account for the apparent contradictions within the poem.

The beginning constitutes one of many passages that evoke the images, vocabulary, and languorous style of *Alcools,* in contrast with other passages whose style is brusquely familiar. All these echoes from the past have meaning, but a changed meaning. The rooster is no longer a sign of defeat, as in "La Chanson du Mal-Aimé." The branches, here, have a shifting significance, suggesting at first victory or a rejoicing of some sort and then transforming themselves, almost cinematically (as is the way with dreams), into a new imagery (3-5) with nightmarish overtones; to the contrary, in *Alcools,* the image of the branch plays a stable, overtly symbolic role, within a specific poem ("La Synagogue," "Lul de Faltenin," "Vendémiaire"). Here, leaves are no longer overtly equated with a postsymbolist image of hands waving farewell ("Rhénane d'automne"). Their comparison to poor sailors may, in fact, be elliptical and may imply the waving of hands; as it stands, however, the comparison seems to transform leaves into faces—again, a startling image which leads one into the next stanza. The sailors (*marins*), on the other hand, may differ little from those lost sailors (destroyed by the Sirens) in "Vendémiaire."

As one proceeds, the images assume an increasingly nightmarish quality. In "Zone," the winged saints and other divinities soar as they follow the flying machine; among them is Icarus, a true flyer. Here, Icarus is false (his wings are only of wax and he will plunge to his death); the other flyers are *tournoyants,* as if disoriented, and they are blind. The transformation of their laughter into bunches of grapes, in line 6, is one more echo from *Alcools,* recalling a recurring image in "Vendémiaire," where grape clusters of men or of heads are frequently fed into the winepress.

Lines 4-5 offer an irrational comparison between blind men and ants and a contradictory shift in terms (the blind seem to see), as in a dream. There is a nightmarish reminiscence of Baudelaire's "Les Aveugles." But also the image recalls and illumines line 2 in "Arbre" (see note). It triggers associations (which become inevitable when one reaches lines 19-20) with blind poets, prophets, kings—Homer, Tirésias, Oedipus. It is as though Apollinaire's unconscious, in his dream, reaching towards a true image of the poet (which would, in itself, constitute a victory), found only its distortion. The blind men seem lost and about to fall, like Icarus. They gesture like ants. Why? Most ants are not blind; they do, however, by waving their antennae about, communicate in a complex manner, and they mechanically follow each other, often into culs-de-sac. Modern poets, in contrast with blind Homer, might well seem like ants to a poet just returned home from a world war; and if the dreamer himself hovered far higher than they attempted to fly, they might, in his eyes, resemble insects. In the same way line 5 exposes the pretense of the blind men who, like Icarus, offer a false appearance: although blind, they admire their reflections like Narcissus, or it might be that they are mirrored; and, although winged, they are tempted by the sight of their own faces not to fly higher.

The themes of sound and of sight, which dominate the poem, are already announced in the first lines, from the opening *Un coq chante* to the superposition of a visual upon an auditive image in line 6. That fusion reoccurs several times (7, 42, 53-54): the talking diamond, the letter that cuts like a tolling bell, the lamps whose glow resembles women laughing—these images contribute to a recurring dreamlike atmosphere; at the same time, the reconciliation they represent between sight and sound illumines the poet's concluding lines.

The landscape of rainy sidewalks peopled by blind men who can see is unlike the Paris landscape of the prewar poems: there, café waiters become savages, peering from the jungle or the bush; posters become parakeets in a rain forest; a sidewalk acrobat miraculously vanishes; the Pied Piper passes by, only to vanish also. The features of the postwar city landscape, in "La Victoire," recall the Paris of Baudelaire in such poems as "Les Sept Vieillards," where mystery suggests nightmare, not moments of enchantment.

Lines 7-11. The poet may wake and, still half-asleep, adress someone he knows intimately—either himself or, more probably, a woman. The diamond could be Jacqueline who, as Tournadre observes, was called "Ruby." Jewel imagery occurs elsewhere during the war years: a letter to Lou compares her eyes to topaz; in a letter to Madeleine, Paris is "une grande améthyste" (*TS*, p. 315). The three possessions named by Apollinaire, like his renewed use of a familiar vocabulary, reveal how much he has changed. His bed, which occurs for the first time in the war poems, may represent a shelter, like the forest or the dugout, a place where the poet can dream. The Mallarméan lamp is essential equipment for a nocturnal poet at work. His helmet and his wound symbolize all that has changed in him and even, perhaps, what isolates him from other men. The preciousness of sight and perhaps the blue eyes may comment on the present. Or line 10, like line 11, may refer to a prolonged past, conjured up by the imperfect tense of *étaient*. Saint-Claude, a hill town in the Jura, is known for its workers in diamonds and other precious stones. The poet suggests that his own eyes, like gem cutters, once shaped the days into an emerald (the stone's greenness, suggestive of youth's eternal summer; its fragility and tendency to crack, suggestive of the difficulty attendant upon mining the matrices of one's art—here, memories, fantasies, emotions). (But see J. Burgos, for whom the three gems symbolize attributes of the poet, in *GA* 8, p. 148.)

Lines 12-16. The journey into the past continues, and visual imagery dominates, although *hoquet* (16) is one of the few sound effects that anticipate the passage on language. After evoking the days of his youth, the poet conjures up the nights. *Ville des météores* may refer to the battlefield of his immediate past, so bright with flares and explosions that it recalls the prewar modern city, while its bombardment may be construed fancifully as seeking to surprise the sky. Or the image of the modern city, lit up like a bombardment at the front, may recall, with its imagery of astronomy and flowers, not only the war poems but, above all, prewar Paris which the poet remembers vividly also in *La Femme Assise* (there Apollinaire's nostalgia for prewar Paris is more explicit). The garden of light, an image of the external world, may also comment on the poet's memory, as does a similar image in "Les Fiançailles" (*Alcools*): "Et les roses de l'électricité s'ouvrent encore / Dans le jardin de ma mémoire" [And the roses of electricity still unfold / In the garden of my memory]. Comparably ambiguous, in line 15, *Tu* may refer to the city or the battlefield—or to the poet. If he invokes the former, the present tense indicates either that he is back in the war or in a prewar world blazing with electricity or, indeed, that he has returned from the past to the present with its wartime blackout; just as the city or battlefield lit up the sky, so the blackout, in its turn, would cause a new surprise. If, on the other hand, the poet addresses himself only, he may be one with the landscape, just as, later in the poem, he becomes the sky or the sea. Or he may refer to himself as a separate entity. In either case, he probably thinks of "L'Esprit Nouveau": the modern poet is a source of surprise to the cosmos.

Lines 17-20. The veteran soldier could well be disillusioned by what he might, rightly or wrongly, consider as a stolid, even exploitive, bourgeoisie. (Some of his contempt is seen in the letters to Lou, in *La Femme Assise,* and conceivably in "Le Medaillon Toujours Fermé.") His own military experience would isolate him from Parisians who had stayed home from the war (17-18). A satiric note may be detected in the two lines that follow, where the poet couches a demand for fresh poetic inspiration in materialistic terms. The imagery and the request itself would seem idealistic. Concerning visions and memories, he would agree with Chirico whose observation, "On ne voit que les yeux fermés" [You can see only with your eyes shut], was to be preempted by the surrealists. Apollinaire combines the ancient image of the blind poet with memories of medieval paintings, particularly of the Rhenish school, where saints fly as easily as angels. The implication of a production line and the phraseology of the request are, however, suspect. The "institute" sounds scientific but also smacks of commercialism. Who is it that asks for that hybrid creature, a blind young man with wings?

The poet who, like Mallarmé in "Salut," looks to the young? Or a prospective buyer from the business world who wants a good ad man? Probably both.

Lines 21-39. Much has been said of the passage on language. On the whole, it has been given a literal interpretation. The opening lines, however, need not be taken literally: poets always look for "a new language"—symbolism, surrealism, concrete poetry. The decrial of grammarians, however, suggests, more specifically, a need for an anti-Cartesian syntax. Again, the "old languages" can be taken as meaning traditional poetic forms and vocabulary. Lines 26-28 were added in *Calligrammes;* they may well indicate Apollinaire's interest in the silent movies and also in mime. At this point the poet's train of thought clearly focuses on concrete aspects of language, but his intention becomes increasingly unclear. He presents us first with the possibility of no language at all and then proceeds to offer us "new sounds" without meaning. Lines 29-41 undoubtedly take, as their point of departure, the contemporary school of "la poésie bruitiste" (which one might translate as "noisism"). The question is: Are these lines heartfelt? (For Davies, they are.) Or does Apollinaire make fun of noise as the Ultima Thule of poetry? (That is the view of Tournadre.) The tone of voice is enthusiastic but lighthearted, with such varied plays on words as *sourdement/sourd* (34, 38), *sons/consonnes/son* (32-35), *pètent/pétiller/pets* (34, 36, 40), where the sounds may not match up precisely but the verbal associations are clear. The two basic ideas offered by the poet are "consonants without vowels" and digestive noises, especially variations on farting, but also on belching, as poetic skills. The first seems absurd (unless one knows the language of the clicks); the second seems a kind of clowning, for a reader cannot help but be reminded of the fart theme in the war poems and also, more generally, of vaudeville stunts where farts imitate other noises (from a sneeze to a trumpet call) or produce a recognizable tune. Indeed the style is reminiscent of *Les Mamelles de Tirésias,* which was receiving its final shaping that same spring. There one finds similar playing with ideas and words, with noises and mime, which echo vaudeville routines and invoke the absurd. Even if one takes these lines as a kind of pontificating with words or wordless poetry, Apollinaire is obviously enjoying himself. In the context of the whole poem, he seems primarily to attempt a depiction of himself as searching for ways to express the changing nature of life and of the present moment.

Lines 40-64. Lines 40-41 continue Apollinaire's observations on language. But already lines 42-43 combine sound and sight to describe memory; not only does Apollinaire reduce the word to a letter instead of a phoneme but the verb *graver* "to cut" recalls his lines on sight (10-11), where he uses a similar verb *tailler.* These lines are immediately followed by the phrase *la joie de voir* "the joy of seeing" and, soon thereafter, by the exhortation *Regarde* "look." In lines 10-11 Apollinaire recalls the past through its visual aspect; here, in the poem's present time, the poet must use his eyes to grasp the newness of things (44-49). Like Baudelaire, he partly bases his aesthetic, as in the prewar period, on modernism (one source, for both poets, of surprise); at the same time he is aware that the most modern phenomena are ephemeral and even that their ephemerality adds to their poetic appropriateness (50-52), an idea already prominent in the war poems.

The image of the lamps dissolving into women's laughter (53-54) is one of several which juxtapose and reconcile sight and sound, as sources of poetry. Laughter, also, and the "ardent mockery" it expresses (56-58) recall, in *Alcools,* the Apollinairean laugh with its conflicting and ambiguous overtones, the poet's fear of the scorn of his friends, his ancient distrust of women. With a brusque change of page, lines 59-60 call for noise. These, in turn, are followed by an invocation of words (61) which is, once more, ambiguous: does the poet desire a meaningful language? or does he relegate the word to the realm of myth? At this point, he presents us with a coinage, *la myrtaie* "the myrtle grove" (Tournadre, *Glossaire*), followed by some erudite games, as if to confuse his trail (62-63). Since myrtle was sacred to Aphrodite, *myrtaie* suggests a sacred wood. *Éros* inevitably sends the reader back to the image of a winged youth, but blindfolded rather than blind. *Antéros* has several meanings: most significantly, Anteors, like Eros, is a god (and this personification in itself seems a comment on the power of words) who plays two different roles: he avenges slighted love and, also, he struggles against Eros. In both roles he may have a private meaning for Apollinaire the poorly loved. Like Eros, too, he sends the reader—or some readers—back to the beginning of the poem: *anteros,* in Pliny's *Naturalis Historiae,* the sort of book Apollinaire was familiar with, is the name of a gem and so provides a link with lines 7-11, where the image of the jewel is associated, as here, with the theme of love and the image of the eye. It is possible that both in this passage on words and in the passage on trains the poet may mourn what he must exile, in the manner of Plato exiling poets or Lucretius exiling the gods. Or the two passages may be seen as forms of praise for what is always ephemeral, whether a modern invention or a current idiom: perhaps all words follow the old words for love into the garden of the ancient goddess of love and so make way for new ones; they pass on, but we continue to love them, as one day we come to love old-fashioned trains. In contrast, the poet is all-encompassing (64), yet he too is limited by his relation to time; he is the sky of *la cité,* which is the medieval center of the sprawling modern city, *la ville,* or the city itself.

Lines 65-69. After an invocation to the sounding sea, the poet describes his own voice (in contrast with the noises he has called for) as faithful as a shadow; but to be faithful to life, which is always renewing itself, the poet's voice must be as fickle as the sea. In a sense, sound equates motion (as for Valéry also).

Lines 70-73. *La mer* is an old image for Apollinaire, of nostalgia in "Le Voyageur" (*Alcools*), of betrayal in "Le Dauphin" (*Le Bestiaire*). The sea is source of both life and death, a Mallarméan betrayer of explorers, and of sailors, like Apollinaire and his brother in "Le Voyageur." The sea offers no support to objects or bodies or to the poet's great godlike cries, only to the impression of movement and swiftness, ephemeral intangible shadows of birds which, as in "Cortège" (*Alcools*), hover between the sun and the earth. In this sense the sea is like a poem, an immediate register of ripples and changes of light.

Lines 74-78. Movement and change are fundamental characteristics of words and poetry as Apollinaire conceives of them. Thus the poet's gift of speech (no longer a matter of cries swallowed by the sea) is *soudaine . . . un Dieu qui tremble*, dynamic like the bird, a god in motion. There may be a suggestion in this line of the spontaneous spoken word on its way to the rigidity imposed by the poem. The word becomes a god and then the god, in turn, seems to be identified with the poet who advances godlike and remembers those who admired him in the past. Who will adore him in the future? The answer may be partly revealed in the refrain from the passage on trains: joy lies in newness.

Lines 79-81. The French word *voix* may mean "voice" or "voices" and refer to the poet's own voice or to others, perhaps voices of the worshipers just invoked or the sea's echoes or the voices of sailors in the taverns. From 65 to 69 to 79 there is a progression: the poet hears the sea, then he desires its qualities, finally he speaks its language. As at the beginning of the poem, there is an interesting use of imagery from *Alcools.* The scene of the port recalls "Le Voyageur." The last taverns may be comparable to the dried-up sirens of "Les Fiançailles." The image of the sea, as in both *Alcools* and *Le Bestiaire*, is accompanied by a classical reference: here, the Hydra that dwelt in the marshes of Lerna. In "Vendémiaire" the Hydra symbolizes earthquakes for Apollinaire. In "La Victoire" he not only plays on its meaning, the Greek word for water (Valéry does the same, in describing the sea), but indulges in more whimsical wordplay. If any one of the Hydra's numerous heads was cut off, others grew in its place: thus *têtu* "stubborn" or "headstrong" (even "heady") is a play on *tête* "head." Classical imagery as a source of verbal play is not new in Apollinaire's poetry; sirens triggered puns in both *Le Bestiaire* and *Alcools.*

Lines 82-89. Abruptly the poet appears, groping like the blind men at the beginning. The street flows past, like a river, or like time. Although the question posed in lines 84-86 is ambivalent, presumably Apollinaire indicates that liveliness and motion in the present moment are what challenge him. A last echo of the passage on trains suggests the swiftness with which the present is immobilized, and separated from us, by the past.

Lines 90-94. The whole final section suggests "L'Esprit Nouveau." The first four lines briefly refer to an image elaborated in "Les Collines" (see note) of lofty heroes who, like Baudelaire's *Phares*, see farther than other men. Sight, in lines 90-91, implies prophetic vision into the future and, in lines 92-93, probably the poet's literal faculty of sight, in present time. In the manuscript at the Doucet, after line 93, Apollinaire started to sign his name, then added two more lines, which later became one line: "Et que tout / Ait un nom nouveau." This last line, added as an afterthought, relates sound to sight thematically and, structurally, the final section to the long passage on language; it points up, as a major preoccupation, the problem of expressing in poetry the rapid changes taking place toward the end of the war. The poet's role as interpreter and *namer* of these changes becomes a point of departure, at the very end of the poem, toward that notion of prophecy which dominates "Les Collines." The emphasis on "a new name" for everything may conceivably be thought of as a demand for linguistic innovation; a less literal interpretation (more related to ideas in "Les Collines" and "La Jolie Rousse") is that the desire for "a new name" represents a hope for a fresh vision of things, in that new postwar world which is about to manifest itself. Thus a synthesis between the poem's polarities may manifest itself in the last line's equation of a new name with a new look.

Reference

Tournadre, C. "A propos de 'La Victoire.'" In *Apollinaire inventeur de langages.* Bibliothèque Guillaume Apollinaire, 7. Minard, 1973, 167-180.

LA JOLIE ROUSSE, page 342

First published in *L'Éventail*, 5 (March 15, 1918).

There could be no more fitting conclusion to *Calligrammes* than this plea for a creative synthesis of tradition and innovation. Apollinaire's formulation of the problem is so relevant to twentieth-century experience that the very terms he uses—Order and Adventure—have passed into general circulation. His case for the innovatory role of the artist in the modern world is persuasive because it is shown to be the fruit, not of impetuous iconoclasm, but of a mature experience of life and a profound respect for the past. The concept of the poet as a heroic explorer of the future has Romantic overtones. Similarly, the relationship that is postulated between poet and audience goes back to the more hopeful Romantic tradition rather than to the later; instead of being the *poète maudit,* the estranged and isolated artist of the symbolist era, the poet here seeks the friendship and understanding of his public. Some incomprehension remains (see the final lines, especially) which makes his position a lonely and poignant one, but the fundamental assumption is that the artist has a socially constructive role to play and deserves the indulgence and support of his fellowmen.

As befits a plea for understanding, the language of the poem is lucid and cogent. In the two other related poems of the final period, "Les Collines" and "La Victoire," a stronger introspective emphasis produces denser imagery and more elliptical expression, but here Apollinaire draws on the fluent, discursive, immediately accessible style that constitutes one of the poles of his modernism (for precedents see "Sur les Prophéties' and war poems such as "Dans l'Abri-Caverne" and "Merveille de la Guerre"). A note of pathos pervades the poem, however, stemming as much from the complexities of his own nature (see introduction, p. 1) as from his sense of the difficulties of his task. This raises the emotional pitch to a high level and gives the whole poem the urgency of a unique personal statement and the moving quality of a poetic testament.

Lines 1-14. Line 1 encapsulates the essential features of the poet's attitude: it is as a man ready to stand openly before the public, and confident in his own wisdom, that he will make his plea. The catalogue of his experience of life in the following lines is more modest and unassertive than the declarations the poet makes about his exceptional powers in "Les Collines," yet by its comprehensive nature, the range of suffering (3, 8, 9) and the special knowledge (2, 10) it involves, it amounts to a similar claim to special status. Despite the measured tone, then, it is as a man of special vision that he presents himself, hence the commanding nature of the concluding verb, *je juge* (13). The sustained rhetorical buildup of lines 1-12 reinforces the proud conclusive note of this statement.

Lines 15-19. Some of the poignancy that begins to enter the poem at this point arises from the fact that the poet, despite his heroic stature, is dependent on the public's indulgence and is aware that, in venturing into the unknown, he is leaving behind models of achieved perfection. The humility expressed toward the public is striking: they are made in the image of divine order (15-16). But, by implication, the poet has to strive to go beyond even that perfection, as well as the perfection of the past.

Lines 20-30. A balance is maintained between the poet as an individual and as a representative of all innovatory artists. Here (beginning in l. 15) he speaks in his public persona, using the first person plural, returning to an individual tone as from line 31. The evocation of the undiscovered realms of art is entirely typical of Apollinaire: the desire to dominate time and manipulate it at will (27), thus escaping from its inexorable flow, is a central impetus in his work; the depiction of the new through images of light, color, and intensity (21-25) reveals the essentially lyric nature of his vision; the emphasis on moral qualities (26) underlines the extent to which he saw avant-garde art as beneficial. But the very sweep of his vision arouses doubts and anxieties about the magnitude of the task, more strongly expressed than before (28-30). These lines correspond to a passage in his lecture, "L'Esprit Nouveau," where he recognizes that there will inevitably be many failures and shortcomings in experimental art.

Lines 31-39. The summer is a long-established image in Apollinaire's work for a period of suffering, or at least severe trial, in the poet's life, frequently taking on extra pathos in that it symbolizes the loss of youth and confrontation with the graver problems of maturity. These anxious associations are present here (31-32), following on from the self-doubt of the previous lines, but they are immediately overlaid with the more positive vision of line 33. The sun is now a force that is welcomed, becoming the perfect symbol of the successful reconciliation of Order (*la Raison*) and Adventure (*ardente*). The symbol then takes on gentler overtones by being identified with a beautiful woman who is the center of the poet's life (34-39). (The woman in question is Jacqueline Kolb whom Apollinaire married in May 1918.) In a graceful compliment the poet combines his aesthetic ideal and personal experience of happiness in one image, and the tone of the poem modulates back to one of enthusiasm and delight in beauty.

Lines 40-43. These lines bring to a simple climax the vision of beauty which *la Raison ardente* has become, and they reveal Apollinaire's gift for sensuous imagery of light, movement, and color. The image of line 41 is particularly significant of happiness in that it suggests an ephemeral vision that has been made permanent. There is a constant preoccupation throughout the volume with images of evanescence which the poet tries to arrest and perpetuate (cf. the significance of flares in the war poems).

Lines 44-48. Revealingly these lines are in a different ink on the manuscript (in the Bibliothèque Littéraire Jacques Doucet) and presumably were added later. They correct the drift of the poem in the previous lines toward a mood of confidence and serenity and restore the equilibrium between optimism and anguish which is an essential feature of Apollinaire's sensibility (see introduction, p. 1). The note of suffering is stronger than previous occurrences because for the first time it springs, not from the poet's realization of the difficulties of his task, but from his fear of the public's incomprehension. Where friendship (l. 12) was sought, mockery is now feared. This shift does not imply a fundamental rift, but it adds to the burden that the poet has to bear and thus to the poignancy of his appeal for help.

Select Bibliography

The bibliography is restricted to works by and on Apollinaire, which are relevant to *Calligrammes.* For more complete listings see *La Revue des Lettres modernes,* Série Guillaume Apollinaire (1962 to date). Place of publication is Paris unless otherwise indicated.

WORKS BY APOLLINAIRE

The abbreviations in parentheses are those used in the introduction and commentaries to identify the work in question.

Anecdotiques. Ed. P. M. Adéma. Gallimard, 1955. (*A*)
Chroniques d'Art (1902-1918). Ed. L. C. Breunig. Gallimard, 1960. (*CA*)
Lettres à Lou. Ed. M. Décaudin. Gallimard, 1969. (*LL*)
Lettres à sa Marraine, 1915-1918. Ed. P. M. Adéma. Gallimard, 1951. (*LM*)
OEuvres Complètes. Ed. P. M. Adéma and M. Décaudin. 4 vols. Balland et Lecat, 1966. (*OC*)
OEuvres Poétiques. Ed. P. M. Adéma and M. Décaudin. Bibliothèque de la Pléiade. Gallimard, 1959. (*OP*)

Les Peintres Cubistes. Méditations Esthétiques. Ed. L. C. Breunig and J. Cl. Chevalier. Hermann, 1965. (*PC*)
Tendre comme le Souvenir. 9th ed. Gallimard, 1952. (*TS*)

ICONOGRAPHICAL DOCUMENTS

Album Apollinaire. Ed. P. M. Adéma and M. Décaudin. Bibliothèque de la Pléiade. Gallimard, 1971.
Guillaume Apollinaire. Documents Iconographiques. Geneva: P. Cailler, 1965.

WORKS ON APOLLINAIRE

Articles in *La Revue des Lettres Modernes,* Série Guillaume Apollinaire, are referred to by the abbreviation *GA* followed by the volume number and the year of publication.

Works referring to specific poems are cited in the relevant commentary.

Adéma, P. M. *Guillaume Apollinaire.* Table Ronde, 1968.
Bassy, A. M. "Forme littéraire et forme graphique: les schématogrammes d'Apollinaire," *Cahiers de recherches de l'Ecole Normale Supérieure,* 3-4 (1973-74), 161-207.
Bates, S. *Guillaume Apollinaire.* Twayne's World Author Series, no. 14. New York: Twayne, 1967.
———. *Petit Glossaire des Mots Libres d'Apollinaire.* Sewanee, Tenn.: privately printed, 1975.
Bergman, P. *"Modernolatria" et "Simultaneità": Recherches sur deux tendances dans l'avant-garde littéraire en Italie et en France à la veille de la première guerre mondiale.* Stockholm: Svenska Bokförlaget (Bonniers), 1962.
Bohn, W. "L'imagination plastique des calligrammes." In *Lecture et interprétation des Calligrammes.* 9th Apollinaire Colloquium. Stavelot, 1977. In press.
Breunig, L. C. "Apollinaire et le Cubisme," *GA* 1 (1962), 7-24.
———. "The Laughter of Apollinaire," *Yale French Studies,* 31 (May 1964), 66-73.
———. *Guillaume Apollinaire.* Columbia Essays on Modern Writers, 46. New York: Columbia University Press, 1969.
Burgos, J. "Sur la thématique d'Apollinaire," *GA* 8 (1969), 141-163.

———. "Pour une approche de l'univers imaginaire d'Apollinaire," *GA* 10 (1971), 35-67.

Butor, M. "Monument de rien pour Apollinaire." In *Répertoire III*. Minuit, 1968.

Caizergues, P. "Apollinaire et la politique pendant la guerre," *GA* 12 (1973), 67-101.

———. *Apollinaire Journaliste*, I-III, Université de Lisle III, 1979.

Carmody, F. J. *The Evolution of Apollinaire's Poetics, 1901-1914*. University of California Publications in Modern Philology, vol. 70. Berkeley and Los Angeles: University of California Press, 1963.

Centre d'Etude du Vocabulaire Français. *G. Apollinaire: Calligrammes, Concordances, Index et Relevés statistiques*. Documents pour l'étude de la langue littéraire, Vol. V. Larousse, 1967.

Chevalier, J. C. "La poésie d'Apollinaire et le calembour," *Europe*, 451-452 (November-December 1966), 56-76.

———. "Quelques remarques sur un index de *Calligrammes*," *GA* 1 (1962), 40-53.

Davies, M. *Apollinaire*. London: Oliver and Boyd, 1964.

———. "L'avenir dans l'œuvre poétique d'Apollinaire." In *Apollinaire inventeur de langages*. Bibliothèque Guillaume Apollinaire, 7. Minard, 1973.

Décaudin, M. "Le changement de front de Guillaume Apollinaire," *La Revue des Sciences humaines*, 60 (October-December 1950), 255-260.

———. "Les *Calligrammes* d'Apollinaire et la tradition du poème figuré," *Bulletin de la Société Toulousaine d'Etudes Classiques* (January-February 1959).

———. "Apollinaire à la recherche de lui-même," *Cahiers du Sud*, 386 (January-March 1966), 3-12.

———. "Apollinaire et le cinéma, image par image." In *Apollinaire*. Ed. M. Bonfantini. Turin: Giappichelli, 1970, pp. 19-28.

———. "Apollinaire: l'espace et le temps," *Quaderni Francesi*, 1 (0000), 667-677.

Delesalle, S. "La guerre, la poésie," *Europe*, 421 (May-June 1964), 174-184.

Dutton, K. R. "Apollinaire and Communication," *Australian Journal of French Studies*, V, 3 (1968), 303-328.

George, E. E. "Calligrammes in Apollinaire and Trakl: A Psycho-stylistic Study," *Language and Style*, 1 (1968), 131-143.

Goldstein, J. P. "Pour un sémiologie du calligramme." In *Lecture et interprétation des Calligrammes*. 9th Apollinaire Colloquium. Stavelot, 1977. In press.

Greet, A. H. "Wordplay in Apollinaire's *Calligrammes*," *L'Esprit Créateur*, X, 4 (Winter 1970), 296-307.

———. "Quelques aspects de l'éphémère dans *Calligrammes.*" In *Apollinaire, inventeur de langages.* Bibliothèque Guillaume Apollinaire, 7. Minard, 1973.

———. *Apollinaire et le livre de peintre.* Minard, 1978.

Hubert, R. R. "L'élan vers l'acuel dans la poésie d'Apollinaire et de Breton," *GA* 7 (1968), 195-206.

———. "Poésie calligrammatique et poésie concrète." In *Lecture et interprétation des Calligrammes.* 9th Apollinaire Colloquium. Stavelot, 1977. In press.

Jutrin, M. "Les *Calligrammes* d'Apollinaire: une transmutation de la guerre et de la poésie," *Marginales,* 139 (June 1971), 1-8.

Levaillant, J. "L'espace dans Calligrammes," *GA* 8 (1969), 48-63.

Lockerbie, S. I. "Le Rôle de l'imagination dans *Calligrammes,*" part 1, *GA* 5 (1966), 6-22; part 2, *GA* 6 (1967), 85-105.

———. "Qu'est-ce que l'Orphisme d'Apollinaire?" In *Apollinaire et la Musique.* Les Amis d'Apollinaire. Stavelot, 1967.

———. "Forme graphique et expressivité dans les *Calligrammes.*" In *Lecture et interprétation des Calligrammes.* 9th Apollinaire Colloquium. Stavelot, 1977. In press.

Longrée, G. H. F. "Elle est fausse et elle ne passe pas. Remarques sur la poésie d'Apollinaire," *Sub-stance,* no. zero (March 1971), 55-60.

———. "L'écriture calligrammatique de Mallarmé à Apollinaire." In *Lecture et interprétation des Calligrammes.* 9th Apollinaire Colloquium. Stavelot, 1977. In press.

Marrow, A. "Form and Meaning in Apollinaire's Picture Poems," *Australian Journal of French Studies,* V, 3 (1968), 295-302.

Martin, M. W. "Futurism, Unanimism and Apollinaire," *Art Journal,* XXVIII, 3 (Spring 1969), 258-268.

Pia, P. *Apollinaire par lui-même.* Seuil, 1954.

Poupon, M. "Remarques à propos d'une iconographie," *GA* 6 (1967), 107-124.

———. *Apollinaire et Cendrars.* Archives des Lettres Modernes, 103. Archives *GA* 2. Minard, 1969.

Renaud, Ph. " 'Ondes' ou les métamorphoses de la musique." In *Apollinaire et la Musique.* Les Amis d'Apollinaire. Stavelot, 1967.

———. *Lecture d'Apollinaire.* Lausanne: Editions L'Age d'Homme, 1969.

Richard, J. P. "Etoiles chez Apollinaire." In *De Ronsard à Breton.* Hommages à M. Raymond. Corti, 1967.

Rinsler, N. "Guillaume Apollinaire's War Poems," *French Studies,* XXV, 2 (April 1971), 109-185.

Roudaut, J. "La Fête d'Apollinaire," *Critique,* 199 (December 1963), 1034-1045.

Rouveyre, A. *Amour et poésie d'Apollinaire.* Seuil, 1955.
Severini, G. "Apollinaire et le Futurisme," *XX Siècle* (June 1972).
Shattuck, R. *The Banquet Years.* New York: Anchor Books, 1961. London: Cape, 1969.
Themerson, S. *Apollinaire's Lyrical Ideograms.* London: Gabberbocchus Press, 1968.
Tournadre, C. *Les Critiques de notre temps et Apollinaire.* Garnier, 1971.
———. "Apollinaire soldat, au jour le jour," *GA* 12 (1973), 7-26.
———. "Apollinaire et les Surréalistes aujourd'hui." In *Surréalisme, Surrealismo.* Quaderni del Novocento Francese, 2. 1974. Rome: Bulzoni. Paris: Nizet.
———. "Notes sur le vocabulaire de la guerre dans *Calligrammes,*" *GA* 13 (1976), 65-75.
———. *Glossaire, Œuvres complètes d'Apollinaire.* In press.

BACKGROUND SOURCES ON APOLLINAIRE'S WAR EXPERIENCE

Dauzat, A. *L'argot de guerre.* Colin, 1918.
Esnault, G. *Le Poilu tel qu'il se parle.* Bossard, 1919.
Meyer, J. *La vie quotidienne des soldats pendant la grande guerre.* Hachette, 1966.

OTHER WORKS

Balakian, A. *Surrealism: The Road to the Absolute.* New York and London: Unwin, 1972.
Bann, S, ed. *Concrete Poetry: An International Anthology.* London: London Magazine ed., 1967.
Décaudin, M. *La crise des valeurs symbolistes.* Toulouse: Privat, 1960.
Garnier, P. *Spatialisme et poésie concrète.* Gallimard, 1968.
Massin, R. *La Lettre et l'Image.* Gallimard, 1970.
Seaman, D. W. *French Concrete Poetry: The Development of a Poetic Form from Its Origins to the Present Day.* Stanford: Stanford University Press, 1970. Ann Arbor: University Microfilms.
Solt, M. E., ed. *Concrete Poetry: A World View.* Bloomington: Indiana University Press, 1968.